NEURAL NETWORKS

in Finance and Investing

Using Artificial Intelligence to
Improve Real-World Performance

Robert R. Trippi
Efraim Turban
E D I T O R S

PROBUS PUBLISHING COMPANY
Chicago, Illinois
Cambridge, England

Authorization to photocopy items for internal or personal use, or the internal or personal use of specific clients, is granted by PROBUS PUBLISHING COMPANY, provided that the U.S. $7.00 per page fee is paid directly to Copyright Clearance Center, 27 Congress Street, Salem, MA 01970, USA, Phone: 1-508-744-3350. For those organizations that have been granted a photocopy license by CCC, a separate system of payment has been arranged. The fee code for users of the Transactional Reporting Service is 1-55738-452-5/93/$00.00 + $7.00.

Library of Congress Cataloging-in-Publication Data

Neural networks in finance and investment : using artificial intelligence to improve real world performance / [edited by] Robert R. Trippi, Efraim Turban.
    p.   cm.
    "A collection of survey and research articles"—Pref.
    Includes bibliographical references and index.
    ISBN 1-55738-452-5 : $65.00
    1. Finance—Decision making—Data processing. 2. Neural networks (Computer science) 3. Artificial intelligence. I. Trippi, Robert R. II. Turban, Efraim.
HG4012.5.N48   1992
332.1'0285'63—dc20   92-28456
                                                  CIP

ISBN 1-55738-452-5

Printed in the United States of America

BC

    4 5 6 7 8 9 0

DEDICATION

To my wife and best friend, Cecilia.

Robert R. Trippi

To my daughters, Daphne and Sharon.

Efraim Turban

CONTENTS

LIST OF FIGURES

LIST OF TABLES

PREFACE

Financial services firms are becoming more and more dependent on advanced computer technologies to establish and maintain competitiveness in a global economy. Neural networks represent an exciting new technology with a wide scope of potential financial applications, ranging from routine credit assessment operations to the driving of large-scale portfolio management strategies. Some of these applications have already resulted in dramatic increases in productivity. This book brings together from diverse sources a collection of survey and research articles that focus on the use of neural network technology to improve financial decision making.

Many of the first neural network researchers were initially inspired by the similarity of neural network architectures and learning paradigms with those of the brain. Although most early attempts to apply neural networks to financial decision making were naive, clumsy, and generally unsuccessful, recent innovations in the technology and improvements in our understanding of the strengths and weaknesses of neural networks vis-à-vis other forms of machine learning and human decision- making processes are now resulting in commercially successful systems. Early neural network research was typically highly product-oriented; today most researchers and system implementors take a much more hardware and software-independent view of neural network-based decision support systems than was formerly the case. In addition, several of the applications discussed here are integrated with expert system technology.

Neural networks are especially suited for simulating intelligence in pattern recognition, association, and classification activities. These problems arise frequently in such areas as credit assessment, security investment, and financial forecasting. It is worth noting that, after the Department of Defense in 1989 embarked on a five-year, multimillion dollar program for neural network research, financial organizations have been the second largest sponsors of research in neural network applications.

It is our hope that a collection of articles such as this — dealing exclusively with investment, risk assessment, forecasting, and other financial applications — will prove to be a useful addition to the libraries of financial analysts, information system professionals interested in or already working on such applications, and managers with financial decision-making responsibilities who wish to keep abreast of new developments in the field.

The authors wish to give thanks for its generous support in this endeavor to the School of Business Administration at California State University, Long Beach. Also, we thank Iva Thomas of the University of Alabama, who helped in proofing this manuscript and Carol Klein from Probus Publishing, who managed the production of this book.

Robert R. Trippi
Efraim Turban

SOURCES AND ACKNOWLEDGMENTS

Chapter 1

"Neural Network Fundamentals for Financial Analysts," by Larry Medsker, Efraim Turban, and Robert R. Trippi. Printed by permission of the authors.

Chapter 2

"Artificial Neural Systems: A New Tool for Financial Decision-Making," by Delvin D. Hawley, John D. Johnson, and Dijjotam Raina. This article originally appeared in *Financial Analysts Journal*, November/December 1990, pp. 63–72. Reprinted with permission.

Chapter 3

"Applying Neural Networks," by Casimir C. "Casey" Klimasauskas. This article originally appeared in *PCAI*, January/February, 1991, pp. 30–33, March/April, 1991, pp. 27–34, and May/June, 1991, pp. 20–24. Reprinted with permission.

Chapter 4

"A Financial Neural-Network Application," by Robert A. Marose. This article originally appeared in *AI Expert*, May 1990, pp. 50–53. Reprinted courtesy of Miller Freeman, Inc.

Chapter 5

"Analyzing Financial Health: Integrating Neural Networks and Expert Systems," by Don Barker. This article originally appeared in *PCAI*, May/June, 1990, pp. 24–27. Reprinted with permission.

Chapter 6

"Applying Neural Networks to the Extraction of Knowledge from Accounting Reports: A Classification Study," by R. H. Berry and Duarte Trigueiros. Printed with permission of the authors.

Chapter 7

"The Use of Neural Computing Technology to Develop Profiles of Chapter 11 Debtors Who Are Likely to Become Tax Delinquents," by George G. Klemic, 1990. Printed with permission of the author.

Chapter 8

"A Neural Network Approach to Bankruptcy Prediction," by Wullianallur Raghupathi, Lawrence L. Schkade, and Bapi S. Raju. Reprinted with permission from *Proceedings of the IEEE 24th Annual Hawaii International Conference on Systems Sciences*, © 1991, IEEE.

Chapter 9

"Bankruptcy Prediction by Neural Network," by Eric Rahimian, Seema Singh, Thongchai Thammachote, and Rajiv Virmani. Printed with permission of the authors.

Chapter 10

"A Neural Network Model for Bankruptcy Prediction," by Marcus D. Odom and Ramesh Sharda. Reprinted with permission from *Proceedings of the IEEE International Conference on Neural Networks*, pp. II163–II168, San Diego, CA, © IEEE.

Chapter 11

"Neural Networks for Bankruptcy Prediction: The Power to Solve Financial Problems," by Kevin G. Coleman, Timothy J. Graettinger, and William F. Lawrence. This article originally appeared in *AI Review*, July/August, 1991, pp. 48–50. Reprinted courtesy of NeuralWare, Inc., Pittsburgh, PA.

Chapter 12

"Managerial Applications of Neural Networks: The Case of Bank Failure Predictions," by Kar Yan Tam and Melody Y. Kiang. This article originally appeared in *Management Science*, Vol. 38, No. 7, July 1992, pp. 926–947, © 1992, The Institute of Management Sciences. Reprinted with permission.

Chapter 13

"Neural Networks: A New Tool for Predicting Thrift Failures," by Linda M. Salchenberger, E. Mine Cinar, and Nicholas A. Lash. This article originally appeared in *Decision Sciences*, Vol. 23, No. 4, July/August, 1992, pp. 899–916. Reprinted with permission.

Chapter 14

"Bond Rating: A Non-Conservative Application of Neural Networks," by Soumitra Dutta and Shashi Shekhar. Reprinted with permission from *Proceedings of the IEEE International Conference on Neural Networks*, pp. II443–II450, © July 1988, IEEE.

Chapter 15

"Neural Networks for Bond Rating Improved by Multiple Hidden Layers," by Alvin J. Surkan and J. Clay Singleton. Reprinted with permission from *Proceedings of the IEEE International Conference on Neural Networks*, pp. II163–II168, San Diego, CA, © 1990, IEEE.

Chapter 16

"An Application of a Multiple Neural Network Learning System to Emulation of Mortgage Underwriting Judgments," by Edward Collins, Sushmito Ghosh, and Christopher Scofield. Reprinted with permission from *Proceedings of the IEEE International Conference on Neural Networks*, pp. II459–II466, © July 1988, IEEE.

Chapter 17

"Risk Assessment of Mortgage Applications with a Neural Network System: An Update as the Test Portfolio Ages," by Douglas L. Reilly, Edward Collins, Christopher Scofield, and Sushmito Ghosh. Reprinted with permission from *Proceedings of the IEEE International Conference on Neural Networks*, pp. II479–II482, © July 1991, IEEE.

Chapter 18

"Economic Prediction Using Neural Networks: The Case of IBM Daily Stock Returns," by Halbert White. Reprinted with permission from *Proceedings of the IEEE International Conference on Neural Networks*, pp. II451–II458, © July 1988, IEEE.

Chapter 19

"Predicting Stock Price Performance: A Neural Network Approach," by Youngohc Yoon and George Swales. Reprinted with permission from *Proceedings of the IEEE 24th Annual Hawaii International Conference of Systems Sciences*, pp. 156–162, © January 1991, IEEE.

Chapter 20

"Stock Market Prediction System with Modular Neural Networks," by Takashi Kimoto, Kazuo Asakawa, Morio Yoda, and Masakazu Takeoka. Reprinted with permission from *Proceedings of the IEEE International Joint Conference on Neural Networks*, pp. I1–I6, San Diego, CA, © 1990, IEEE.

Chapter 21

"Stock Price Pattern Recognition: A Recurrent Neural Network Approach," by Ken-ichi Kamijo and Tetsuji Tanigawa. Reprinted with permission from *Proceedings of the IEEE International Joint Conference on Neural Networks*, pp. I215–I221, San Diego, CA, © 1990, IEEE.

Chapter 22

"Adaptive Processes to Exploit the Non-Linear Structure of Financial Markets," by W. E. Bosarge, Jr. This paper was presented at the Santa Fe Institute of Complexity Conference: *Neural Networks and Pattern Recognition in Forecasting Financial Markets*, February 15, 1991. Reprinted with permission.

Chapter 23

"A Commodity Trading Model Based on a Neural Network-Expert System Hybrid," by Karl Bergerson and Donald C. Wunsch, II. Reprinted with permission from *Proceedings of the IEEE International Conference on Neural Networks*, pp. I289–I293, Seattle, WA, © 1991, IEEE.

Chapter 24

"Commodity Trading with a Three Year Old," by J. E. Collard. Printed with permission of the author acknowledging support from Gerber Inc., Schwieterman Inc., and Martingale Research Corp.

Chapter 25

"Testability of the Arbitrage Pricing Theory by Neural Network," by Hamid Ahmadi. Reprinted with permission from *Proceedings of the IEEE International Conference on Neural Networks,* pp. I385–I393, San Diego, CA, © 1990, IEEE.

Chapter 26

"Neural Network Models as an Alternative to Regression," by Leorey Marquez, Tim Hill, Reginald Worthley, and William Remus. A modified version of a paper is reprinted with permission from *Proceedings of the IEEE 24th Annual Hawaii International Conference on Systems Sciences,* pp. 129–135, Vol. VI, © 1991, IEEE.

Chapter 27

"A Connectionist Approach to Time: Time Series Prediction—An Empirical Test," by Ramesh Sharda and Rajendra B. Patil. This article appeared in the *Journal of Intelligent Manufacturing,* published by Chapman and Hall, 1992. Reprinted with permission.

Chapter 28

"Constructive Learning and Its Application to Currency Exchange Rate Forecasting," by A. N. Refenes. Printed with permission of the author.

CONTRIBUTORS

Hamid Ahmadi, California State University, Sacramento
Kazuo Asakawa, Fujitsu Laboratories Ltd.
Don Barker, Gonzaga University
Karl Bergerson, Neural Trading Company
R. H. Berry, University of East Anglia
W. E. Bosarge, Jr., Frontier Financial Corporation
E. Mine Cinar, Loyola University of Chicago
Kevin G. Coleman, Neuralware, Inc.
J. E. Collard, GIST Technologies Corp.
Edward Collins, Nestor, Inc.
Soumitra Dutta, University of California, Berkeley
Sushmito Ghosh, Nestor, Inc.
Timothy J. Graettinger, Neuralware, Inc.
Delvin D. Hawley, University of Mississippi
Tim Hill, University of Hawaii
John D. Johnson, University of Mississippi, Oxford
Ken-ichi Kamijo, NEC Corporation
Melody Y. Kiang, University of Texas at Austin
Takashi Kimoto, Fujitsu Laboratories Ltd.
George G. Klemic, San Mateo, California
Casimir C. Klimasauskas, Neuralware, Inc.
Nicholas A. Lash, Loyola University of Chicago

William F. Lawrence, Neuralware, Inc.
Robert A. Marose, Hofstra University
Leorey Marquez, University of Hawaii
Larry Medsker, American University
Marcus D. Odom, Oklahoma State University, Stillwater
Rajendra B. Patil, University of Oklahoma
Wullianallur Raghupathi, California State University, Chico
Eric Rahimian, Alabama A&M University
Dijjotam Raina, Mobile Telecommunications Technology, Inc.
Bapi S. Raju, University of Texas at Arlington
A. N. Refenes, University College London
Douglas L. Reilly, Nestor, Inc.
William Remus, University of Hawaii
Linda M. Salchenberger, Loyola University of Chicago
Lawrence L. Schkade, University of Texas at Arlington
Christopher Scofield, Nestor, Inc.
Ramesh Sharda, Oklahoma State University, Stillwater
Shashi Shekhar, University of California, Berkeley
Seema Singh, University of Alabama at Huntsville
J. Clay Singleton, University of Nebraska
Alvin J. Surkan, University of Nebraska
George Swales, Southwest Missouri State University
Masakazu Takeoka, The Nikko Securities Co., Ltd.
Kar Yan Tam, Hong Kong University of Science and Technology
Tetsuji Tanigawa, NEC Corporation
Thongchai Thammachote, University of Alabama at Huntsville
Duarte Trigueiros, University of East Anglia
Robert R. Trippi, California State University, Long Beach
Efraim Turban, California State University, Long Beach
Rajiv Virmani, University of Alabama at Huntsville
Halbert White, University of California, San Diego
Reginald Worthley, University of Hawaii
Donald C. Wunsch II, Neural Trading Company
Morio Yoda, The Nikko Securities Co., Ltd.
Youngohc Yoon, Southwest Missouri State University

PART 1

NEURAL NETWORK OVERVIEW

1

NEURAL NETWORK FUNDAMENTALS FOR FINANCIAL ANALYSTS

Larry Medsker, Efraim Turban, and Robert R. Trippi[1]

INTRODUCTION

Over the past four decades, the field of artificial intelligence has made great progress toward computerizing human reasoning. Nevertheless, the tools of AI have been mostly restricted to sequential processing and only certain representations of knowledge and logic. A different approach to intelligent systems involves constructing computers with architectures and processing capabilities that mimic the processing characteristics of the brain. The results may be knowledge representations based on massive parallel processing, fast retrieval of large amounts of information, and the ability to recognize patterns based on

3

experience. The technology that attempts to achieve these results is called *neural computing,* or *artificial neural networks* (ANN).

Artificial neural networks are an information processing technology inspired by studies of the brain and nervous system. After falling into disfavor in the 1970s, the field of neural networks experienced a dramatic resurgence in the late 1980s. The renewed interest developed because of the need for brainlike information processing, advances in computer technology, and progress in neuroscience toward better understanding of the mechanisms of the brain. Declared the Decade of the Brain by the U. S. government, the 1990s look extremely promising for understanding the brain and the mind. Neural computing should have an important role in this research area, which initially was oriented toward medical research. In many financial decision making as well as other application areas, ANN are supplementing or taking the place of statistical and conventional expert systems (ES) approaches, as the ANN approach provides features and performance advantages not available in the other types of systems.

THE BIOLOGICAL ANALOGY

Biological Neural Networks

The human (and animal) brain is composed of cells called *neurons,* which are unique in that they do not die—all other cells reproduce to replace themselves, then die. This phenomenon may explain why we retain information. Estimates of the number of neurons in a human brain range up to 100 billion, and more than a hundred different kinds of neurons are known. Neurons function in groups called networks. Each group contains several thousand highly interconnected neurons. Thus, the brain can be viewed as a collection of neural networks.

Thinking and intelligent behavior are controlled by the brain and the central nervous system. The ability to learn and react to changes in our environment requires intelligence. Those who suffer brain damage, for example, have difficulty learning and reacting to changing environments.

A portion of a network composed of two cells is shown in Figure 1.1. The cell itself includes a *nucleus* (at the center). On the left of Neuron 1, note the *dendrites,* which provide inputs to the cell. On the right is the *axon,* which sends signals (outputs) via the axon terminals to Neuron

Figure 1.1
Two Interconnected Biological Cells

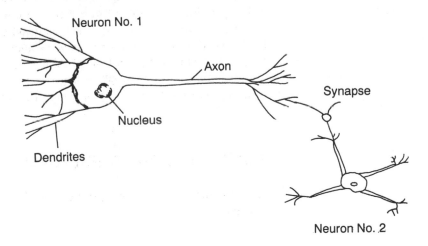

2. These axon terminals are shown merging with the dendrites of Neuron 2. Signals can be transmitted unchanged, or they can be transmitted over synapses. A *synapse* is able to increase or decrease its strength of connection and causes excitation or inhibition of a subsequent neuron.

Artificial Neural Networks

An *artificial* neural network is a *model* that emulates a biological neural network. Today's neural computing uses a very limited set of concepts based on our knowledge of biological neural systems. The concepts are used to implement software simulations of massively parallel processes involving processing elements (also called artificial neurons or neurodes) interconnected in a network architecture. The artificial neuron is analogous to the biological neuron. It receives inputs analogous to the electrochemical impulses that the dendrites of biological neurons receive from other neurons. The output of the artificial neuron corresponds to signals sent out from a biological neuron over its axon. These artificial signals can be changed similarly to the change occurring at the synapses.

The state of the art in neural computing is not necessarily limited by our understanding of biological neural networks. Despite extensive research in neurobiology and psychology, important questions remain about how the brain and the mind work. This is just one reason why neural computing models are not very close to actual biological systems. Nevertheless, research and development in the area of ANN are producing interesting and useful systems that borrow some features from the biological systems, even though we are far from having an artificial brainlike machine.

NEURAL NETWORK COMPONENTS AND STRUCTURES

A network is composed of processing elements that can be organized in different ways or architectures.

Processing Elements

An ANN is composed of artificial neurons (to be referred to as neurons); these are the *processing elements* (PEs). Each of the neurons receives input(s), processes the input(s), and delivers a single output. This process is shown in Figure 1.2. The input can be raw data or output of other processing elements. The output can be the final product, or it can be an input to another neuron.

A Network

Each ANN is composed of a collection of neurons grouped in layers. A basic structure is shown in Figure 1.3. Note the three layers in this example: input, intermediate (called the hidden layer), and output.

Network Structure

Similar to biological networks, an ANN can be organized in several different ways (topologies); that is, the neurons can be interconnected in different ways. Therefore, ANN appear in many shapes. In processing

Figure 1.2

A Neural Processing Element

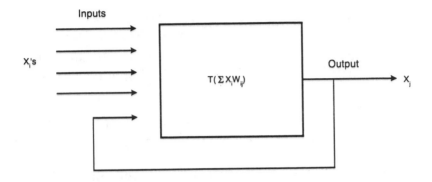

Figure 1.3

Three-Layer Network

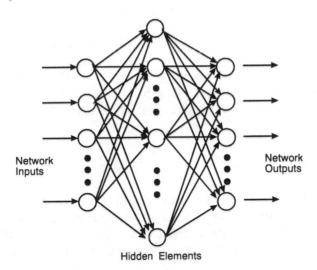

information, many of the processing elements perform their computations simultaneously. This *parallel processing* resembles the way the brain works, and contrasts with the serial processing of conventional computing.

Processing Information in the Network

Once the structure of a network is established, the relevant information can be processed. The major elements participating in the processing are:

Inputs. Each input corresponds to a single attribute. For example, if the problem is to decide on the approval or disapproval of a loan, an attribute can be an income level, age, or ownership of a house. The *value* of an attribute is the input to the network. Although input data are numerically valued, in some applications numbers may actually represent qualitative data such as "yes," "no"; "up," "down"; or "pass," "fail."

Outputs. The output of the network is the solution to a problem. For example, in the case of a loan application it may be "yes" or "no." The ANN assigns numeric values, for example, +1 for yes and 0 for no. The purpose of the network is to compute the value of the output.

Weights. Key elements in an ANN, *weights* express the *relative strength* (or mathematical value) of the initial entering data or the various connections that transfer data from layer to layer. In other words, weights express the *relative importance* of each input to a processing element. Weights are crucial; it is through repeated adjustments of weights that the network "learns."

Summation Function

The *summation function* finds the weighted average of all the input elements to each processing element. A summation function multiplies the input values (Xs) by the weights (Ws) and totals them together for a weighted sum, Y. For N inputs i into one processing element j, we have:

$$Y_j = \sum_{j}^{n} X_i W_{ij}$$

Transformation (Transfer) Function

The summation function computes the internal stimulation, or activation level, of the neuron. (Sometimes it is referred to as the activation function.) Based on this level, the neuron may or may not produce an output. The relationship between the internal activation level and the output may be linear or nonlinear. Such relationships are expressed by a *transformation (transfer) function*, and there are several different types. The selection of the specific function determines the network's operation. One very popular nonlinear transfer function is called a *sigmoid function*:

$$Y_T = \frac{1}{1 + e^{-y}}$$

where Y_T is the transformed (or normalized) value of Y.

The purpose of this transformation is to modify the output levels to a reasonable value (e.g., between 0 and 1). This transformation is done *before* the output reaches the next level. Without such transformation, the value of the output may be very large, especially when several layers are involved. Sometimes instead of a continuous transformation function, a *threshold detector* is used. For example, any value of 0.5 (or other fixed number) or less is changed to zero; any value above 0.5 is changed to one. A transformation can occur at the output of each processing element, or it can be performed at the final output of the network. An example of a PE using a sigmoid transfer function is the following:

$x_1 = 3$ $w_1 = .2$

$x_2 = 1$ $w_2 = .4$ PE $y = .77$

$x_3 = 2$ $w_3 = .1$

Note that the summation function results in:

$$y = 3(.2) + 1 \ (.4) + 2(.1) = 1.2$$

and the sigmoid transformation results in:

$$Y_T = \frac{1}{1 + e^{-1.2}} = .77$$

Learning

An ANN learns from its mistakes. The usual process of learning (or training) involves three tasks:

1. Compute outputs.

2. Compare outputs with desired answers.

3. Adjust the weights and repeat the process.

The learning process usually starts by setting the weights randomly. The difference between the actual output (Y or Y_T) and the desired output (Z) is called Δ. The objective is to minimize Δ (or better, to reduce it to zero). The reduction of Δ is done by incrementally changing the weights.

Information processing with ANN consists of analyzing patterns of activities (*pattern recognition*) with learned information stored as the neuron's connection weights. A common characteristic of systems is the ability to classify streams of input data without the explicit knowledge of rules and to use arbitrary patterns of weights to represent the memory of categories. During the learning stages, the interconnection weights change in response to training data presented to the system. Different ANN compute the error in different ways depending on the learning algorithm that is being used. More than a hundred learning algorithms are available for various situations and configurations. In training a network, the training data set is divided into two categories: test cases and training cases.

ANN STRENGTHS AND WEAKNESSES

Neural network technology has significant advantages over conventional, rule or frame-based, ES approaches in some applications. For one, since neural networks do not require knowledge to be formalized, they are appropriate to domains in which knowledge is scanty. Conventional expert systems map input responses into progressively refined, but linearly separable spaces. Neural networks, on the other hand, can develop input/output map boundaries that are highly nonlinear (Figure 1.4). Some types of problems benefit from this capability. Also, although most conventional ES software permits classification probabilities to be incorporated into rules, ordinarily they must be explicitly entered. Some types of neural networks are able to deduce these probabilities through training. It is difficult for rule-based ESs to develop rules from historical data when the inputs are highly correlated. Neural network learning paradigms do not suffer from this problem. Finally, the per-case processing time of neural networks can be faster than that of conventional systems, since the network examines all of the information available about a problem at once. This facilitates a more highly automated input interface.

Neural networks have several other benefits:

❖ *Fault tolerance.* Since there are many processing nodes, each with primarily local connections, damage to a few nodes or links does not bring the system to a halt.

❖ *Generalization.* When a neural network is presented with noisy, incomplete, or previously unseen input, it generates a reasonable response.

❖ *Adaptability.* Since the network learns in new environments, training can occur continuously over its useful life, and occur concurrently with the deployment of the network.

Neural networks have their weaknesses. Not every potential ES application will benefit from the advantages of neural networks, or be worth the additional cost and complexity. A vexing and sometimes unacceptable characteristic of neural network ESs is that they can identify as important for decision-making factors that appear to be irrelevant, or even factors that conflict with traditional theories in the knowledge domain. Since the scope of training is always to some extent limited by economics and time, networks that contradict accepted theory run the risk of lacking generality, functioning well only on data with a structure similar to that of the training set.

Most neural network systems lack explanation facilities. Justifications for results are difficult to obtain because the connection weights

Figure 1.4

Input-Output Maps (with outputs A, B, C, D)

A.

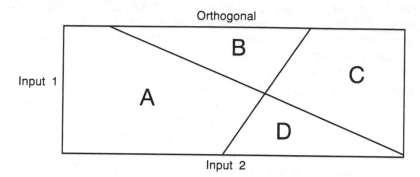

B.

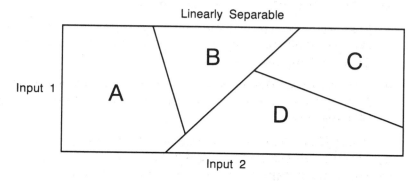

C.

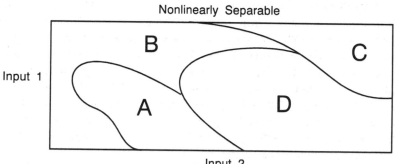

Source: R. R. Trippi and E. Turban, "Auto-Learning Approaches for Building Expert Systems," *Computers and Operations Research,* 17:6 (June 1990), pp. 553–560.

do not usually have obvious interpretations. This is particularly true in pattern recognition where it is very difficult or even impossible to explain the logic behind specific decisions. With current technologies, training times can be excessive and tedious; thus, the need for frequent retraining may make a particular application impractical. The best way to represent input data and the choice of architecture is still mostly subject to trial and error. Neural computing usually requires large amounts of data and lengthy training times.

Also, most neural networks cannot guarantee an optimal solution to a problem, a completely certain solution, or sometimes even repeatability with the same input data. However, properly configured and trained neural networks can often make consistently good classifications, generalizations, or decisions, in a statistical sense.

Neural networks can be used effectively to automate both routine and ad-hoc financial analysis tasks. Prototype neural network-based decision aids have been built for the following applications:

- ❖ Credit authorization screening

- ❖ Mortgage risk assessment

- ❖ Project management and bidding strategy

- ❖ Financial and economic forecasting

- ❖ Risk rating of exchange-traded fixed-income investments

- ❖ Detection of regularities in security price movements

- ❖ Prediction of default and bankruptcy

Other potential applications meriting further research, development, and evaluation are the following:

- ❖ Portfolio selection and diversification

- ❖ Simulation of market behavior

- ❖ Index construction

- ❖ Identification of explanatory economic factors

- ❖ "Mining" of financial and economic databases

DEVELOPING NEURAL NETWORK APPLICATIONS

Neural network applications are in use enough to allow identification of practical guidelines for their development. The first two steps in the ANN development process involve collecting data and separating it into a training set and a test set. These tasks must be based on a thorough analysis of the application so that the problem is well bounded, and the functionality of the system and the context of the neural networks are well understood.

In conjunction with a domain expert, the developer must identify and clarify data relevant to the problem. This means formulating and conceptualizing the task in a data-oriented way that will be amenable to a neural network solution. For example, textual descriptions need to be reformulated to allow the knowledge to be described numerically. The developer needs to avoid biases due to the particular way the data are represented. Other considerations are the stability of the input and the extent to which environmental conditions might require changes in the number of input nodes to the neural network. At this point, a difficulty in expressing data in the form needed for a neural network might lead to cancellation of the project.

The anticipated structure of the neural network and the learning algorithm determine the data type, such as binary or continuous. High-quality data collection requires care to minimize ambiguity, errors, and randomness in data. The data should be collected to cover the widest range of the problem domain; it should cover not only routine operations, but also exceptions and conditions at the boundaries of the problem domain. Another task is to confirm reliability by using multiple sources of data; even so, ambiguities will have to be resolved. In general, the more data used, the better—as long as quality is not sacrificed. Larger data sets increase processing times during training, but better data improve the accuracy of the training and could lead to faster convergence to a good set of weights.

Normally, training a neural network begins with *data separation*. The data sets are randomly separated into two categories: training cases and testing cases. The training cases are used to adjust the weights. The test cases are used for validation of the network. The number of cases needed for each category can be computed by considering several factors.[2-4]

NETWORK STRUCTURES

Many different neural network models and implementations are being developed and studied today.[3, 5] Three representative architectures are shown in Figure 1.5 and are discussed below.

Associative Memory Systems

Associative memory is the ability to recall complete situations from partial information. These systems correlate input data with information stored in memory. Information can be recalled from incomplete or "noisy" input, and performance degrades only slowly as neurons fail. Associative memory systems can detect similarities between new input and stored patterns. Most neural network architectures can be used as associative memories, and a prime example of a single-layer system is the Hopfield network,[6] which uses the collective properties of the network and minimization of an energy function to classify input patterns.

Hidden Layer

Associative memory systems can have one or more intermediate (hidden) layers. An example of a simple network was shown in Figure 1.3.

Figure 1.5

Neural Network Structures

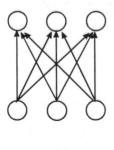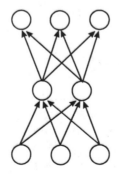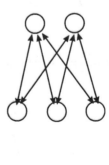

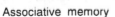

Associative memory   Hidden layer   Double layer

Many of today's multilayer networks use the back-propagation learning algorithm. Another type of unsupervised learning, competitive filter associative memory, is capable of learning by changing its weights in recognition of categories of input data without being provided examples by an external trainer. A leading example of such a single-layer, self-organizing system for a fixed number of classes in the inputs is the Kohonen network.[7]

Double-Layer Structure

A double-layer structure, exemplified by the adaptive resonance theory (ART) approach, does not require the knowledge of a precise number of classes in the training data.[8] Instead, it uses feed-forward and feed-backward to adjust parameters as data are analyzed to establish arbitrary numbers of categories that represent the data presented to the system. Parameters can be adjusted to tune the sensitivity of the system and produce meaningful categories.

For more complex neural computing applications, neurons are combined in various architectures useful for information processing. Practical applications require one or more (hidden) layers between the input and output neurons and a correspondingly large number of weights. Most commercial ANN include three, and rarely four or five layers, with each containing from ten to a thousand processing elements. Some experimental ANN include millions of processing elements. The use of more than three layers is not necessary in most commercial systems. The amount of computation added with each layer increases very rapidly.

LEARNING ALGORITHMS

An important consideration in ANN is the appropriate use of algorithms for learning (or training). Such algorithms are called learning algorithms (or paradigms), and more than a hundred of them are known. A taxonomy of these algorithms has been proposed by Lippman,[9] who distinguishes between two major categories based on the input format: binary-valued input (0's and 1's) or continuous-valued input. Each of these can be further divided into two basic categories: *supervised learning* and *unsupervised learning*.

Supervised learning uses a set of inputs for which the appropriate (desired) outputs are known. In one type, the difference between the desired and actual output is used to calculate corrections to the weights of the neural network. A variation of that approach simply acknowledges for each input trial whether or not the output is correct as the network adjusts weights in an attempt to achieve correct results. Examples of this type of learning are back-propagation and Hopfield network.

In unsupervised learning, only input stimuli are shown to the network. The network is self-organizing; that is, it organizes itself internally so that each hidden processing element responds strategically to a different set of input stimuli (or groups of stimuli). No knowledge is supplied about what classifications (outputs) are correct, and those that the network derives may or may not be meaningful to the person training the network. However, the number of categories into which the network classifies the inputs can be controlled by varying certain parameters in the model. In any case, a human must examine the final categories to assign meaning and to determine the usefulness of the results. Examples of this type of learning are the adaptive resonance theory and Kohonen self-organizing feature maps.

HOW A NETWORK LEARNS

Consider a single neuron that learns the inclusive OR operation—a classic problem in symbolic logic. Consider two input elements, X_1 and X_2. If either of them or both have a positive value (or a certain value), then the result is also positive. This can be shown as follows:

Case	Inputs		Desired
	X_1	X_2	Results
1	0	0	0
2	0	1	1 (positive)
3	1	0	1 (positive)
4	1	1	1 (positive)

The neuron must be trained to recognize the input patterns and classify them to give the corresponding outputs. The procedure is to present to the neuron the sequence of the four input patterns so that the weights are adjusted by the computer after each iteration. This operation is repeated until the weights converge to one set of values that allows the neuron to correctly classify each of the four inputs. The results shown in Table 1.1 were produced by using a spreadsheet to execute the calculations.

In this simple example, a step function is used to evaluate the summation of input values. After calculating outputs, a measure of the error Δ between the output and the desired values is used to update

Table 1.1

Example of Supervised Learning

Parameters: $\alpha = 0.2$; Threshold $= 0.5$

Iteration	X_1	X_2	Z	Initial		Y	Δ	Final	
				W_1	W_2			W_1	W_2
1	0	0	0	0.1	0.3	0	0.0	0.1	0.3
	0	1	1	0.1	0.3	0	1.0	0.1	0.5
	1	0	1	0.1	0.5	0	1.0	0.3	0.5
	1	1	1	0.3	0.5	1	0.0	0.3	0.5
2	0	0	0	0.3	0.5	0	0.0	0.3	0.5
	0	1	1	0.3	0.5	0	1.0	0.3	0.7
	1	0	1	0.3	0.7	0	1.0	0.5	0.7
	1	1	1	0.5	0.7	1	0.0	0.5	0.7
3	0	0	0	0.5	0.7	0	0.0	0.5	0.7
	0	1	1	0.5	0.7	1	0.0	0.5	0.7
	1	0	1	0.5	0.7	0	1.0	0.7	0.7
	1	1	1	0.7	0.7	1	0.0	0.7	0.7
4	0	0	0	0.7	0.7	0	0.0	0.7	0.7
	0	1	1	0.7	0.7	1	0.0	0.7	0.7
	1	0	1	0.7	0.7	1	0.0	0.7	0.7
	1	1	1	0.7	0.7	1	0.0	0.7	0.7

the weights, subsequently reinforcing correct results. At any iteration in the process for a neuron, j, we get

$$\Delta = Z_j - Y_j$$

where Z and Y are the desired and actual outputs, respectively. Then, the updated weights are:

$$W_i \text{ (Final)} = W_i \text{ (Initial)} + \alpha \Delta X_i$$

where α is a parameter that controls how fast the learning takes place.

As shown in Table 1.1, each calculation uses one of the X_1 and X_2 pairs and the corresponding value for the OR operation along with initial values, W_1 and W_2, of the neuron's weights. In this example, the weights are assigned random values at the beginning and a *learning rate* (a parameter), α, is set to be relatively low. Δ is used to derive the final weights, which then become the initial weights in the next row.

The initial values of weights for each input are transformed using the equation above to values that are used with the next input (row). The threshold value (another parameter) causes the Y value to be 1 in the next row if the weighted sum of inputs is greater than 0.5; otherwise, the output is set to 0. In this example, in the first iteration two of the four outputs are incorrect ($\Delta = 1$) and no consistent set of weights has been found. In the subsequent iterations, the learning algorithm improves the results until it finally produces a set of weights that give the correct results. Once determined, a neuron with those weight values can quickly perform the OR operation.

In developing ANN, an attempt is made to fit the problem characteristic to one of the known learning algorithms. Software exists for all the most common algorithms, but it is best to use a well-known and well-characterized one, such as back-propagation.

TRAINING THE NETWORK

This phase consists of presenting the training data set to the network so that the weights can be adjusted to produce the desired output for each of the inputs. Weights are adjusted after each input vector is presented, so several iterations of the complete training set will be required until a consistent set of weights that works for *all* the training data is derived.

The choice of the network's structure (e.g., the number of nodes and layers), as well as the selection of the initial conditions of the network, determines the time needed for training. Therefore, these choices are important and require careful consideration at the outset of the process.

In the ideal case, the network can learn the features of the input data without learning irrelevant details. Thus, with the presentation of novel inputs that are not identical to those in the training set, the network would be able to make correct classifications.

In the first step of the development process, the available data are divided into training and testing data. After the training has been performed, it is necessary to test the network. The testing phase examines the performance of the network using the derived weights by measuring the ability of the network to classify the test data correctly. Black-box testing (comparing test results to actual historical results) is the primary approach to verify that inputs produce appropriate outputs.

In many cases, the network is not expected to perform perfectly, and only a certain level of quality is required. Usually, the neural network application is an alternative to another method that can be used as a standard. For example, a statistical technique or other quantitative methods may be known to classify inputs correctly 70 percent of the time. The neural network implementation often improves on that percentage. If the neural network is replacing manual operations, performance levels of human processing may be the standard for deciding if the testing phase is successful.

The test plan should include routine cases as well as potentially problematic situations, for example, at the boundaries of the problem domain. If the testing reveals large deviations, the training set needs to be reexamined and the training process may have to be reactivated.

In some cases, other methods can supplement straightforward black-box testing. For example, the weights can be analyzed statistically to look for unusually large values that indicate overtraining or unusually small weights that indicate unnecessary nodes, which can be eliminated. Also, certain weights that represent major factors in the input vector can be selectively activated to make sure that corresponding outputs respond properly.

Even at a performance level equal to that of a traditional method, the ANN may have other advantages. For example, the network is easily modified by retraining with new data. Other computerized techniques may require extensive reprogramming when changes are needed.

IMPLEMENTATION

The implementation of an ANN frequently requires proper interfaces to other computer-based information systems and training of the users. Ongoing monitoring and feedback to the developers are recommended for system improvements and long-term success. An important consideration is to gain confidence of the users and management early in the deployment to ensure that the system is accepted and used properly.

If it is a part of a larger system, the ANN will need convenient interfaces to other information systems, input/output (I/O) devices, and manual operations of the users. The system may need I/O manipulation subsystems such as signal digitizers and file conversion modules. Good documentation and user training are necessary to ensure successful integration into the mainstream operations. A convenient procedure must be planned for updating the training sets and initiating periodic retraining of the network. This includes the ability to recognize and include new cases that are discovered when the system is used routinely.

Ongoing monitoring and feedback to the developers is necessary for maintaining the neural network system. Periodic evaluation of system performance may reveal environmental changes or previously missed bugs that require changes in the network. Enhancements may be suggested as users become more familiar with the system, and feedback may be useful in the design of future versions or in new products.

NEURAL COMPUTING PARADIGMS

In building an artificial neural network, the builder must make many decisions. The most important decisions are:

❖ Size of training and test data

❖ Learning algorithms

❖ Topology—Number of processing elements and their configurations (inputs, layers, outputs)

❖ Transformation (transfer) function to be used

❖ Learning rate for each layer

❖ Select diagnostic and validation tools

A specific collection of configurations determined by these decisions is referred to as the network's paradigm.

PROGRAMMING NEURAL NETWORKS

Artificial neural networks are basically software applications that need to be programmed. Like any other application, ANN can be programmed with a programming language, a tool, or both.

A major portion of the programming deals with the training algorithms and the transfer and summation functions. It makes sense, therefore, to use development tools in which these standard computations are preprogrammed. Indeed, several dozen development tools are on the market. Some of these tools are similar to expert system shells. Even with the help of ANN tools, however, the job of developing a neural network may not be so simple. Specifically, it may be necessary to program the layout of the database, to partition the data (test data, training data), and to transfer the data to files suitable for input to an ANN tool.

Most development tools can support several network paradigms (up to several dozens). In addition to the standard products, many specialized products are available. For example, several products are based on spreadsheets (e.g., NNetSheet). Other products are designed to work with expert systems as hybrid development products.

The user of these tools is constrained by the configuration of the tool. Therefore, builders may prefer to use programming languages such as C, or to use spreadsheets to program the model and execute the calculations.

NEURAL NETWORK HARDWARE

Most current neural network applications involve software simulations that run on conventional sequential processors. Simulating a neural network means mathematically defining the nodes and weights assigned to it. So instead of using one CPU for each neuron, one CPU is used for all of the neurons. This simulation may require long processing times. Advances in hardware technology will greatly enhance the performance of future neural network systems by exploiting the inherent advantage of *massively parallel processing*. Hardware improvements will meet the higher requirements for memory and processing speed and thus allow shorter training times of larger networks.

Each processing element computes node outputs from the weights and input signals from other processors. Together, the network of neurons can store information that may be recalled to interpret and classify future inputs to the network.

To reduce the computational work of ANN, which can consist of hundreds of thousands of manipulations when the work is done on regular computers, one of three approaches is applicable:

1. *Faster machines.* For example, a machine supplemented by a faster math coprocessor can expedite work, but not too much (e.g., two to ten times faster).

2. *Neural chips.* Most of today's special semiconductor chips can execute computations very fast, but they cannot be used to train the network. So it is necessary to train "off the chip." This problem is expected to be overcome soon; in the interim, acceleration boards are useful. The idea is to provide implementation of neural network data structures through hardware rather than software, using an analog device (e.g., Intel 80170 Electronically Trainable ANN) or a digital device, or even an optical one.[10] (See Caudill [1991] for details.) Most hardware-implemented neural networks are still in the developmental stage.

3. *Accelerator boards.* These are dedicated multichip processors that can be added to regular computers; they function similarly to a math coprocessor. Because they are especially designed for ANN, they are very fast in this application. (For example, such a processor can be ten to 100 times faster than the 80486 processor.) Acceleration boards are currently the good approach to speeding up computations. Some examples are the BrainMaker Accelerator Board, Balboa/860 boards, and NeuroBoard, which is at least 100 times faster than the 80486 processor. Accelerator boards are extremely useful because they reduce training time, which usually is long. For ex-

ample, independent testing with the NeuroBoard accelerator showed a reduced training time from seven minutes to one second.

CONCLUSION

Artificial neural networks represent a radically different form of computation from the more common algorithmic model. Neural computation is massively parallel, typically employing from several thousand to many millions of individual simple processors, arranged in a communicative network. ANN technology can deliver performance demonstrably superior to conventional problem-solving approaches in a wide variety of areas. Although numerous neural network models and products supporting those models are currently available, the deployment of neural network-based systems to aid in making business decisions is at a relatively early stage of development, with much of the current activity still taking place at the research level.

The unique learning capabilities of ANN promise benefits in many aspects of investment and financial decision-making which involve the recognition of patterns, and in which adequate representation of knowledge is difficult or impossible. Commercial applications likely to be most successful are those that directly assist finance professionals in one or more specific aspects of their work, such as implementation of a particular strategy, or that provide improved results relative to statistical and other conventional forms of analysis when used for more routine operations such as credit, risk, and exception assessment.

ENDNOTES

1. The material in this chapter is based largely on the work of L. Medsker as it appears in E. Turban, *Expert Systems and Applied Artificial Intelligence* (New York: Macmillan Publishing Co., 1992) Chapter 18; and in part on the work of R. R. Trippi, "Intelligent Systems for Investment Decision Making," in *Managing Institutional Assets*, ed. F. Fabozzi, (Harper and Row, 1990).

2. M. Caudill and C. Butler, *Naturally Intelligent Systems* (Cambridge, Mass.: MIT Press, 1990).

3. R. Hecht-Nielson, *Neurocomputing* (Reading, Mass.: Addison Wesley, 1990).

4. T. Khanna, *Foundations of Neural Networks* (Reading, Mass.: Addison Wesley, 1990).

5. R. Beale and T. Jackson, *Neural Computing* (Bristol, England: Adam Hilger, 1990).

6. J. Hopfield, "Neural Networks and Physical Systems with Emergent Collective Computational Abilities," *Proceedings of the National Academy of Science USA*, 1985, 79, pp. 141–152.

7. T. Kohonen, *Self-Organization and Associative Memory* (Berlin: Springer-Verlag, 1984).

8. G. Carpenter and S. Grossberg, "A Massively Parallel Architecture for a Self-Organizing Neural Pattern Recognition Machine," *Computer Vision, Graphics and Image Processing*, 1987, 37, pp. 54–115.

9. R. P. Lippman, "Review of Neural Networks for Speech Recognition," *Neural Computation, 1989*, 1:1, pp. 1–38.

10. M. Caudill, "Embedded Neural Networks," *AI Expert*, December 1989, April 1990, June 1990, July 1990, September 1990, December 1990, April 1991.

2

ARTIFICIAL NEURAL SYSTEMS: A NEW TOOL FOR FINANCIAL DECISION-MAKING

Delvin D. Hawley, John D. Johnson, Dijjotam Raina

INTRODUCTION

The financial press has largely confined its coverage of artificial intelligence applications to so-called "expert systems." While expert systems have been successfully applied to some financial decision tasks, many others are beyond the scope of expert systems technology. The disadvantages of expert systems include the difficulty of programming and maintaining the system, the enormous time and effort required to extract the knowledge base from human experts and translate it into the IF-THEN rules upon which the system is based, and the inability of an

This article originally appeared in *Financial Analysts Journal*, November/December 1990, pp. 63–72. Reprinted with permission.

expert system to use inductive learning and inference to adapt the rule base to changing situations. These problems may be particularly troublesome in financial analysis and management environments.

Many of these problems could be overcome with another product of artificial intelligence research—the artificial neural system, also known as an artificial neural network, electronic neural network, or simply neural net. Neural networks attempt to model human intuition by simulating the physical process upon which intuition is based—that is, by simulating the process of adaptive biological learning (although on a much less complex scale). A neural network is theoretically capable of producing a proper response to a given problem (or the best possible response when more than one response is applicable) even when the information is noisy or incomplete, or when no set procedure exists for solving the problem.

THE DECISION ENVIRONMENT

Simon has classified managerial decisions along a continuum from highly structured to highly unstructured.[1] In structured decisions, the procedures for obtaining the best (or at least a good enough) solution are best known in advance, and the objectives are clearly specified. Managers can call on predefined models, whether conceptual or computer-based, to assist in the decision process. In unstructured problems, however, intuition plays a larger role in decision-making. The manager may seek help from experts, but the final decision generally involves ad hoc analysis and a substantial subjective element.

Many highly structured, routine tasks can be handled effectively by basic computer systems, readily available commercial software, and lower-level management or even clerical personnel. Most decisions faced by top-level financial managers, however, are highly unstructured in nature and not easily adapted to conventional methods of computer-aided analysis and decision support. In addition, many of these decisions are largely unique in character.

In such cases, the manager may have to draw upon incomplete, ambiguous, partially incorrect, or irrelevant information and analyze it in a highly subjective and ad hoc manner. The manager may not be able to objectify his decision process, or to break it down in a step-by-step manner.

Computer technology, at its current state of development, has little to offer decision-makers faced with unstructured problems. CFOs, for example, may call on corporate computer information systems or external on-line data sources such as Dow-Jones News Retrieval to acquire information and spreadsheet programs or other software to analyze the information. If more formal or complicated software is required, however, it must be created from scratch by internal or external programmers. This can take many weeks or months and usually involves great expense. In addition, the resulting program may have to be reworked each time it is applied to a new problem. Because most financial decisions must be made very quickly, this is simply not a viable alternative for decision-makers in many cases.

As a consequence, top-level financial decision-makers have obtained very little direct benefit from the tremendous advances in computer technology over the past decade, despite the arrival of decision support systems and expert systems. Decision support systems aim to assist the decision-maker without constraining the decision process. Expert systems attempt to model the decision-making ability of human experts. The intuition or knowledge base of the experts must be programmed into an expert system, however, and the creation of the knowledge base is a long and expensive process. Expert systems thus simply are not economical for one-time decision problems. Furthermore, it is rarely clear what an expert's knowledge base includes and what heuristics must be used to model it.

In unstructured decision environments, artificial neural systems offer distinct advantages over decision support and expert systems. Neural nets can be defined as "highly simplified models of the human nervous system, exhibiting abilities such as learning, generalization, and abstraction."[2] While the concept of such systems is not new, only recently have technological advances made artificial neural systems a viable alternative for many financial problems.

NEURAL NETWORKS

An artificial neural system (ANS) models, in a very simplified way, the biological systems of the human brain. It does so by mimicking the basic functions of the major component of the human brain—the neuron. Simulated neurons serve as the basic functional unit of the ANS in much the same way that binary electronic switches serve as the basic units in digital computers.

A neuron, illustrated in Figure 2.1, is a simple structure that performs three basic functions—the input, processing, and output of signals. The input components (called dendrites) receive electrochemical impulses (through synaptic links) from the output components (called axons) of other neurons. Each neuron may be connected to 1,000 or more neighbors via a network of dendrites and axons.

The processor component of the neuron (called the nucleus or soma) works very simply. The neuron's many dendrites receive impulses from other neurons and transfer these impulses to the soma. (All dendrites do not receive impulses simultaneously; each dendrite can receive an impulse at any point in time from any of the axons to which it is connected.) The soma collects these impulses, sums them, and compares the sum to an output threshold or "action potential." This action potential is the level of stimulation (called the "activation level") necessary for the neuron to "fire" or send an impulse through its axon to other connected neurons.

A neuron is a much slower mechanism (possibly a thousand times slower) than the digital switches in conventional computers. Even so, the brain is capable of solving difficult pattern-recognition problems

---

Figure 2.1

A Single Neuron

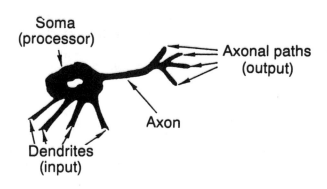

(vision and language, for example) in about one-half second, while even simple pattern-recognition tasks are beyond the capabilities of conventional digital computers. The brain achieves its processing speed and power by linking tremendous numbers of inherently slow neurons into an immensely complex network that allows many individual neurons to function simultaneously. (This process of sub-dividing tasks for simultaneous completion is referred to as "parallel distributed processing.")

Artificial Neurons

Like the brain itself, an ANS depends for power and speed on the simultaneous functioning of its individual neural units. In most cases, the ANS requires computer hardware with parallel processing (as opposed to the standard serial) capabilities. Because the outputs of an ANS are parallel (involving simultaneous transmission of data vectors), ANS implementations usually require specialized hardware, sometimes referred to as "neurocomputers," designed to facilitate parallel processing. The parallel inputs required by neural networks may also require the installation of special-purpose preprocessors, or "front-ends."[3]

Neural net systems differ from traditional computer applications, including most expert systems, in many other ways. Neural nets are not "programmed" in the traditional sense. An ANS is not provided with quantitative descriptions of objects or patterns to be recognized, or with logical criteria for distinguishing such objects from similar objects. Instead, it is presented with repetitive examples that display variety; cars come in all shapes and sizes, mammals include cows and mice but not alligators, etc. The ANS "discovers" the relationships between inputs by observing the examples and progressively refining an internal matrix of weights governing the relationships between its simulated neurons. The ANS thus learns through adaptation—the major difference between ANS and expert system applications. Expert systems are based on inference from accurate representation of the problem environment; they generally have little or no learning capability.

An ANS has three major components—a network topology, a spreading activation method, and a training mechanism. The network topology consists of a set of nodes connected via links. Nodes directly linked to one another are said to be "neighbors." Nodes are connected in parallel—that is, each node is connected to many others. Furthermore, the flow of information through the system need not be unidirectional; information can flow in either direction along any link.

Figure 2.2 shows a simple artificial neuron consisting of a node (Y) and its associated links. Input signals—the ys in Figure 2.2—are received from the node's links, assigned weights (the ws) and added. The value of the node, Y, is the sum of all the weighted input signals. This value is compared with the node's threshold activation level. When the value meets the threshold level, the node transmits a signal to its neighbors.

The activation level of any node depends on the node's previous activation level and on the activation levels of its neighbors. A node's activation level is communicated to its neighbors at each point in time via the system's spreading activation method. The neighbors use the activation level to update their own levels of activation. Weights, which are numeric estimates of connection strengths, are assigned to the links between nodes.

If the activation level of one node tends to increase (decrease) the activation level of a neighboring node, then the connection is designated as an excitatory (inhibitory) link and is assigned a positive (negative) weight. These weights—numeric estimates of the direction and strength of connections between nodes—are the instrumental elements of the ANS "learning" process.[4]

Figure 2.2

A Single Artificial Neuron

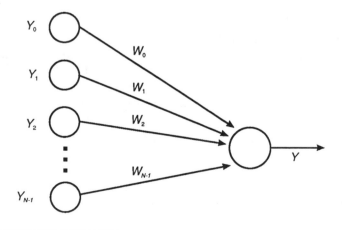

The learning process of an ANS is actually a training process. An animal can be trained by rewarding desired responses and punishing undesired responses. The ANS training process can also be thought of as involving rewards and punishments. When the system responds correctly to an input, the "reward" consists of a strengthening of the current matrix of nodal weights. This makes it more likely that a similar response will be produced by similar inputs in the future. When the system responds incorrectly, the "punishment" calls for the adjustment of the nodal weights based on the particular learning algorithm employed, so that the system will respond differently when it encounters similar inputs again. Desirable actions are thus progressively reinforced, while undesirable actions are progressively inhibited.

An ANS can be trained using either a supervised or an unsupervised methodology. In supervised training, an input information vector is paired with a desired output or target vector.[5] For example, the input vector might contain a series of numbers, while the output vector contains the product of the numbers. The objective of the training process in this case would be for the ANS to discover the pattern underlying the relationship between the input and the target output.

Prior to training, the system may have no knowledge of numbers, their relative magnitudes or mathematical operations; in the terminology of psychology, it is a *tabula rasa* or "blank slate" consisting only of a matrix of arbitrarily assigned nodal weights. The system would need to discover that the symbol "6" implies something different from the symbol "2," and that the symbol "12" is related to them in some consistent manner. It would also need to discover that the symbol "12" can be related to "3" and "4" in a similar and consistent manner.

In unsupervised training, the system is presented with only the input vector; no target vector exists. The ANS objective is to detect and identify patterns in the input. The system self-organizes until a consistent output is produced whenever the input vector is applied. The characteristics of the output may be quite unpredictable prior to training.[6] As with supervised learning, the system in unsupervised training discovers recurring patterns in the input information, but it must do so without any information about the desirable or correct output. Such a system could be trained, for example, to recognize and identify specific musicians in recordings of symphonic music.

ANS VERSUS ES

An expert system (ES) depends on the representation of the expert's knowledge as a series of IF-THEN conditions or rules, known as the knowledge base. These rules must first be determined by observing human experts, then programmed into the ES using special languages such as PROLOG or shells such as Knowledge Craft, ART, or KEE. This process can be time-consuming and expensive. Coats points out that ES programmers, or knowledge engineers, "spend weeks, months, sometimes years with experts, coaxing them to articulate the objective and subjective factors, rules, and thought processes used in problem solving . . . The fact is that extracting knowledge from the experts presents a very serious bottleneck."[7] Furthermore, once the system is functional, making even minor changes to the knowledge base can be a complex and expensive process because of the intricate relations between the rules forming the knowledge base.[8] Thus, expert systems are generally cost effective only for frequently recurring problems of a very narrow scope that can be solved by a knowledge base that is essentially static.

Neural net systems do not exhibit these same shortcomings, primarily because they do not require a predefined knowledge base. Changes in the problem do not require reprogramming the ANS; the system simply retrains itself based on the new information. The ANS creates its own knowledge system based on the inputs (and possibly outputs) to which it is exposed. It is also self-maintaining, responding automatically to changes in the problem environment by adjusting nodal weights. Best of all, it is fundamentally a dynamic, rather than a static, system. It continues to adapt and improve as it is exposed to new information.

Neural nets will certainly not replace programmers in the foreseeable future, but they do offer a much more powerful and expedient alternative in some applications, particularly those involving pattern recognition.[9] The abilities of an ANS to self-organize and to function without a preprogrammed knowledge base give it an important additional advantage in business applications—protection of sensitive information.

Another problem with expert systems, as pointed out by Coats, is that "ES cannot really deal with erroneous, inconsistent, or incomplete knowledge because most ES rely on rules that represent abstracted knowledge of the domain [i.e., the problem space] and thus the ES are not able to reason from basic principles."[10] In other words, a fairly complete understanding of the human expert's knowledge is a prerequisite to creating the knowledge base for the ES. The system is not able to make "educated guesses" or employ "common sense" as a human expert would when presented with a problem that did not have a clear solution path. It is also unable to perform effectively when the input information is incomplete, ambiguous (noisy), or partially erroneous.

It is in this area that neural net systems may offer the clearest advantage over expert systems. The ANS can accommodate variations in inputs. That is to say, the ANS is very good at filtering out noise and isolating useful input information. People are very good at this, too. A human reader, for example, can often make sense of a text that is largely illegible or incorrect.

The real world rarely obliges financial decision-makers by presenting them with clearly defined and precise information. Much of the information they receive is noisy, incomplete, and full of error. Conventional computers and expert systems can be programmed to tolerate noisy inputs, but the necessary algorithms involve such an enormous computational load that their use is often impractical. Neural networks, however, can work with noisy and incomplete inputs and produce the correct output by making use of context and generalizing or "filling in the gaps" in incomplete information. This ability to generalize is based on the adaptive structure of the neural net system, rather than on complex programming.

Neural nets are also capable of abstraction—i.e., inferring the "ideal set" from a non-ideal training set. This process involves determining the most prominent characteristics of the training set, then using those characteristics to construct an internal representation of the ideal or archetypical pattern.[11]

It is the nature of an ANS to make "educated guesses," inferring as much as possible from previous inputs and experience. In the early training stages of an ANS, the educated guesses will undoubtedly range very wide of the mark because the system has had very little education. As the training process progresses, however, the experiential basis for the educated guesses will become more refined, and the quality of the guesses will, on average, improve. In fact, an ANS, unlike an ES, can potentially exceed the ability of human experts. A well-trained ANS, for example, may be able to discern patterns that human experts would miss, and to recognize patterns with a higher degree of consistency.

ANS Disadvantages

A major and inherent problem of artificial neural systems is that the internal structure of the neural network makes it difficult to trace the steps by which the output is reached. In other words, an ANS cannot tell the user how it processed the input information or reached a conclusion. That process is represented only in the matrix of connected weights, which, at least at present, cannot be translated into an algorithm that would be intelligible or useful outside the ANS.[12] The output cannot be decomposed into discrete steps or series of operations, as would be possible with an ES rule base or any conventional computer program.[13] It is thus not possible to check intermediate computations or to debug an ANS in the traditional sense. The only way to test the system for consistency and reliability is to monitor the output.

The absence of a clearly identifiable internal logic could be a severe stumbling block in the acceptance of neural networks, at least for some applications. Where is the accountability? How does the user know if the system malfunctions? It would be ill-advised, given the current state of technology, to use an ANS to control nuclear weapons on a warship.

Many important business decisions made by humans suffer from the same shortcoming. An executive can rarely recognize and understand *all* the steps that went into a given decision, let alone be able to explain the process to another person. It is the average effectiveness of the executive's decisions—the dependability of the output—that counts, not the intricacies of the intermediate processes. Although this standard may apply to human decision-makers, however, many people are going to be uncomfortable applying it to computer-based systems.

Finally, the ANS learning process requires a large number of training examples, hence can involve substantial time and effort. For most conceivable financial applications, however, ample training examples would be readily available, so relatively little time or effort would be involved in data collection. Furthermore, the time and effort required to train an ANS would be much less than that required to extract and translate an expert's knowledge base for an ES.

ANS APPLICATIONS

Neural net systems are most effectively applied to three tasks (all based primarily on pattern recognition)—classification, associative memory, and clustering.[14] Classification involves the assignment of input vectors to *predefined* groups or classes based on patterns that exist in the input information. An ANS should be successful in this task even if the inputs are incomplete or have been corrupted. If the input vector consists of sounds of a musician playing an instrument in a busy subway station, for example, an ANS should be able to pick out the sounds of the instrument and classify it as a saxophone, piano, or a bagpipe.

The recognition of handwritten characters is another example of a classification task. The recognition and identification of underwater targets by sonar would be a very appropriate ANS application.[15] In finance, an example of classification would be the grouping of bonds, based on patterns in the issuers' financial data, into categories that match the agency ratings assigned to those bonds.

An ANS can also function as associative memory (also referred to as content-addressable memory). In this task, the class exemplar is desired and the input pattern is used to determine which exemplar to produce. Content-addressable memory is useful when only part of a pattern is available and the complete pattern is required. As an example, the input vector may consist of a digitized picture of a smudged fingerprint and the desired output would be a reconstruction of the complete fingerprint.

In clustering, the ANS is used to group or "vector-quantize" a large number of diverse inputs, each of which has elements of similarity with other inputs. This function is useful in compressing or filtering input data without losing important information. An example would be clustering corporate bonds into homogeneous risk classes based on financial statement data. In this case, the number and composition of the risk classes would be determined by the ANS, not by the user. This differs from classification, discussed above, in that the categories are not predefined.

ANS in Use

Researchers are currently working on many projects using ANS technology. Sejnowski and Rosenberg have created a neural network, NET-talk, that learned the correct pronunciation of words from written text (ASCII characters) even though it began with no linguistic rules.[16] The ANS taught itself pronunciation skills (approximately equivalent to those of a six-year-old child) *overnight*, simply by listening to the correct pronunciation of speech from text. In contrast, Digital Equipment Corporation designed an expert system called DECtalk that serves the same function but required 20 years of linguistic research to devise the necessary knowledge base.[17] Current ANS research is directed toward the recognition of radar and sonar targets and the detection of plastic explosives in airline baggage.[18] In the business and finance areas, researchers are working on the development of neural networks that can assess the risk of mortgage loans and rate the quality of corporate bonds.[19]

While a good deal of ANS research has focused on the behavior of stock prices, it has had only moderate success to date. Halbert White of the University of California at San Diego, for example, provided an ANS with daily returns for IBM common stock over 500 days in the mid-1970s, the objective being to extract predictable fluctuations in the stock price.[20] However, only random movements were evident. White points out that "it won't be easy to uncover predictable stock market fluctuations with neural nets, and if you succeed, you'll want to keep it secret." Of course, this application presupposes that predictable patterns in stock prices exist, contrary to a preponderance of empirical evidence supporting weak-form market efficiency.

The inability of an ANS to discover stock price patterns does not necessarily imply a failure of the system; it could be construed simply as additional evidence supporting market efficiency. Unfortunately, there is no way to know which conclusion is correct. The situation is similar to that of scientists monitoring radio signals in space. The absence of nonrandom signals does not necessarily imply that intelligent extraterrestrial life does not exist; the search may simply not be focused in the proper place, or the technology may be incorrectly applied.

APPLICATIONS IN FINANCE

Tasks requiring accuracy of computational results or intensive calculations are best left to conventional computer applications. As we have noted, artificial neural networks are best applied to problem environments that are highly unstructured, require some form of pattern recognition, and may involve incomplete or corrupted data. Below, we outline some potential applications of ANS to problems faced by corporate financial managers, financial institutions, and professional investors.

Corporate Finance

Financial Simulation. The financial structure of any business operation constitutes an immensely complex and dynamic environment. While financial management tasks can be broken down conceptually and functionally into a number of subtasks, the interrelations between these subtasks are still enormously complex. Artificial neural systems can be used to create models of segments of the corporate financial environment. Such models can be: (1) specific to a particular company, (2) dynamic with respect to changes in the financial structure of the company over time, and (3) reflective of the relations between the segment modeled, other financial and nonfinancial segments of the company, and the external environment.

An ANS might, for example, be created to simulate the behavior of a firm's credit customers as economic conditions change. The input vectors could consist of economic data and customer-specific data, and the output could be the expected purchase/payment behavior of the customer given the input conditions. Training data would be based on actual behavior of customers in the past. Such a system would be useful for planning for bad-debt expenses and the cyclical expansion and contraction of accounts receivable and for evaluating the credit terms and limits assigned to individual customers.

Neural net simulations might also be designed for many other segments of the firm's financial environment, such as cash management, evaluation of capital investments, asset and personnel risk management (insurance), exchange rate risk management, and prediction of credit costs and availability based on the firm's financial data. The richest potential for ANS applications in corporate financial management may well lie in simulations of this sort.

Prediction. Some tasks involving financial forecasting can be performed more efficiently using conventional computers and software rather than neural networks. This is particularly true of those tasks involving complex numerical calculations in well-identified models. However, the financial analyst is always concerned with the effects of certain actions on the behavior of investors.

Investors do not react to isolated bits of information about a company; they are, rather, influenced by the comprehensive body of information concerning all aspects of the company. It may be possible to train an ANS to mimic the behavior of investors in response to changes in the collective financial condition or policies of the company. Using actual investors as training models, one might create an ANS that could simulate investors' reactions to, say, changes in dividend policy, accounting methods, reported earnings, capital structure, or any other items of interest. Past studies of this sort have relied primarily on changes in stock price to gauge investor reaction, but investors may react in many ways other than buying or selling stock. An ANS could improve the financial analyst's ability to predict investor reactions to changes in corporate financial policy.

Evaluation. It should be possible to train an ANS to estimate a value for acquisition targets based on the target's financial information. The training procedure would involve both an input vector consisting of financial information concerning the target company and a target output consisting of the acquisition value estimate of a human expert. The objective of the ANS would be to simulate the valuation processes used by the human expert in order to derive for any target a value estimate that would be comparable to the estimates of a human expert.

The system could also be trained to select desirable acquisition targets on the basis of criteria other than simple valuation—criteria, for example, known only to the human expert and involving perhaps "hunches" or personal preferences. That is, the system would learn to mimic the idiosyncrasies and intuition of the human expert without depending on definable rules or programmable logic in the process. The numerous benefits of such a system would include the following.

1. The system could be used to screen a very large number of companies for undervaluation or desirability for acquisition. The decision-maker would save much time by looking only at companies that were closest to the "ideal" acquisition target.

2. Because the system would not depend on preprogrammed rules or a set knowledge base, it could easily adapt to mimic the evaluation techniques of any decision-maker.

3. The system would automatically adapt to changes in a decision-maker's analytical procedures and selection criteria over time.

An expert system could conceivably perform a similar task, but it would be severely limited in comparison with an ANS. The ES would require a knowledge base extracted from the human expert, and it is unlikely that such a knowledge base would incorporate all of the subjective elements and idiosyncracies of the expert's decision process. Even if it did, the resulting ES could not adapt to changes in personal preferences or selection criteria (or could not be adapted without substantial reprogramming costs and delays).

Credit Approval. While the task of approving customers for credit and assigning credit limits is generally delegated to lower-level financial staff, it is still a labor-intensive and time-consuming process that has a significant impact on the profitability of most companies. Approval procedures based on credit scoring can be successfully implemented with conventional computer equipment and software, but such systems cannot incorporate the subjective and otherwise nonquantifiable elements of a human's decision process. In addition, much of the information concerning customers does not come to the decision-maker in a standard format (e.g., Dun & Bradstreet credit reports have a standardized form, but financial statements display a remarkable diversity).

An ANS could be trained using customer data as the input vector and the actual decisions of the credit analyst as the desired output vector. The objective of the system would be to mimic the human decision-maker in granting or revoking credit and setting credit limits. In addition, the system would be able to deal with the diversity of input information without requiring that the information be restated in a standard form.

Financial Institutions

Assessing Lending/Bankruptcy Risk. The credit-approval system described above would be applicable in commercial and consumer lending as well. The diversity of loan applicants and lending arrangements encountered by most lending institutions could be handled quite efficiently in an ANS environment. While the ANS may not be used to make the final decision on loans of major importance to the institution, its output could be viewed as one more expert opinion included in the decision process.

Security/Asset Portfolio Management. Financial institutions must manage a wide variety of investment portfolios involving many types of assets—stocks, bonds, mortgages, real estate, etc. Decisions concerning risk adjustments, market timing, tax effects, maturity structure and many other variables must be made almost continuously. For trust departments in large banks, this can be an enormously complex tax involving many people. The task is complicated even more by the constant fluctuation of the financial and economic environment. Given the unstructured nature of the portfolio manager's decision processes, the uncertainty of the economic environment and the diversity of information involved, this would be an appropriate arena for a neural network implementation.

Pricing IPOs. The pricing of new securities by investment bankers is always a difficult and complicated process that has a direct impact on the profitability of the firm. For initial public offerings of common stock, however, the pricing process is most difficult. Information concerning the issuer may be incomplete, in a non-standard format, and cover only a short time period. Information about similar companies and the industry will need to be considered, as well as information about current and future economic conditions. In addition, there are many subjective elements involved in gauging investors' level of receptiveness and in determining the most opportune time to release the issue.

Here again, an ANS could be trained to mimic the decisions of the expert(s) by observing the inputs and outputs of actual decisions made in the past. In addition, in this environment, the system has the potential to improve on the expert's performance, because the input data can include actual price performance and selling activity subsequent to a security's issuance. The system thus has the potential for learning directly from the decision-maker and also from the actual results in the decision. The ANS might thus discover relationships that were overlooked or misinterpreted by the expert. In addition, such a system will continue to serve the firm even if the human expert leaves, thus perpetuating the expert's knowledge and valuable experience.

Professional Investors

Identification of Arbitrage Opportunities. Consider an analyst who specializes in the identification of hostile takeover targets in advance of tender offer announcements. This analyst's selection of likely targets, and therefore desirable investments, depends on many bits of information and a good amount of personal experience and judgment. An ANS could be trained to assist the analyst in the identification task by observing the actual decisions he/she makes and the errors that those decisions have produced. After training, the ANS could improve upon the efficiency of the analyst by increasing the number of companies that can be examined in a given time span, thus allowing more thorough screening and more frequent updating of each company's evaluation. Even a small improvement in the performance of the decision-maker could result in a substantial improvement in profitability.

Technical Analysis. Technical analysis, with the objective of predicting future short-term movements in stock prices based on patterns in *ex post* price and volume data, has been the subject of much research but has achieved almost no empirical support. Even so, many professional and private investors use technical analysis as a primary investment-selection tool. This group has long voiced the opinion that empirical studies of technical analysis have failed to corroborate its usefulness because they applied it in an isolated, incomplete or erroneous manner and because the researchers lack the necessary level of experience, and the intuition it brings, to use technical analysis effectively. These investors believe that the intuition of the experienced analyst, not the blind application of a selection procedure or formula, is the key to success; someone has to interpret the data, recognize the important patterns and make the predictions. Market technicians may also argue that a successful technical analyst is unlikely to divulge the nature of his or her techniques to researchers, because any "edge" the techniques afford the analyst may be destroyed if other investors begin to use them. Consequently, researchers may have been studying a set of analysis tools that is missing the most important parts.

While the pattern-recognition capabilities of neural nets suggest possibilities for the application of ANS technology to research studies concerning technical analysis, it is likely that the most beneficial applications would be designed by and for the technicians themselves. If an ANS could be trained to simulate the experience-based intuition of a successful technician, it could result in a substantial increase in the number of stocks that could be analyzed in real time. While a similar result could probably be achieved with an expert system, the technician would have to divulge valuable information to a knowledge engineer and the resulting system could not be easily adapted to changes in the market environment or the prerogatives of the analyst. The special abilities of neural nets would be very well adapted to this particular application.

Fundamental Analysis. Insofar as fundamental analysis also requires judgment and intuition based on experience (although possibly to a lesser extent than technical analysis), this area also offers great promise for successful ANS applications. Given the vast amount of information that can be involved for each company at each time point, the parallel processing capability of artificial neural systems offer a very important potential advantage in this area. Much more so than for technical analysis, the inputs for fundamental analysis are parallel in nature. An input data vector for one company could include all the raw data from many years of financial statements, current and historical market and economic data, industry averages, and more. The ANS could be trained to evaluate stocks using these inputs and the analyst's own evaluations as the target output vector. As with technical analysis, the goal of the system would be to improve upon the efficiency of the analyst by allowing analysis of a greater number of stocks and more frequent updates.

CONCLUSION

We hope that the preceding discussion will stimulate financial managers and researchers to recognize that artificial neural nets offer great potential for improvements in productivity and efficiency. The necessary technology exists, and significant improvements will certainly continue in the years ahead. It is quite possible that the development of artificial neural networks will prove to be one of the most important, practical and fruitful endeavors in finance in the next decade. There would seem to be no area of business management that is better suited for successful ANS applications, nor any that is so likely to benefit from them.[21]

ENDNOTES

1. H. Simon, *The New Science of Management Decision* (New York: Harper and Row, 1960).

2. P. D. Wasserman and T. Schwartz, "Neural Network, Part 1," *IEEE Expert*, Winter 1987, p. 10.

3. It should be noted that neural network topologies can be simulated with software in order to build working prototypes. For a list of

available software and hardware products, see the August 1989 issue of *Byte*.

4. A technical discussion of the ANS training process is available from the authors on request.

5. P. D. Wasserman and T. Schwartz, "Neural Network, Part 2," *IEEE Expert*, Spring 1988, p. 12.

6. *Ibid.*

7. P. K. Coats, "Why Expert Systems Fail," *Financial Management*, August 1988, p. 81.

8. *Ibid.*, p. 80.

9. Wasserman and Schwartz, "Neural Network, Part 2," *op. cit.*, p. 11.

10. Coats, "Why Expert Systems Fail," *op. cit.*, p. 80.

11. Wasserman and Schwartz, "Neural Network, Park 2," *op. cit.*, p. 11.

12. It should be noted that a number of researchers are currently addressing this problem.

13. See Y. S. Abu-Mostafa and D. Pslatis, "Optical Neural Computers," *Scientific American*, March 1989 and J. A. Anderson, E. J. Wisniewski and S. R. Viscuso, "Software for Neural Networks," *ACM Computer Architecture Transactions*, forthcoming.

14. Simon, *The New Science of Management Decision, op. cit.*

15. K. K. Obermeier and J. J. Barron, "Time to Get Fired Up," *Byte*, August 1989.

16. T. Sejnowski and C. R. Rosenberg, "NETtalk: A Parallel Network that Learns to Read Aloud" (John Hopkins University Technical Report, 1, 1986).

17. J. Giarratano and G. Riley, *Expert Systems* (Boston: PWS-KENT Publishing, 1989).

18. *Ibid.*, and Obermeier and Barron, "Time to Get Fired Up," *op. cit.*, p. 220.

19. B. Bower, "Neural Networks: The buck stops here," *Science*, August 6, 1988.

20. H. White, "Neural Network Learning and Statistics," *AI Expert*, December 1989.

21. The authors of Chapter Two thank Pamela Coats, Van Harlow, and colleagues at the University of Mississippi for their helpful comments.

3

APPLYING NEURAL NETWORKS

Part I: An Overview

Casimir C. "Casey" Klimasauskas

BASIC CONCEPTS IN NEURAL NETWORKS

Before looking at the application process, let us establish some basic concepts. First, a definition. *Neural networks* (artificial neural systems) are an information processing technology inspired by studies of the brain and nervous system.

As an information processing technology, a neural network accepts several inputs, performs a series of operations on them, and produces one or more outputs. In this sense, they are just like a subroutine.

Where does the term neural network come from? In personal computers, a local area network connects several computers into an inter-

This article originally appeared in *PCAI*, January/February, 1991, pp. 30–33, March/April, 1991, pp. 27–34, and May/June, 1991, pp. 20–24. Reprinted with permission.

related, functioning whole. Within the brain, the elemental computing units called neurons are connected together into a functioning whole as well. Technologies inspired by studies of the brain use the basic concept of neurons connected together into a functioning whole. Hence the term, neural networks.

One key difference between neural networks and other technologies (database, expert systems, programming languages) is that the method for how the inputs are processed is developed by showing the network examples of inputs and what the outputs should be. You might think of an untrained neural network as a lump of clay on the potter's wheel. As the network is shown examples of how it should respond to various inputs, the clay is shaped until it reflects the subtle relationships between the inputs and the outputs. The actual process which occurs is that the neural network designer selects a basic architecture in which the problem is to be solved. This basic architecture is shown an example set of inputs. It uses these inputs to devise an output (actual output). The network output (actual output) is compared to what the answer should have been (desired output). The difference between these is the error. The error is used to adjust various parameters in the basic architecture so that the next time the neural network is shown this example, it will produce more nearly the correct answer. This process is repeated several times for each example in the training set.

WHAT PROBLEMS SHOULD NEURAL NETWORKS BE CONSIDERED FOR?

It is important to recognize that neural networks are an evolutionary technology. They are able to improve the performance of several existing technologies. When used in conjunction with or as a replacement to these technologies in high-value or high-volume applications, the financial impact can be tremendous. Examples of the areas where neural networks work best include: Classifying data, modeling and forecasting, and signal processing.

Classifying data is currently one of the most widely used capabilities of neural networks. Examples include targeted marketing (deciding who to send mail-order catalogs to), credit approval (deciding who gets credit or how much credit should be granted to an individual), stock picking (ranking by predicted performance), automated trading, picking winning football teams, predicting future job performance based on aptitude tests, classifying sonar signals (deciding if the sonar return signal is from an underwater mine or a rock), predicting solar flares (very important to the power industry), sorting syringes (needles) into good or bad, testing electric motors for proper operation, diagnosing problems with automobile engines, and so forth. Neural networks used in these applications typically replace statistically based systems or a variety of other pattern classification systems. Performance improvements range from 5 percent to 50 percent reduction in error. In some instances where the problem is well understood, although neural networks will match or approximate the performance of statistical or pattern classification systems, they may not do any better.

Modeling and forecasting are concerned with developing mathematical relationships between several continuous input variables and typically one, though possibly more, output variables. In forecasting, the input variables consist of samples of the data to predict at several points back in time. Examples of modeling include developing models of chemical processes for optimizing performance, building models of very complex programs for designing electric generators, or predicting interest rates or inventory levels. The technologies currently used in these applications include linear and polynomial regression techniques, auto-regressive (integrated) moving average (ARMA & ARIMA), and Box-Jenkins. Where these techniques are being used or considered, neural networks should also be considered. As an example of how well these techniques do, Lapedes & Farber at Los Alamos National Laboratories found that neural network approaches substantially outperformed all existing techniques for forecasting chaotic time series. In another instance, a neural network was trained to predict the direction of a fractal dimension 13 time series (stock price) two steps in advance. It was successful in doing this 87 percent of the time. This is quite a feat!

In the area of signal processing, neural networks, in particular backpropagation and related networks, may be thought of as techniques for developing a multilevel convolver. This results in the ability to create better signal discriminant systems, which can be used in classifying sounds, for speech recognition, and as a replacement for various single-level convolutional filters.

In summary, the most exciting aspect of neural network technology is that it represents a fundamental breakthrough in the ability to approximate complex mathematical mappings. The practical side of this is the wide range of applications that incrementally benefit from this breakthrough.

AN OVERVIEW OF THE APPLICATION PROCESS

In this chapter, we will focus on a pattern classification application: solving the credit approval problem. This particular problem was chosen for the richness of the concepts that it can be used to illustrate.

The basic application process consists of the following steps:

1. Collect all the data in one place.

2. Separate the data into training and test sets.

3. Transform the data into network-appropriate inputs.

4. Select, train, and test the network. Repeat steps 1, 2, 3, and 4 as required.

5. Deploy the developed network in your application.

To begin the process, examine the credit approval problem and see briefly how each of these steps applies.

THE CREDIT APPROVAL PROBLEM

Figure 3.1 shows a basic credit card application. Data are abstracted from this application and entered into a database. The database definition for a basic credit card application is shown in Figure 3.2. For purposes of this example, these are assumed to be fixed-length records. If data are not available, the field will be blank (if character type) or zero (if numeric type). All data are stored in ASCII. Note, however, that this example makes quite a number of simplifying assumptions about the credit approval problem for purposes of illustrating the neural network application process.

Comparing the fields in the database, notice that they do not correspond exactly to what is on the credit card application. The credit cards have been counted by type and entered into the database. The total monthly expenses have been computed by adding up the monthly credit card payments plus the mortgage payment. The occupation is entered into the database along with a "standard occupation code"

Figure 3.1

A Simplified Application Designed for Illustrating How Neural Networks Are Applied

Name:_____ Home Tel:_____Work Tel:_____

Address:_____

      City:_____ State:_____ Zip:_____

      Social Security Number:_____ Sex: __M __F

      Marital Status:__Single __Married __Widowed __Divorced

      Number of Children:____

Job Information:

      Employer:_____ Years:____

      Occupation:_____

Financial Information:

      Home: __Own __Rent Purchase Price:_____ Date:____

      Monthly Income:_____

      Checking Account: Number:_____ Bank:_____

                       Balance:_____

      Savings Account: Number:_____ Bank:_____

                       Balance:_____

	Total Amount	Monthly Payment
Mortgage Expense:		
Car Loans:		
_____	_____	_____
_____	_____	_____
Credit Cards:		
_____	_____	_____
_____	_____	_____
_____	_____	_____
_____	_____	_____

derived from a standard job description catalog. All of this "prepro-cessing" of the application has been done manually prior to data entry.

The field "Late Payments" indicates the number of weeks late a particular payment was. Each field corresponds to one of the past 12 months. Each month, the field is shifted over one digit and the current month's status appended. This field will be used to determine whether

Figure 3.2

Database Description for Credit Card Application

The data in this record are collected directly from the credit card application itself.

Field Name	Len	Type	Description
Name:	24	char	Last, first
Address:	32	char	
Zip Code:	5	digits	
Home Tel:	10	char	
Work Tel:	10	char	
SS#:	11	char	Social security number
Sex:	1	char	M/F
Marital Status:	1	char	Single, married, widowed, divorced
Children:	1	digit	Number of children under 18 at home
Occupation:	12	char	Description of occupation
Occ Code:	4	digits	Standard occupation code
Home:	1	letter	Own/rent
Monthly Income:	6	digits	
Monthly Expenses:	6	digits	
Checking Account:	1	char	Y/N
Savings Account:	1	char	Y/N
Master Card:	1	digit	Number of MCs
Visa:	1	digit	Number of Visas
American Express:	1	digit	Number of AMEX (Amex, Optima, etc.)
Merchant Cards:	1	digit	Number of merchant cards
Late Payments:	12	digit	1 digit for each of past 12 months

this person is a good risk. The neural network will be trained so that when it sees a particular set of input data, it will learn how to predict whether this individual will be a good-paying or poor-paying (good risk or poor risk) customer.

The process used to build the neural network credit authorizer is:

1. Collect the data. The first step is to gather all of the pertinent data in one place. In this example, all of the data already are in a single database. However, since redlining (denying credit based on geographic location) is illegal, it might be helpful to learn more about the individual by using a "zip code overlay" of census data. If a zip code overlay of census data were used, it would be necessary to append the applicable census data fields to the credit data record (or at least make them readily accessible on the same machine).

2. Separate the data into training and test sets. Since neural networks learn from experience, it is important to provide them both with experience and a way to see if they have "learned" ("Generalize Well") or "memorized" ("Generalize Poorly") what they have been shown. The only way to do this is to divide the available data into two (or more) sets. This procedure will be described further in Part III.

3. Transform the data into network-appropriate inputs. Neural networks *only* accept numeric inputs. How do you convert "Occupation" into a number? The process of transforming numeric and symbolic inputs into purely numeric inputs is called preprocessing. For me, this was the one area that seemed like magic. In Part II, the magic will be dispelled.

4. Select, train, and test a network. Picking the right network configuration can have a substantial impact on the performance of the resulting system. The process of debugging a neural network is still an art, but much easier with the powerful tools that are becoming commercially available. Part III describes this process and provides a number of helpful hints to get the most out of your neural network.

5. Deploy the developed network in your application. Once the development is done, how do you make a neural network part of an application?

Part II: A Walk Through the Application Process

REVIEW

The basic process of developing a neural network consists of the following steps:

1. Collect all the data in one place.

2. Separate the data into training and testing sets.

3. Transform the data into network-appropriate inputs.

4. Select, train, and test the network. Repeat steps 1, 2, 3, 4 as required.

5. Deploy the developed network in your application.

Actually, before taking any of these steps, we need to know what our objective is. The problem selected to illustrate these steps is the credit approval problem: Who should we give credit to? In an ideal world, the resulting neural network should give us a simple approve-disapprove signal.

GATHERING ALL THE DATA IN ONE PLACE

The process of training a neural network entails looking at all of the possible or potentially useful information about the problem, and using that to predict a certain behavior or other characteristic. For purposes of generating training and test sets, all of this information must be brought together. This process is similar to what is required to develop statistically based or behavioral scoring models.

In many applications, where the objective is to predict the behavior of a specific individual, zip-code or block-code overlays are used to provide additional information about the individual. Block-code overlays typically start with the U.S. Census Bureau data. The census bureau has divided the entire United States into "blocks." Each "block" consists of approximately 30 families. When census data is collected every ten years, it is summarized by "block." This data is available directly from the census bureau as well as various third-party companies who merge other information into it. The census data includes estimates of income, number of children, type of employment, and so on—everything that is asked on the census report. However, in accord with privacy laws, the data provided by the census bureau does not reference individuals. The third-party companies start with the census data and will rent mailing lists from various magazines, clubs, and other organizations and match them against the "block groups" to enhance the amount of information known about a "block group."

Credit bureaus often match customers in their database to block groups and incorporate specific fields from the census data into the customer record for purposes of developing credit-worthiness or bankruptcy-likely scores. In a large company, various components of the customer database may be managed by different groups within the company. For purposes of developing a neural network model, selected fields from the various databases may need to be merged.

Sometimes, information might be captured at one point, then stripped from the master record and archived. If you think this information is pertinent, it should be re-merged into the master records.

SEPARATE THE DATABASE INTO TRAINING AND TEST SETS

Why not use all of the data available to train and test a neural network? First, doing so prevents determining whether the neural network has memorized the data or learned something about the relationships between the inputs and the predicted output. Memorizing the relationship between the inputs and outputs may result in poor or erratic response to new or novel situations. Setting aside a certain number of examples increases our confidence in the performance of the trained neural network. Second, depending on the particular problem, certain neural networks may not learn well if the data is not properly distributed between possible outcomes. As such, it becomes important to carefully select the cases to be used for training. For testing purposes, an "Nth" item subset provides the best picture of how the network will perform overall.

Why is it so important to have about the same numbers of training items in each output category? Part of the answer is that many neural networks are basically lazy. They will attempt to find the easiest way to solve a particular problem. If 95 percent of the examples are "good" and 5 percent "bad," the network may discover that it is right most of the time by classifying everything as "good." This kind of swamping effect is even more pronounced when the boundaries between "good" and "bad" are fuzzy.

What is the ideal training set? For the most popular class of neural networks, back-propagation, the ideal training set is equally distributed among each of the possible outcomes. The ideal test set is one that is representative of the data as a whole. In practical terms, it is often easier to extract a test set first, then select a training set from the remaining examples.

For example, suppose that the database has about 31,000 examples in it. Each of the examples has been categorized into one of three possible outcomes: Good Risk, Poor Risk, and Indeterminate Risk. An analysis of the frequency of each of these is shown in column 2 of Figure 3.3.

The first step is to extract a test set. For our purposes, 10 percent will be sufficient. The test set will be extracted by sequentially going through the data and picking out every tenth example. The results are shown in column 3 of Figure 3.3.

The second step is to select the training set. The smallest single outcome is "Poor Risk." After selecting the test set, there are 6,179 (6,851–672) Poor Risk examples left. Of the remaining elements, randomly pick examples until 6,179 of each category are selected. When a particular category is full, reject any new examples picked for it. Include

Figure 3.3

Frequency of Occurrence of Each of the Three Possible Outcomes in the Database Distributed Among the Test and Training Sets

Category	Initial Data	Test Dataset	Training Dataset	Unused Examples
Good Risk	17,284	1,739	6,179	9,366
Indeterminate Risk	7,523	755	6,179	589
Poor Risk	6,851	672	6,179	0
Total:	31,658	3,166	18,537	9,955

all of the examples for the "Poor Risk" category. The results are shown in column 4 of Figure 3.3. Training examples are picked randomly to remove any bias that might exist in the natural ordering of the master database.

As a general rule, the more training examples available, the better the network will ultimately perform. For a variety of problems that we have solved using neural networks, 30,000 to 40,000 training examples have been adequate. Little additional improvement has been seen with more examples. For simple problems with few inputs and well-defined boundaries, as few as 50 or 100 examples may be adequate.

TRANSFORM THE DATA INTO NETWORK-APPROPRIATE INPUTS

When I began to learn about neural networks, this was perhaps the most bewildering element of the application process. It seemed like magic that symbolic and numeric data could be mapped into a vector of numbers. As with most "magic," when understood, the process is straightforward.

As described elsewhere, neural networks typically work with inputs in the range 0 to 1 or –1 to +1. Each of the fields in our database must be mapped into one or more network inputs, each in the appropriate range. This section covers basic concepts in mapping data into a neural network.

A description of the database is provided in Listing 1 in the Appendix to this part. Our mission is to find a way to map that database into a form suitable for input to a neural network. Notice that the database consists primarily of three types of data: numeric (income, expense, # of MCs, etc.), category (Sex, Rent/Own, Checking Account, etc.); and free-form text (Occupation, Name, Address, etc.). Let us go through each of the database fields individually and see how we can use them.

"NameCA" identifies the individual and probably does not have a significant bearing on the creditworthiness of the person. Address ("AddrCA") and zip code ("ZipCA") could be useful for integrating geographic block-code over-lay data. However, it is illegal to use zip-code as an input by itself. (This is known as redlining.) Social Security number ("SSNCA") could be useful as a key into other databases, but is not directly useful. Sex ("SexC") is another field that cannot be used as network input, because it is illegal to discriminate against an individual based on sex when issuing credit.

Marital Status ("MStatusC") can take on one of four values (M=Married, S=Single, W=Widowed, D=Divorced). This type of "category" record is typically encoded using a "one of N" coding. In a "one of N" coding, each category will be assigned to a separate neural network input. Since there are four categories, this database element would map to four inputs. For these four inputs, only one of them would be "on" (its value set to 1) at a time. All of the others would be off (value set to 0).

Number of children ("NChildrenC") will range from 0 to 9. Since this is a number, it can be re-scaled into the range 0 to 1 and input directly to the network.

Occupation creates some problems. In this database, there are several occupations. A listing of them is shown in Figure 3.4. One way of approaching the encoding of occupation is to use the "one of N" encoding used for marital status. The difficulty with that approach is that there are over 3,000 standard occupations and likely very few examples of most in the database. Another solution is to group them into some larger set of categories such as: Principal, Management, Professional, Skilled Labor, Unskilled Labor. These categories were chosen because they "seem" like they might be significant in determining creditworthiness. Since they were chosen somewhat intuitively, and the grouping of titles under each category is somewhat arbitrary, other categories and groupings may work better. However, this is a start.

Home ownership takes on one of two categories: Rent or Own. This encodes nicely into a "one of N" encoding.

Monthly income and expenses are both numbers and could be re-scaled and passed directly to the network as inputs.

Checking Account and Savings Account contain either a Y=Yes or N=No flag. In the mapping program, Y=Yes is translated to a "1," and N=No to a 0. Another way these fields could be treated is to consider them as each containing two categories and encode them each into two inputs. This has advantages in some instances.

The number of credit cards of each category has been directly passed through to the training file, with the expectation that they will be appropriately scaled by the neural network development tool.

Payment history has already been preprocessed into a rating. If more than nine out of 12 payments were made on-time, the rating is G=Good. If fewer than 6, the rating is poor. Otherwise it is indetermi-

---

Figure 3.4

A Listing of the Kinds of Occupations that Occur in the Credit Database and One Possible Way of Grouping Them Together

Principal:	President
	Store Owner
	Contractor

Management:	Vice President
	Senior Manager
	Manager
	Plant Manager
	Office Manager
	EDP Manager

Professional:	Software Engineer
	Accountant
	Doctor
	Professor

Skilled Labor:	Draftsman
	Mechanic
	Electrician
	Plumber

Unskilled Labor:	Laborer
	Farmhand
	Trucker
	Cabbie

---

nate. The "RatingC" field is mapped to three outputs, one for each of the possible categories of Good, Poor, or Indeterminate.

To review the process of mapping database inputs to neural network inputs:

1. Do not attempt to map information that does not seem likely to apply nor that may otherwise be illegal to use in making a decision.

2. Numeric inputs can be used directly as is.

3. Symbolic fields may be mapped directly with a "1 of N" code or indirectly by regrouping them into larger conceptual groups first.

4. Network "desired outputs" are mapped in much the same way as network inputs.

SELECTING A NETWORK ARCHITECTURE

Back-propagation has almost universally become the standard network paradigm for modeling, forecasting, and classification. Selecting an optimal back-propagation architecture is one of the areas that is receiving substantial research. Some of the key questions are: How many hidden units? Which transfer function? Which learning rule? What should the learning rates be?

TRAINING AND TESTING THE NETWORK

Depending on the dataset, the training process may be very slow. The basic training process consists of showing the network a set of inputs, and what the output should be. The network uses the current inputs to produce an output. This is compared to what the network should have produced. The error is used to modify the weights so that the network gives a more nearly correct answer the next time. During training, several diagnostic tools are helpful, in particular: (1) measuring the mean square error of the entire output layer, (2) a histogram of all of the weights in the network, and (3) Pearson's R coefficient for each of the outputs. These diagnostic tools facilitate understanding how the network is training.

During the testing process, the test database is used to determine how well the network performs on data it has not seen before during training. A properly architected and trained network will exhibit similar levels of performance on *both* the training and testing sets. If performance differs widely, appropriate corrective action should be taken to the architecture, composition, or size of the training and testing sets.

DEPLOYING THE NETWORK

Once trained to your satisfaction, the final step is to convert the network into a form that can be deployed with your application.

SUMMARY

Selecting appropriate test and training sets is an essential step in developing a neural network application. Once selected, developing a mapping from the symbolic and numeric fields in the database is relatively straight-forward.

APPENDIX TO PART II

Listing 1 - "network.h" describes the layout of the database

```
/* 12:00 14-Jan-91 (Network.H) "credit card" database definition */
/****************************************************************************
**
*Database Record Description*
**
****************************************************************************
*/
typedef struct_cdb {/* credit card database record */
char NameCA[24];/* name */
char AddrCA[32];/* address */
char ZipCA[5];/* zip code */
char SSNCA[11];/* social security code number */
char SexC;/* sex (M/F) */
char MStatusC;/* marital status */
char NChildrenC;/* # of children */
char OccupationCA[12];/* occupation */
char HomeOwnC;/* Rent/Own */
char IncomeCA[6];/* monthly income */
char ExpenseCA[6];/* monthly expenses */
char CheckingActC;/* Checking Account Y/N */
char SavingsActC;/* Savings Account Y/N */
char NMCsC;/* # of Master cards */
char NVISAsC;/* # of Visa cards */
char NAmexC;/* # of American Express cards */
char NMerchC;/* # of Merchant cards */
char PmtHisCA[12];/* Payment regularity for past 12 mos */
char RatingC;/* G=good risk, P=poor risk, I=indeterminate */
char LFCharC;/* line-feed at end of record */
}CDB;
```

Compiling and Running Programs for Generating Test and Training Sets

1. Compile the program. The author used Zortech "C" version 2.00.

   C>ztc select.c

2. Execute the select program to create the test and training databases. The main database is "db."

   C>select db test.db train.db

3. Compile the conversion program to map the test and training databases into network input files.

   C>ztc xformc.c

4. Transform the test database into network inputs. The resulting ".nna" file is suitable for input to NeuralWare's NeuralWorks Explorer or NeuralWorks Professional II; Ward System's NeuroShell; or California Scientific's BrainMaker.

   C>xformc test.db test.nna

5. Transform the training database into network inputs.

   C>xformc train.db train.nna

6. You are now ready to train the network of your choice. This will be described in more detail in Part III of this chapter.

Part III: Training a Neural Network

THE TRAINING PROCESS

In Part I, a database for credit application evaluation was described. In Part II, various techniques were described and applied to convert the various symbolic and numeric fields into values appropriate for neural network input. In particular, each of the fields in the database was converted to a numeric value. Prior to conversion, the database was divided into two parts: *training* and a *testing* set. The training set was chosen so that it represented equally the likelihood of each outcome. The test set was chosen to represent the entire population.

After transforming the database, there were 20 numeric inputs and three numeric outputs. Any network built to learn the relationship between the inputs and the outputs will have 20 inputs and three outputs. The outputs represented a Poor, Good, or Indeterminate risk. This was based on a very primitive analysis of payment history. The training data was written to an ASCII file (using xformc.exe) in a format suitable for input to a variety of neural network tools readily available.

Architecting the Network

When building a back-propagation network, a series of decisions must be made. These are listed in Table 3.1. The Problem Specific Parameters are defined by the problem. In particular, the number of inputs is 20; the number of outputs, 3; and a min-max table is required to automatically scale all of the data into the appropriate range for input to the network. (Table 3.2.)

The Network Decisions are determined by a combination of analysis of the data and trial-and-error.

Transfer Function

Selecting a transfer function is determined by the nature of the data and what the network is trying to learn. The key observation which leads to the selection of a transfer function is to observe that when the

Table 3.1	
Parameters for Back-Propagation Networks	

Network Decisions:

Transfer Functions:	Sigmoid Hyperbolic Tangent Sine
Learning Rules:	Delta Rule Cumulative Delta Rule Normalized Cumulative Delta Rule
Topology:	Number of Hidden Layers Number of PEs per Layer Functional Link Layer (if any) Connection to Prior Layers
Learning Rates:	Learning Rates for Each Layer

Problem Specific Parameters:

Number of Input PEs:	Number of Inputs to Network
Number of Output PEs:	Number of Outputs from the Network
Min-Max Table:	Required to Normalize Data
Instruments:	RMS Error, Confusion Matrix

input to a processing element is 0, no learning occurs on that particular connection. In a typical application, several of the inputs will be coded as either 0 or 1. With sigmoidal transfer functions, the limits of the output of the processing element are 0 and 1. With a hyperbolic tangent transfer function, the limits are –1 and 1. As a result, if the problem involves learning about "average" behavior, sigmoid transfer functions work best. However, if the problem involves learning about "deviations" from the average, hyperbolic tangent works best. For example, bankruptcy prediction and stock picking are examples of problems where the objective is to learn to pick out "exceptional" situations, and hyperbolic tangent works best. In the case of learning to classify respondents from nonrespondents for a direct mail application, the sigmoid

Table 3.2
Initial Network Decisions

The following table shows the experience of the author in developing an initial design for a back-propagation neural network.

1. Create the training and test sets.

2. Transform the training and test sets to numeric values suitable for network inputs.

3. Select a transfer function:
    Exceptions are more important than average: Hyperbolic tangent
    average is more important than exceptions: Sigmoid

4. Select a learning rule:
    Normalized cumulative delta rule.
    Default learning parameters. (Optimize later)
    Epoch = 16 (Optimize later)

5. Topology:
    One hidden layer.
    Number of hidden units selected so total weights are much less than the number of training examples.

6. Diagnostic tools:
    RMS error for output layer.
    Confusion matrix for each output.
    Histogram of weights for each layer.

works well. In this case, the sigmoid transfer function is a good starting point.

Learning Rule

The original learning rule developed by Rummelhart and described in Chapter 8 of *Parallel Distributed Processing: Explorations in the Microstructure of Cognition*, Volume I (MIT Press, 1986) is the delta rule. Two very popular extensions of this are the cumulative delta rule (which accumulates weight changes over several examples), and the normalized cumulative delta rule. In general, the normalized cumulative delta rule works very well. Typically, the Epoch (the number of presentations over which weight changes are accumulated) is set to 16. In circumstances where the data are very noisy, this may need to be adjusted.

Epoch Size

The procedure for adjusting the epoch size is as follows: (1) Pick an initial value. (2) Train the network for 10,000 (or some preestablished number) interactions. (3) Test the network and record the accuracy (or Pearson's R-Coefficient). Repeat this process three or four times for each of several epoch sizes. If you plot out the results, you will discover that the network performance peaks for a certain epoch size. This represents the fundamental "frequency" of certain dominant components of the underlying noise. Use this new epoch size for all further training.

Topology Issues

Three basic questions arise under topology issues. The first is, "How many hidden layers?" Closely associated with this is, "How many PEs in each hidden layer?" Typically, start with a single hidden layer. Most problems can be solved with a single hidden layer. If you do use more than one hidden layer, make sure to connect each layer to all prior layers. This promotes learning and increases the complexity of patterns that can be learned without adding additional processing elements. When starting out on solving a problem, it is usually helpful to try connecting the output layer directly to the input layer (connect prior layers). If the problem was reasonably solved using conventional statistical methods, this is often very effective.

How many hidden units? In general, the fewer the number of processing elements in the hidden layers, the better the network will "generalize." Generalization is the ability to interpolate between previously seen examples. Procedures have been developed to "prune" out superfluous hidden units as well as methods for adding additional hidden units to improve performance. From an information perspective, a theoretical upper bound for the number of hidden units can be determined by the number of training examples. The rule is that there should be at least five examples for each weight. In a network with 20 inputs, five hidden units, and three outputs, there are $(20+1)*5 + (5+1)*3 = 123$ weights. There are 264 examples in the training set, so five hidden units may be a bit many. Even so, for this example we will use one hidden layer with five hidden units.

Functional Link Layer

Pao made the observation that the hidden layer in a back-propagation network "transforms" the input space into a new space in which the classes are more nearly linearly separable. Based on this, he suggested that this could be done artificially by computing the pairwise product of each of the inputs. Sometimes this works very well. When using Functional Links, the first step is to use no hidden layer, and to connect all processing elements to both the input as well as the functional link layer (Connect Prior). This in essence augments the input layer with $N^*(N-1)$ additional parameters representing the pairwise product of the inputs. If this does not work well, it is usually better to not use a functional link layer at all.

Learning rates are the final key decision that must be made. Most vendors provide a set of "ready-made" learning rates. These typically work. As a rule of thumb the learning rate for the last hidden layer should be twice that of the output layer. If there are no connections that jump layers, the learning rates for each prior hidden layer should be twice that of the prior hidden layer. If connections do jump layers (prior layer connections), learning rates should be 20 percent to 30 percent less than the hidden layer above. Optimal learning rates (those that result in networks with maximum performance) result in smooth RMS error graphs and weight histograms for each layer which spread at about the same rate. If the weights for one layer grow larger faster than another layer, the network may get caught in a very long, shallow trough. The learning rates for the layer that is growing faster can be reduced to balance out the evolution of the network. If the RMS error graph jumps around a lot, reduce the learning rates for all layers proportionately. This in a nutshell is the condensed wisdom of several thousand tests.

Figure 3.5 shows how NeuralWorks Professional II/PLUS can be used to build a network for solving the credit approval problem. The learning coefficients and momentum parameters are the manufacturer's default values. The training and testing files have been selected along with other options.

GAME PLAN FOR NETWORK OPTIMIZATION

Once the network is built, there are three key areas that need to be optimized: learning rates, epoch size, and hidden layer size (Table 3.3).

Figure 3.5

Setting up a Back-Propagation Network to Solve the Credit Rating Problem Using NeuralWorks Professional II PLUS "Back-Prop Builder"

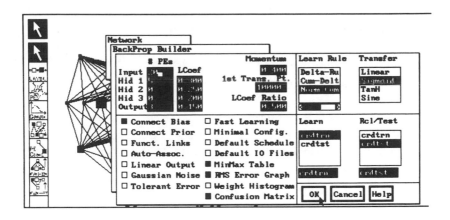

There are a series of heuristics for optimizing each of these parameters for a particular problem. The basic principles for optimizing learning rates and epoch size have already been discussed above. There are two basic approaches to optimizing hidden layer size: constructive and destructive.

The constructive approach to hidden layer size is to start with a network with no hidden units. The inputs are connected directly to the outputs. Train the weights until the error "stabilizes." Fix these weights and add a hidden unit connected to the input and all prior hidden layers. The output of this new unit is connected to the output. Continue training. Eventually, the network will make no mistakes on the training data. One of the keys to the constructive approach is to decide when to stop adding hidden units. The answer is that at each decision point, the network is tested on both the training and test sets. Performance on both is plotted. If the performance on both does not improve, remove the last hidden unit added and stop. Why? The network is starting to "memorize" the training set to the detriment of the test set.

Table 3.3
Optimizing the Network Parameters

1. **Optimize learning rates:**
   Initialize the network and train it for 10,000 iterations.
   Simultaneously:
   Lower all of the learning rates so that the RMS error plot is smooth.
   Change the relative magnitude of the learning rates so that the weight histograms for each layer spread at the same rates.

2. **Optimize the epoch size:**
   Start with an initial epoch.
   Train the network for 10,000 iterations.
   Test the network and record the "R-Coefficient" for each output.
   Repeat the above process for a variety of epoch sizes.
   Plot out the R-Coefficients and pick the epoch which produces the highest value.

3. **Optimize the hidden layer size:**
   Use one of the following procedures:
   Start with a "minimum" number of hidden units and add more as the training process proceeds.
   Start with the "maximum" number of hidden units and prune out marginal ones.

The destructive approach to hidden layer size is to start with a network with a large population of hidden units. Train the network for a while, and then test it on both the training and test sets. For each unit in the hidden layer: (1) disable the unit, setting its output to zero; (2) re-test the network on both the training and test sets; and (3) record the results. If disabling the unit improved *both* the performance on both the training and test sets, leave it disabled. Use the new results for the standard to measure the effect of each succeeding unit. Then, continue the training process.

During training, a few common problems often occur. The first is that the weights in the network grow large very rapidly. This shows up very graphically on the weight histogram and is usually easily detected in the RMS error plot as well. The underlying cause of this problem is that the learning rates are set too high, the training set is not adequately randomized, or the inputs are not properly scaled. First, make sure that the training presentations are randomized. If they are not, the network may very quickly learn about how to classify data in one particular mode (all good) and, due to the effects of momentum, move quickly in that direction. When data of another class eventually appear, the network has become "locked" up and does not effectively learn the new data. The second check is to see that the inputs have all been scaled into a range appropriate for the type of network (0 to 1 for sigmoid or –1 to 1 for hyperbolic tangent). An easy way to do this is to use a min-max table that will compute the minimum and maximum of each training example. These values are used to scale the inputs into the appropriate range automatically. Finally, try reducing the learning rates.

Another problem which sometimes occurs is that the RMS error does not seem to decrease. Sometimes this is a problem and sometimes it is not. If the training data are particularly noisy, the RMS error may not decrease much over the training process. In this case, the confusion matrix can be used to determine where the problem is. In some cases, the error may be caused by one particular output which is of little concern.

Figure 3.6 shows a network that has been trained for 16,000 iterations. (This problem actually requires about 50,000 iterations for best performance.) This took about 10 minutes on a Toshiba 5200. Notice that the RMS error has not dropped very much and that it is quite "jagged." From prior discussions, the learning rates should be reduced. Though it would be helpful, weight histograms for each of the layers are not being used. For each output, there is a confusion matrix. The confusion matrix is a graphical way of understanding how the network is performing. Along the x-axis is the "desired output": what the network should be producing. Along the y-axis is the actual output of the network. Both the desired output and the actual outputs have been discretized into bins. The bars in one column of the interior of the confusion matrix show the distribution of actual network outputs for a particular desired output. If the network were performing perfectly, the only interior quadrants would be the lower left and upper right of the interior area. From this, the network is starting to learn to distinguish good from non-good (Conf. Matrix 3). However, it is quite confused in both of the other categories.

The number along the y-axis is Pearson's R-coefficient. This is a correlation coefficient that measures how well the desired output and

Figure 3.6
Trained Network

This network has run through 50,000 training iterations. The RMS error graph shows how well the network is performing.

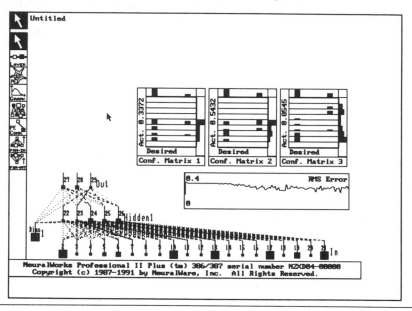

actual outputs are correlated. A perfect correlation results in a score of 1.0. The scores shown are: Poor = 0.3372; Indeterminate = 0.5432; Good = 0.8545. This is a numerical method to represent what is happening graphically.

SUMMARY

In Part III, the basic process of architecting and training a network has been discussed. The procedures used are those that have been developed by the author through trial and error. Following the steps outlined usually results in success.

Sources, sample data, and copies of the network shown are available from the author.

PART 2

ANALYSIS OF FINANCIAL CONDITION

4

A FINANCIAL NEURAL NETWORK APPLICATION

Robert A. Marose

INTRODUCTION

A statistical-based hybrid neural network at Chase Manhattan Bank is one of the largest and most successful AI applications in the United States. It addresses a critical success factor in the bank's strategic plan: reducing losses on loans made to public and private corporations.

Most of Chase's business for corporations involves assessing their creditworthiness. Chase loans $300 million annually and has long searched for tools to improve loan assessment. This assessment allows Chase to mitigate risk and seek out new business opportunities. Financial-restructuring deals are promising business opportunities for the bank.

Reprinted with permission from *AI Expert*, May 1990, pp. 50–53.

In 1985 Chase began a search for new quantitative techniques to assist senior loan officers in forecasting the creditworthiness of corporate loan candidates. Chase located Inductive Inference Inc. (headed by Dr. David Rothenberg), a New York City company with a history of successfully applying neural-network technology to statistical pattern analysis. A test model was built, evaluated, and independently audited. The results were reviewed by the Chase CEO committee in 1987 and Inductive Inference was granted a multimillion dollar contract. Consequently, Chase established a 36-member internal consulting organization called Chase Financial Technologies to oversee the development of pattern-analysis network models for evaluating corporate loan risk.

The resulting models, called the Creditview system, perform three-year forecasts that indicate the likelihood of a company being assigned a Chase risk classification of *good, criticized,* or *charged-off*. In addition to the overall forecast, Creditview provides a detailed listing of the items that significantly contributed to the forecast, an expert-system generated interpretation of those items, and several comparison reports. This article focuses on the public company loan model (PCLM).

Creditview models run on a Chase Financial Technologies host computer. A user system resides at each user's PC and communicates with the host through telephone lines. In addition, conventional financial statement analysis may be performed using Chase's Financial Reporting System, an independent financial spreading and analysis package designed for conventional financial statement analysis. The Financial Reporting System also resides on the user's PC and permits a company's standard financial statements to be accessed and displayed. System data is obtained from COMPUSTAT.

It took 15 years for Inductive Inference to develop ADAM, a tool that generates the models such as those used in Creditview. ADAM is a statistically based technique that extracts a collection of Boolean formulae from historical data and captures rules most significant in determining the obligor's creditworthiness. ADAM identifies rules and their combinations that, based on historical data, may be expected to do three-year forecasts reliably. The historical data are also used to embed the Boolean formula in a network that evaluates the significance of each possible formula combination that may be satisfied by a particular company.

ADAM's pattern-analysis technology provides the ability to construct a hybrid neural network (the Forecaster), if enough high-quality historical data are available. Each forecaster represents a separate "model" produced by ADAM (Figure 4.1). PCLM, the first model implemented at Chase, derives from Chase's extensive loan history of large, publicly traded companies and their past financial data. (Chase has both publicly and privately owned corporations in its base of clients and prospects. Separate credit-risk forecasting models will be developed for public and private companies because their particular characteristics will probably mandate separate assessments and analysis by the bank.)

The input to ADAM includes:

❖ Historical financial-statement data on *good* and *bad* obligors (the learning sample)

❖ Industry norms calculated using financial-statement data from companies in specific industries (obtained from COMPUSTAT). These norms reflect industry characteristics.

The historical data analyzed by ADAM to produce forecasting models consist of a large collection of data units. Each data unit contains as much as six years of consecutive financial data for a particular company, corresponding industry norms, and the company's status three years

Figure 4.1

ADAM and PCLM

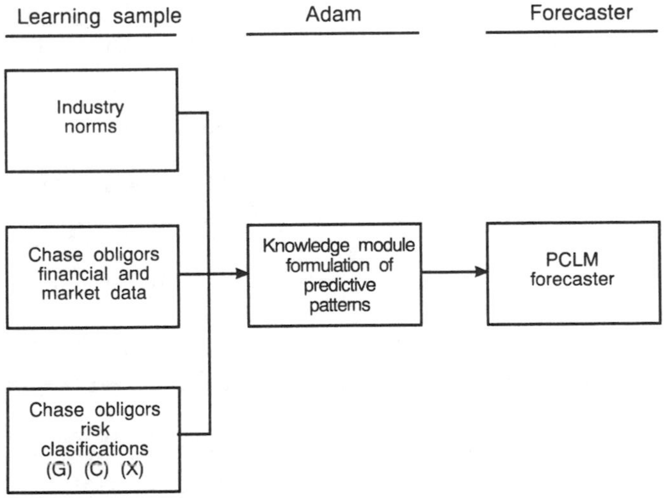

after the last year of data. (The last of the six years is called the "year of the data unit.") The data unit's status is the company's rating — G stands for *good*, C stands for *criticized*, and X stands for *charged-off*.

ADAM uses this data to construct a large set (say, 1,000) of candidate variables that may or may not indicate a company's future financial condition. These variables are used to form patterns.

DEFINITION OF PATTERNS

A pattern is fundamentally a statement about the value of a particular financial variable or set of variables. A very simple pattern may have the form:

$$C1 < V1 < C2$$

or

$$V1 < C1$$

where *V1* is a financial variable and *C1* and *C2* are constants. For example:

$$1.75 < \text{QuickRatio} < 2.00$$

could be a simple pattern. Typically, patterns are more complex; they have several elements of this kind and are combined by using AND, OR, and NOT. This example could be one of a small complex pattern:

$$C1 < V1 < C2$$
$$V2 < C3$$
$$C4 < V3 < C5 \text{ .AND. } C6 < V4 < C7$$
$$C8 \leq V5 \leq C9$$

where all the Cs are constants and the Vs financial variables.

Candidate variables are arranged into thousands of complex patterns and analyzed by ADAM to produce an optimal set of variables and patterns that form a pattern network called the Forecaster. The criteria for selection of patterns include:

Score. The score (as observed in the historical data) measures the ability of the pattern to differentiate between the categories *good, criticized,* and *charged-off*—in other words, the ability of the pattern to classify correctly.

Complexity. Complexity is a measure of how complicated the pattern is (in terms of number of variables), simple patterns within it, and the amount of historical data it satisfies.

Spuriousness. A measure of the likelihood that the pattern's score (how well it predicts) is due solely to chance.

These statistics are used to evaluate the predictive power of the patterns and ensure that whatever predictive power is uncovered is not by chance. To each pattern and status a probability (called the "precision") exists that a data unit corresponding to the pattern will have that status. ADAM uses a proprietary network-balancing technique that selects the patterns for the network to maximize precision and minimize bias.

ADAM was used to develop the PCLM, an expert system based on historical data that can predict the likelihood of a public firm being rated *good, criticized,* or *charged-off* three years in advance. Among other features, PCLM:

❖ Accepts six years of past financial data for the firm under consideration.

❖ Uses the lattice (network) of Boolean expressions developed by ADAM to determine nodes that best match the firm under analysis.

❖ Calculates the probability for each rating based on the expressions matched and the characteristics of these patterns.

❖ Produces extensive reports, including a text explanation of the analysis, based on the characteristics of the matched pattern and other companies that have matched these expressions.

The PCLM comprises two parts: the Forecaster, built by the ADAM technology from large publicly traded companies (residing on a Chase host computer), and a PC-based user system that allows access to the model on the host computer to generate forecasts for particular companies, perform various analyses, and print reports (Figure 4.2). Note that information about an obligor's specific credit facility (whether the facility is secured, covenants, and so on) is not considered by the PCLM. The system evaluates the company itself rather than the risk of its defaulting in specific credit payments.

PCLM MODEL OUTPUT

The PCLM produces these reports: Contributing Variables, Expert-System Interpretation, Two-Year Comparison: Items of Increased Significance, Two-Year Comparison: Items of Decreased Significance, and Two-Year Comparison: Items That Changed Risk Category. Of these reports, Contributing Variables contains PCLM's primary output; the others derive from the data contained in it. Contributing Variables comprises an overall forecast for the company in question along with a list of the variables that most strongly contributed to the forecast. The basic report consists of these sections:

Figure 4.2

PCLM Model Process

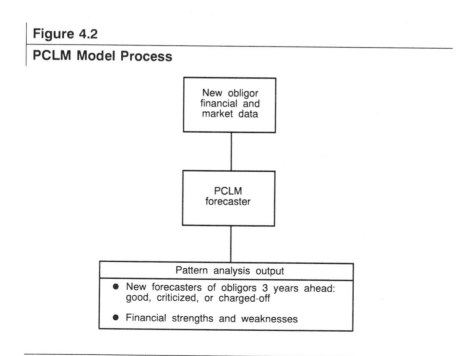

Section 1. General information. Contains the company name, forecast year, standard industrial classification (SIC), data source, date, and years of data that were used in generating the forecast.

Section 2. Industry peer group. Defines the industry peer group as determined by the model for the company. The company's asset size and geographic location are shown in this section. Information on the industry peer group consists of its SIC, the latest year for which industry norms were calculated, the number of firms in the peer group, and the peer-group reference number (useful in determining the peer group's members).

Section 3. Overall forecast. Shows the forecast rating for the company (G, C, or X). These ratings are mathematically combined into a single "vulnerability index" that helps compare the relative risk among different forecasts (different companies or years for the same company). In addition, to assist the analyst in evaluating the forecast's significance, the company's forecast compared to others in Chase's experience is shown in several ways. Chase Rank shows the relative percentile of this company's *good* rating compared to all Chase obligors in the years 1986 through 1988. For example, if the company's Chase Rank was 25 percent, for all Chase obligors from 1986 through 1988, 75 percent have a higher and 25 percent have a lower rating for good. Percent Going to Criticized and Charged-off shows the historical outcome of similarly ranked companies.

Section 4. A list of contributing variables most strongly influencing the forecast. These variables are organized into categories and by contributions to strength and weakness within each category: *profitability, asset efficiency, cash flow, capital structure and liquidity,* and *market.*

Section 5. A list of contributing variables compared to the best or worst quartile of companies in the industry (defined as its peer group) that most strongly influence the forecast.

Other reports can be generated by the user system:

Expert system interpretation. The PCLM can use its network to output the various factors accounting for its conclusions. This output permits the model to explain its decision in an understandable, text-generated manner.

Two-year comparison reports. These reports automatically compare the forecasts for two (not necessarily consecutive) years and show items that appear in the second but not the first year (Items of Increased Significance Report), items that appear in the first but not the second year (Items of Decreased Significance Report), and items that appear in both years but have changed their risk category (Items That Changed Risk Category Report).

SYSTEM SUCCESS

PCLM benefits the user because it identifies the strengths and vulnerabilities in the financial structure of the obligor and forecasts the impact of these factors on the firm's financial health three years into the future. Chase tested the system extensively and, having identified many potentially troublesome loans, the bank is now implementing it.

From a statistician's viewpoint, a major distinction between ADAM and classical neural networks, as shown in Table 4.1, is that neural networks weigh values that maximize the accuracy in the classification of the historical data. ADAM, however, maximizes the accuracy of the classification after discounting bias.

A new, more robust PCLM is being developed as a sister model for private companies, and a user-friendly shell has been created to facilitate the use of both models by bank officers from their PCs. Feasibility studies have concluded that the ADAM technology can be applied successfully to corporate planning, investment portfolio analysis, and oil-exploration models.

Table 4.1

ADAM, Expert Systems, and Neural Networks

Feature	Expert System	Neural Network	ADAM Model
Model financial data and use the results to evaluate new information.	No	Yes	Yes
Automatically model and use the unconscious knowledge and experience of experts.	No	Yes	Yes
Automatically adapt to changing economic and market conditions.	No	Yes	Yes
Explain, in English, the reason for their evaluations.	Yes	No	Yes
Accommodate missing information.	Yes	Yes	Yes
Discover unknown significant rare events.	No	Yes	Yes
Is resistant to data errors.	Sometimes	Sometimes	Yes

5

ANALYZING FINANCIAL HEALTH: INTEGRATING NEURAL NETWORKS AND EXPERT SYSTEMS

Don Barker

INTRODUCTION

The application presented here was developed using KnowledgePro, NeuroShell, and dBase III Plus. These software environments require little programming experience and provide for quick and simple data exchanges. As a result, practically anyone wishing to employ the flexibility and power of integrated knowledge processing would be able to exploit the concepts detailed below.

As we begin the last decade of this millennium, true machine intelligence still eludes us and remains confined to the imaginations of

This article originally appeared in *PCAI*, May/June, 1990, pp. 24–27. Reprinted with permission.

science fiction writers. Unquestionably, significant strides have been made in developing systems for solving problems that previously required human reasoning. Feigenbaum, McCorduck, and Nil document hundreds of such programs in their book *The Rise of the Expert Company*. The expert systems they describe work by storing the knowledge of human specialists in the form of rules and applying the tenets of logic to produce answers to a myriad of business concerns.

Although expert systems function well within their limited areas of competency, they perform quite poorly outside these boundaries. When confronted with circumstances where heuristics are either unclear or questionable, expert systems, because of their deterministic nature, are simply impractical solutions for automating the reasoning process. Since many "real world" problems lack a distinct set of decision rules, it is little wonder that AI has progressed slowly.

Fortunately, a new genre of AI software, neural networks, is now making itself felt in the marketplace. These programs rely on classification and association to reach likely solutions. They are able to "learn" from a set of sample decisions and classify new cases according to the similarities associated with the "memorized" patterns. The method by which these patterns are stored and identified is called parallel distributed processing (PDP). It is termed "parallel" because multiple aspects of a pattern are considered simultaneously, and "distributed" because the results are stored throughout the network.

However, neural networks suffer from several limitations of their own. They lack the capacity to explain their conclusions and, perhaps more important, they are unable to reason in a sequential or stepwise manner that results in precise conclusions. These restrictions can be critical when dealing with situations that demand exact answers and lucid justifications. Because expert systems use symbolic processing to logically derive a conclusion, they excel at explaining their line of reasoning and producing precise recommendations.

From the previous discussion, it should now be apparent that symbolic and parallel distributed processing are not competing AI strategies but complimentary. By uniting them we can avoid many of the weaknesses inherent in each method while capitalizing on their unique strengths. The program described below provides an example of effectively combining these two dissimilar knowledge processing strategies.

RATIO ANALYSIS OF SMALL BUSINESS

Like large corporations, every small business must produce financial statements, if for no other reason than tax purposes. However, these statements can provide useful information about the financial health of the company. One common way of analyzing the data in financial statements is to convert them into ratios. A ratio is simply a means of transforming two numbers into one. Interpretation of the new number depends upon comparisons. Comparing a firm's ratios to industry-wide average ratios can reveal the relative financial condition of the company.

We are going to examine a system that analyzes the ratios of small firms. It performs two main tasks: (1) interpreting the ratios of a company and (2) estimating the likelihood that a firm will be able to acquire additional capital through borrowing. Both the heuristics and the facts necessary for performing the first task are unambiguous and reliable, making it an ideal choice for an expert system solution.

However, estimating a company's borrowing ability is a bit more tricky. Rules for making a loan decision are obscure and, although sample cases do exist, they have inconsistencies. (These inconsistencies result from the various lending institutions applying different criteria in making loan decisions.) In the absence of clear rules or precise data, a neural network approach has the best chance of producing plausible results.

Figure 5.1 shows the design for a hybrid expert system that addresses all the facets of our problem. It contains elements for communicating with the user and for processing knowledge in both a symbolic and parallel distributed fashion, and a database to store relevant facts. Notice that the symbolic processing component has access to both its rule base and a shared database. Access to the database is necessary because the industry average ratios required for analysis are stored there. The rule base contains the expertise necessary to interpret a company's ratios by comparing them with the average ratios obtained from the database.

The parallel distributed processing segment also shares a connection with the database. This allows the neural network to train on sample loan decisions stored in the database. The PDP element uses the trained neural network to classify new cases in order to make predictions about loan possibilities.

Figure 5.1

Diagram of a Hybrid Expert System for Evaluating Business Ratios

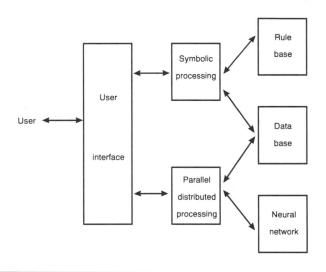

PUTTING THE SYSTEM ON THE COMPUTER

Since there is presently no software package that incorporates symbolic processing, PDP, and a database, three separate development tools are necessary for putting our hybrid expert system on the computer. These programs must communicate with each other and transfer relevant data. They should also allow for the creation of a "seamless" interface to minimize user confusion. Finally, to reduce development time and make this technology more widely available, it is desirable that the programs provide most of the procedural code necessary to implement the system.

NeuroShell, by Ward Systems, Inc., is used to construct the neural network portion of the program. It employs one of the most powerful algorithms for performing parallel distributed processing (backward error propagation). NeuroShell stores data in standard ASCII files, making data transfer a simple operation. Another important feature is a run-time version that can be evoked from inside another program and run in the background. This contributes greatly to the goal of a seamless user interface. NeuroShell is constructed around the same idea that has made expert system shells so popular. By including all the fundamental components necessary for building a neural network and offering menu-driven controls, it releases the developer to concentrate on the critical job of crafting a quality neural network.

KnowledgePro, a product of Knowledge Garden, Inc., is an expert system shell with an extensive command language for manipulating symbols. These commands enable data from imported files to be parsed and organized for symbolic processing. They also make it possible to format data for export to other programs with different file structures. In addition, facilities exist for executing external programs from within a KnowledgePro application. Like other expert system shells, KnowledgePro comes with an inference mechanism for directing reasoning efforts and a user interface for communicating with the outside world. This allows the developer to ignore the procedural aspects of building an expert system and focus on gathering the expertise necessary to create a rule base for solving a particular problem.

KnowledgePro uses the concept of "topics" for organizing and processing related "chunks" of knowledge. Topics are similar to procedures in traditional programming languages in that they act to separate tasks or functions within a program. For instance, Figure 5.2 displays the topic named "main." Its purpose is to control the execution of all the other topics that comprise our hybrid expert system. When Knowledge-Pro encounters the command "do (main)," it begins execution of the topic. This, in turn, causes the sequential activation of the eight topics contained in "main." As each topic terminates, control is returned to "main" so that the next topic can be run.

The first topic to be executed is "instructions." This topic presents the user with an explanation of how the system operates. When the user finishes reading these instructions, the topic "identify business type" is activated. Here the user is asked to select the industry category that most closely matches the business being evaluated. (This information is used later to search the database for the industry average ratios that correspond to the business.) The third topic, "gather financial facts," queries the user for a series of numbers drawn from the financial statements of the company under examination. These numbers are converted into ratios in the topic "compute ratios for firm" (see the Appendix—Business Ratios). The next three topics in "main" are the heart of the system. We will investigate them in more detail.

Figure 5.2

The "Main" Topic (routine) for the Hybrid Expert System Dubbed the "Ratio Evaluator"

```
(* Ratio evaluator *)

do (main).

topic main. (* driver routine for system *)

    window ('Ratio Evaluator', white, blue, yellow, 2,2,78,19).

    do (instructions).
    do ('identify business type').
    do ('gather financial facts').
    do ('compute ratios for firm').
    do ('get industry ratios').
    do ('estimate borrowing probability').
    do ('interpret ratios').
    do (continue).

end. (* main *)
```

SEARCHING THE DATABASE

Figure 5.3 is a listing of the topic "get industry ratios." Its function, as the name implies, is to retrieve industry average ratios from a database. dBase III Plus was chosen to create the data files for this program because both KnowledgePro and NeuroShell are able (through additional utilities) to read these files. Figure 5.4 shows the structure and some sample records from the database "RATIOS.DBF." The "TYPE" field holds the name of each industry category, while the other four fields contain the associated ratios.

The first instruction in Figure 5.3 tells KnowledgePro to open the file "c:\garden\ratios" and read its structure. The subsequent line stores the field names from the database in the variable "field_list." These field names are used in the subtopic "locate," which is activated by the command "locate( )." (A question mark appearing in front of a word

---

Figure 5.3

A Procedure for Extracting Database Records

Topic 'get industry ratios'. (* data base access *)

```
db_desc = open_dbf('c:\garden\ratios').
field_list = element(?db_desc,5).
locate().
close_dbf(?db_desc).

topic locate ().

    eof = number_to_char(26).
    data_list = #s.
    data = read_dbf(?db_desc).
    While ?data<>?eof
        then ?field_list is _c ?data and
        (If ?TYPE = ?business_type
        then data_string gets
        [?QUICK,?DEBT_WORTH,?SALES_REC,?PROFIT_WTH]
        and data = number_to_char(26)
        else data = read_dbf(?db_desc)).

end. (* locate *)

record_list = string_to_list (?data_string).

average_quick_ratio is element (?record_list,1).
average_debt_to_worth is element (?record_list,2).
average_sales_to_receivables is element (?record_list,3).
average_profit_to_worth is element (?record_list,4).

end. (* get industry ratios *)
```

---

or phrase signifies that it is a variable name and causes the program to examine the value assigned to it and not the variable name itself.)

Topic "locate" performs a sequential search of the database to find the record that matches the industry type identified earlier. Once the record is found, its contents are stored in the variable "data_string" and the subtopic terminates. The database is then closed and the data string is converted into a list. This is done so that each ratio can be extracted from the list and assigned to a variable (see the lower portion of Figure 5.4). The procedure for accessing the database then concludes, and control is returned to the topic "main."

PARALLEL DISTRIBUTED PROCESSING

The next step in our analysis is to estimate the probability of the firm obtaining capital through additional debt. A neural network is used to

---

Figure 5.4

The File Structure and Sample Listing of the Database Containing the Industry Financial Ratios

Structure for database: C: ratios, dbf
Number of data record: 7
Date of last update: 12/15/89

Field	Field Name	Type	Width	Dec
1	TYPE	Character	20	
2	QUICK	Numeric	5	1
3	DEBT_WORTH	Numeric	5	1
4	SALES_REC	Numeric	5	1
5	PROFIT_WTH	Numeric	5	1
Total			41	

Record #	TYPE	QUICK	DEBT_ WORTH	SALES_ REC	PROFIT_ WTH
1	Apparel	0.8	66.1	16.0	20.6
2	Computer Stores	0.8	97.6	11.5	38.2
3	Farm Equipment	0.6	123.4	24.8	16.1
4	Fuel Oil	1.6	60.8	19.6	14.1
5	Gift Shops	0.9	63.9	11.2	36.3
6	Hardware	0.9	76.0	13.6	13.6
7	Office Supplies	1.2	90.1	10.6	16.1

process the firm's ratios and produce a plausible guess concerning the likelihood of a loan. The training set for this network is shown in Figure 5.5. (These sample cases are only for demonstration purposes. A much larger set of actual cases would be needed to accurately train a network.) As you look at Figure 5.5, notice that when the debt-to-worth ratio is high, the loan is denied. This is because an elevated debt-to-worth means that creditors are sharing a greater degree of risk than the owners. Future creditors are quite reluctant to extend more financing in this situation. Thus, we can safely expect the neural network to assign a low borrowing probability to companies with an elevated debt-to-worth ratio.

Figure 5.6 lists the topic "estimate borrowing probability." The first four lines of code instruct the program to create a file and place the ratios for the firm in it. The commands "#s" and "#x" are used to format the values in the file so that NeuroShell will be able to read it. The purpose of the next group of instructions is to invoke the batch version of NeuroShell, telling it to process the file "ratios.in" and then call a subtopic to read the results. In this subtopic, the rounded output from the neural network is assigned to the variable "estimation." This ends the parallel distributed processing portion of the program and reinstates control to the "main" topic.

Figure 5.5

Training Cases for the Neural Network

Quick Ratio	Debt to Worth	Sales to Receivables	Profit to Worth	Loan Probability
0.5	220.0	25.0	140.0	0.0
0.6	41.2	22.7	61.4	100.0
0.5	261.4	27.8	159.1	0.0
0.8	35.0	20.8	58.3	100.0
0.5	243.5	31.3	152.2	0.0
1.0	34.1	16.7	56.9	100.0

0.0 = Loan Denied
100.0 = Loan Approved

Figure 5.6

The Procedure for Accessing the Neural Network from within
KnowledgePro

```
topic 'estimate borrowing probability'. (* parallel distributed
processing *)

    new_file ('ratios.in').
    write(['ratios.in'],#x1,?quick_ratio,#s#x10,?debt_to_worth,#s#x20,
    ?sales_to_receivables,#s#x30,?profit_to_worth,#s#x40).
    close_all().

    NeuroShell = ('c:\garden\banalog.exe ratios').
    if run (?NeuroShell)<0
    then say ('Sorry, it was impossible to load NeuroShell')
    else do ('get output patterns from ratios').

topic 'get output patterns from ratios'.
    output is read_line ('ratios.prn').
    close_all().

    number = string_to_list (?output).
    estimation = ((?number + 0.5) div 1).
end. (* topic get output patterns from ratios *)

end. (* estimate borrowing probability *)
```

SYMBOLIC PROCESSING

With all the necessary data gathered, it is now possible to complete the
ratio evaluation. Figure 5.7 provides a complete picture of the rules for
interpreting a firm's ratios in comparison with industry averages. The
rules are displayed in the form of a decision table. Decision tables are
extremely useful devices for viewing judgments in a very compact form.

Figure 5.7

Decision Table for Ratio Analysis

	1	2	3	4	5	6	7	8	9	10	11	12	13	14	15	16
Quick Ratio	F	U	U	U	U	F	F	F	F	U	F	F	F	U	U	U
Debt Worth	F	F	U	U	U	F	F	U	U	F	F	U	U	F	F	U
Sales Receivables	F	F	F	U	U	F	U	U	U	F	U	F	F	U	U	F
Profit/Worth	F	F	F	F	U	U	U	U	F	U	F	F	U	F	U	U
Liquidity	F	U	U	U	U	F	F	F	F	U	F	F	F	U	U	U
Leverage	F	F	U	U	U	F	F	U	U	F	F	U	U	F	F	U
Activity	F	F	F	U	U	F	U	U	U	F	U	F	F	U	U	F
Profitability	F	F	F	F	U	U	U	U	F	U	F	F	U	F	U	U

F = Favorable
U = Unfavorable

Each column in the table represents a complete and sometimes complex rule. For example, column 1 of the decision table is read as follows:

> If the Quick-Ratio is favorable
>   and Debt-to-Worth is favorable
>   and Sales-to-Receivables is favorable
>   and Profit-to-Worth is favorable
> then Liquidity is favorable
>   and Leverage is favorable
>   and Activity is favorable
>   and Profitability is favorable

Since there are four conditions in the IF part or antecedent of each conditional, our decision table needs to cover 16 possible combinations or rules (4^2). Columns 2 through 16 cover the remaining possibilities. KnowledgePro processes rules derived from the decision table. For example, one rule checks to see if the company's ratios are favorable in comparison to the industry ratios. When all four ratios are favorable, the rule fires and the procedure displays the results of the analysis to the user along with an estimation of the company's chances of acquiring a loan.

At this point, the last theme in the topic "main" is executed. This final topic prompts the user to either end the session or continue by submitting another case.

CONSULTING THE SYSTEM

Let us now step through a consultation with the system to see how it appears from the outside. We'll use the imaginary company "Computers R US" to test the program. The relevant financial data for the business are exhibited in Figure 5.8. The first display to appear contains information about the system (Figure 5.9). Once familiar with this overview, the <Enter> key is pressed to begin the session. We are then asked to select the business sector that most closely matches the firm under study (Figure 5.10). Because "Computers R US" is a small storefront operation selling directly to the public, the "Retailers" option is chosen. We are then presented with another list containing a further breakdown of the selected business sector. Picking "Computer Stores" starts a series of window prompts that collect all the necessary numbers for completing the ratio evaluation (see Figure 5.11 as an example of these query windows).

After all the entries have been made, the program analyzes the inputs by executing its parallel distributed and symbolic processing components. Figure 5.12 displays the system's final conclusion. Observe that in every case, with the exception of the debt-to-worth ratio (137.2 percent), our computer company has favorable ratios in comparison with the industry averages. But because the debt-to-worth rating carries a great deal of weight with creditors, the firm's other positive ratios have only managed to garner it a 52 percent chance of acquiring capital through new loans. This concludes the consultation. One last screen appears giving us the opportunity to either evaluate another company or exit the program.

CONCLUSION

Our example application has shown that instead of being mutually exclusive, expert systems and neural networks are actually complimen-

Figure 5.8

Financial Data for the Imaginary Company "Computers R US"

COMPUTERS R US INCOME DATA

Sales	$250,000
Cost of Goods Sold	$120,000
Gross Margin	$130,000
Expenses	$60,000
Profit (pretax)	$70,000
Income Tax	$28,000
Profit (after tax)	$42,000

ASSETS

Inventory	$90,000
Accounts Receivable	$15,000
Current Assets	$105,000
Leasehold Improvements	$50,000
Equipment	$30,000
Fixed Assets	$80,000
Total Assets	$185,000

LIABILITIES AND CAPITAL

Accounts Payable	$7,000
Short-Term Bank Loans	$10,000
Current Debt	$17,000
Notes Payable	$20,000
Long-Term Bank Loans	$70,000
Long-Term Debt	$90,000
Total Debt	$107,000
Common Stock	$36,000
Retained Earnings	$42,000
Net Worth	$78,000

Figure 5.9

Information about the System

Ratio Evaluator

Welcome to the Ratio Evaluator. This system is only for the purposes of demonstration and its recommendations should not be taken seriously. It is designed to show how neural technology can be used in concert with a rule-based expert system and a data base to provide a more complete decision support system.

A consultant with the Ratio Evaluator begins with the system asking you for financial numbers from the firm under study. This information is used to compute a set of ratios designed to reveal the financial health of the firm. These ratios are evaluated in comparison to numbers drawn from a data base of industry average ratios. Some of these figures are also used to produce an estimate of how likely it is that the company will be able to acquire additional debt in the near future. Important variances are noted and a final report is issued containing the results of the analysis.

Press the Enter key to begin the consultation.

| F1 Help | F5 Evaluate | F7 Edit | Pg 1 of 1 |
| Space Cont. | F6 Display KB | F8 DOS | F10 Quit |

---

tary reasoning mechanisms that can be joined to form a versatile tool for tackling especially perplexing problems, that, because of their diverse nature, have resisted solution by any single AI technology.

This chapter only touches on one possible application of integrating these two approaches to problem solving. Perhaps the ideas presented here will encourage further investigation of other interesting combinations for automating the reasoning process.

Figure 5.10

List of the Possible Business Sectors a Firm Might "Fit" in

Ratio Evaluator
Please choose a general business sector:

> Retailers
> Wholesalers
> Services
> Contractors
> Professional Services
> Manufacturers

F1 Help	F5 Evaluate	F7 Edit	
	F6 Display KB	F8 DOS	F10 Quit

Figure 5.11

The Numbers Required to Compute the Firm's Ratios

Ratio Evaluator

> Query
> Enter current assets:
> => 105000

F1 Help	F5 Evaluate	F7 Edit	
Enter Accept	F6 Display KB	F8 DOS	F10 Quit

Figure 5.12

Results of the Analysis

Ratio Evaluator

ASSESSMENT

	Quick Ratio	Debt/Worth	Sales/Receivables	Profit/Worth
Firm:	0.9	137.2	16.7	89.7
Std:	0.8	97.6	11.5	38.2

The quick ratio is greater than or equal to the industry average signaling that the firm should have the liquidity to meet its short term obligations.

The debt to worth ratio is greater than the industry average indicating that the firm is heavily leveraged which increases the risk to the creditors.

The sales/receivables ratio is greater than or equal to the industry average which implies a sound receivables' management policy.

The profit/worth ratio is greater than or equal to the industry average signaling that the owners are getting a solid return on their investments.

The likelihood of raising capital by borrowing is 52 percent.

F1 Help	F5 Evaluate	F7 Edit	Pg 1 of 1
Space Cont.	F6 Display KB	F8 DOS	F10 Quit

APPENDIX

Business Ratios

Although there are many types of ratios, they can generally by placed into one of four categories depending on what they are trying to measure: liquidity, leveraging, activity, and profitability. Liquidity ratios test a firm's ability to meet its short-term or current financial obligations; leverage ratios indicate the proportion of funds provided by owners and creditors; activity ratios reveal how effectively a firm utilizes the resources at its disposal; and profitability ratios measure the overall net effect of the managerial efficiency of a firm. For our purposes here, we will use only a single ratio from each of the four categories. They are listed below with a brief description of each:

$$\text{Quick ratio} = \frac{\text{Current assets} - \text{Inventory}}{\text{Current debt}}$$

The quick ratio indicates the amount of liquid assets available to meet a firm's current obligations. Assuming current assets can be liquidated at or near book value, the higher the ratio, the greater the firm's liquidity.

$$\text{Debt to worth} = \frac{\text{Total debt}}{\text{Net worth}} \times 100\%$$

The debt-to-worth ratio shows the proportion of capital contributed by creditors as compared to the funds contributed by the owners. A high value indicates that the firm is strongly leveraged; indicating a greater risk for the creditors. Servicing an inordinate amount of debt can strain the resources of any organization.

$$\text{Sales to receivables} = \frac{\text{Sales}}{\text{Receivables}}$$

The sales/receivables ratio measures an important business activity; it relates the revenues generated to the level of outstanding receivables carried. A high number implies a sound receivables management policy. By turning over receivables quickly and keeping noncash sales to a minimum, a company benefits in terms of an improved cash flow and fewer collection problems.

$$\text{Profit to worth} = \frac{\text{Profit (pretax)}}{\text{Net worth}} \times 100\%$$

The profit-to-worth ratio shows the return the owners are receiving on their investment. The higher the ratio, the more profitable their investment.

6

APPLYING NEURAL NETWORKS TO THE EXTRACTION OF KNOWLEDGE FROM ACCOUNTING REPORTS: A CLASSIFICATION STUDY

R. H. Berry and Duarte Trigueiros

INTRODUCTION

This study develops a new approach to the problem of extracting meaningful information from samples of accounting reports. Neural networks are shown to be capable of building structures similar to financial ratios, which are optimal in the context of the particular problem being

Printed with permission of the authors.

dealt with. This approach removes the need for an analyst to search for appropriate ratios before model building can begin.

The internal organization of a neural network model helps identify key features of accounting data and provides new insights into the relative importance of variables for particular modeling tasks. The lack of interpretability of neural network parameters so often reported in other applications of the approach is removed in the accounting context. Much of the internal operation of the networks involves the construction of generalizations of the ratio concepts with which accountants are familiar. Thus, traditional modes of understanding can be brought to bear.

ACCOUNTING DECISION MODELS

Accounting reports are an important source of information for managers, investors, and financial analysts. Statistical techniques have often been used to extract information from them. The aim of such exercises is to construct models suitable for predictive or classification purposes, or for isolating key features of the data. Well-known examples include, in the U.S. context, Altman et al[1] and, in the U.K. context, Taffler.[2]

The procedures used in this vast body of literature are generally similar. The first stage consists of forming a set of ratios from selected items in a set of accounting reports. This selection typically is made in accordance with the prior beliefs of researchers. Next, the normality of these ratio variables is examined and transformations applied, where necessary, to bring it about. Finally, some linear modeling technique is used to find optimal parameters in the least-square sense. Linear regression and Fisher's multiple discriminant analysis are the most popular algorithms. However, logistic regression can also be found in some studies. Foster[3] provides a review of the general area of statistical modeling applied to accounting variables.

The widespread use of ratios as input variables is particularly significant in the present context. This seems to be an extension of their normal use in financial statement analysis. However, there is a problem; there are many possible ratios. Consequently, some researchers utilize a large number of ratios as explanatory variables, others use representative ratios, and still others use factor analysis to cope with the mass of ratio variables and their linear dependence.

THE STATISTICAL CHARACTERIZATION OF ACCOUNTING VARIABLES

The statistical distribution of accounting ratios has been the object of considerable study. The common finding is that ratio distributions are skewed. Horrigan[4] in an early work on this subject, reports positive skewness of ratios and explains it as the result of effective lower limits of zero on many ratios. Barnes[5] in a discussion of the link between firm size and ratio values, suggests that skewness of ratios could be the result of deviations from strict proportionality between the numerator and the denominator variables in the ratio. The underlying idea here, that interest should center on the behavior of the component accounting variables, and not on the ratios that they have traditionally been used to form, is basic to the present research.

Mcleay,[6] in one of the few studies of distributions of accounting variables as opposed to ratios of such variables, reports that accounting variables which are sums of similar transactions with the same sign, such as Sales, Stocks, Creditors, or Current Assets, exhibit cross-section lognormality. Empirical work carried out during the current research project confirms this finding and suggests that the phenomenon of lognormality is much more widespread. Many other positive-valued accounting variables have cross-section distributions that are approximately log normal. Furthermore, where variables can take on positive and negative values, then lognormality can be observed in the subset of positive values and also in the absolute values of the negative subset. Size-related nonfinancial variables such as number of employees also seem to exhibit lognormality. Distributional evidence for 18 accounting and other items, for 14 industry groups over a five-year period, can be found in Trigueiros.[7] In this chapter, lognormality is viewed as a universal distributional form for the cross-section behavior of those variables used as inputs to the neural networks that have been built.

The lognormal distribution is characterized by a lower bound of zero and a tail consisting of a few relatively large values. In any statistical analysis of such variables, based on the least-squares criterion, these few large values will dominate coefficient estimates. Consequently, an analyst is well advised to apply the logarithmic transformation to accounting variables that are to be inputs to least-squares-based techniques to counteract this effect. In what follows, logs of accounting variables will appear in various linear combinations, having the general form:

$$z = a_1\log(x_1) + a_2\log(x_2) - b_1\log(y_1) - b_2\log(y_2) \tag{1}$$

If the logarithmic transformation is reversed, this linear combination is seen to be equivalent to:

$$k = \frac{x_1^{a_1} \; x_2^{a_2}}{y_1^{b_1} \; y_2^{b_2}} \tag{2}$$

This is a complex ratio form. Had the linear combination been restricted to the difference between two variables, and the coefficients to the value one, then a simple ratio of two variables would have been produced by reversing the logarithmic transformation. The observation that a linear combination, including both positive and negative coefficients, in log space, is equivalent to a ratio form in ordinary space, is fundamental to the interpretation of the neural network coefficients presented in this chapter.

NEURAL NETWORKS

A neural network is a collection of simple computational elements, neurons, that are interconnected. The connections between neurons have weights attached to them. A neuron can receive inputs from other neurons or from sources outside the network, form a weighted combination of these inputs (often called NET), the weights being those assigned to the connections along with the inputs travel, and produce an output (often called OUT) that is sent to other neurons. The output may be simply the weighted combination of inputs, NET, or a nonlinear transformation of NET. This nonlinear transformation is known as a transfer, or squashing, function. The number and pattern of interconnection of the neurons in a network determine the task a network is capable of performing.

The particular network form used in this chapter is known as a multilayer perceptron (MLP). A simple example is shown in Figure 6.1. There are three layers of neurons (each neuron being represented by a rectangle): an input layer, a hidden layer, and an output layer. The

Figure 6.1

A Multilayer Perceptron

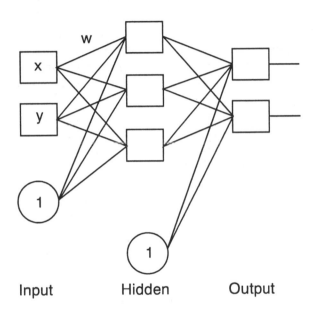

Input   Hidden   Output

neurons in the input layer do not perform weighting or non-linear transformation. They simply send inputs from the world outside the network to the hidden-layer neurons. In Figure 6.1, each input neuron sends its signal to each of the neurons in the hidden-layer. Each of these hidden layer neurons forms a weighted linear combination of the input values and then applies a nonlinear transformation to generate its own output. A common transfer function is the sigmoid, which generates a signal $0 \leq OUT \leq 1$:

$$OUT = \frac{1}{1 + e^{-NET}} \tag{3}$$

The signals from the hidden-layer neurons are sent to the output layer neurons. In Figure 6.1, each output-layer neuron receives input from each hidden-layer neuron. The neurons in the output layer each form linear combinations of their inputs and apply a nonlinear transformation before sending their own signals onwards, in their case to the outside world. The sigmoid function again serves as the nonlinear transformation. The circles in Figure 6.1 do not represent neurons. They each send a signal that has a constant value of 1 along weighted connections. This weighted signal becomes part of NET for each receiving neuron. This has the effect of generating a threshold value of NET in each neuron's OUT calculation, above which OUT rises rapidly.

The particular MLP shown in Figure 6.1 is capable of performing a relatively complex classification task, given that appropriate weights have been attached to the interconnections between neurons. Figure 6.2 shows a convex set of (x,y) values. The convex region is formed by the intersection of three half-spaces, each defined by a linear inequality. Each of the three linear relations that define the convex set can be represented by a linear combination of (x,y) values. Thus, each can be represented by one of the three neurons in the hidden layer of the MLP shown in Figure 6.1. Each output-layer neuron then receives over/under signals from the hidden-layer neurons, and, again by weighting and transforming the signals, carries out AND/OR operations to produce an output.

In the network shown in Figure 6.1, one output neuron will produce a value close to 1 if the (x,y) pair being input lies within the convex

Figure 6.2

Classification Problem

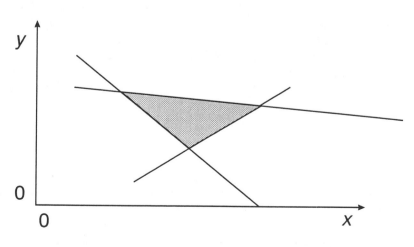

region. The other will produce a value close to 0 in these circumstances. The input of an (x,y) pair outside the convex region will cause a reversal of this output pattern. (Given the binary nature of the output signal required, one output neuron could theoretically do the job. However, computational experience shows that economizing on output neurons is a mistake.) In order to model more difficult nonlinear boundaries, additional hidden layers of neurons might have to be added to the network.

The problem left unresolved in the preceding description of the operation of the MLP is, where do the values of the interconnection weights come from? To carry out the classification task appropriately, each interconnection must have an appropriate weight.

The network learns these weights during a training process. To build a network capable of performing a particular classification task, the following actions must be undertaken:

1. The network topology (number of layers and number of neurons in each layer) must be specified.

2. A data set must be collected to allow network training. In the example under discussion, this training set would consist of (x,y) pairs and for each pair, a target value vector $(1,0)$ if the pair lies in the convex region of interest, $(0,1)$ if it does not.

3. Random, small weights are assigned to each interconnection.

4. An (x,y) pair is input to the network.

5. The vector of OUT values from the output neurons is compared with the appropriate target value vector.

6. Any errors are used to revise the interconnection weights.

The training set is processed repeatedly until a measure of network performance based on prediction errors for the whole training set reaches an acceptably low level. Once training has been completed, the network can be used for predictive purposes. There are two styles of training. In the first, weight updating occurs after each individual element of the training set is processed through the MLP. In the second, the entire training set is processed before updating occurs.

The algorithm used to adjust interconnection weights, known as the generalized delta rule, or as the back-propagation method, is usually associated with Rumelhart et al.[8] This algorithm is an enhanced version of the stochastic gradient-descent optimization procedure. Its virtue is that it is able to propagate deviations backwards through more than one layer of nodes. Thus, it can train networks with one or more hidden layers. For the algorithm to work, the transfer function used in the MLP must be differentiable. Good descriptions of the algorithm exist in several sources, including Pao[9] and Wasserman.[10] Wasserman's approach plays down the mathematics and emphasizes the computational steps.

Minimum least-squares deviation is one possible success criterion that could be used to decide when to curtail the training process. However, there are others such as likelihood maximization. In this case the weights are adjusted to maximize the probability of obtaining the input/output data that constitute the training set.

In general, if the number of nodes in hidden layers is large compared with the number of important features in the data, the MLP behaves just like a storage device. It learns the noise present in the training set, as well as the key structures. No generalization ability can be expected in these circumstances. Restricting the number of hidden-layer neurons, however, makes the MLP extract only the main features of the training set. Thus, a generalization ability appears.

It is its hidden layers of neurons that make the multilayer perceptron attractive as a statistical modeling tool. The outputs of hidden neurons can be considered as new variables, which can contain interesting information about the relationship being modeled. Such new variables, known as internal representations, along with the net topology, can make the modeling process self-explanatory, and so the neural network approach becomes attractive as a form of machine learning.

As stated earlier, if variables are subjected to a logarithmic transformation, then a linear combination of such variables is equivalent to a complex ratio form. If the values input to an MLP are the logs of variable values, then the neurons in the (first, if there are more than one) hidden layer produce NETs that represent complex ratios. The nonlinear transformation effectively reverses the logarithmic transformation, so these complex ratios are inputs to the next layer of neurons where they are linearly combined to model the relation being investigated.

The hidden layer of neurons in the MLP discussed in this chapter is, then, dedicated to building appropriate ratios. The problem of choosing the best ratios for a particular task, which has taxed so many researchers, is thus avoided. The best ratios are discovered by the modeling algorithm, not imposed by the analyst. It will be shown later that by using an appropriate training scheme these extended ratios can be encouraged to assume a simple and therefore potentially more interpretable form.

AN APPLICATION: MODELING INDUSTRY HOMOGENEITY

The approach described above is now applied to the problem of classifying firms to industries on the basis of financial statement data. The neural network's performance is compared to that of a more traditional discriminant analysis-based approach. To ensure that the discriminant analysis exercise is more than a "straw man," an existing, reputable study based on discriminant analysis is replicated. The neural network approach is then applied using the same raw data.

All companies quoted on the London Stock Exchange are classified into different industry groups according to the Stock Exchange Industrial Classification (SEIC), which groups together companies whose results are likely to be affected by the same economic, political, and trade influences.[11] Although the declared criteria are ambitious, the practice seems to be more trivial, consisting of classifying firms mainly on a end-product basis. The aim here is to attempt to mimic the classification process using accounting variables.

The data for exercises were drawn from the Micro-EXSTAT database of company financial information provided by EXTEL Statistical Services Ltd. This covers the top 70 percent of U.K. industrial companies. Fourteen manufacturing groups were selected according to the SEIC criteria. The list of member firms was then pruned to exclude firms known to be distressed, nonmanufacturing representatives of foreign companies, recently merged, or highly diversified. After pruning, data on 297 firms remained for a six-year period (1982–1987) and a bigger sample (502 cases) for the year 1984. The distribution of firms by industry in this sample is shown in Table 6.1.

The initial analysis of this data followed the traditional statistical modeling approach. This consisted of, first, "forming 18 financial ratios chosen as to reflect a broad range of important characteristics relating to the economic, financial and trade structure of industries."[12] Eight principal components were then extracted to form new variables. Next, these new variables were used as inputs to a multiple discriminant analysis. Only a randomly selected half of the data set was used during this estimation phase of the discriminant analysis.

Table 6.1

Industry Groups and Number of Cases in the One-Year (1984) Data Set

Group	Name	Cases	Percent (%)
1	Building Mat.	31	6.2
2	Metallurgy	19	3.8
3	Paper, Pack	46	9.2
4	Chemicals	45	9.0
5	Electrical	34	6.8
6	Industrial Pl.	17	3.4
7	Machine Tools	21	4.2
8	Electronics	79	15.7
9	Motor Comp.	23	4.6
10	Clothing	42	8.4
11	Wool	19	3.8
12	Misc. Text.	30	6.0
13	Leather	16	3.2
14	Food	80	15.9

The other half was used as a holdout sample to measure the classification accuracy of the resulting model. The exercise was repeated reversing the role of the two half data sets. Lack of consistency of results here would have raised doubts about the appropriateness of the sampling activity undertaken. A detailed description of the ratios used and the modeling procedure adopted can be found in Sundarsanam and Taffler.[12] The results of this exercise were found to be similar to those achieved by Sundarsanam and Taffler.[12] Thus, it was decided that they were an acceptable base case against which to compare the results achieved by an MLP constructed with the same data.

The input data for the neural network approach consisted of eight of the accounting variables that had been building blocks for the 18 ratios previously calculated. The number eight was selected simply to mimic the number of explanatory variables in the discriminant analysis. It must be emphasized that basic accounting variables, not ratios, were used. The selected items were Fixed Assets (FA), Inventory (I), Debtors (D), Creditors (C), Long-Term Debt (DB), Net Worth (NW), Wages (W), and Operating Expenses Less Wages (EX). The variables were chosen to represent the key balance sheet elements and a rudimentary picture of cost structure.

A logarithmic transformation was applied to these variables. Many of these accounting variables were well suited for a logarithmic transformation. However, some caused problems because of the presence of zero or negative values. In order to transform the negative values of such variables, the following rule was applied:

$$x \rightarrow \quad \log(x), \qquad \text{for } x > 0$$
$$x \rightarrow \quad -\log(|x|), \quad \text{for } x < 0$$

This corresponds to the assumption that negative cases are lognormally distributed in a negative direction.

To avoid the problem of zero values, instead of log 0, a very small number, log 1 = 0, was used. Such an approach is acceptable if the unit of measurement is not far away from the typical value in the data set. An alternative approach to (some) such problem variables would be to ensure that their pattern of variation is reflected in the model by using as input variables some, that in combination define the problem variable, but which are themselves amenable to the logarithmic transformation. The variability of Profit, say, could be brought to the model by the introduction of both Sales and Expenses.

The base of logarithms to be used can be selected in a way that avoids the need for further scaling. The aim of the transformation is to avoid extreme values. With natural logs, the transformed values of the variables being examined ranged from 2 to 18 approximately. Base 10 logs generated a range between 3 and 7. Given the transfer function in use, 2 to 18 is too great a range. The training process would break down. Thus, base 10 logs were used, and the resulting variable values centered on zero for submission to the network.

The eight variables were then input to a succession of differently structured MLPs. The basic format consisted of an input layer of eight neurons, one or two hidden layers with relatively few neurons in each, and an output layer with 14 neurons. Once again the networks were trained using only half the data set, the other half being used to test classification performance. As with the discriminant analysis, the roles of training and testing set were reversed and the consistency of the resulting models examined. The most successful network topology involved one hidden layer with six nodes. The method of determining this optimal topology, its performance, and the interpretation of its weights is discussed below.

INTERPRETING AND POSTPROCESSING THE OUTPUTS OF AN MLP

There is a problem when using an MLP with multiple output neurons. The implied industry classification, given a set of inputs, may not be easy to identify. This has implications for both network training and use. Each output neuron produces an output value between 0 and 1. It would be most unusual to find 13 zeros and a single 1 in the vector of outputs. Therefore, identifying the predicted classification when overlapping distributions are present requires a probabilistic interpretation of outputs. In accounting applications, population proportions generally bear no relation to the proportions observed in the sample. Therefore, the approaches adopted by other neural network researchers in other application areas, where population and sample probabilities coincide, may not be appropriate. In particular it is most unlikely that sample proportions can be viewed as good estimates of prior probabilities.

Following Baum and Wilczek,[13] several authors advocate a direct interpretation of outputs as probabilities, and show how the usual squared-error criterion can be corrected to achieve likelihood maximization.[14,15] In such cases, the connection weights in the network are adjusted in the gradient direction of the log-likelihood rather than the squared error.

An alternative approach is to interpret the outputs of the MLP as a multidimensional measure of distance to targets. If departures from normality are not severe, this interpretation can be carried out using conventional statistics such as chi-square, Penrose, or Mahalanobis distances. Such measures can be regarded as scores, and conditional probabilities can be deduced from them allowing further Bayesian corrections if required, independent of the proportions observed in the sample. A Bayesian correction independent of the sample proportions could of course also be applied directly to the MLP's outputs if they were interpreted as probabilities.

In this application it was found that interpreting neuron outputs directly as probabilities produced a clear reduction in classification accuracy. There was a severe loss of ability to identify firms belonging to the smaller industry groups. A Bayesian correction independent of sample proportions was not pursued.

Results are reported in Figure 6.3. Direct interpretation, shown in Figure 6.3(a), ignores nine of the 14 industry groups, but finally achieves a good global performance by classifying the remaining five groups, which are the bigger ones, very well. Figure 6.3(b) shows classification performance when neuron outputs are postprocessed to produce a multidimensional distance measure. As can be seen, this allows the smaller industry groupings to appear. Therefore, although for the sake of efficiency of convergence the likelihood cost function was adopted during training, node outputs were postprocessed as distances.

A relatively simple approach was taken to the definition of a multidimensional distance. For a training set with N cases, consider o_{im}, the output signal produced in output layer neuron m, $1 \leq m \leq M$ by case i, $1 \leq i \leq N$. Compute K square deviations, d_{kim}, between neuron m's output for that input vector and each possible target value, t_{km} for that neuron: $d_{kim} = (t_{km} - o_{im})^2$, with k, $1 \leq k \leq K$. The mean sum of squared deviations from the kth target at neuron m over the whole training set will be:

$$\sigma^2_{km} = \sum_{i=1}^{N} \frac{d_{kim}}{(N-1)} \tag{4}$$

The standardized distances between a neuron's output and the kth target can be added over all nodes to give:

$$D_{ki} = \sum_{m=1}^{M} \frac{d_{kim}}{\sigma^2_{km}} \tag{5}$$

D_{ki} is then the distance between the output vector generated by the ith case in the training set and the kth target. The minimum of these distances identifies the appropriate classification if no Bayesian corrections are needed, that is, if the assumption of equal prior probabilities is acceptable. As part of this research effort, this distance measure's performance has been compared with that of a more elaborate measure, the Mahalanobis distance. The use of the Mahalanobis distance did not produce improved performance.

Figure 6.3

The Impact of Postprocessing Outputs on Classifications

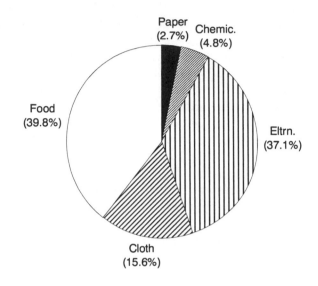

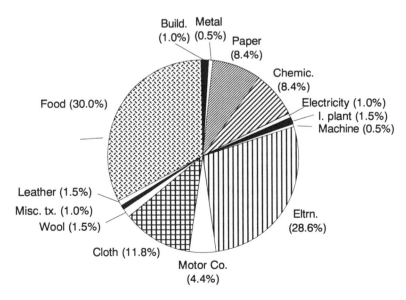

DETERMINING NETWORK TOPOLOGY

The literature gives little guidance on selecting the number of hidden layers, or the number of nodes per hidden layer. Nor is there much advice on the number of times the training set should pass through the network before training is complete. The most common approach to the latter problem is to choose a target value for the training set error and repeat submission of the training set until this target value is achieved.

For the former problem a reasonable approach would seem to be to subdivide the training set into two parts, A and B. Training set A is used in the connection weight updating procedure as usual. Different topologies can be trained using this training set. The classification performance of each of these topologies on training set B can then be examined. The topology that gives best performance is then selected for further work. It is this topology that can then be retrained to generate a simplified structure as described in the next section. The true generalization ability of the network topology can then be checked on the as yet unused testing set.

THE PROCESS OF NETWORK TRAINING

One of the major goals of this research was the evaluation and improvement of the interpretability of multilayer perceptron models. MLPs are often considered unsuitable in applications where self-explanatory power is required. However, in the case of accounting variables, it seems possible to interpret the way the relation has been modeled by looking at the weights connecting input variables with the hidden layer's neurons. These weights are the exponents of the extended ratios involved in the optimal solution.

In order to enhance interpretability, the normal process of training interconnection weights was amended in two ways. First, it was decided to assign to one hidden-layer neuron the task of dealing with the scale effect in financial variables. The failure of ratios to cope with scale effects has been widely discussed in the literature. The weights on connections from input neurons to this hidden-layer neuron were fixed at either 0 or 1 from the outset. Connections with unit weights linked the hidden-layer neuron to only those inputs that were seen as size related. Dedicating one neuron of the hidden layer to representing this scale effect generated as a bonus an improvement in speed of convergence of the training process.

The weight generation process was also amended in a second way. During training, whenever a new presentation of the entire training set was to begin, one of the neurons of the hidden layer was randomly selected and the connection weights linking it to the input neurons were examined. Any inhibitory weights (close to 0) were penalized by a small factor, typically 0.98. As has been said, the aim was to reduce the number of variables featuring in each of the complex ratios being formed. In a neural network each neuron acts as a modeling unit with a certain number of free parameters. The same output can be obtained with very different combinations of these parameters. Inhibitory weights connecting inputs with the hidden layer appear when the network tries to weaken the contribution of a variable. Therefore, by randomly introducing small penalizations of inhibitory weights during the training the inhibitory weights were encouraged to remain inhibitory. As a by-product, the noninhibitory weights were encouraged to become even less inhibitory. Before the end of training, all the weights connecting inputs to the hidden layer and exhibiting strong inhibitory values were set to 0 and fixed. While this procedure served its purpose, it should only be applied when the basic network topology is known with some confidence.

The results produced in the neural network can be seen in Table 6.2. This shows the extended ratios formed in an MLP with eight inputs, six nodes in one hidden layer, and 14 output nodes, trained with 1984 data. Only two hidden-layer neurons produce ratio forms of substantial complexity. The relative simplicity of the ratio structures achieved bodes well for other applications in the accounting and finance area.

Interpretation of the resulting ratios unfortunately is unclear. One possible explanation for this is that the data set being used does not include an economic basis for the classification decision. Financial statement data is hardly an ideal data set for the application in question; variables such as product type are obviously more relevant. However, the fact that traditional ratios have not been formed does not indicate a failure of the approach. It indicates the unsuitability of these traditional ratio constructs and the need for alternatives.

Apart from these nonstandard training features that stem from the particular application area, two further enhancements to the training process described in the literature were also applied. The first was the utilization of a learning rate particular to each weight.[16,17] The second

Table 6.2

Values of Weights Connecting Input Variables Hidden Nodes after Training with Penalties

	Node number				
Variable	2	3	4	5	6
DB			−6		
NW	8				
W	1			−6	
I	8				
D	2				−2
C				3	
FA	−9	−4		6	−4
EX	−10	4	8	−2	3

was, as has already been mentioned, likelihood maximization instead of squared-deviations minimization.

MLP CLASSIFICATION PERFORMANCE

In order to obtain an estimate of the generalization capacity associated with the MLPs examined here, the original samples were divided randomly into two subsamples of approximately equal size. All models were constructed twice, first with one half of the sample and a check carried out with the other half, and again reversing the roles of the two half-data sets. Results were considered acceptable if both models, when validated with the half sample not used to build them, produced consistent results.

All classification results reported here concern the test set, not the training set. That is, they were obtained by measuring the rate of correct classification the model produced when evaluated by the half set not used to train it. The classification performance on the set used for training depends solely on the number of free parameters and can be increased simply by introducing more neurons into the hidden layers. Such results are therefore uninteresting and are not presented here.

The normal approach to testing a model, by deleting a single observation and predicting its value with the model estimated on the rest of the data set, and repeating this procedure, is infeasible here. This is because the training of a neural network is time consuming. However, the procedure adopted here will work acceptably with a large enough data set.

It was found that the generalization capacity of the neural MLP was very much dependent on the topology of the net. The number of nodes in the hidden layer seemed to determine the ability of the net to properly generalize. Persistently, good generalizations were obtained whenever the hidden layer had six nodes. Both the 1984 and the six-year data sets exhibited such a feature. Figure 6.4 shows some classification results for different numbers of nodes in the hidden layer when using the six-year data set. Similar patterns, though not showing so great a contrast, were observed when using the 1984 set.

Table 6.3 shows the best generalization results achieved with the traditional methodology (discriminant analysis and ratios) and also with the neural network. As can be seen, the neural network achieved a better performance, with half the number of input variables and within a much simpler framework.

Figure 6.4

Proportion of Correct Classifications versus Hidden-Layer Structure: 6-Year Data Set

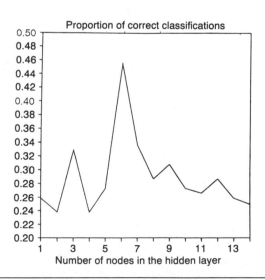

Table 6.3

Classification Results of MLP (Multilayer Perceptron) Compared with MDA (Multiple Discriminant Analysis)

	1984 Data (%)		Six-Year Data (%)	
Input	MDA	MLP	MDA	MLP
18 ratios	29		30	
8 variables		38		45

The need for forming appropriate ratios was avoided as well as the blind pruning of outliers and the extraction of an arbitrary number of factors.

CONCLUSIONS

So far, most applications of neural networks have related to the modeling of difficult relations (pattern recognition) or the mimicking of brain functions. There has been little emphasis on their potential explanatory power. Here, however, it has been argued that in accounting-based applications networks could generate meaningful internal representations. Numerical, continuous-valued observations such as those found in stock returns, or data organized in accounting reports, cannot be efficiently used by traditional expert systems knowledge acquisition tools. Neural networks can now be seen as an alternative self-explanatory tool. In this application hidden units formed ratios very different to those commonly used. If repeated in other application areas, this could shed light on many important issues.

The emphasis on interpretation should not obscure the other finding of the study. The MLP proved able to outperform the classification performance of a traditional discriminant analysis approach. Neither method came close to adequately classifying the testing sets, but there was a substantial improvement when the MLP was used. The fact that there was a potential for improvement was a key fact in determining the particular application area to be studied. It is perhaps worth pointing out that redoing the discriminant analysis, using representations of the ratios produced by the MLP, captured some but not all of the

MLP-based improvement. The remainder may well have related to the ability of the MLP to cope with nonlinear boundaries.

The importance of the MLP's topology cannot be overemphasized. The number of hidden layers, and hidden-layer neurons, can be selected by splitting the training set and adopting a two-phase training process. However, the principle of parsimony should always be borne in mind. If there are too many hidden neurons, the MLP will fail to identify key features and will model the noise in the data set as well. Generalization ability will then be lost.

ENDNOTES

1. A. Altman, R. Haldeman, P. Narayanan, "Zeta Analysis: A New Model for Bankruptcy Risk of Corporations," *Journal of Banking and Finance*, 1977.

2. R. Taffler, "Forecasting Company Failure in the U.K. Using Discriminant Analysis and Financial Ratios Data," *Journal of the Royal Statistical Society*, 1982.

3. G. Foster, *Financial Statement Analysis*, Prentice-Hall, (1986).

4. J. Horrigan, "The Determination of Long-term Credit Standing with Financial Ratios," *Journal of Accounting Research, Supplement. Empirical Research in Accounting: Selected Studies*, 1966.

5. P. Barnes, "Methodological Implications of Non-Normally Distributed Financial Ratios," *Journal of Business, Finance and Accounting*, 1982.

6. S. Mcleay, "The Ratio of Means, the Mean of Ratios and Other Benchmarks," *Finance, Journal of the French Finance Society*, 1986.

7. D. Trigueiros, "The Cross-Section Distribution of Accounting Variables" University of East Anglia: unpublished working paper, 1991.

8. D. Rumelhart, G. Hinton, and R. Williams, "Learning Internal Representations by Error Propagation," in *Parallel Distributed Processing*, (MIT Press, 1986).

9. Y. H. Pao, *Adaptive Pattern Recognition and Neural Networks*, Addison-Wesley, 1989.

10. P. D. Wasserman, *Neural Computing: Theory and Practice,* Van Nostrand Reinhold, 1989.

11. J. Plymen, "Classification of Stock Exchange Securities by Industry," *Journal of the Institute of Actuaries,* 1971.

12. P. Sudarsanam, and R. Taffler, "Industrial Classification in U.K. Capital Markets: A Test of Economic Homogeneity," *Applied Economics* 1985.

13. E. Baum, and F. Wilkzek, "Supervised Learning of Probability Distributions by Neural Networks," *IEEE Conference on Neural Information Processing Systems—Nulural and Synthetic,* Denver, 1987.

14. J. Hopfield, "Learning Algorithms and Probability Distributions in Feed-forward and Feed-back Networks," *Proceedings of the National Academy of Science USA,* 1987.

15. S. Solla, E. Levin, and M. Fleisher, "Accelerated Learning in Layered Neural Networks," *Complex Systems,* 1988.

16. R. Jacobs, "Increased Rates of Convergence Through Learning Rate Adaptation," *Neural Networks,* 1988.

17. F. Silva, and L. Almeida, "Speeding Up Backpropagation," INESC, (Lisbon: R. Alves Redol, 1990).

## 7

THE USE OF NEURAL COMPUTING TECHNOLOGY TO DEVELOP PROFILES OF CHAPTER 11 DEBTORS WHO ARE LIKELY TO BECOME TAX DELINQUENTS

George G. Klemic

INTRODUCTION

Each year the Internal Revenue Service (IRS) assigns to special agents all of the cases opened because of a taxpayer filing for the protection

Printed with permission of the author.

of the court under Chapter 11 of the Bankruptcy Act. This can amount to up to several thousand new cases a year, in addition to those cases remaining open.

The taxpayer-debtors (debtors) typically are businesses with employees and continue to operate after filing for the court's protection. With cash scarce, some of the debtors withhold income and social security tax from their employees and use it for current operations, rather than remitting it as a Federal Tax Deposit (FTD). These unremitted FTDs accumulate rapidly and represent a large accounts receivable inventory to the IRS, amounting to millions of dollars a year for each district. While these unpaid, postpetition amounts are granted priority for payment as an expense of administration of the debtors' estates, there usually are insufficient funds to pay such claims. Also, such claims reduce the amount of funds available to general creditors.

It is long-standing government policy to credit the employees of such debtors with the withheld amounts even though the withheld amounts were not remitted. Prevention of delinquency of payment is therefore a very high priority for the Service. Current systems identify such delinquencies only many weeks, sometimes months, after they begin to occur. The only way to prevent or minimize delinquency is by close individual monitoring of debtor activity and petitioning the court for immediate payment or a conversion of the proceedings to a Chapter 7 liquidation upon the discovery of delinquency. The Service calls this process referral for adjudication (referral).

Typically, only very limited resources are available to monitor these cases, with three to five advisory revenue officers (advisors) assigned to these cases per district. Even in the best-case scenario with five advisors, a few clerks, and 900 to 1,000 cases, the ratio of cases to advisors (180) exceeds their ideal span of control by almost 120 cases.

The advisors who are responsible for these cases have no profile or delinquency model to follow. The cases must be worked blind. The combination of scarce resources and nonexistence of a model or profile to identify the likely delinquents causes a large district to expend many staff hours working cases that will not become delinquent, and never would have, even if unworked.

It is important that a method of identifying the debtors who are likely to become delinquent be devised, so the scarce resources can be applied in the most effective fashion.

Traditional IRS methods of developing models and profiling would take many months to implement and are done on a nationwide basis.

Conditions vary greatly from jurisdiction to jurisdiction, so a nation-wide model or profile would be considerably less than optimal. There is a need to develop locally valid profiles of debtors likely to become postpetition delinquents. The method needs to be simple and quick enough to be iterated frequently to allow for updating necessitated by changes in conditions.

THE NEURAL PROCESS

Since traditional IRS modeling techniques did not appear appropriate, consideration was given to the use of more current technology. The more traditional forms of artificial intelligence involve the identification and use of rules, drawn from the knowledge of domain experts. Were such a means to be used, we would spend several weeks to months attempting to identify and analyze the rules. This would consume analyst time and domain expert production time. Application of the rules to the data would then require a system design effort, potential acquisition of hardware and software, a programming effort, debugging, execution of the program, and analysis and testing of the results.

Neural computing, on the other hand, entails the teaching of the system by example. The teaching is done with existing databases. Neural computing has several advantages over traditional artificial intelligence methods, as shown in Table 7.1.

Table 7.1

Comparison of Neural Networks and Expert Systems

Neural Networks	Expert Systems
Example based	Rule based
Domain free	Domain specific
Finds rules	Needs rules
Little programming needed	Much programming needed
Easy to maintain	Difficult to maintain
Fault tolerant	Not fault tolerant
Needs (only) a database	Needs a human expert
Fuzzy logic	Rigid logic
Adaptive system	Requires reprogramming

Source: Samdani.[1]

PROBLEM STATEMENT

Can neural computing technologies be used to provide the needed profiles? While much has been written about neural computing, relatively little has been written about the application of neural computing to financial problems. The few articles that have been published all lean to shallow discussion of the same few applications.

Klimasauskas,[2] Zeidenberg,[3] and Smith[4] write about several neural computing applications, including the teaching of a system to evaluate loan applications for creditworthiness and grant credit approval. Zeidenberg[3] also discussed neural nets that forecast the rate of business bankruptcies and that predict T-Bill yield curves. Brody[5] writes about measuring mortgage loan risk and about a system that identifies fraudulent credit card transactions. Smith[4] discusses systems designed to read checks into databases, thus eliminating the need for keyboard entry of the data. Rochester[6] looks to the use of neural nets for "database mining," which explores the strategic value that has been buried in corporate databases. Ring[7] writes of Cambridge Consultant's development of a trader's interface to help differentiate spoof bids from genuine ones.

A search of the literature on the topic of applications of neural networks to Chapter 11 situations revealed that nothing has been indexed on this specific topic. Although this specific problem has not been addressed in the literature, the considerable discussion in related subjects suggests that there is a good possibility that neural computing could be used to resolve the IRS problem.

METHODOLOGY

The IRS Western Regional Office (WR) has some experience with neural computing. Scheduling and routine problems, as well as some simple case profiling situations have been successfully addressed with neural nets.

The problem to be addressed here is considerably more complex, but the methodology is basically the same. The hardware and software will be selected, available data will be analyzed, and duplicate items and nonvariables will be culled from the database. The database will be preprocessed and augmented, as needed. The appropriate neural network architecture will be selected, trained, tested, evaluated, and deployed.

Selecting the Application

The WR has been experimenting with neural networks and similar technology for about a year, having had successes with Knowledgeseeker, a statistical analysis package product that identifies patterns in data and presents them in tree form. WR also acquired the the Hecht-Nielson Corporation (HNC) product Explorenet I and has arranged for acquisition of Explorenet II and NeuralWare products. An analyst has been thoroughly trained in the use of these products and has used them for several simple applications. These products are capable of assimilating data and establishing the connections between the variables. The use of any of these would be at no additional cost to WR.

Product specifications and articles describing successful application elsewhere indicate that HNC products can provide the utility needed to address the problem at hand. WR's training and experience with these products is somewhat stronger than the other products. These technical, training, and experience considerations, when linked with availability of the software at no additional cost, drive WR to use the HNC products for the project.

To run any of these applications with a database as large as those needed for our largest districts, Laguna Nigel and Los Angeles, requires a fast microcomputer, 16 MB of RAM, and 1.2 GB of storage.

Data Analysis

Two automated databases might be used to teach a neural net, the Service's own database and that of the federal court. Both databases are standardized in accordance with direction from national administrative heads of the IRS and the judiciary.

The Service's database is stored on microcomputers of various vintage, including Zilgos, Pyramids, and Sequents. The database language used is INFORMIX.

The court's database is stored on Unisys 5090 series machines or on microcomputer local area networks (LANs), depending on the court district size. The database language used is UNIFY for the Unisys and FOXBASE for the microcomputer LANs. All of the FOXBASE courts are migrating to the UNIFY systems, so this chapter addresses the problem as if the UNIFY system were the only one in use.

For purposes of testing this approach to the problem, a large district, Seattle, was selected. This district was selected because its size, number of cases (25,500, occupying 635 MB of space), and average dollar value of cases are significant. The success of this approach to the problem, if achieved, will reap significant cost savings and revenue gains.

The Service's database occupies 172 MB of space on the storage devices of the microcomputers. The court's database contains entity information, tax data provided by the Service, and considerable financial information. The Service's database contains entity information, tax data, and data provided by the court. Scanning of the data dictionaries of the two databases demonstrates considerable overlap.

Culling. The data used to train the system should be representative of data encountered in actual operation. It will be necessary to examine the universe of data and remove cases that are not Chapter 11 cases. This will be done with C language scripts. The 25,000-case universe can probably be cut down to 2,000. These 2,000 represent those cases which are currently Chapter 11s and those which were Chapter 11s but which the court converted to other proceedings or which were dismissed.

It will be appropriate to cull duplicate data from the databases. The court is the book of original entry for all of the data except the tax data, and the tax data that the IRS enters into its database is provided to the court. The IRS database therefore will not be used to train the neural network.

The court's database, now culled of non-Chapter 11 cases, will be examined for fields that do not represent variables (for example, docket narratives in the court's database, telephone numbers, and so forth). These will likewise be culled.

The purified database will contain entity identifying information and variables that may be linked to or contribute to postpetition delinquency.

The data dictionary was analyzed to identify variables, as shown in Table 7.2. The number of variables may be further reduced by consolidation to increase processing potential and speed as necessary.

Preprocessing and Augmenting. The results of the culling must be defined for the system. This will be done by key entry for the test. If any of the variables to be used are not present in sufficient quantity to train

Table 7.2

Variables in the Data Dictionary

Total fields	1,072
Field representing variables	33
Fields that can be eliminated	1,039
Total characters/case	12,364
Characters eliminated/case	11,983
Characters to be taught /case	381
Chapter 11 cases	924
Total characters to be taught	351,682

the system, it will be necessary to augment the data. Since court processing is meticulous, we do not anticipate experiencing deficiencies with the variables.

If execution reveals deficiencies to be present, we will request that the court provide archive tapes from earlier years to augment those variables. If such archive tapes are not available, tapes from other courts can be used, but this will have the effect of de-localizing the process.

Picking an Architecture

There are 16 or more architectures available for projects such as this. Some of these architectures are more esoteric than others. WR has more experience in back-propagation than in other architectures, so back-propagation will be used.

The trained system will permit use to look backward from those instances of debtors failing to pay the taxes that have accrued after the petitioning of the bankruptcy court to the variables common to these debtors. From this, a profile can be prepared. Also, when IRS is notified of the existence of a new debtor, the data on that debtor can be run against the neural network to determine likelihood of delinquency.

Training the Network

The network is trained by permitting it to iterate readings of the data. With each of these iterations, the network assigns weights to the variables in order to establish the relationships between the variables. As the iterations occur, the mean squared error in establishing the relationships is continually reduced, until a predetermined acceptable level is reached.

The vendor recommends 300 to 1,000 iterations, although our experience has shown that the system can learn with considerably fewer iterations.

It is anticipated that the training of the network may take a weekend or more. Although training a network will tie up one microcomputer, only set-up time and occasional checking will be required of an analyst.

Testing the Network

It is anticipated that the relationships of variables identified by the net will be molded into a profile for use in the State of Washington.

There will be two levels of testing of the profile and of the network, a training test and a real-world test. The training test will be accomplished by using the network's output on an archived database and on the database from another court district. If the net-based profile can identify the debtors who became delinquent, with a false-positive and false-negative rate of 10 percent or less, the training test will be deemed to have been passed.

The real-world test will be accomplished by using the profile on new, live cases from the State of Washington. Current monitoring methods will be suspended for six months. As new cases are received, they will be profiled. Those profiled as positive (likely to become postpetition delinquents) will be subject to close monitoring. The District will be asked to report when, if at all, these debtors become delinquent. The District will also be asked to report on negative cases that become delinquent. As with the training test, a 10 percent error rate will be considered to be acceptable for both false-positive and false-negative findings.

The 10 percent error rate is arbitrary, but considered an ambitious starting point. With a universal approach, IRS monitors far more compliant debtors than delinquent ones.

Final Evaluation of the Network

Final evaluation of the network will be based on the results of the real-world test, the cost of the exercise, and the benefit, in terms of the dollar value of the hours saved per referral.

Explaining the System. This step is newly inserted into the routine. HNC's products now include one classed Knowledgenet. This product explains the results of the neural computing program's efforts. Although such explanation is not necessary for the functioning of the system, it may be helpful as a marketing tool for sharing the process with other locations. Also, given the litigious nature of IRS' customers, it is likely that one or more debtors will challenge IRS' close monitoring of their payroll and tax depositing activities.

Deploying the Network. The test network will be deployed to the Seattle District in a remote fashion, with WR in control. If successful, the network will be deployed to our largest districts first (to maximize the benefit), as budget and district preparedness for this technology allow.

COST-BENEFIT ANALYSIS

This analysis is predicated on the assumption that the neural computing approach will be applied to the problem in the Western Region alone. Neural computing will be used only for those court districts that volunteer copies of their databases. Execution will be accomplished by one analyst on the staff. Costs to execute are presented in Table 7.3.

BENEFITS

The Service monitors the activities of debtors and does collect from delinquent debtors. The Service also petitions the court to convert delinquent debtor Chapter 11s to Chapter 7 liquidations. In many cases, however, the delinquent taxes accrue, a conversion occurs, and no payment is forthcoming because of the debtor's poor financial position.

Table 7.3	
Costs to Execute	
80486 microprocessor, monitor, and printer	$10,000 Sunk cost, purchased previously
Neural software	Sunk cost, purchased previously
Analyst, $26 per hour * 8 hours programming time, extraction	$ 208
Training costs	Sunk cost, accomplished previously
Additional disk space	$ 2,500
Blank tapes	$ 25
Total cost	$12,733

To accomplish the above activities, the Service devotes many staff years, as described in Table 7.4. Additional data can be found in the Appendix.

As reflected by the number of referrals, the 5,213 hours in 1989 and 8,754 hours in 1990 were used to blindly attempt to monitor 1,420 and 924 debtors while looking for the 91 and 35 debtors who would become delinquent.

The benefit to be reaped would be the ability to identify the potential delinquents without the need to monitor the other cases. We know from years of practice that a manageable inventory of cases amounts to about 65. If we can pre-identify the target cases, we could concentrate our energies there and save 4,904 hours. At $20 an hour, this would represent a savings of $98,080.

Benefit	$98,080
Cost	12,733
Gain (deficit)	85,347

Iteration of the process for the other ten districts of the WR would bring the annual benefit of the neural net to $938,707.

Table 7.4

Cost of Efforts over Two Years

	1989	1990	Average
New cases	453	347	400
Inventory	1,420	924	1,172
Total hours	10,236	12,571	11,404
Referrals	91	35	63
Monitoring time	5,213	8,754	6.984
Average salary/hour	$ 20	$ 20	$ 20
Cost to monitor	$ 104,260	$ 175,080	$ 139,670
Cost per referral	$ 1,146	$ 5,002	$ 2,217

DISCUSSION

The problem discussed in this chapter has been faced by the IRS for many years. With advances in neural computing a method now exists for development of a profile in relatively little time and at very low cost. The anticipated $0.94 million annual benefits in WR will be augmented by additional productivity gained by shifting of staff hours savings to other work. The profiling method, if applied to the other six regional areas, could reap similar benefits.

It is anticipated that the project will be executed this year. If the results are not as anticipated, the process can be repeated with an updated database to identify the adjustments needed. If and when the results are as anticipated, WR will have a need to share the process with the other regions.

The process, of course, depends heavily on the accuracy of the database. Data entry at the court level may be inaccurate or tardy. Debtors may err or perjure themselves in the preparation of their schedules. Should either of these problems occur as other than isolated instances, will the profiling be accurate? Perhaps of equal importance, if real-world experience shows the profiles to be inaccurate, will that be a clue to use neural computing to identify erroneously prepared or entered schedules?

ENDNOTES

1. G. Samdani, "Neural Nets: They Learn From Examples," *Chemical Engineering*, vol. 97(8), August 1990, pp. 37–45.

2. C. C. Klimasauskas, "Applying Neural Networks," *PC AI*, vol. 5(1), January/February 1991, pp. 30–33.

3. J. Zeidenberg, "I Think, Therefore ICON," *CA Magazine*, vol. 123(8), 1990, pp. 36–42.

4. J. C. Smith, "A Neural Network—Could It Work for You?" *Financial Executive*, vol. 6(3), May/June 1990, pp. 26–30.

5. H. Brody, "The Neural Computer," *Technology Review*, vol. 93(6), August/September 1990, pp. 43–49.

6. J. B. Rochester, "New Business Uses for Neurocomputing," *I/S Analyzer*, vol. 28(2), February 1990, pp. 1–11.

7. K. Ring, "Neural Networks, Knowledge Systems, Genetic Algorithms at Cambridge Consultants," *Computergram International*, July 1989, pp. 439–512.

APPENDIX

Table A7.1
Seattle Data

	1989	1990	Average
New cases	453	347	400
Inventory	1,420	924	1,172
Claims	698	483	591
Total hours	10,236	12,571	11,404
Collections	$4,959,344	$5,954,415	$5,456,880
Referrals	91	35	63
Hours/new case	1	1	1
Research	1	1	1
Claim time	3	3	3
Plan analysis	4	4	4
Closing time	2	2	2
Total nonmonitor time	11	11	11
New cases × 11	4,983	3,817	4,400
Monitoring time	5,213	8,754	6,984
Average salary/hour	$ 20	$ 20	$ 20
Cost to monitor	$ 104,260	$ 175,080	$ 139,670
Cost per referral	$ 1,146	$ 5,002	$ 2,217

PART 3

BUSINESS FAILURE PREDICTION

8

A NEURAL NETWORK APPROACH TO BANKRUPTCY PREDICTION

Wullianallur Raghupathi, Lawrence L. Schkade, and Bapi S. Raju

INTRODUCTION

The domain of this exploratory research is in financial analysis. Specifically, the research develops and models the bankruptcy prediction process using a neural network approach. The application can assist auditors, individual investors, portfolio managers, bankers, and other investment advisors in making decisions about investments.

Auditors generally verify financial statements of companies to see if they have been prepared according to generally accepted accounting principles and present fairly the financial picture of the company. Interpretation and prediction are left to the user of the statements. However, it is believed that the auditor's responsibility goes beyond mere verification of the statement. The Statement on Auditing Standards (SAS) 59 deals with the assessment of going concern status. An entity is assumed to be a going concern if it is expected to continue in existence for the foreseeable future. The auditor has a responsibility to evaluate whether there is substantial doubt about the entity's ability to continue as a going concern for a reasonable period of time, not to exceed one year beyond the date of the financial statement. If the auditor has a doubt about the likelihood of continued existence, possible or potential mitigating factors must be examined before giving a final opinion. The auditor's work in this respect is made difficult by uncertainty and fuzziness in the financial statement information, laws, and guidelines. This necessitates a good decision support system that the auditors can use to make confident predictions about the future status of a company: for example, will the company go bankrupt or remain a going concern.[1]

The following section briefly reviews some of the prior research in the domain of bankruptcy prediction.

LITERATURE REVIEW

Much research has been done utilizing financial statement data for bankruptcy prediction with an emphasis on ratio analysis. McKinley et al.[2] state that ratios are the best known and most widely used of financial analysis tools. They allow the analyst to study the relationships among various components and to compare a company's performance to that of similar enterprises. Miller[3] believes that some ratios represent cause and some represent effect. Gibson and Frishkoff[4] caution that ratios will differ across industry groups and according to accounting methods used. For a more detailed discussion on this issue see Horrigan.[5]

The primary focus has been on using standard statistical techniques in which it appears that the financial ratios are generally valid discriminators between bankrupt and nonbankrupt firms. Previous researchers have represented nonquantitative items by indicator variables or by regressing one variable on others to reflect trends.

The principal tools in this regard have been discriminant analysis, logit analysis, and recursive partitioning. The problem is generally treated as a classification problem.

Collins and Green[6] compare and contrast the three statistical models most frequently used for bankruptcy prediction: multiple discriminant analysis (MDA), linear probability models (LPM), and logistic regression (logit analysis). Multiple discriminant analysis is a statistical technique used to classify an observation into one of two or more a priori groups. In the case of bankruptcy prediction, there are two predefined groups: bankrupt and nonbankrupt firms. Classification is accomplished through development of a discriminant function, which is generally a linear combination of independent variables. The discriminant function is derived in such a way as to minimize the possibility of misclassification. In order for inferences of MDA to be valid, certain assumptions have to be met. In applying MDA, part of the data set is used as an analysis sample to develop the discriminant function. A cutting score is derived to determine group classification for each observation, and the resultant function is then applied to the remainder of the data set (a holdout sample) for validation. A classification matrix is derived for both the analysis sample and holdout sample. This matrix (also called a confusion matrix) shows the number of observations correctly and incorrectly classified. From this, a hit ratio may be computed, indicating the percentage of observations correctly classified.

In logit analysis the logit model is based on the cumulative logistic probability function. It has been found appropriate in many situations involving a binary dependent variable (e.g., bankrupt or nonbankrupt). In comparing logit analysis to MDA, Collins and Green[6] assert that the logit model appears to produce lower Type 1 errors (classifying as healthy a firm that subsequently fails) but is not significantly better at classification accuracy. Furthermore, they maintain that MDA seems fairly robust to violations of model assumptions. Therefore, unless the cost of Type 1 errors is large, the additional computational effort of the logit model compared to MDA may not be worthwhile.

Recursive partitioning algorithm (RPA) is a computerized nonparametric classification technique based on pattern recognition. The model is in the form of a binary classification tree that assigns objects to predefined groups in such a way as to minimize misclassification costs. Classification accuracy of a function may be determined by the use of a test sample whose correct classification is known. For instance, in a bankruptcy prediction model, the classification tree may be constructed using a portion of the data and tested with the remainder. Or the model may be built with data from one time period and tested with data from a comparable period. Altman[7] tested his discriminant analysis model on a holdout sample of 66 nonbankrupt firms, of which 65 percent had incurred two or three years of losses. Of the firms, 79 percent were correctly classified. Gentry et al.[8] tested two logit models on a sample of 23 financially weak firms (based on a credit-watch list) and obtained accuracy rates of 70 percent and 78 percent).

Harris[1] performed MDA, logit analysis, and RPA tests on a sample of 100 bankrupt and 100 nonbankrupt companies matched by asset size, industry, and year. Each model was analyzed with the entire data set, then with the set split into analysis and holdout samples of equal size. For discriminant analysis, overall classification accuracy was 84.5 percent for the analysis sample of 100 companies (50 bankrupt and 50 nonbankrupt); pooled and nonpooled versions yielded the same overall classification accuracy of 86 percent, while the holdout sample with pooled variance-covariance matrices had an accuracy rate of 85 percent. In logit analysis, overall classification accuracy was 87 percent; for the analysis sample, 95 percent, and for the holdout sample, 78 percent. In RPA using CART (Classification and Regression Trees, software for RPA), classification accuracy was 77 percent for bankrupt firms and 86 percent for nonbankrupt on the full data set; 80 percent and 94 percent for bankrupt and nonbankrupt respectively in the analysis sample; and 76 percent for bankrupt and 90 percent for nonbankrupt for the holdout sample.[1]

Individuals generally rely on auditor judgment and financial ratios for important investment decisions. However, not all variables are known completely, and some others are difficult to characterize precisely. In the following section, we briefly discuss the limitations of the statistical techniques and the potential of a neural network model.

PROBLEM STATEMENT

Developing a robust and reliable model for bankruptcy prediction is important as it enables investors, auditors, and others to independently evaluate the risk of investment. The task of predicting bankruptcy of a company can be posed as a classification problem: given a set of classes (here, bankrupt and nonbankrupt) and a set of input data vectors, the task is to assign each input data vector to one of the classes. For this study, the different financial ratios form the set of input data vectors and the two possible values (bankrupt and nonbankrupt) form the set of possible classes to which the new input belongs.

Conventional statistical approaches are of limited use in deriving an appropriate prediction model in the absence of well-defined domain models.[9] Statistical techniques always require the assumption of a certain functional form for relating dependent variables to independent variables. When the assumed functional form is not correct, the statistical techniques merely confirm that, but do not predict the right functional form. Additionally, quantitative models suffer from the weakness of being sample specific. Generalizations can be made only with caution. A few atypical companies can skew the results. Further, sample variances can be large.

Neural networks do provide a more general framework for determining relationships in the data and do not require the specification of any functional form.

NEURAL NETWORKS

Neural networks are networks of simple processing units called nodes that interact with each other using weighted connections. There are various ways of connecting them. Each node sums up the activations of all the nodes connected to it. And, depending on the paradigm of choice, they can have different activation functions to transform the input and different error correcting rules to guide the learning process. Typically, knowledge in neural networks is stored in the set of weights on the interconnections between various nodes. Therefore, the design of a neural network algorithm for a given problem must address three issues: (1) the type of intralayer and interlayer connectivity between different nodes; (2) the activation function for the nodes for transforming the inputs; and (3) an error-correcting algorithm for training.

The network paradigm of choice in this research is the PDP backpropagation (BP) algorithm.[10] In this BP network, the nodes in adjacent layers are fully connected and there are no intralayer connections. A nonlinear activation function (sigmoid) transforms the inputs at each node. The generalized delta rule is used for error correction. Apart from the input and output layers, another layer (called the hidden layer) between the input and output may be needed. Hidden layers can extract higher level features and facilitate generalization if the input vectors have low-level features of the problem domain or if the input/output relationship is complex. Given a set of input vectors and the desired output for each input vector, the back-propagation learning algorithm can iteratively find a set of weights that will perform the mapping, if such a set exists.

In order to verify how well the neural network has learned the underlying domain model, the same set of weights (on the connections) learned during the learning phase must be used to check the accuracy of the predicted outcome. The success of the predictions of the neural network depends on the range of values covered by the input/output vectors. The neural network model helps us in determining the functional mapping between the input/output exemplar sets.

METHODOLOGY

The following sections describe the various steps in the design and experiment phases of the research.

Selection of Variables

Table 8.1 lists the 13 financial ratios used in the current study. This list is selected from ratios proven popular (and useful) in earlier research on bankruptcy prediction and is by no means exhaustive. Table 8.2 gives the generally accepted interpretations of the various ratios selected. Karels and Prakash[11] believe that the large diversity of ratios in use is because of the limited theoretical basis for choosing them. The selected ratios do have a bearing on the going concern issue.[1] Since the financial ratios used in this research have proven useful in previous studies, it is expected that they will be good discriminators between bankrupt and nonbankrupt firms. These ratios have been used in earlier studies of bankruptcy prediction.[1,7,8,11] In addition to the financial ratios, a trend variable was included showing how many of the three years prior to bankruptcy a company incurred a loss.[1]

Data Collection

Financial statement data was collected for a total of 102 companies. In keeping with the methods of earlier researchers, these companies consist of 51 pairs of bankrupt and nonbankrupt companies of the same industry and approximately the same asset size. The asset size is taken

Table 8.1

Financial Ratios Used

X1 — Total current assets / Total current liabilities
X2 — [Cash + STI + Net receivables] / Total current liabilities
X3 — [Income from continuing operations + DDA] / [Total CL + Long-term debt]
X4 — [Total CL + Long-term debt / Total assets
X5 — [Total current assets − Total current liabilities] / Total assets
X6 — Income from continuing operations / Total assets
X7 — [ICO + Income taxes + Interest expense] / Total assets
X8 — Net sales / Total assets
X9 — Retained earnings / Total assets
X10 — Total current assets / Net sales
X11 — [Total current assets − Total current liabilities] / Net sales
X12 — Total current assets / Total assets
X13 — [Cash + Short-term investments] / Total assets

Notes:
STI — Short-term investments
DDA — Depreciation, depletion, amortization
CL — Current liabilities
ICO — Income from continuing operations

Source: Harris.[1]

three years prior to bankruptcy to offset any effects of impending failure on this factor.

Bankrupt firms were chosen from listings in the Wall Street Journal Index for the years 1980 through 1988 and from a list of deleted companies in the *Moody's Industrial Manual*. Utilities, transportation companies, and financial services were excluded because these firms are structurally different and have a different bankruptcy environment. Financial statement information is obtained from COMPUSTAT, *Moody's Industrial Manual*, *Moody's OTC Manual*, annual reports, and 10-K reports for the three years preceding bankruptcy. Data for non-bankrupt companies were obtained from the same sources for the same three-year period as that of the corresponding bankrupt firms.

Table 8.2

Interpretation of Ratios

X1 — Short-term liquidity
X2 — Short-term liquidity (more rigorous test)
X3 — Availability of funds
X4 — Financial leverage
X5 — Working capital relative to total capitalization
X6 — Return on investment
X7 — Productivity, irrespective of financing
X8 — Sales-generating ability of assets
X9 — Cumulative profitability
X10 — Inventory turnover
X11 — Working capital turnover
X12 — Relative liquidity of assets
X13 — Cash position

Source: Harris.[1]

Experiment

The experiment consisted of two parts, training and testing. There are 14 input nodes representing the 14 variables and one output node representing the binary classification decision (0 for bankrupt and 1 for nonbankrupt).

Learning. Since the back-propagation algorithm uses the sigmoid activation function for each node with the function values ranging between 0 and 1, the input data need to be normalized. The values for the 14 variables for each company were input into a LOTUS worksheet and normalized using the following formula:

$$Y = (X - X_1) / (X_2 - X_1)$$

where

Y : Normalized value of X
X : Actual value for each variable
X_1 : Minimum value for each variable
X_2 : Maximum value for each variable

From the total normalized data set of 51 pairs of asset-matched firms (one bankrupt and one nonbankrupt in each pair), 25 pairs were selected at random for the learning phase. Table 8.3 lists the mean and standard deviation of all the 14 variables for the 102 companies.

Since there is no standard criterion for selecting the number of hidden layers and hidden nodes, the learning phase involved experimentation with two different neural network configurations. Table 8.4 lists the values for various parameters kept constant during the training and testing phases. In this experiment, the two different configurations are (1) one hidden layer with 10, 15, and 20 nodes and (2) two hidden

Table 8.3

Statistical Information on the Financial Ratios

	Mean	Standard Deviation
X1 —	2.047	1.428
X2 —	1.125	0.879
X3 —	-0.276	1.954
X4 —	0.601	0.294
X5 —	0.176	0.363
X6 —	-0.14	0.382
X7 —	-0.08	0.379
X8 —	1.402	1.016
X9 —	-0.086	0.859
X10—	0.553	0.392
X11—	-0.002	0.941

Table 8.4

Parameters for the Neural Network Model

Upper Threshold	:	0.8
Lower Threshold	:	0.3
Learning Rate	:	0.9
Momentum Term	:	0.65

layers with 10 and 15 nodes. For each configuration, the training was halted either after 10,000 iterations were run through the training set or when the network had learned all the training examples, whichever occurred earlier.

Testing. Once the neural network was trained with the training exemplars, each of the two configurations was tested with the remaining 52 companies for classification as either bankrupt or nonbankrupt. The learned weights on the connections between nodes were kept constant during the testing phase. For each company, the 14-variable input was fed to the network and an output (value between 0 and 1) was generated in one pass through the network. Now, based on the upper and lower thresholds used for learning, the output was interpreted as a 0 or a 1 (bankrupt or nonbankrupt).

RESULTS

Figures 8.1 and 8.2 display the six different trends for the change in total average error over the number of iterations in the learning phase for the two configurations with a different number of nodes. Figures 8.3 and 8.4 show the number of examples learned over the number of iterations. As can be seen, the average error decreased and the number learned increased with successive iterations. The different trends do not indicate any noticeable variation in learning capability. Therefore, the decision to select a particular configuration as the more suitable one for prediction was postponed until the testing phase.

Figure 8.5 illustrates the relative performance of the different configurations in terms of the classification accuracy during the testing phase. The configuration with 15 nodes in the first hidden layer and two in the second seems to have the best percentage of correct classifications (86 percent).

Discussion

Though the training phase did not indicate the best configuration, the testing phase seems to suggest that the one with 15 nodes in the first hidden layer and two nodes in the second hidden layer was able to generalize better. This supports the intuition that financial ratios are

Figure 8.1

Training with One Hidden Layer (Average Error versus Number of Iterations)

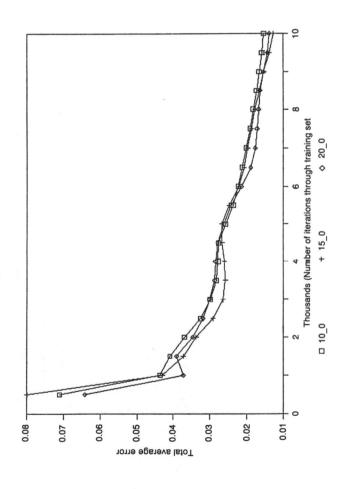

Figure 8.2

Training with Two Hidden Layers (Average Error versus Number of Iterations)

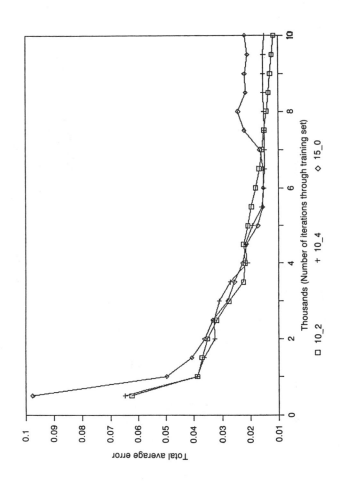

Figure 8.3
Training with One Hidden Layer (Patterns Learned versus Number of Iterations)

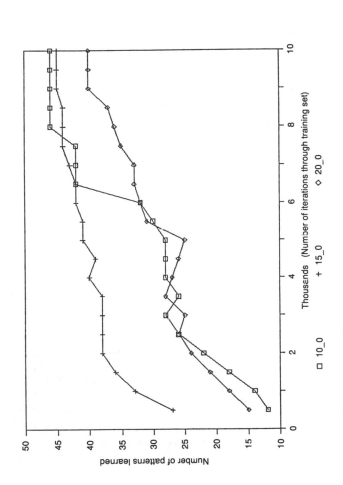

Figure 8.4

Training with Two Hidden Layers (Patterns Learned versus Number of Iterations)

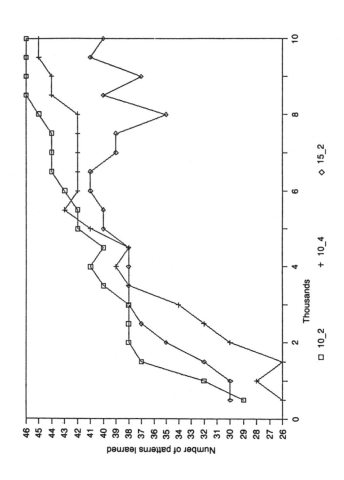

Figure 8.5

Results of Testing Phase

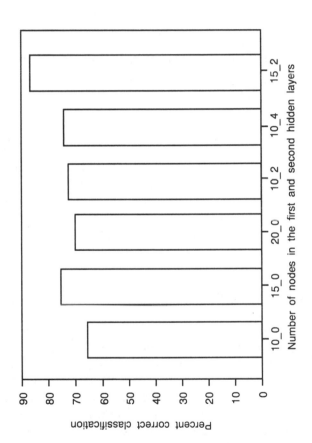

mere low features representing the dynamics of the bankruptcy prediction problem. The results suggest that the functional mapping between financial ratios and the bankruptcy decision is more complex than can be captured by a one-layered BP network. Various financial ratios may be giving some intermediate features such as immediate financial health of the company, long-term financial health, recent revenue generating trends, and others. Based on these higher-level features, the network may be arriving at a categorizing decision. Though this is only speculative, the fact that the two-layered network fared better leads to a possible conclusion of hierarchical feature extraction involved before categorization. This means a potential bankruptcy prediction network needs to extract higher-level features for better generalization.[9]

Assumptions

The financial ratios selected for consideration in this study were based on the previous research in the field of bankruptcy prediction applying standard statistical procedures. The use of these quantitative variables precludes the possible influence of qualitative factors such as litigation, taxes, or other unforeseen situations. Further, the analysis and results are accurate to the extent that the reported data reflect the actual financial condition of the firm.

FUTURE RESEARCH

First, one needs to focus on obtaining a representative data set that encompasses the range of possible values for the financial ratios. Second, more complex configurations need to be considered. Third, the sample size must be increased to accommodate a larger variety of companies in different industries. Fourth, a neural network offers the unique advantage of recognizing the relative importance of the various financial ratios leading to parsimony in selection of variables for bankruptcy prediction. Fifth, in this study the output reflected either a correct classification or a misclassification. In this regard, we need to address the issue of possible relation between misclassified output values and inconsistencies in the financial ratios. Finally, another concern not addressed in this study that needs to be examined is the possibility of random variation making the categorization more complex. In the future, we intend to test the traditional statistical techniques with the same data for more meaningful comparisons.[12]

CONCLUSIONS

In this exploratory research we have examined a neural network application for bankruptcy prediction. Preliminary results indicate that neural networks might provide suitable models for the bankruptcy prediction process. In the long run, a neural network-based decision support system for bankruptcy prediction can be developed to assist auditors and other potentially interested parties.

ENDNOTES

1. C. Harris, "An Expert Decision Support System for Auditor Going Concern Evaluation," Ph.D. dissertation, The University of Texas at Arlington, 1989.

2. J. E. McKinley, R. L. Johnson, G. R. Downey, Jr., C. S. Zimmerman, and M. D. Bloom, *Analyzing Financial Statements.* (Washington: American Bankers Association, 1983.)

3. D. E. Miller, *The Meaningful Interpretation of Financial Statements,* Rev. ed. (New York: American Management Association, 1972.)

4. C. H. Gibson and P. A. Frishkoff, *Financial Statement Analysis: Using Financial Accounting Information,* 3rd ed. (Boston: Kent Publishing Company, 1986.)

5. J. O. Horrigan, "A Short History of Financial Ratio Analysis," *The Accounting Review,* vol. 43, April 1968, pp. 284–294.

6. R. A. Collins and R. D. Green, "Statistical Methods for Bankruptcy Forecasting," *Journal of Economics and Business,* vol. 32, 1982, pp. 349–354.

7. E. L. Altman, "Financial Ratios, Discriminant Analysis and the Prediction of Corporate Bankruptcy," *The Journal of Finance,* vol. 23, September 1968, pp. 589–609.

8. J. A. Gentry, P. Newbold, and D. T. Whitford, "Classifying Bankrupt Firms with Funds Flow Components," *Journal of Accounting Research,* vol. 23, Spring 1985, pp. 146–160.

9. S. Dutta, and S. Shekar, "Bond Ratings: A Non-Conservative Application of Neural Networks," *Proceedings of the ICNN,* 1988, pp. II-443–II-450.

10. D. E. Rumelhart, G. E., Hinton, and R. J. Williams, "Learning Internal Representations by Error Propagation," (D. E. Rumelhart, and J. L. McClelland. *Parallel Distributed Processing: Exploration in the Microstructure of Cognition,* eds. (Cambridge, Mass. MIT Press, 1986.)

11. G. V. Karels and A. J. Prakash, "Multivariate Normality and Forecasting of Business Bankruptcy," *Journal of Business Finance & Accounting,* vol. 14, Winter 1987, pp. 573–593.

12. The neural network simulator used in this study was made available by the character recognition group of the Computer Science and Engineering Department of the University of Texas at Arlington. We thank Dr. Carolyn Harris for providing data and other background material in the bankruptcy prediction domain.

9

BANKRUPTCY PREDICTION BY NEURAL NETWORK

Eric Rahimian, Seema Singh,
Thongchai Thammachote, and Rajiv Virmani

BANKRUPTCY AND FINANCIAL DISTRICT ANALYSIS

For the past 22 years, linear discriminant functions have been used to analyze financial data for bankruptcy or financial distress analysis. A pioneer study of bankruptcy analysis was done by Altman in 1968.[1] Altman compared the financial data of 33 manufacturers who filed for bankruptcy with the data of 33 nonbankrupt firms on the basis of similar industry and asset size. Asset size ranged between $1 million to $25

Printed with permission of the authors.

million. He used 22 financial variables to compile five explanatory variables for bankruptcy. These included:

X_1 = Working capital/Total assets
X_2 = Retained earnings/Total assets
X_3 = EBIT/Total assets (where EBIT is earnings before interest and tax)
X_4 = MVE/Total debt (where MVE is the market value of equity)
X_5 = Sales/Total assets

Altman classified the sample using z-score analysis. The description of z-score is beyond the scope of this study. Z-score computation uses discriminant analysis.[2,3] All firms having a z-score greater than 2.99 fell in the category of nonbankrupt, whereas all firms having a z-score below 1.81 were bankrupt. The area between 1.81 and 2.99 was defined as the zone of "ignorance" or the "gray" area.

Odom and Sharda[4] have recently used the back-propagation neural network model to predict bankruptcy. The purpose of their study was to compare the predictive ability of the neural network and multivariate discriminant analysis model. Many other studies including Deakin,[5] Blum,[6] Moyer,[7] Altman, et al.[8] and Karels and Prakash[9] also have used discriminant analysis of financial data.

This chapter takes advantage of the comparative study of Odom and Sharda.[4] Briefly, three different paradigms of neural networks are utilized. The efficiency (number of cycles and computation time) and predictive capability of these paradigms for bankruptcy prediction are compared with each other as well as with the performance of Odom and Sharda's back-propagation and the discriminant analysis.

THEORETICAL COMPARISON OF TRADITIONAL MODELS VERSUS A NEURAL NETWORK MODEL

Discriminant analysis requires certain restrictive assumptions. The distribution of discriminating variables is assumed to be jointly multivariate normal. Karels and Prakash[9] have indicated that the results of discriminant analysis procedure are erroneous when this requirement is violated. Neural networks are not under normality constraints, so if they produce comparable predictive results they are safer to use.

Also, a close relationship exists between two-group discriminant analysis and regression with binary-valued dependent variable (the dummy regression method). Several assumptions such as the normality of the disturbance term U_i and homoscedasticity of variances of the disturbances usually are not satisfied for real-world financial ratios used in discriminant analysis.[10] Hence, the prediction of discriminant analysis or dummy regression analysis should be taken with a grain of salt.

DATA

The data used for this study are the same as the ones used by Odom and Sharda.[4] Our variables are the same financial ratios employed by Altman.[1] We used the sample data that was obtained from Moody's *Industrial Manuals* for 129 firms, where 65 firms went bankrupt during the period 1975 through 1982. Two subsamples were used. The training subsample consisted of 74 firms, 36 nonbankrupt and 38 bankrupt firms. The testing subsample consisted of 55 firms, 28 nonbankrupt and 27 bankrupt firms. Using the same data as the ones of Odom and Sharda made it possible to compare the results of the paradigms of our chapter with the ones of the NeuroShell network and the discriminant analysis of Odom and Sharda.

MODELS FOR BANKRUPTCY PREDICTION

We used three paradigms in our study as follows:

1. Back-propagation

2. Athena

3. Perceptron (like back-propagation but without any hidden layer)

Back-Propagation

Generally, this is a multilayered neural network. It uses the sigmoidal activation (squashing) function.

$$OUT = F(X.W) = F(NET) = 1/(1 + e^{-NET}) \qquad (1)$$

where

W = Weight vector w between neuron i in layer k and
      neuron j in layer $k + 1$
X = The input vector
OUT = The final output of a neuron in the output layer

where range of OUT is bounded by (0,1). Other activation functions that are differentiable may also be employed. Back-propagation uses supervised learning. Weights are adjusted to produce desired (target) output. Training pairs consist of input vectors and target output values. As the weights are changed, they perform steepest descent on a surface in weight space whose height at any point in weight space is equal to the error measure. As in the case of perceptron, a learning-rate parameter is used for weight adjustments. In addition, another parameter called momentum is recommended in spaces containing long ravines with sharp curvature across the ravine. The momentum term filters out high curvature and allows weight adjustment steps to be larger. In practice the best momentum and learning rates are selected in repeated runs of trial and error, where one is trying to optimize the number of cycles (time) and the performance of the model. A bias term also may be introduced for each neuron. This functions the same way as adjusting the threshold of the perceptron.

Stornetta and Huberman[11] have discussed the impact of changing the value of the binary inputs and outputs to a range of [−1/2, +1/2]. They have shown that the convergence time can be reduced by 30 percent to 50 percent. This will modify the output function as follows:

$$OUT = -1/2 + 1/(1 + e^{-NET}). \qquad (2)$$

Notice that this will reduce the value of output by 0.5.

The network topology used by us is the same as employed by Odom and Sharda and is shown in Figure 9.1. In our application, we learned that normalization of input data to a range of −.5 to +.5 and using the values of −.5 and +.5 instead of 0 and 1 for target output reduced the training time dramatically. Actually, in the best result, the number of cycles was reduced to 95 cycles, which was much smaller than the 191,400 reported by Odom and Sharda. With the ANSim (Artificial Neural Network Simulator) package we ran the original model of Odom and Sharda without such adjustments and after several days and over 40,000 cycles (ANSim is slower than NeuroShell), it did not converge. Introducing the above modifications allowed us to get much

Figure 9.1

Back-Propagation Network

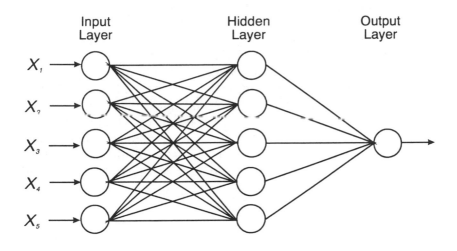

better performance and faster convergence, as is discussed in more detail in comparison of test results, below.

It is notable that small learning rates cause slow and inefficient convergence, whereas large learning rates cause paralysis or instability. Network paralysis will occur when weights become very large, producing large outputs and small error adjustment signals, which may cause the training to come to a virtual halt.

Athena

Athena is a neural network for pattern classification based on an entropy measure.[12,13] It uses supervised learning. The model uses hyperplanes to partition the object space into groups of convex sets, each of which contains objects of the same class. The net consists of a group of neurons, each of which corresponds to one of the partition's hyperplanes, $P = \{ X \mid X$ is an element of the object space R and $W'X = T\}$; where X is the input vector, W is the weight vector and T is the threshold. The weight vector determines the orientation of the hyperplane, and the threshold determines its distance from the origin. The network is formed dynamically, and the training is a one-shot procedure that uses an entropy measure to optimize the partition.

Each hyperplane divides the object space into two regions: the upper half space, P^u above the hyperplane and the lower half space P^l below the hyperplane. For training, each neuron identifies a weight vector and a threshold value, which define a separating hyperplane. As the separation by a neuron is completed and the result is passed to the children neurons, a tree of neurons is built, where the upper half space of a neuron is assigned to the right child and the lower half space assigned to the left child neuron. Either way, linearly separable training instances are completely separated by the hyperplane or a hyperplane is selected so as to optimize an entropy measure for the quality of the separation. This process continues until each leaf neuron is associated with objects of only one class.

Perceptron

Generally speaking, a single-layer neural network with binary outputs is called a perceptron. Perceptron uses a non-linear threshold unit:

If *NET* output ≥ Threshold, *OUT* = 1
Otherwise   *OUT* = 0

Perceptron training occurs through supervised learning. A set of input patterns and target outputs are presented to the network, and the weights applied to inputs are adjusted until the desired output occurs for each input pattern. The input may be binary or continuous.

In this chapter, we have utilized a modified continuous version of the perceptron learning algorithm. The continuous version is called the Δ rule.[14] The perceptron may be summarized as follows:

1. Apply an input pattern, *X*, and calculate the output.

2. If output is correct, change nothing and go to 1. Else, if output is in correct use the Δ rule to adjust the weights. The weight adjustment using the Δ rule in this step is explained as follows:

    Δ = *T* – *A* (where *T* = target output and *A* = actual output)
    If Δ = 0, no weight adjustment is required.

Else if $\Delta \neq 0$, compute
$\Delta_i = \alpha \, \Delta \, X_i$ where α is a positive learning rate < 1.
Notice that Δ may be negative.
$W_i \, (n + 1) = W_i(n) + \Delta_i$

3. Go to step 1.

In practice a small value of Δ is acceptable and an exit from the given algorithm can be made if Δ reaches below a predetermined value. In ANSim the tolerable root mean square error may be set to 0.1, and training is continued until convergence is achieved.[14]

This modified perceptron was realized by using the back-propagation model of ANSim, removing the hidden layer but keeping the values of target output at −.5 and +.5, and using the squashing function of equation (2).

COMPARISON OF TEST RESULTS

By using the same data as the ones used by Odom and Sharda, we are able to directly compare the performance of the paradigms utilized by us with the performance of both discriminant analysis and the back-propagation paradigm used by them.

Two subsamples of the firms were available, one with 74 firms for training the networks and the other with 55 firms for testing the models. The training and testing with Athena were extremely efficient. Because Athena was able to separate the training set with only one hyperplane, it suggested that the bankruptcy prediction problem at hand may be linearly separable. Both training and testing times with Athena were less than one minute, and the number of erroneous predictions was ten out of 55 — the same number as for Odom and Sharda's back-propagation; normalized back-propagation and number of cycles may be assumed to be one. The testing results of Athena are presented in Table 9.1a and b, which also give the values of data in the testing subsample.

The back-propagation model with binary target output value as used by Odom and Sharda proved to be extremely slow on our ANSim software using the IBM PC 386. Odom and Sharda used NeuroShell Network release 1.1. Their model, as they confirmed, was tedious and slow in convergence (24 hours and 191,400 cycles). Even this result was obtained by modification of learning rate from 0.6 to 0.1 and change of momentum from 0.9 to 0.8 during the test run.

Table 9.1a
Nonbankrupt Firms

WC / TA	RE / TA	EBIT / TA	MVE / TD	S / TA	NB	
.2234	.3931	.1168	1.1371	1.7523	1	
.1725	.3238	.1040	.8847	.5576	1	
.2955	.1959	.2245	1.1606	1.8478	1	
.5542	.4316	.1065	.8375	1.6678	1	
.2489	.4014	.1669	1.4609	7.1658	1	
.3813	.3194	.2044	2.8513	.9851	1	
.4512	.4114	.1146	1.7185	1.5543	1	
.1904	.2011	.1329	.5586	1.6623	1	
.5248	.6437	.2478	6.3501	1.2542	1	
.4058	.4497	.1497	1.1076	1.7428	1	
.2947	.3724	.1104	.9410	1.3568	1	
.4327	.6494	.2996	8.2982	1.2865	1	
.1630	.3555	.0110	.3730	2.8307	1	# @
.5189	.3627	.1015	.9764	.7466	1	
.4792	.3495	.1076	.8105	1.7224	1	
.0669	.2904	.0978	.7659	4.3912	1	
.3449	.1270	−.0083	.1059	.8611	1	*#%&@
.0272	.0503	.0184	.1413	1.2008	1	*#%&@
.6302	.3324	.1524	1.1259	1.5579	1	
.2170	.2507	.0826	.3404	1.9889	1	
.4078	.1316	.1095	.3233	1.8226	1	# % &
.2864	.2823	.1856	2.7709	2.7730	1	
.1841	.3344	.0857	2.1230	2.1686	1	
.0732	.3526	.0587	.2349	1.7432	1	
.0106	.0200	.0226	1.887	1.2274	1	*#%&@
.6398	.1723	.2019	34.5032	1.1388	1	
.3750	.3326	.1290	.9487	1.2529	1	
.2921	.2390	.0673	.3402	.7596	1	

WC / TA = Working capital / Total assets
RE / TA   = Retained earnings / Total assets
EBIT / TA = Earnings before interest and tax / Total assets
MVE / TD= Market value of equity / Total debt
S / TA   = Sales / Total assets
NB   = Nonbankrupt

*   Misclassified by Discriminant Analysis
\#   Misclassified by Odom and Sharda Model
%   Misclassified by Back-propagation Model
&   Misclassified by Perceptron Model
@ Misclassified by Athena Model

Table 9.1b

Bankrupt Firms

WC / TA	RE / TA	EBIT / TA	MVE / TD	S / TA	BR	
.0471	.1506	−.0150	.1039	.6253	0	
.2770	−.0417	.0904	.5245	1.9380	0	
.4958	.2199	.0219	.1267	3.0305	0	
.1070	.0787	.0433	.1083	1.2051	0	
.1936	.0778	−.1830	.6531	2.4263	0	
.1611	.0954	.0307	.2113	1.4529	0	
.3732	.3484	−.0139	.3483	1.8223	0	* %
.2653	.2683	.0235	.5118	1.8350	0	* %
−.1599	−.5018	−.0889	.1748	2.1608	0	
.1123	.2288	.0100	.1884	2.7186	0	
.3696	.2917	.0621	.5554	1.7326	0	*#%&@
.2702	.1402	.1668	.2717	2.1121	0	*# &@
.1144	−.0194	.0074	.2940	1.5734	0	
.4044	−.1878	.0768	.2846	1.3489	0	
.2787	.1767	.0305	.1797	5.3003	0	
−.0357	−.9814	−.0031	.3291	2.1088	0	
−.0179	−.2902	.0984	2.2848	2.1803	0	
.4067	.2972	.0454	.5001	2.0631	0	*%&@
.2260	.1620	.0965	.2737	1.9199	0	*
.0780	−.2451	.0627	.0453	.1451	0	
.3422	.2865	.0778	.5300	1.5564	0	*#%&@
.3440	.1725	.1386	.2775	2.0030	0	*#&@
.1756	.1233	.1046	.7468	1.6774	0	*
.1186	.1849	−.0718	.2117	.1376	0	
.3617	.1312	.0413	.3706	2.1890	0	
.1162	.3026	.0863	.9220	.9513	0	*#%&@
.2323	.1095	.1054	.4661	.9193	0	*

WC / TA = Working capital / Total assets
RE / TA = Retained earnings / Total assets
EBIT / TA = Earnings before interest and tax / Total assets
MVE / TD = Market value of equity / Total debt
S / TA   = Sales / Total assets
BR   = Bankrupt

*   Misclassified by Discriminant Analysis
#   Misclassified by Odom and Sharda Model
% Misclassified by Back-propagation Model
&   Misclassified by Perceptron Model
@ Misclassified by Athena Model

We chose to normalize the input data to values between −.5 and .5 for our back-propagation training and testing. This model is consistent with the modification of output values from 0 and 1 to −.5 and .5. As anticipated these modifications produced results that were very encouraging. The lowest training time after such modifications occurred in 14 minutes with the screen display on during the training. This consisted of 95 training cycles only. The learning rate and the momentum term were 0.40 and 0.86, respectively. The accuracy of the prediction remained the same as the test by Odom and Sharda, whereas the training time for our back-propagation paradigm was only about 1 percent of their training time. The number of cycles with other training parameters for the normalized back-propagation paradigm are presented in Table 9.2.

Since the test results of Athena indicated potential linear separability, we removed the hidden layer of the back-propagation network to convert it to a perceptron. The same target output values of −0.5 and 0.5 were used in this model. This modification produced a training time of 17 minutes with 934 cycles for a learning rate equal to 0.175 and momentum rate of 0.8. A comparative result of performance and efficiency of this modified perceptron is presented in Table 9.3. As this table indicates, the use of a learning rate of 0.20, which is more than 0.175 used in the best output result, increased the number of cycles. The same is true when a learning rate lower than 0.175 is used.

The results of the selected test runs are included in the Appendix.

CONCLUSION

The results of our analysis have indicated that the formulated bankruptcy problem is potentially linearly separable. The best performance

Table 9.2

Back-Propagation Comparison of Different Parameter Values

Set No.	Learning Rate	Momentum	Number of Cycles
1	0.4	0.86	95 (Best case)
2	0.3	0.84	135
3	0.2	0.70	160
4	0.1	0.80	198
5	0.5	0.00	403
6	0.6	0.00	560

Table 9.3

Perceptron Comparison of Different Parameter Values

Set No.	Learning Rate	Momentum	Number of Cycles
1	0.175	0.8	934 (Best case)
2	0.15	0.8	1,320
3	0.20	0.8	1,379
4	0.10	0.6	4,423
5	0.225	0.0	3,636

was achieved by Athena paradigm (time used was 35 to 45 seconds and the accuracy was the same as other models) (see Table 9.4). The normalization of input data to values between –.5 and .5 and modification of output target values from 0 and 1 to –.5 and .5 in the back-propagation model reduced the training time to 14 minutes and number of cycles to 95, an enormous improvement over the regular back-propagation paradigm utilized by Odom and Sharda. As a final conclusion, one may like to assess the importance of the discriminant factors used by comparing the weights assigned to these factors by Athena paradigm. The weights of the last two variables were negligible (0.0 and

Table 9.4

Comparison of Different Models

	Training Time	Number of Cycles	# Correct/ # Total
Discriminant analysis test	—	Not available	41/55
Odom and Sharda test	24 hours	191,400	45/55
Athena	35–45 seconds	Not available	45/55
Perceptron	17 minutes	934 with display on	45/55
Backprop	14 minutes	95	45/55

–0.0), whereas the weights of X_1, X_2, and X_3 were 0.01, 0.05, and 0.11—an indication of the discriminatory power of these variables. Note also that although the weights assigned by the modified perceptron model are much larger (–2.66, 40.28, 29.64, 15.07, –1.27), their predictive powers as indicated by & and @ signs in Table 9.1a and b are very similar. Despite the similarity of performance of Athena and the perceptron model, these latter weights are different from the weights of Athena because this perceptron was a back-propagation model without a hidden layer and with a squashing function and used target output values of –.5 to +.5. This makes the meaning of the modified perceptron's weights more difficult to analyze than that of Athena's.

ENDNOTES

1. E. L. Altman, "Financial Ratios, Discriminant Analysis and the Prediction of Corporate Bankruptcy," *Journal of Finance,* vol. 23, 1968, p. 596.

2. C. F. Lee, "Financial Analysis and Planning Theory and Applications," (Reading, Mass.: Addison Wesley Publishing, 1985), pp. 97–102.

3. H. D. Platt, *Why Companies Fail,* (Lexington, MA: Lexington Books, 1985), pp. 88–91.

4. M. D. Odom, and R. Sharda, "A Neural Network for Bankruptcy Prediction," *International Joint Conference on Neural Networks,* June 17–21, 1990, vol. II (San Diego, Calif.), pp. 163–168.

5. E. B. Deakin, "A Discriminant Analysis of Predictors of Business Failure," *Journal of Accounting Research,* Spring 1972, pp. 167–179.

6. M. Blum, "Failing Company Discriminant Analysis," *Journal of Accounting Research,* Spring 1974, pp. 1–25.

7. R. C. Moyer, "Forecasting Financial Failure: A Reexamination," *Financial Management,* Spring 1977, pp. 11–17.

8. E. L. Altman, R. G. Haldeman, and P. Narayanan, "Zeta Analysis," *Journal of Banking and Finance,* June 1977, pp. 29–51.

9. G. V. Karels, and A. Prakash, "Multivariate Normality and Forecasting of Business Bankruptcy," *Journal of Business Finance & Accounting,* Winter 1987, pp. 573–593.

10. D. Gujarati, *Econometrics,* (New York: McGraw-Hill Book Company, 1978), pp. 312–319.

11. W. S. Stornetta and B. A. Huberman, "An Improved Three Layered Backprop Algorithm," in *Proceedings of the IEEE First International Conference on Neural Networks,* eds. M. Caudill and C. Butler. (San Diego, Calif.: SOS Printing, 1988).

12. C. Koutsougeras and G. Papachristou, "Training of a Neural Network for Pattern Classification Based on an Entropy Measure," *Proceedings of IEEE ICNN,* 1988.

13. C. Koutsougeras and G. Papachristou, "Learning Discrete Mappings—Athena's Approach," IEEE, CH 2636-Sept 1988, pp. 31–36.

14. P. D. Wasserman, *Neural Computing: Theory and Practice.* (New York: Van Nostrand Reinhold, 1989).

APPENDIX to CHAPTER NINE

Table A9.1

The Training Data

BR=0 NB=1	WC/TA	RE/TA	EBIT/TA	MVE/TD	S/TA
1	.3922	.3778	.1316	1.0911	1.2784
1	.0574	.2783	.1166	1.3441	.2216
1	.1650	.1192	.2035	.8130	1.6702
1	.3073	.6070	.2040	14.4090	.9844
1	.2574	.5334	.1650	8.0734	1.3474
1	.1415	.3868	.0681	.5755	1.0579
1	.3363	.3312	.2157	3.0679	2.0899
1	.3378	.0130	.2366	2.4709	1.2230
1	.4870	.6970	.2994	5.4383	1.7200
1	.4455	.4980	.0952	1.9338	1.7696
1	.4704	.2772	.0964	.4268	1.9317
1	.5804	.3331	.0810	1.1964	1.3572
1	.2073	.3611	.1472	.0417	1.1985
1	.1801	.1635	.0908	.4094	.4566
1	.1778	.3668	.0779	.9742	.5075
1	.2304	.2960	.1225	.4102	3.0809
1	.4328	.5136	.2059	1.9721	1.3194
1	.6674	.4047	.1796	1.0069	1.2968
1	.3255	.5583	.1600	2.2889	1.3146
1	.3684	.3913	.0524	.1658	1.1533
1	.1527	.3344	.0783	.7736	1.5046
1	.4147	.3983	.1532	1.3148	1.3745
1	.1126	.3071	.0839	1.3429	1.5736
1	.0141	.2366	.0905	.5863	1.4651
1	.4135	.3120	.1861	1.1743	1.0319
1	.0140	.2862	.0741	30.6486	1.9606
1	.3735	.4980	.1604	1.8366	2.3793
1	.4934	.3416	.2200	.8144	2.1937
1	.1332	.4077	.0543	1.4921	1.4826
1	.2220	.1797	.1526	.3459	1.7237
1	.3720	.3446	.2124	.8888	1.9241
1	.2776	.2567	.1612	.2968	1.8904
1	.1445	.3808	.1780	1.4796	1.4811
1	.3907	.6482	.1408	3.0489	1.5255
1	.1862	.1687	.1298	.9498	4.9548
1	.1663	.4291	.1133	1.1745	1.6831

BR = Bankrupt
NB = Nonbankrupt
WC/TA = Working capital / Total assets
RE/TA = Retained earnings / Total assets
EBIT/TA = Earnings before interest and tax / Total assets
MVE/TD = Market value of equity / Total debt
S/TA = Sales / Total assets

Table A9.2

The Training Data

BR=0 NB=1	WC/TA	RE/TA	EBIT/TA	MVE/TD	S/TA
0	.4422	.1379	.0104	.2460	1.2492
0	−.0643	.1094	−.1230	.1725	1.3752
0	.2975	−.3719	−.1390	.9627	2.2774
0	.0478	.0632	−.0016	.4744	1.8928
0	.0718	.0422	.0006	3.2964	2.1331
0	.2689	.1729	.0287	.1224	.9277
0	−.3107	−.8780	−.2969	.1945	1.0493
0	.0766	−.0734	.0076	.1681	1.0789
0	.3899	.0809	.0447	.2186	.9273
0	.0664	−.1266	−.1556	.1471	3.6192
0	.0147	−.1443	−.0498	.1431	6.5145
0	.1321	.0686	.0008	.3544	2.3224
0	.2039	−.0476	.1263	.8965	1.0457
0	.0549	.0592	−.2279	.0913	1.6016
0	−.5359	−.3487	−.0322	.4595	.9191
0	−.0801	−.0835	.0036	.0481	.7730
0	.3294	.0171	.0371	.2877	3.1382
0	.5056	−.1951	.2026	.5380	1.9514
0	.1759	.1343	.0946	.1955	1.9218
0	−.2772	.1619	−.0302	.1225	2.3250
0	.2551	−.3442	−.1108	1.2212	2.2815
0	−.1294	.0085	−.0971	.1764	1.3113
0	.2027	−.1169	−.0261	.5965	.7892
0	−.0901	−.2710	.0014	.1473	2.5064
0	−.3757	−1.6945	−.4504	1.2197	2.2685
0	.3424	−.1104	.0541	1.5052	1.0416
0	.0234	−.0246	.0320	.6406	1.1091
0	.3579	.1515	.0812	.1991	1.4582
0	−.0888	−.0371	.0197	.1931	1.3767
0	.2845	.2038	.0171	.3357	1.3258
0	.0011	−.0631	−.2225	.3891	1.7680
0	.1209	.2823	−.0113	.3157	2.3219
0	.2525	−.1730	−.4861	.1656	1.4441
0	.3181	−.1093	−.0857	.3755	1.9789
0	.1254	.1956	.0079	.2073	1.4890
0	.1777	.0891	.0695	.1924	1.6871
0	.2409	.1660	.0746	.2516	1.8524
0	.2496	.1260	−.2474	.1660	3.0950

BR = Bankrupt
NB = Nonbankrupt
WC/TA = Working capital / Total assets
RE/TA = Retained earnings / Total assets
EBIT/TA = Earnings before interest and tax / Total assets
MVE/TD = Market value of equity / Total debt
S/TA = Sales / Total assets

Table A9.3

Back-Propagation Network

Number of layers = 3
  layers numbered from 1 (input) to 3 (output)

Layer dimensions:
  layer 1: (1, 5)
  layer 2: (1, 5)
  layer 3: (1, 1)

Cycles trained = 95

Weights initialized from −0.300 to 0.300

Noise = 0.00000, decay = 0.00000

Tolerance = 0.00000

Learning rates for layers:
  layer 2: 0.40000
  layer 3: 0.40000

Momentum terms for layers:
  layer 2: 0.86000
  layer 3: 0.86000

Biases for hidden and output layers:
layer 2 biases:
  0.07636   −1.41765 −3.74051   2.88704   0.31603
layer 3 biases:
−2.45347

Weight matrices: (to unit I from unit J, J changing fastest)
layer 1 to 2 weights:
−0.29914   −1.12996 −0.94523 −1.05204   0.18254   0.00316   10.80784   9.43302
−0.78687   0.01702 −0.02624 12.85093   9.72821   1.17494   −0.49308   −0.81009
−7.56186   −8.20073 −8.32964   0.94388   0.10122 −1.40391   −1.54195   −1.43610
  0.11747
layer 2 to 3 weights:
−0.58688   5.63501   6.35895 −6.80284 −0.87855

Table A9.4

Modified Perceptron Network

Number of layer = 2
  layers numbered from 1 (input) to 2 (output)

Layer dimensions:
  layer 1:   (1, 5)
  layer 2:   (1, 1)

Cycles trained = 934

Weights initialized from −0.300 to 0.300

Noise = 0.00000, decay = 0.00000

Tolerance = 0.00000

Learning rates for layers:
  layer 2: 0.17500

Momentum terms for layers:
  layer 2: 0.80000

Biases for hidden and output layers:
layer 2 biases:
  −6.01205

Weight matrices: (to unit I from unit J, J changing fastest)
layer 1 to 2 weights:
  −1.47879   19.58733   29.66311   1.27743   −0.23120

10

A NEURAL NETWORK MODEL FOR BANKRUPTCY PREDICTION

Marcus D. Odom and Ramesh Sharda

INTRODUCTION

Neural networks have proven to be good at solving many tasks. They may have the most practical effect in the following three areas: modeling and forecasting, signal processing, and expert systems.[1] The predictive ability of neural networks falls into the forecasting area. Predictive type problems relate to the autoassociative memory of certain neural networks. The method used for neural network prediction is called generalization.[2] Generalization is different from autoassociative memory, in that once the network has been trained, new data are input for the network to predict the output. Previous business applications of neural networks include predicting the ratings of corporate bonds,[2] and emulating mortgage underwriting judgments.[3]

The purpose of this study is to compare the predictive ability of a neural network and multivariate discriminant analysis models in bankruptcy risk prediction. This area has been studied extensively in accounting literature. The first studies were performed to determine whether financial ratios provide useful information.[4,5] Many different studies have used financial ratios for bankruptcy prediction since that first study by Beaver.[4] Most of these later studies use a discriminant analysis approach instead of the univariate approach used by Beaver. Studies that applied discriminant analysis include Altman,[5] Deakin,[6] Blum,[7] Moyer,[8] Altman et al.,[9] and Karels and Prakash.[10] Discriminant analysis is valid only under certain restrictive assumptions including the requirement for the discriminating variables to be jointly multivariate normal. This multivariate normality of the variables is critical to the discriminant analysis procedure; otherwise, the results obtained may be erroneous.[10] Neural networks are not subject to the restriction of normality. A comparison of a neural network model and a discriminant analysis model in bankruptcy prediction is worthwhile in that we will be able to compare a new, more robust approach against an established model that makes a priori assumptions about the discriminatory variables.

The importance of failure analysis provides another motivation for this study. Failure analysis using financial ratios is very important for several reasons. First, management can use it to identify potential problems that need attention.[11] Second, investors use ratios to evaluate a firm. Last, auditors use it as a tool in going-concern evaluation.[12] The American Accounting Association, in *A Statement of Basic Accounting Theory*, defines accounting as "the process of identifying, measuring, and communicating economic information to permit informed judgments and decisions by users of the information."[13] Ratio analysis is just one means of using accounting data for this purpose. This chapter will see whether neural networks are better predictors of business performance when these same ratios are presented to them.

METHODOLOGY

This chapter performs analysis on ratios using both discriminant analysis and a neural network. The Altman study[5] is used as the standard for comparison for subsequent bankruptcy classification studies using discriminant analysis. For this reason, we have chosen to use the same financial ratios that Altman used in his 1968 study. These ratios are:

X_1 Working capital / Total assets
X_2 Retained earnings / Total assets
X_3 Earnings before interest and taxes / Total assets
X_4 Market value of equity / Total debt
X_5 Sales / Total assets

The sample of firms from which the ratios were obtained consisted of firms that went bankrupt between 1975 and 1982. The sample, obtained from *Moody's Industrial Manuals*, consisted of a total of 129 firms, 65 of which went bankrupt during the period and 64 nonbankrupt firms matched on industry and year. Two subsamples were developed from this sample of 129 firms. The first (training) subsample of 74 firms' data (38 bankrupt firms and 36 nonbankrupt firms) was used as the training set for both methods. The second subsample consisted of 55 firms (27 bankrupt firms and 28 nonbankrupt firms) and was used as the holdout sample. Data used for the bankrupt firms are from the last financial statements issued before the firms declared bankruptcy.

Ratios computed from the data for each original subsample were entered into both a conventional discriminant analysis program and a neural network. The models derived from this original subsample were used to predict the classification for both the training subsample and the holdout subsample.

MODELS FOR BANKRUPTCY PREDICTION

Discriminant Analysis

The multivariate statistical technique known as discriminant analysis is by far the most widely used method for bankruptcy risk analysis. The program used in this study was SAS DISCRIM.

The discriminant analysis method correctly classified 33 of the 38 bankrupt firms for a correct classification rate of 86.84 percent when using the training subsample. The model correctly classified all of the nonbankrupt firms in the training subsample. While this looks promising, the classification results are based on the same data used in model formulation. Therefore, caution should be exercised in assessing the validity of the model at this point.

Neural Network

The neural network used for training was a three-perceptron network consisting of an input layer, a hidden layer, and the output layer (Figure 10.1). The input layer consisted of the five nodes, one for each of the ratios. The hidden layer consisted of 5 nodes. The output layer consisted of only one neuron with a response of 0, representing bankrupt, and 1, representing nonbankrupt. The network was presented with the ratios for the firms. The network classified the data on a scale between 0 and 1. Firms with output below .5 were classified as bankrupt. Firms with output greater than .5 were classified as nonbankrupt.

The neural network was trained by presenting the five ratios for each of the firms in the first subsample and the correct output for each to the network. The learning threshold for the network was .075. The initial learning rate and momentum were .6 and .9, respectively. The learning rate and momentum were adjusted downward as suggested by Lippmann[1] to improve performance during training. The learning rate and momentum at the time of convergence were .1 and .8 respectively.

Figure 10.1

Neural Network

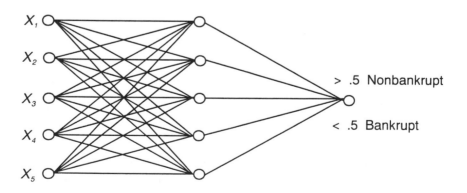

One problem with the back-propagation rule, as explained in Caudill,[14] is the number of iterations needed to learn the data. This criticism held true in this project. Convergence was reached after 191,400 iterations. All of the training was performed on a PC-XT. The average time for training was approximately 24 hours. The software used was NeuroShell, release 1.1, a commercial neural network simulator package available for the microcomputer from Ward System Group, Inc. This program uses a back-propagation rule neural network. For more in-depth description of the back-propagation rule refer to Lippmann[1] and Rummelhart et al.[15]

The neural network correctly predicted all 36 of the nonbankrupt firms in the training subsample as nonbankrupt. The trained network also correctly predicted all 38 of the bankrupt firms as bankrupt. This was very promising when compared to the discriminant analysis prediction rates for the training subsample.

COMPARISON OF RESULTS

The results of the multivariate discriminant analysis method and the neural network are presented in Table 10.1 for the holdout sample only. An analysis of the incorrect classifications that were made by the neural network is presented after explaining Table 10.1. In order to test the robustness of the discriminant analysis model and the neural network, the training sets were randomly adjusted to be more realistic of the real-world ratio of nonbankrupt firms to bankrupt firms. Three separate groups were formed, the original sample with the 50/50 proportion. The second consisted of 36 (80 percent) nonbankrupt firms and 9 (20 percent) bankrupt firms. The third group had 36 (90 percent) nonbankrupt firms and 4 (10 percent) bankrupt firms. These will be referred to as the 80/20 and 90/10 training sets.

A comparison of the results from the models' predictions for the holdout subsample with the 50/50 training set shows that the discriminant analysis has a correct prediction rate of 59.26 percent for the bankrupt firms, which is well below the correct prediction rate of 81.48 percent for the neural network. When the training sample was changed to the 80/20 proportion of nonbankrupt to bankrupt firms, the discriminant analysis had a correct prediction rate of 70.37 percent for the bankrupt firms as compared to the neural network's correct prediction of 77.78 percent. When the training sample was reduced to the 90/10

Table 10.1

Comparison of Discriminant Analysis and Neural Networks on Holdout Sample

Training Sample Proportion		50/50		80/20		90/10	
Model	Actual / Predicted	BR (27)	NBR (28)	BR (27)	NBR (28)	BR (27)	NBR (28)
Neural Network	BR	22 (81.48)	5 (18.51)	21 (77.78)	6 (22.22)	21 (77.78)	6 (22.22)
	NBR	5 (17.86)	23 (82.14)	6 (21.43)	22 (78.57)	4 (14.29)	24 (85.71)
Discriminant Analysis	BR	16 (59.26)	11 (40.74)	19 (70.37)	8 (29.63)	16 (59.26)	11 (40.74)
	NBR	3 (10.71)	25 (89.29)	4 (14.29)	24 (85.71)	6 (21.43)	22 (78.57)

BR = Bankrupt
NB = Nonbankrupt
% in parenthesis

proportion, the discriminant analysis had a correct prediction rate of 59.26 percent and the neural network had a correct prediction rate of 77.78 percent for the holdout subsample. The neural network appears to be more robust, performing better than the discriminant analysis method in each of the three situations. The neural network also appears to be more consistent that the discriminant analysis method.

The discriminant analysis method correctly predicted 89.29 percent of the nonbankrupt firms while the neural network predicted 82.14 percent correctly when trained with the 50/50 sample. Using the 80/20 sample, the discriminant analysis method correctly predicted 85.71 percent as compared to the neural network's correct prediction rate of 78.57 percent. However, when the 90/10 sample was used for training, the neural network did better, correctly predicting 85.71 percent of the holdout subsample, while the discriminant analysis method predicted only 78.57 percent.

Further analysis of the incorrect predictions of the neural network revealed that the five bankrupt firms incorrectly classified as nonbankrupt were also misclassified by the discriminant analysis model.

Of the five nonbankrupt firms incorrectly classified by the neural network as bankrupt, three were also misclassified by the discriminant analysis model and one more was nearly misclassified by this model because it received only a 51.31 percent probability of membership in the nonbankrupt group. These results show that the firms misclassified by the neural network were also a problem for the discriminant analysis method.

It is more costly to classify a failed firm as nonfailed than to classify a nonfailed firm as failed.[16] The accountant will be more interested in getting an early indication of a firm heading towards bankruptcy. Figure 10.2 exhibits the performance of the two models in predicting bankruptcy of a firm as the training set proportions are varied. It clearly states that regardless of the training sample proportions, the neural

Figure 10.2

Prediction of Bankrupt Firms versus Distribution of Training Set

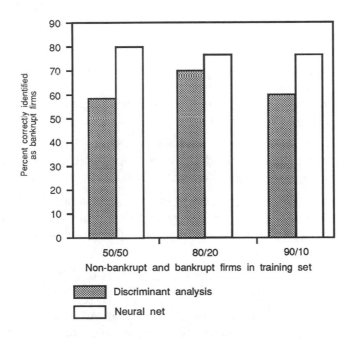

network model predicted more accurately the likelihood of a firm declaring bankruptcy.

CONCLUSIONS

The results obtained from this project show promise in using neural networks for prediction purposes. This research compared neural networks against a method that has become the gold standard in bankruptcy prediction, and the neural network performed better on both the original set of data and on predicting the bankrupt firms in the holdout sample. The neural network proved to be more robust than the discriminant analysis method on reduced sample sizes.

Further research should be done in this area using different ratios to see if the prediction accuracy can be increased. The ratios in this study were based on a study completed in 1968, different ratios may perform better today.[9] Another area for future research may be in applying different neural network architectures to this problem. Comparison of these other architectures may help to identify the best architecture for this type of problem.

ENDNOTES

1. R. P. Lippmann, "An Introduction to Computing with Neural Nets," *IEEE ASSP Magazine*, April 1987, pp. 4–22.

2. S. Dutta, and S. Shekhar, "Bond Rating: A Non-Conservative Application of Neural Networks," Working paper (University of California: Computer Science Division, 1989).

3. E. Collins, S. Ghosh, and C. Scofield, "An Application of a Multiple Neural Network Learning System to Emulation of Mortgage Underwriting Judgments," Working paper (Providence, R.I.: Nestor, Inc.), 1989.

4. W. H. Beaver, "Financial Ratios as Predictors of Failure," *Empirical Research in Accounting: Selected Studies*, 1966, pp. 71–111.

5. E. L. Altman, "Financial Ratios, Discriminant Analysis and the Prediction of Corporate Bankruptcy," *The Journal of Finance*, September 1968, pp. 589–609.

6. E. B. Deakin, "A Discriminant Analysis of Predictors of Business Failure," *Journal of Accounting Research*, Spring 1972, pp. 167–179.

7. M. Blum, "Failing Company Discriminant Analysis," *Journal of Accounting Research*, Spring 1974, pp. 1–25.

8. R. C. Moyer, "Forecasting Financial Failure: A Reexamination," *Financial Management*, Spring 1977, pp. 11–17.

9. E. I. Altman, R. G. Haldeman, and P. Narayanan, "Zeta Analysis," *Journal of Banking and Finance*, June 1977, pp. 29–51.

10. G. V. Karels, and A. Prakash, "Multivariate Normality and Forecasting of Business Bankruptcy," *Journal of Business Finance & Accounting*, Winter 1987, pp. 573–593.

11. J. G. Siegel, "Warning Signs of Impending Business Failure and Means to Counteract Such Prospective Failure," *The National Public Accountant*, April 1981, pp. 9–13.

12. E. I. Altman, "Accounting Implications of Failure Prediction Models," *Journal of Accounting Auditing & Finance*, Fall 1982, pp. 4–19.

13. American Accounting Association, *A Statement of Basic Accounting Theory*, (AAA), 1966.

14. M. Caudill, "Neural Networks Primer, Part III," *AI Expert*, June 1988, pp. 53–59.

15. D. E. Rumelhart, G. E. Hinton, and R. J. Williams, "Learning Internal Representation by Error Propagation," in *Parallel Distributed Processing*, vol. 1, (Cambridge, Mass.: MIT Press, 1986).

16. R. L. Watts, and J. L. Zimmerman, *Positive Accounting Theory*, (Prentice-Hall, Inc., 1986).

11

NEURAL NETWORKS FOR BANKRUPTCY PREDICTION: THE POWER TO SOLVE FINANCIAL PROBLEMS

Kevin G. Coleman, Timothy J. Graettinger, and
William F. Lawrence

INTRODUCTION

One cannot pick up a newspaper or tune into a news broadcast without being painfully aware of the rising number of bankruptcies. Within the realm of finance, the FDIC reported that 1,000 banks closed over the past five years. The disaster within the savings and loan industry has been a national issue.

Neural Networks for Bankruptcy Prediction appears courtesy of NeuralWare, Inc., Pittsburgh, PA. This article appeared in *AI Review*, July/August, 1991, pp. 48–50.

Financial institutions are not alone in suffering. As Figure 11.1 shows, commercial and individual bankruptcies are also steadily rising. In 1990 there were about 725,000 filings for Chapter 7 or Chapter 11 bankruptcies. As a natural result, debt associated with bankruptcies is at its largest point in our history.

While bankruptcies pose grave problems for credit institutions, they are also a nightmare for accounting firms. Aside from losing the income from a paying client, accounting firms can share the liability for bankruptcies. Liability was one of the major reasons for the Laventhal liquidation. The state of California sought to have Ernst & Young's accounting license suspended for their role in the collapse of the Lincoln Savings & Loan Association.

NEURAL NETWORK SOLUTIONS

Clearly the ability to accurately predict if an institution, company, or individual will become bankrupt is of paramount importance.

Figure 11.1

Rise in Bankruptcy Filings, 1981 through 1989

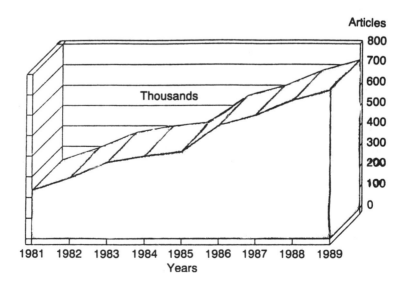

NeuralWare's Applications Development Service and Support (ADSS) group has been involved with a number of successful bankruptcy prediction applications. These applications were built using the NeuralWorks Professional neural network development system. One of the highlights of the NeuralWorks development system is that, after development, NeuralWare Designer Pack can be used to port the network to an ANSI standard "C" module for deployment in a customer's computing system.

Both applications discussed in this chapter used standard back-propagation networks, with the addition of a proprietary error function created by the ADSS staff. The first application was developed for Peat Marwick, and was used to predict banks that were certain to fail within a year. The predicted certainty of failure was then given to bank examiners dealing with the bank in question.

The back-propagation network the ADSS engineers developed had 11 inputs, each of which was a ratio developed by Peat Marwick. Figure 11.2 shows an example of one of these ratios. The inputs were connected to a single hidden layer, which in turn was connected to a single node in the output layer. The network output was a single value denoting whether the bank would or would not fail within that calendar year. The network employed the normalized-cumulative-delta learning rule

---

Figure 11.2

The Derivation of PRMCAPAS

One of the Ratios Used as an Input to the Network Developed for Peat Marwick.

Numerator:	Total Equity Capital
	+ Minority Interest
	+ Total Mand. Conv. in Capital
	- Allowance for Losses
Denominator:	- Total Assets
	Allowances

---

and the hyperbolic-tangent transfer function, both standard choices within the development system. In fact, with the exception of applying the custom error function, the entire network could be constructed from within a single dialog box in the NeuralWorks Professional II/PLUS development system.

The network was trained on a set of about 1,000 examples, 900 of which were viable banks and 100 of which were banks that had actually gone bankrupt. Training consisted of about 50,000 iterations of the training set.

Peat Marwick has published[2] that the model can predict 50 percent of the population of banks that are viable, and predict failed banks with an accuracy of 99 percent (with an accepted error of 1 percent). If the accepted error is increased to 10 percent, the network can predict both viable and bankrupt banking institutions with an accuracy of 90 percent.

NeuralWare's ADSS has also developed a bankruptcy prediction application for one of the nation's leading credit card institutions. This prediction application is currently used in identifying those credit card holders who have a 100 percent probability of going bankrupt, allowing the institution to take action before this occurs.

NeuralWare isn't the only group that has had success in applying neural computing to bankruptcy prediction. Odom and Sharda,[1] at the Oklahoma State University, have compared the prediction capabilities of a back-propagation neural network with a discriminant analysis technique. Using a training set divided into 10 percent bankrupt firms and 90 percent nonbankrupt firms, the neural network was able to predict bankruptcy with an accuracy of 77.78 percent. This was opposed to an accuracy of 59.26 percent produced by discriminant analysis. By changing the ratio of the bankrupt to nonbankrupt firms in the training set to 50 percent each, the bankruptcy predicting accuracy of the neural network improved 81.48 percent. Through techniques developed by the ADSS group, NeuralWare has further improved accuracy over that reported by Odom and Sharda.

WHAT LIES AHEAD?

Figure 11.3 shows a bankruptcy prediction system that incorporates a neural network and an expert system. This hybrid application feeds data from conventional programs (data entry screens, links to external databases, etc.) to both the database and the neural network. The neural

Figure 11.3

**A Hybrid Neural Network and Expert System Bankruptcy
Detection Application**

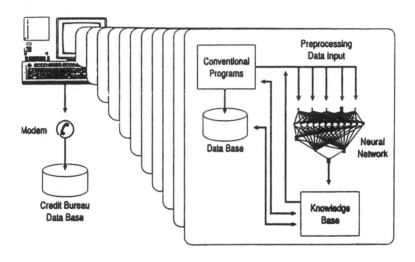

network then produces a single output value, which is actually a probability of whether or not the company, institution, or individual will declare bankruptcy. Using the Explain Net function, a unique feature in the NeuralWorks Professional II/PLUS development system, the neural network can also inform the knowledge base about which of the input parameters had the most effect on its prediction.

The expert system can then apply its rule-based decision-making capabilities and recommend remedial actions to improve the financial condition of the company, institution, or individual. It can also recommend a course of action to be taken by its owner, i.e., a credit institution or accounting firm. This is a vital capability, as the system is not only able to pinpoint potential problems, but it also can suggest ways to avoid problems or at least minimize losses.

A fascinating feature of this system is its ability to play "what-if" games to determine the efficacy of remedial action. Because the knowledge base also has access to the conventional programs supplying data to the neural network, it can then vary the parameters that were originally fed into the neural network. By experimenting with changes to the most significant parameters, and then checking the resultant probability of bankruptcy, the system can actually establish what suggested actions are likely to have the most effect.

Finally, the probability of bankruptcy and the suggested actions are added to the database. The result is a self-contained system that both predicts bankruptcy and advises the credit institution or accounting firm on what to do.

SUMMARY

Neural networks are already having a positive impact on the rising problems of institutional, company, and individual bankruptcies. Combined neural network and expert system applications can take a further step in quelling the problem of bankruptcies, by not only predicting the occurrence of bankruptcy but also recommending courses of action that have been tested against the neural network model.

ENDNOTES

1. M. D. Odom, and R. Sharda, "A Neural Network Model for Bankruptcy Prediction," *Proceedings of the IJCNN*, June 1990, pp.II-163–II-168.

2. T. B. Bell, G. S. Ribar, and J. R. Verchio, "Neural Nets vs. Logistic Regression: A Comparison of Each Model's Ability to Predict Commercial Bank Failures." Deloitte & Touche/University of Kansas Auditing Symposium, May 1990.

12

Managerial Applications of Neural Networks: The Case of Bank Failure Predictions

Kar Yan Tam and Melody Y. Kiang

INTRODUCTION

Many managerial decisions involve classifying an observation into one of several groups. A special case of this problem is binary classification in which the number of groups is limited to two. Extensive literature has been devoted to studying this problem under various contexts, including credit scoring, default prediction, merger and acquisition, and

© 1992, The Institute of Management Sciences. This article originally appeared in *Management Science*, Vol. 38, No. 7, July 1992, pp. 926–947. Reprinted with permission.

bond rating, just to name a few. The solution to this problem is a discriminant function from the variable space in which observations are defined into a binary set.

Since Fisher's seminal work,[1] numerous methods have been developed for classification purposes. They are typically referred to as multivariate discriminant analysis (hereafter referred to as DA). In general, these methods accept a random sample of observations defined by a chosen set of variables and generate a discriminant function that serves as a classifier. They differ in two major aspects: (1) assumption on group distribution, and (2) functional form of the discriminant function. In the current study, we have taken a neural-net approach to the binary classification problem and compared it with popular DA methods. Our goal is to identify the potentials and limitations of neural nets as a tool to do discriminant analysis in business research.

The subject of neural nets, once viewed as the theoretical foundation for building artificial intelligent systems in the 1950s and 1960s, was proven to be too limited by Minsky and Papert.[2] Using simple examples, Minsky and Papert showed that only a few functions are guaranteed to be learned by a neural net. In the case of the well-known exclusive or (XOR)[3] function, they showed that the function cannot be learned by a two-layer network; however, recent breakthroughs in neural nets research have overcome some of the limitations cited earlier. For example, Rumelhart, Hinton, and Williams[4] have developed a back-propagation learning algorithm to train a multilayer network that can reproduce the XOR function.

The resurgent interest in neural nets has been manifested in the study of a new class of computation models called the *connectionist models*, which have limited analogy, if any, to their neurophysiology origin.[5] Connectionist systems provide massive parallel processing capabilities that are essential in many domains, such as pattern recognition, concept classification, speech processing, and real-time process control.[6,7] Fault-tolerance is another appealing property that has profound implications in the design and fabrication of integrated circuits. A connectionist system can tolerate minor component failures without impairing the entire system. Existing computers are serial machines based on the Von Neumann architecture proposed some 40 years ago. These machines are designed to execute serial threads of instructions and are vulnerable even to minute component failures. Because our main concert is not in the biological isomorphism of connectionist models nor their implications in computer architecture design, we shall focus on the modeling capability of neural nets as inspired by these computation models. In particular, we shall compare the performance of classification models developed by popular DA methods and by neural nets along the following dimensions: robustness, predictive accuracy, adaptability, and explanatory capability.

The testbed used in our comparative study consists of bank-bankruptcy cases reported in the state of Texas. The increasing numbers of commercial bank failures have evolved into an economic crisis that has received much attention in recent years. It is therefore both desirable and warranted to explore new predictive techniques and to provide early warnings to regulatory agencies. Tam and Kiang[8] introduced a neural net approach for bank failure prediction. However, there are methodological problems that limit the generalization of the findings. For instance, not all information about a bank was used, and the final results may be biased by the holdout samples chosen. In this study, we have extended our previous work by incorporating misclassification costs and prior probabilities in the neural net models. We have included additional classification techniques for comparison and have taken a rigorous approach in validating the results.[9]

MULTIVARIATE DISCRIMINANT ANALYSIS

Linear Discriminant Model

Perhaps the most widely used DA method is the one due to Fisher.[1] The Fisher procedure constructs a discriminant function by maximizing the ratio of between-groups and within-groups variances. Classifiers derived from the Fisher procedure are known to be optimal in minimizing the expected costs of misclassifications, provided the following conditions are satisfied:

1. Each group follows a multivariate normal distribution.

2. The covariance matrices of each group are identical.

3. The mean vectors, covariance matrices, prior probabilities, and misclassification costs are known.

In the case of binary classification, the discriminant function is stated as

$$D(X) = X'\Sigma^{-1}(\mu_1 - \mu_2) - \frac{1}{2}(\mu_1 - \mu_2)^T \Sigma^{-1}(\mu_1 + \mu_2)$$

where μ_1, μ_2, and Σ^{-1} are the mean vectors and inverse of the common covariance matrix, respectively. The threshold value of the decision rule is ln $(C_{21}\pi_1/C_{12}\pi_2)$ where C_{12}, C_{21}, π_1, and π_2 are the misclassification costs and prior probabilities of each group. This method yields a linear function relating a set of independent variables to a scoring variable. It represents a hyperplane that divides the variable space into two partitions with each assigned to a group.

DA minimizes the expected misclassification cost provided the normality and equal dispersion assumptions are satisfied. Unfortunately, violations of these assumptions occur regularly. It is common that individual variables are not normally distributed.[10] Examples can be found where variables are bounded or assume category values. Transformations, such as taking the natural logarithm, are suggested to approximate normal distribution; however, the transformed variables may be difficult to interpret. If the covariance matrices are different, quadratic instead of linear functions should be employed. Quadratic classifiers may be quite accurate in classifying the training sample, but they do not perform well as linear models in holdout sample tests.[11] Lachenbruch, Sneeringer, and Revo[12] reported a similar conclusion after comparing the two methods under various nonmultivariate normal distributions. Whether the function is linear or quadratic, a fundamental condition that must be satisfied is that the two groups are discrete and identifiable. Situations deviating from this condition can be found where observations of each group form clusters in different regions of the variable space. Depending on the number of clusters in each group, the discriminant functions (linear or quadratic) may incur a high error rate for both the training and holdout sample.

Altman et al.[11] identified four related problems in the use of DA techniques in classification: (1) relative significance of the individual variables, (2) reduction of dimensionality, (3) elimination of insignificant variables, and (4) existence of time series relationships. Recognizing the limitations of linear classifiers, a common practice is to accept the results as if the assumptions were satisfied.

Logistic Regression

An alternative to the linear DA model is logistic regression. A nonlinear logistic function having the following form is used

$$Y = \frac{1}{1 + e^{y}}, \qquad y = c_0 + \sum_{i=1}^{n} c_i X_i$$

where X_i, $1 \leq i \leq n$, represent the set of individual variables, c_i is the coefficient of the ith variable, and Y is the dependent variable. Because Y falls between 0 and 1, it is usually interpreted as the probability of a class outcome. In practice, it has been suggested that the logistic regression approach is often preferred over DA.[13] Harrell and Lee[14] contended that even when all the assumptions of DA hold, a logit model is virtually as efficient as a linear classifier.

k Nearest Neighbor

Distribution-free techniques are applicable under less restrictive conditions regarding the underlying population distribution and data measurement scales. kNN is a nonparametric method for classifying observations into one or several groups based on one or more quantitative variables. It not only relaxes the normality assumption, it also eliminates the functional form required in DA and logistic regression. The group assignment of an observation is decided by the group assignments of its first k nearest neighbor. The distance $d(x, y)$ between any two observations x and y is usually defined by the Mahalanobis distance between x and y. Using the nearest neighbor decision rule, an observation is assigned to the group to which the majority of its k nearest neighbors belong. This method has the merits of better approximating the sample distribution by dividing the variable space into any arbitrary number of decision regions, with the maximum bounded by the total number of observations.

Decision Tree (ID3)

Instead of generating a decision rule in the form of a discriminant function, the ID3 method creates a decision tree that properly classifies the training sample.[15,16,17] This tree induction method has been applied in credit scoring,[18] corporate failures prediction,[19] and stock portfolio construction.[20] Frydman, Altman and Kao[21] applied a similar technique, called *recursive partitioning*, to generate a discriminant tree. Both ID3 and recursive partitioning employ a nonbacktracking splitting procedure that recursively partitions a set of examples into disjointed subsets. These methods differ in their splitting criteria. The ID3 method intends to maximize the entropy of the split subsets, whereas the recursive partitioning technique is designed to minimize the expected cost of misclassifications.

The five techniques compared in this study can be categorized into two groups: machine learning (neural nets and ID3) and statistical techniques (DA, logit, and kNN). Although previous research has focused mainly on a single method, the mix of techniques employed in this study allows a more comprehensive comparison of the different approaches to the problem.

NEURAL NETWORKS

A neural net consists of a number of interconnected homogeneous processing units. Each unit is a simple computation device. Its behavior can be modeled by simple mathematical functions. A unit i receives input signals from other units, aggregates these signals based on an input function I_i, and generates an output signal based on an output function O_i (sometimes called a transfer function). The output signal is then routed to other units as directed by the topology of the network. Although no assumption is imposed on the form of input/output functions at each node other than to be continuous and differentiable, we will use the following functions as suggested in Rumelhart et al.[5]:

$$I_i = \sum_j w_{ij}O_j + \varphi_i \quad \text{and} \quad O_i = \frac{1}{1 + e^{I_i}}$$

where

I_i = input of unit i,
O_i = output of unit i,
w_{ij} = connection weight between unit i and j,
φ_i = bias of unit i.

Feedforward Networks

The configuration of a neural net is represented by a weighted directed graph (WDG) with nodes representing units and links representing connections. Each link is assigned a numerical value representing the weight of the connection. Variations of the general WDG topology are found in a number of connectionist models.[22,23] A special class of neural nets called feedforward networks is used here.

In a feedforward network, there are three types of processing units: input units, output units, and hidden units. Input units accept signals from the environment and reside in the lowest layer of the network. Output units send signals to the environment and reside in the highest layer. Hidden units are units which do not interact directly with the environment, hence are invisible (i.e., hidden from the environment). Connections within a layer or from a higher layer to a lower are prohibited, but they can skip several layers.

The pattern of connectivity of a feedforward network is described by its weight vector W—weights associated with the connections. It is W that constitutes what a neural net knows and determines how it will respond to any arbitrary input from the environment. A feedforward network with an appropriate W can be used to model the casual relationship between a set of variables. Changing the model is accomplished by modifying the weight associated with each connection.

Back-propagation Learning Algorithm

It is very difficult to assign an appropriate W for a classification task, especially when there is little information about the population distribution. A general solution is to let the network learn the task by training it with examples.[24] A typical learning algorithm will search through the space of W for a set of weights offering the best fit with the given examples. Notable learning algorithms are the perceptron convergence procedure[25] and the back-propagation algorithm.[4]

The back-propagation learning algorithm, designed to train a feedforward network, overcomes some of perceptron's limitations by making it possible to train a multiple-layer network. It is an effective learning technique that is capable of exploiting the regularities and exceptions in the training sample. A flow chart of the algorithm is shown in Figure 12.1. The back-propagation algorithm consists of two phases:

Figure 12.1

Flowchart of the Back-Propagation Algorithm

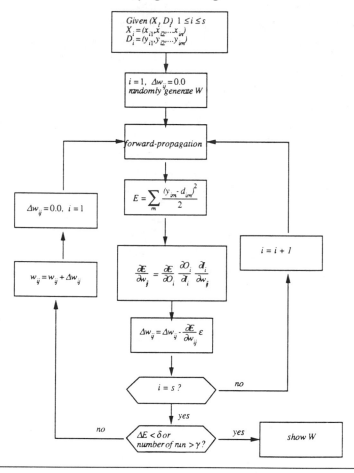

forward-propagation and backward-propagation. Suppose we have s examples, each described by an input vector $X_i = (x_{i1}, x_{i2},...,x_{im})$ and an output vector $D_i = (d_{i1}, d_{i2},...,d_{in})$, $1 \leq i \leq s$. In forward-propagation, X_i is fed into the input layer, and an output $Y_i = (y_{i1}, y_{i2},...,y_{in})$ is generated on the basis of the current W. The value of Y_i is then compared with the actual (or desired) output D_i by calculating the squared error $(y_{ij} -$

$d_{ij})^2$, $1 \leq i \leq n$, at each output unit. Output differences are summed up to generate an error function E defined as

$$E = \sum_{i=1}^{s} \sum_{j=1}^{n} \frac{(y_{ij} - d_{ij})^2}{2}.$$

The objective is to minimize E by changing W so that all input vectors are correctly mapped to their corresponding output vectors. Thus, the learning process can be cast as a minimization problem with objective function E defined in the space of W.

The second phase performs a gradient descent in the weight space to locate the optimal solution. The direction and magnitude change Δw_{ij} of each w_{ij} can be calculated as

$$\Delta w_{ij} = -\frac{\partial E}{\partial w_{ij}} \varepsilon,$$

where $0 < \varepsilon < 1$ is a parameter controlling the convergence rate of the algorithm.

The total squared error calculated in the first phase is propagated back, layer by layer, from the output units to the input units in the second phase. Weight adjustments are determined on the way propagation at each level. Because I_i, O_i, and E are all continuous and differentiable, the value of $\partial E / \partial w_{ij}$ at each level can be calculated by applying the chain rule

$$\frac{\partial E}{\partial w_{ij}} = \frac{\partial E}{\partial O_i} \frac{\partial O_i}{\partial I_i} \frac{\partial I_i}{\partial w_{ij}}$$

W can be updated in two ways. Either W is updated for each (X_i, D_i) pair, or Δw_{ij} are accumulated and updated after a complete run of all examples. The two phases are executed in each iteration of the back-propagation algorithm until E converges. Although the back-propagation algorithm does not guarantee optimal solution, Rumelhart et al.[5] reported that solutions obtained from the algorithm come close to the optimal ones in their experiments.

BANK BANKRUPTCY PREDICTION

The number of financial distresses in the banking industry has reached a historic high unparalleled since the Great Depression. The number of bankruptcy cases filed under the Federal Deposit Insurance Corporation (FDIC) has increased from less than 50 in 1984 to an estimate of over 400 in 1991. To monitor the member banks and to assure their proper compliance with federal regulations, the FDIC has committed substantial efforts to both on-site examinations and off-site surveillance activities. Since the mid-1970s, the FDIC has been operating an "early warning" system that facilitates the rating process by identifying troubled banks and alerting the agency for early inspection.[26] This is accomplished by statistically evaluating the reports filed by each bank on a regular basis. According to West[27] "performance ratios of banks are compared to some standard, or arranged to some sort of statistical cut-off. Banks that "fail" these ratio tests are singled out for more careful scrutiny."

Given the importance of this subject at both the micro and macro level, numerous models have been developed to predict bank failure. These models employ statistical techniques which include regression analysis,[28] multivariate discriminant analysis,[29,30,31] multivariate probit or logic analysis,[32,33] arctangent regression analysis,[34] and Factor-logistic analysis.[27] Although widely practiced, these models have been criticized for their problematic methodologies,[35] and a satisfactory model has yet to be developed.

DATA SAMPLE AND MODEL CONSTRUCTION

Data Sample

The data sample consists of Texas banks that failed in the period 1985–1987.[36] Texas banks were selected for two reasons. First, more than one quarter of the failed banks in 1987 were located in Texas.[37] Not surprisingly, the high bankruptcy rate coincides with the general economic conditions in the Southwestern region, especially in the energy and real estate sectors of the economy. Thus, it is interesting to develop a prediction model specifically tailored to the economic environment in this region. Second, involving banks from the same region, instead of those from other states, increases the sample's homogeneity.

The data sample consists of bank data one year and two years prior to failure. As a control measure, a failed bank was matched with a nonfailed bank in terms of (1) asset size, (2) number of branches, (3) age, and (4) charter status. In each period, 118 banks (59 failed and 59 nonfailed) were selected as the training sample.

Each bank is described by 19 financial ratios that have been used in previous studies. The list of ratios is shown in Table 12.1. The selection of variables followed closely the CAMEL criteria used by the FDIC. CAMEL is an acronym for Capital, Asset, Management, Equity, and Liquidity which is generally adopted by all U.S. bank regulatory agencies. An assessor rates a bank according to its scores in each of these five areas, and the composite ratings are taken to reflect the financial conditions of the bank. Rating results provide early warnings to an agency, drawing its attention to those banks that have a high likelihood of failure in the coming one or two years.

The 19 ratios can be grouped into four of these five criteria. The first ratio represents the capital adequacy of the bank; ratios 2–10 mea-

Table 12.1

A List of Financial Variables

Name	Description
capas	capital/assets
agfas	(agricultural production & farm loans + real estate loans secured by farm land)/net loans & leases
comas	(commercial and industrial loans)/net loans & leases
indas	(loans to individuals)/net loan & leases
resas	(real estate loans)/net loan & leases
pasln	(total loans 90 days or more past due)/net loans & leases
nonln	(total nonaccrual loans & leases)/net loans & leases
losln	(provision for loan losses)/average loans
netln	(net charge-offs)/average loans
rtoas	return on average assets
intdp	(total interest paid on deposits)/total deposits
expas	(total expense)/total assets
incas	(net income)/total assets
infln	(interests and fees on loans + income from lease financing rec)/net loans & leases
incex	(total income)/total expense
curas	(cash + U.S. treasury & government agency obligations)/total assets
govas	(federal funds sold + securities)/total assets
llnas	(total loans & leases)/total assets
llndp	(total loans & leases)/total deposits

sure asset quality; the bank's earnings are captured by ratios 11–15, and liquidity is represented by ratios 16–19. No explicit ratio was used for the Management criterion because the quality of management, which is difficult to quantify, will eventually be reflected by the above-mentioned ratios.

Linear Discriminant Model

The Kolmogorov-Smirnov test[38] was performed for each of the 19 financial ratios in the data sample to check if the normal distribution assumption was satisfied. The test indicated that 15 out of 19 ratios were not normally distributed in the one-year period. In the two-year period, only one ratio was shown to be normally distributed. For those ratios that failed the test, the natural logarithm transformation was performed. The Kolmogorov-Smirnov test was then repeated for the transformed ratios. The results showed that 13 out of 19 ratios in the one-year period and 14 out of 19 in the two-year period were still not normally distributed. Because no significant improvement was observed, we decided to use the original ratios to construct the DA models. The DA models were implemented using FORTRAN with embedded IMSL procedure calls.

Logistic Model

Like the DA model, no variable transformation was performed. All 19 variables were used to estimate the logit model for the one- and two-year period.[39] A bank will be classified as a failed bank if the value of the dependent variables is less than 0.5, and as a nonfailed bank otherwise.

kNN models

Two kNN models, one with $k = 1$ and the other with $k = 3$, were constructed for each period.[40] For $k = 1$, a bank was assigned to the group that contains its nearest neighbor, whereas in $k = 3$, the bank was assigned to the group that contained the majority of its three closest neighbors. Even values of k were not included due to the possibility of a tie.

ID3

The ID3 algorithm was implemented in CommonLisp. A chi-square stopping rule with a significance level of 5 percent was used to reduce the effects of noisy data. The classification trees generated by using ID3 for both periods are shown in Figures 12.2a and 12.2b. The *F* and *NF* in each leaf of the tree denote the number of failed and nonfailed banks, respectively. The number of variables has been reduced from 19 to 6 in the one-year period and to 8 in the second-year period. The classification tree for the former exhibits a more balanced and less complex structure than the latter, indicating that observations in the two-year period may intermesh more uniformly than in the one-year period. In addition, two-thirds of the variables in the one-year period (nonln, expas, pasln, rtoas) representing mainly asset quality and earnings also appear in the two-year period.

Figure 12.2a
Classification Tree for One-Year Period

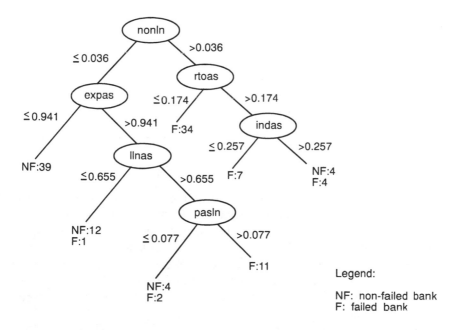

Legend:

NF: non-failed bank
F: failed bank

Figure 12.2b

Classification Tree for Two-Year Period

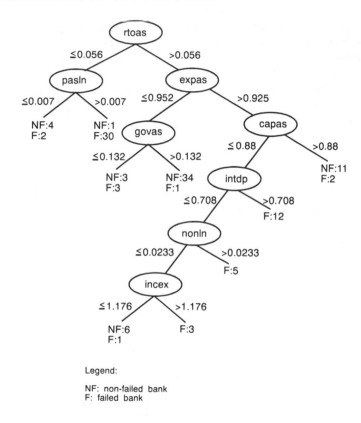

Legend:

NF: non-failed bank
F: failed bank

Neural Network Models

We have performed some exploratory experiments to decide on the configuration of the neural nets used in our study. This is a required step because there is yet a formal algorithm to be developed to map a task to a configuration. We have constructed 2-layer and 3-layer networks; for 3-layer networks, different numbers of hidden units were tried. Finally two configurations, one with no hidden unit (2-layer) and the other with 10 hidden units (3-layer), were constructed for each period (see Figures 12.3a and 12.3b).

Figure 12.3a

The Network Configuration of Net$_0$

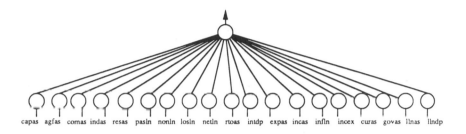

Figure 12.3b

The Network Configuration of Net$_{10}$

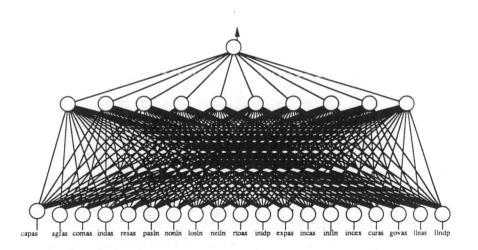

The original back-propagation algorithm does not take into account the prior probabilities of each group and their misclassification costs. To incorporate them into the learning algorithm, the objective function E is generalized to E_w defined as

$$E_w = \sum_{i=1}^{2} Z_i \sum_{j=1}^{n_i} \frac{(y_{ij} - d_{ij})^2}{2}$$

where $Z_2 = C_{12}\pi_2$ represents type I misclassification error, $Z_1 = C_{21}\pi_1$ represents type II misclassification error and n_i ($i = 1, 2$) is the number of examples in group i. The type I error is defined as the event of assigning an observation to group 1 that should be in group 2, while the type II error involves assigning an observation to group 2 that should be in group 1. The value of Z_i is treated as the weight of the squared error incurred by each observation. It is clear that the initial objective function E is a special case of E_w by setting $C_{12}\pi_2 = C_{21}\pi_1$. In the current study, we will refer to nonfailed banks as group 1 and failed banks as group 2.

Because we are concerned with dichotomous classification (failure versus nonfailure), only a single output unit is needed. The decision is stated as

output unit > 0.5 → group 1 (nonfailed banks),

output unit ≤ 0.5 → group 2 (failed banks).

Instead of using $\Delta w_{ij} = - \partial E / \partial w_{ij}\varepsilon$, which may be slow in terms of convergence, we use an accelerated version as shown:

$$\Delta w_{ij}(t) = - \varepsilon \frac{\partial E}{\partial w(t)} + \alpha \Delta w_{ij}(t - 1)$$

where $0 \le \alpha \le 1$ is an exponential decay factor determining the contribution of the previous gradient descent.

To smooth out drastic changes to W by some outlining examples, we prefer the accumulated weights updating scheme. No prior information is available as to how units should be connected in the three-layer network, so all hidden units are fully connected to the input units.

The back-propagation procedure was implemented in Pascal and run on an EMX machine. Five different sets of weights were generated and five different runs were done for each neural net model. Each run was allocated a maximum of 2000 iterations. The classification accuracy obtained by each run was ranked by total misclassifications, and the median run was taken as the result.

COMPUTATION RESULTS

The classification accuracy of neural nets is first compared with that of DA using different prior probabilities and misclassification costs. Two prior probabilities for failed banks (π_2), 0.01 and 0.02, and eight misclassification costs were used. We followed the distribution of misclassification costs used previously by Frydman et al.,[21] where the misclassification cost of nonfailed banks (i.e., C_{21}) is kept to 1, whereas the misclassification costs of failed banks (i.e., C_{12}) are set to 1, 5, 25, 40, 50, 60, 75, and 100. The values of ε, α, and δ are set to 0.7, 0.5 and 0.01, respectively.

Results of this comparison are shown in Tables 12.2–12.5. In Tables 12.2 and 12.3, the type I and type II errors of each model are given for each combination of prior probability and misclassification cost. The resubstitution risks for each combination are also calculated and displayed in Tables 12.4–12.5. According to Frydman et al. (1985), the resubstitution risk is the observed expected cost of misclassification defined as

$$C_{12}\pi_2\frac{n_2}{N_2} + C_{21}\pi_1\frac{n_1}{N_1} ,$$

where n_i is the total number of type i misclassifications and N_i is the sample size of the ith group.

The numbers in Tables 12.2–12.3 indicate that neural nets transcend smoothly from minimizing type I errors to type II errors as C_{12} increases. In the contrary, there is a sharp transition from $C_{12} = 5$ to $C_{12} = 25$ in DA. The proportion of DA's type I and type II errors remains virtually the same as C_{12} increases beyond 25, and its resubstitution risk starts to level off at this value. As shown, DA models are not sensitive to changes in C_{12} and π_2. This can be explained by the fact that the training

Table 12.2

Misclassification Errors in the Training Sample for Different Misclassification Costs and Prior Probabilities (One-Year Period)

$C_{12}=$	1			5			25			40			50			60			75			100		
Model	I	II	T	I	II	T	I	II	T	I	II	T	I	II	T	I	II	T	I	II	T	I	II	T
$\pi_2 = 0.01$																								(*)
DA	8	7	(15)	4	8	(12)	0	11	(11)	0	12	(12)	0	12	(12)	0	12	(12)	0	13	(13)	0	13	(13)
Net$_0$	11	1	(12)	9	1	(10)	8	1	(9)	6	2	(8)	6	3	(9)	4	6	(10)	4	7	(11)	0	8	(8)
Net$_{10}$	16	0	(16)	11	0	(11)	10	0	(10)	8	0	(8)	5	0	(5)	4	0	(4)	3	0	(3)	0	2	(2)
$\pi_2 = 0.02$															(*)									
DA	6	8	(14)	3	9	(12)	0	12	(12)	0	13	(13)	0	13	(13)	0	14	(14)	0	14	(14)	0	14	(14)
Net$_0$	17	1	(18)	9	2	(11)	8	3	(11)	8	3	(11)	6	5	(11)	0	7	(7)	0	11	(11)	0	15	(15)
Net$_{10}$	11	0	(11)	10	0	(10)	10	0	(10)	0	6	(6)	0	7	(7)	0	9	(9)	0	10	(10)	0	13	(13)

Notes:

(*) $\pi_2 C_{12} \approx \pi_1 C_{21}$

I — Number of type I misclassifications

II — Number of type II misclassifications

T — Total number of misclassifications (in parentheses)

Table 12.3
Misclassification Errors in the Training Sample for Different Misclassification Costs and Prior Probabilities (Two-Year Period)

Model	$C_{12} =$ 1 I	II	T	5 I	II	T	25 I	II	T	40 I	II	T	50 I	II	T	60 I	II	T	75 I	II	T	100 I	II	T
$\pi_2 = 0.01$																							(*)	
DA	34	5	(39)	20	6	(26)	5	8	(13)	5	10	(15)	5	10	(15)	5	10	(15)	5	10	(15)	4	10	(14)
Net$_0$	39	0	(39)	30	0	(30)	17	1	(18)	16	1	(17)	11	2	(13)	12	4	(16)	10	6	(16)	8	6	(14)
Net$_{10}$	35	0	(35)	19	0	(19)	19	0	(19)	14	2	(16)	12	3	(15)	9	3	(12)	6	5	(11)	5	6	(11)
$\pi_2 = 0.02$																(*)								
DA	27	5	(32)	13	8	(21)	5	10	(15)	5	10	(15)	4	10	(14)	4	10	(14)	3	10	(13)	3	11	(14)
Net$_0$	35	0	(35)	20	0	(20)	16	1	(17)	4	8	(12)	4	8	(12)	4	8	(12)	4	10	(14)	3	13	(16)
Net$_{1c}$	29	0	(29)	13	0	(13)	11	3	(14)	10	4	(14)	3	6	(9)	3	6	(9)	3	6	(9)	0	17	(17)

Notes:
(*) $\pi_2 C_{12} \approx \pi_1 C_{21}$
I — Number of type I misclassifications
II — Number of type II misclassifications
T — Total number of misclassifications (in parentheses)

Table 12.4

Resubstitution Risks of the Training Sample (One-Year Period)

	$C_{12} =$	1	5	25	40	50	60	75	100
Model	$\pi_2 = 0.01$								(*)
DA		0.119	0.138	0.185	0.201	0.201	0.201	0.218	0.218
Net_0		0.019	0.024	0.051	0.074	0.101	0.141	0.168	0.134
Net_{10}		0.003	0.009	0.042	0.054	0.042	0.041	0.038	0.034
	$\pi_2 = 0.02$					(*)			
DA		0.135	0.155	0.199	0.216	0.216	0.233	0.233	0.233
Net_0		0.022	0.019	0.117	0.158	0.185	0.116	0.183	0.249
Net_{10}		0.004	0.017	0.085	0.100	0.116	0.150	0.166	0.216

Notes:
(1) Resubstitution risk = $\pi_1 C_{21} n_1 / N_1 + \pi_2 C_{12} n_2 / N_2$ where n_i = total number of type i misclassifications, N_i = sample size of the i th group.
(2) (*) $\pi_2 C_{12} \cong \pi_1 C_{21}$.

Table 12.5

Resubstitution Risks of the Training Sample (Two-Year Period)

	$C_{12} =$	1	5	25	40	50	60	75	100
Model	$\pi_2 = 0.01$								(*)
DA		0.089	0.118	0.155	0.202	0.210	0.219	0.231	0.236
Net_0		0.007	0.025	0.089	0.125	0.127	0.189	0.228	0.236
Net_{10}		0.006	0.016	0.081	0.128	0.152	0.142	0.160	0.185
	$\pi_2 = 0.02$					(*)			
DA		0.092	0.155	0.208	0.234	0.234	0.247	0.242	0.284
Net_0		0.012	0.034	0.152	0.187	0.203	0.214	0.268	0.318
Net_{10}		0.010	0.022	0.143	0.202	0.151	0.161	0.176	0.282

Notes:
(1) Resubstitution risk = $\pi_1 C_{21} n_1 / N_1 + \pi_2 C_{12} n_2 / N_2$ where n_i = total number of type i misclassifications, N_i = sample size of the i th group.
(2) (*) $\pi_2 C_{12} \cong \pi_1 C_{21}$.

samples are not normally distributed. There is evidence that nonfailed banks have a multimodal distribution that is particularly apparent in the one-year period. For example, looking at the first and fourth rows in Table 12.2, there is a distinct cluster of 12 to 13 nonfailed banks that fall into the decision region of the failed group. Similarly, a cluster of about 10 nonfailed banks is observed in Table 12.3.

In Table 12.2, there are several occasions where Net_0 and Net_{10} generate inconsistent results. For example, the values of Z_i are known to be identical for both $C_{12} = 100$, $\pi_2 = 0.01$ and $C_{12} = 50$, $\pi_2 = 0.02$. One should expect similar results in both cases, but both their number and proportion of errors are quite different. This is indirectly due to the initial weights assigned to Net_0 and Net_{10}. Because the time a net takes to converge varies according to the starting point, the search may have yet to settle on a local optimum when the program halts, resulting in a different number of misclassification errors. We have rerun the algorithm to validate this argument by lifting the iteration bound in some of these inconsistent cases. Similar results were obtained this time. Rumelhart et al.[5] and many other researchers have mentioned in their work that initial weights are used to break up the symmetry of a net.[41] They do not have a major effect on the final results if sufficient time is allowed for the net to converge. The use of five random weights is designed to average out the discrepancy in convergence periods.

In both periods, Net_0 and Net_{10} dominate DA with lower resubstitution risk across all combinations of π_2 and C_{12}. The results of Tables 12.4 and 12.5 also illustrate that Net_{10} outperforms Net_0 in most cases with a few exceptions. These exceptions can be explained by the different running times associated with the initial weights and can be eliminated by allowing a net to run to convergence. The better performance of Net_{10} can be explained by the incorporation of hidden units, which provides a better fit with the training sample distribution. The resubstitution risks of Net_{10} and Net_0 are almost identical in the two-year period for small C_{12}. The dominating performance of Net_{10}, however, starts to degrade in the two-year period. The percentage reduction in resubstitution risk over Net_0 decreases from an average of 44 percent in the first period to 16.2 percent in the second period.

Table 12.6 depicts the misclassification rates of each method in predicting the training samples. Because logit, kNN, and ID3 do not account for prior probabilities and misclassification costs, the comparison is made possible by setting approximately $C_{12}\pi_2 \approx C_{21}\pi_1$ in DA and the neural nets.

Table 12.6

Misclassification Rates of the Various Models Using the Training Sample

Model	One-year Prior			Two-year Prior		
	I	II	T	I	II	T
DA	0.0	22.0	(11.0)	10.2	1.7	(6.0)
Logit	8.5	6.8	(7.7)	13.6	13.6	(13.6)
1NN	37.3	23.7	(30.5)	32.2	32.2	(32.2)
3NN	35.6	25.4	(30.5)	37.3	32.3	(34.8)
ID3	10.2	5.1	(7.7)	13.5	5.1	(9.3)
Net_0	5.0	11.0	(8.0)	10.2	11.9	(11.0)
Net_{10}	0.0	7.6	(3.8)	6.7	10.2	(8.5)

Percentage (%)

Note:
(1) The type I and type II misclassification rates of DA, Net_0 and Net_{10} are based on the average of ($C_{12} = 100$, $\pi_2 = 0.01$) and ($C_{12} = 50$, $\pi_2 = 0.02$).

In the one-year period, Net_{10} outperforms other methods with lower type I and total misclassification rates. This is followed by logit, ID3, Net_0, DA, 1NN, and 3NN. In the two-year period, DA is the best classifier, scoring the lowest type II and total misclassification errors. Net_{10} is the second best, which is followed by ID3, Net_0, logit, 1NN and 3NN.

Misclassification rates based on the training sample are often over-estimated and need further validation. The predictive accuracy of each method is validated by a holdout sample. The sample consists of 44 banks (22 failed and 22 nonfailed) and 40 banks (20 failed and 20 nonfailed) in the one- and two-year periods, respectively. Selection is made according to a similar matching procedure for the training sample. To facilitate comparison, the expected costs of misclassification for both type I and type II errors are approximately identical (i.e., $C_{12}\pi_2 \approx C_{21}\pi_1$). The validation results of the holdout sample are reported in Table 12.7.

The performance ranking in Table 12.7 is different from that of Table 6. In the one-year period, Net_{10} remains the best classifier in terms of fewer type II and total errors. This is followed by DA, Net_0, logit, ID3,

Table 12.7

Misclassification Rates of the Various Models Using the Hold-Out Sample

| | Percentage (%) | | | | | |
| | One-year Prior | | | Two-year Prior | | |
Model	I	II	T	I	II	T
DA	18.2	13.6	(15.9)	30.0	5.0	(17.5)
Logit	31.8	4.5	(18.2)	15.0	0.0	(7.5)
1NN	40.9	4.6	(22.8)	20.0	25.0	(22.5)
3NN	36.4	9.1	(22.8)	30.0	10.0	(20.0)
ID3	22.7	18.2	(20.5)	40.0	5.0	(22.5)
Net_0	31.8	4.5	(18.2)	20.0	12.6	(16.3)
Net_{10}	18.2	11.4	(14.8)	2.5	20.0	(11.3)

Note:
(1) The type I and type II misclassification rates of DA, Net_0 and Net_{10} are based on the average of (C_{12} = 100, π_2 = 0.01) and (C_{12} = 50, π_2 = 0.02).

1NN and 3NN. To our surprise, logit scores the lowest type II and total errors in the two-year period. Net_{10} comes next and is followed by Net_0, DA, 3NN, ID3, and 1NN.

The performances of DA and logit are not stable in both tests. In the first test, DA ranks the fifth in the one-year period and becomes the best classifier in the two-year period. In the holdout sample test, DA scores the second lowest misclassification rates but degrades to the fourth place in the two-year period. Logit behaves in a similar way. In the first test, it ranks second to Net_{10} in the first period, and drops to the fifth place in second period. In the validation test, it jumps from the fourth place in the one-year period to the first in the two-year period. The performances of other methods are relatively stable. Although Net_{10} remains high in the ranking list, kNN performs the worst in both tests. Net_0 and ID3 reside in the middle of the list with their positions interchanged in Tables 12.6 and 12.7.

Five out of seven methods in Table 12.7 have lower misclassification rates in predicting bank failures two years ahead. This is contrary to our intuition, because the earlier the prediction, the more uncertain it is, and one should expect a higher misclassification rate. It is difficult to conceive that the logit model can reduce more than half of its misclassification errors (18.2 percent in the one-year and 7.5 percent in two-year period) one year earlier. Furthermore, the ratios of type I to type II errors in the holdout sample test are not consistent with those in Table 12.6. The number and ratio of type I and type II errors vary widely in both tables. The only explanation is that the hold-out sample (probably both training and holdout samples) is not a representative sample of the group distributions.

Depending on the samples chosen, error rates estimated by the holdout sample may be biased. An alternative estimation method is the jackknife method that Lachenbruch[9] has shown to produce unbiased estimates for the probability of misclassification. The method involves holding one example out of the training set and using the estimated discriminant function to predict the extracted example. This is repeated for each example in the training set, and the proportion of misclassifications in each class is reported as its misclassification rate. The training and holdout samples are pooled to form one single training sample which consists of 162 (81 failed and 81 nonfailed) and 158 (79 failed, 79 nonfailed) examples in the one- and two-year periods, respectively. Descriptive statistics of the training samples are shown in Appendices I and II. The neural nets are allowed to run until convergence this time.

As shown in Table 12.8, Net_{10} scores the lowest total misclassification rates in both periods. This is followed by Net_0, DA, logit, ID3, 3NN and 1NN. The relative ranking remains virtually the same in both periods. The only difference is between DA and Net_0, which have their

Table 12.8
Misclassification Rates Estimated Using the Jackknife Method

| | Percentage (%) | | | | | |
| | One-year Prior | | | Two-year Prior | | |
Model	I	II	T	I	II	T
DA	17.3	11.1	(14.2)	17.3	13.9	(15.6)
Logit	12.3	17.3	(14.8)	15.2	20.3	(17.7)
1NN	17.3	38.3	(27.8)	31.6	29.1	(30.4)
3NN	18.5	30.9	(24.7)	19.0	26.6	(22.8)
ID3	21.0	17.3	(19.2)	20.3	25.3	(22.8)
Net_0	8.6	13.5	(11.1)	8.9	25.3	(17.1)
Net_{10}	8.6	12.3	(10.5)	8.9	12.7	(10.8)

positions interchanged. The performance of logit is not as superior as in the holdout sample test. It ranks in the fourth place behind Net_{10}, Net_0, and DA. 1NN and 3NN remain the worst classifiers after ID3 in both periods. When compared between predictive periods, all methods except 3NN have lower total misclassification rates in the one-year period than in the two-year period. This is consistent with our intuition.

Misclassification rates estimated from both validation tests are compared. The proportions between type I and type II errors are less extreme in the jackknife test. For example, in the two-year period, the ratio of type I and type II errors changed from 6 to 1.24 in DA and from 0.13 to 1 in Net_{10}. Holdout test overestimates the total misclassification rates of 1NN, 3NN, logit (one-year), and Net_0 (two-year) and underestimate that of DA, Net_{10}, logit (two-year), and Net_0 (one-year). The results of ID3 are quite consistent, although its type I and type II error compositions are very different in the two tests. Furthermore, the absolute difference between total misclassification rates estimated by the two tests are relatively small for most methods.

Because the misclassification rates estimated by the jackknife method have been shown to be unbiased, there is evidence that the neural net approach provides better predictive accuracy than DA methods. We have also eliminated the effects of premature termination of the learning procedure by allowing each net in the jackknife method to run until convergence. As shown in both tests, a net with no hidden unit has a performance similar to a DA, but the incorporation of a layer of hidden units improves considerably its predictive accuracy. This can best be explained by viewing the partitioning structure induced by a DA method. Each method divides the variable space into disjointed partitions in very different ways. For instance, a DA model cuts the space into two partitions with a hyperplane, whereas an ID3 model divides the space into a number of recursive rectangular partitions. The sensitivity of a partitioning structure to the distribution of the training sample varies among methods, resulting in very different misclassification rates. Net_{10}, with the lowest total misclassification rates, offers a structure that best matches the training examples. In fact, it has been shown that a three-layer net can be used as a universal approximate for any continuous function in a multidimensional space. Geometrically, a network is capable of generating nonlinear partitioning structures that very often fit better a given training sample than other DA methods.

DISCUSSION

The neural-net approach presented in this paper offers an alternative to existing bankruptcy prediction models. Empirical results show that neural nets offer better predictive accuracy than DA, logit, kNN and ID3. The original back-propagation algorithm is modified to include prior probabilities and misclassification costs. Depending on the classification tasks, the tradeoff between type I and type II errors may be very different and needs to be accounted for. It is essential to allow an assessor to state his own preference in deciding such a tradeoff. For example, the error of misclassifying a failed bank to the nonfailed group (type I error) is generally accepted to be more severe than the other way. The original function E is generalized to E_w by multiplying each error term by Z_i. It is worthwhile to note that minimizing E_w is not equivalent to minimizing the expected misclassification cost. Although the results in Tables 12.2–12.5 show that the nets do behave in this direction and outperform linear classifiers in minimizing resubstitution risks, more empirical studies are needed to validate this result.

Our comparison is based on a training set with an equal proportion of failed and nonfailed banks. In many cases, the number of defaults constitutes only a small portion of the whole population. The matching process may introduce biases to the model. To avoid this, the entire population should be used as the training set. There are many application domains (for example, handwritten character recognition) for which a neural net is an appropriate choice for identifying a single group from a large set of alternatives. It has been proved that a net with a hidden layer can compute any Boolean function with k variables.[42] It is therefore possible to identify a group out of a total of 2^k cases. As illustrated in the XOR example, this is not possible for a linear DA model.

In terms of explanatory capability, it has been shown that the coefficients of a linear discriminant function convey little information about the relative importance of individual variables. Unlike logit analysis, there is no rigorous statistical test on the significance of individual coefficients. The same criticism is also applicable to kNN and neural nets, the results of which are difficult to interpret. On the other hand, the symbolic approach of ID3 sheds some light on the importance of individual variables. A variable is selected as the splitting variable when it can partition a set of examples into the most homogeneous subgroups. Homogeneity is measured by the weighted entropy of the result subgroups. For example, in Figure 12.2a, the root node nonln (nonln > 0.036 ?) correctly identifies 93.22 percent of the nonfailed banks and 76.27 percent of the failed banks, and, in Figure 12.2b, the root node rtoas (rtoas > 0.056 ?) accounts for 91.5 percent of the nonfailed banks and 54.32 percent of the failed banks.

Dimension reduction is another problem associated with existing DA techniques. West[27] extended the logit approach by augmenting it with factor analysis. The factor-logistic method reduces the number of dimensions by transforming the space of initial variables into one composed of important factors that account for a large portion of the variance (for example, 90 percent). Observations are described by their factor scores in the new factor space. The factor scores are then put into a logistic regression model with a dichotomy dependent variable. This combined factor-logistic approach has proven effective in predicting bank bankruptcy; however, the meaning of each factor is subject to interpretation, and the actual number of variables for describing each observation remains the same. In the ID3 approach, Quinlan[17] showed that minimizing the entropy of a decision tree is equivalent to minimizing the expected number of tests to make a decision. Thus, the ID3 method has a built-in mechanism to reduce the dimensions of the variable space. For example, in Figures 12.2a and 12.2b, the number of variables is reduced by 66.67 percent and 57.89 percent in the one-year and two-year periods, respectively. In feedforward nets, the number of dimensions equals the number of input units.

A neural net allows adaptive adjustment to the predictive model as new examples become available. This is an attractive property, especially when the underlying group distributions are changing. Statistical methods assume old and new examples are equally valid, and the entire training set is used to construct a new model. The batch update is necessary if the distributions do not change. However, in situations where the new sample is drawn from a new distribution, retaining the old examples may result in a predictive model with low accuracy. An important feature of a neural net is that past information is not ignored; instead, its importance will be reduced (or strengthened) incrementally as new examples are fed into the network. In actual implementation, a sliding window scheme is needed to retain part of the old sample and combine it with the new sample to create a new training set. The exact proportion of old sample to be retained depends on the stability of the distribution and the level of noise in the sample.

Although the study reported here is far from sufficient to generate any conclusive statements about the applicability of neural nets in general, it does provide some insights into their potentials and limitations. Based on the comparison reported above, the neural net approach offers a comparative alternative to classification techniques, especially under the following conditions:

1. Multimodal distribution: the nonlinear discriminant function represented by a neural net provides a better approximation of the sample distribution, especially when the latter is multimodal. Many classification tasks have been reported to have a nonlinear relationship between variables. Whitred and Zimmer[43] suggest that loan officers may have a higher prediction accuracy than linear DA models because of their ability to relate variables and loan outcome in a nonlinear manner. In another experiment conducted by Shepanski,[44] it was reported that human judgments are better approximated by a nonlinear function.

2. Adaptive model adjustment: The ability to adaptively adjust the model is a virtue of a neural net. This allows the model to respond swiftly to changes in the real world.

3. Robustness: The network does not assume any probability distribution or equal dispersion. There is also no rigid restriction on the use of input/output functions other than that they be continuous and differentiable.

Despite the successful applications of neural nets reported recently, their usage is still rather ad hoc. Some of their limitations are summarized here.

Network Topology

There is no formal method to derive a network configuration for a given classification task. Although it was shown that only one hidden layer is enough to approximate any continuous functions,[45,46,47] the number of hidden units can be arbitrarily large. In addition, there is a possibility of overfitting the network. This problem arises when the number of hidden units is relatively large with respect to the size of the training sample.[48] Unless the whole population is used for training, one has to be cautious in selecting the number of hidden units in order to avoid this problem. Currently, deciding how many hidden units to use is part of the modeling process itself.

Computational Efficiency

Training a neural net demands more computation time than the other methods. In the current study, computation time ranges from a few minutes to 3 hours on an EMX minicomputer. One strategy we have employed to reduce computation time is to allocate five different sets of weights and to restrict each run to an acceptable number of iterations. It seems to be an effective strategy in most cases, but inconsistent results are generated occasionally. All statistical methods took at most half a minute on an IBM 3081 mainframe. ID3 required on average 8 minutes on a Mac II microcomputer.

Explanatory Capability

The discriminant capability of a neural net is difficult to express in symbolic form. This may not be a serious drawback if one is concerned primarily with predictive accuracy. However, a neural net is limited if one wants to test the significance of individual inputs. There is no formal method to derive the relative importance of an input from the weights of a neural net.

Continuous improvements are being made in all these directions. Recently, Miller, Todd and Hedge[49] suggested applying genetic algorithms to the design of network configurations. Genetic algorithms adopt an evolutionary approach in which a pool of networks, called the *population*, is continuously being modified by using genetic operators such as crossover and mutation.[50] Each synthesized network, which corresponds to a possible configuration, is evaluated using the back-propagation algorithm. Genetic algorithms have a built-in bias towards retaining and combining good configurations in the next generation. The evolutionary nature of the algorithm enables the search for good configurations to proceed in a parallel fashion, thus reducing the possibility of trapping in local optimal configuration.

The problem of lengthy computation time is attributed to our implementation, which is basically a simulation that runs on a serial machine. The intrinsic parallel processing capability of a network is not exploited in our study. Progress is underway to implement neural nets on silicon, which will significantly reduce computation time.[51]

Heuristics have been developed to give the modeler some insights into the relative importance of variables with respect to a single example. A method using the partial derivative of the error function has been suggested in Tam and Kiang.[8] In addition, the limited explanatory capability of neural nets can be explained by linking them with fuzzy logic. The latter provides a means of combining symbolic and numeric computations in inference processing. The linkage between neural nets and symbolic reasoning can be established through the membership function of fuzzy logic. The function measures the degree of possibility of a concept as related to a numeric quantity. A neural net can be used to synthesize a membership function by training it with instances of the relation. In our present case, a neural net may represent the membership function of the concept "high likelihood of failure." Such a representation can be easily combined with other symbolic conditions appearing in the rules of an expert system. By using neural nets as frontends in rules definition, one can take advantage of the explanatory capability of expert systems as well as the subsymbolic computational capability offered by neural nets.[52]

CONCLUSION

We have presented a new approach to bank bankruptcy prediction using neural nets. We believe neural nets can be extended to other managerial applications, particularly those involving classification. Furthermore, a neural net may supplement a rule-based expert system in real-time applications. While rule-based expert systems are satisfactory for off-line processing, a neural net-based system offers on-line capabilities. More work needs to be done in prototype development, and actual applications need to be empirically tested before the full potential of neural nets can be asserted.[53]

APPENDIX

Table A12.1
Descriptive Statistics of Variables (One-Year Ahead)

Name	Nonfailed		Failed	
	Mean	St. Dev.	Mean	St. Dev.
capas	10.76	5.45	5.53	2.98
agfas	0.09	0.15	0.09	0.15
comas	0.29	0.16	0.35	0.16
indas	0.28	0.16	0.26	0.16
resas	0.36	0.16	0.34	0.16
pasln	0.01	0.01	0.05	0.07
nonln	0.01	0.02	0.08	0.06
losln	1.80	1.92	5.31	3.71
netln	1.45	1.72	4.18	3.51
rtoas	−0.14	2.10	−3.19	2.79
intdp	0.06	0.01	0.07	0.01
expas	0.09	0.02	0.12	0.02
incas	0.00	0.02	−0.04	0.03
infln	0.12	0.03	0.13	0.02
incex	1.11	0.19	1.00	0.17
curas	0.27	0.12	0.20	0.11
govas	0.28	0.15	0.17	0.10
llnas	0.53	0.14	0.67	0.11
llndp	0.61	0.16	0.71	0.18

Table A12.2

Descriptive Statistics of Variables (Two-Years Ahead)

Name	Nonfailed		Failed	
	Mean	St. Dev.	Mean	St. Dev.
capas	9.87	4.03	7.87	2.54
agfas	0.08	0.14	0.10	0.16
comas	0.30	0.14	0.36	0.14
indas	0.28	0.15	0.25	0.14
resas	0.35	0.15	0.31	0.15
pasln	0.01	0.01	0.02	0.03
nonln	0.01	0.01	0.04	0.05
losln	1.16	1.15	3.01	2.99
netln	0.81	1.04	2.51	2.78
rtoas	0.69	1.44	−1.44	2.51
intdp	0.06	0.01	0.07	0.01
expas	0.09	0.01	0.11	0.02
incas	0.01	0.01	−0.01	0.03
infln	0.12	0.02	0.13	0.02
incex	1.16	0.12	1.05	0.15
curas	0.25	0.13	0.21	0.09
govas	0.28	0.15	0.17	0.09
llnas	0.55	0.14	0.66	0.10
llndp	0.62	0.17	0.73	0.11

ENDNOTES

1. R. A. Fisher, "The Use of Multiple Measurements in Taxonomic Problems," *Ann. Eugenics*, 7, 1936, pp. 179–188.

2. M. Minsky and S. Papert, *Perceptrons*, (Cambridge, MA: MIT Press, 1969).

3. XOR is a binary function that returns true when only one of its inputs is true, and false otherwise.

4. D. E. Rumelhart, G. Hinton, and R. Williams, "Learning Representation by Back-Propagating Errors," *Nature*, 323, 9, 1986, pp. 533–536.

5. D. E. Rumelhart, J. McClelland, and the PDP Research Group (Eds.), *Parallel Distributed Processing: Explorations in the Microstructure of Cognition*, (Bradford Books, 1986).

6. D. L. Waltz, "Applications of the Connection Machine," *IEEE Computer*, January 1987, pp. 85–97.

7. L. W. Tucker and G. Robertson, "Architecture and Applications of the Connection Machine," *IEEE Computer*, August 1988, pp. 26–38.

8. K. Y. Tam and M. Kiang, "Predicting Bank Failures: A Neural Network Approach," *Applied Artificial Intelligence*, 4, 4, 1990, pp. 265–282.

9. P. A. Lachenbruch, "An Almost Unbiased Method of Obtaining Confidence Intervals for the Probability of Misclassification in Discriminant Analysis," *Biometrics*, December 1967, pp. 639–645.

10. E. B. Deakin, "Distributions of Financial Accounting Ratios: Some Empirical Evidence," *Accounting Review*, January 1976, pp. 90–96.

11. E. L. Altman, R. A. Eisenbeis, and J. Sinkey, *Applications of Classification Techniques in Business, Banking, and Finance* (Greenwich, CT: JAI Press, 1981).

12. P. A. Lachenbruch, C. Sneeringer and L. Revo, "Robustness of the Linear and Quadratic Discriminant Function to Certain Type of Non-Normality," *Commun. Statistics*, 1, 1, 1973, pp. 39–56.

13. S. J. Press and S. Wilson, "Choosing between Logistic Regression and Discriminant Analysis," *Journal American Statistical Association*, 73, 1978, pp. 699–705.

14. F. E. Harrell and K. L. Lee, "A Comparison of the Discrimination of Discriminant Analysis and Logistic Regression under Multivariate Normality," in *Biostatistics: Statistics in Biomedical, Public Health, and Environmental Sciences*, (P. K. Sen, Ed.), (Amsterdam, North Holland, 1985).

15. J. R. Quinlan, "Discovering Rules by Induction from Large Collection of Examples," in *Expert Systems in the Micro Electronic Age*, (D. Michie, Ed.), (Edinburgh: Edinburgh University Press, 1979).

16. J. R. Quinlan, "Learning Efficient Classification Procedures and Their Applications to Chess End Games," in *Machine Learning: An Artificial Intelligence Approach*, Vol. I., (R. S. Michalski, J. Carbonell,

and T. Mitchell, Eds.) (Palo Alto, CA: Tioga Publishing Company, 1983).

17. J. R. Quinlan, "Induction of Decision Trees," *Machine Learning*, 1, 1986, pp. 81–106.

18. C. Carter and J. Catlett, "Assessing Credit Card Applications Using Machine Learning," *IEEE Expert*, Fall 1987, pp. 71–79.

19. W. F. Messier and J. Hansen, "Inducing Rules for Expert System Development: An Example Using Default and Bankruptcy Data," *Management Sci.*, 34, 12, 1988, pp. 1403–1415.

20. K. Y. Tam, M. Kiang, and R. Chi, "Inducing Stock Screening Rules for Portfolio Construction," *Journal Operational Research Society*, 49, 9, pp. 747–757.

21. H. Frydman, E. Altman, and D. Kao, "Introducing Recursive Partitioning for Financial Classification: The Case of Financial Distress," *Journal Finance*, 40, 1, 1985, pp. 269–291.

22. D. S. Broomhead and D. Lowe, "Multivariate Functional Interpolation and Adaptive Networks," *Complex Systems*, 2, 1988, pp. 321–355.

23. J. Moody and C. Darken, "Fast Learning in Networks of Locally-Tuned Processing Units," *Neural Computing*, 1, 2, 1989, pp. 281–294.

24. G. E. Hinton, "Connectionist Learning Procedures," *Artificial Intelligence*, 40, 1989, pp. 185–234.

25. F. Rosenblatt, *Principle of Neurodynamics*, (New York: Spartan, 1962).

26. Similar early warning systems have been operated in the Office of Comptroller of the Currency (OCC) and the Federal Reserve System (Fed).

27. R. G. West, "A Factor-Analytic Approach to Bank Condition," *Journal Banking and Finance*, 9, 2, 1985, pp. 253–266.

28. P. A. Meyer and H. Pifer, "Prediction of Bank Failures," *Journal Finance*, 25, September 1970, pp. 853–868.

29. E. L. Altman, "Financial Ratios, Discriminant Analysis and the Prediction of Corporate Bankruptcy," *Journal Finance*, 23, 3, 1968, pp. 589–609.

30. J. F. Sinkey, "A Multivariate Statistical Analysis of the Characteristics of Problem Banks," *Journal Finance*, 30, 1, 1975, pp. 21–36.

31. A. M. Santomero and J. Vinso, "Estimating the Probability of Failure for Commercial Banks and the Banking System," *Journal Banking and Finance*, 1, 2, 1977, pp. 185–205.

32. G. A. Hanweck, "Predicting Bank Failures," *Research Papers in Banking and Financial Economics*, Financial Studies Section, Board of Governors of the Federal Research System, Washington, DC, 1977.

33. D. Martin, "Early Warning of Bank Failure, A Logit Regression Approach," *Journal Banking and Finance*, 1, 3, 1977, pp. 249–276.

34. L. Korobow and D. Stuhr, "Performance Measurement of Early Warning Models," *Journal Banking and Finance*, 9, 1985, pp. 267–273.

35. R. A. Eisenbeis, "Pitfalls in the Application of Discriminant Analysis in Business, Finance, and Economics," *Journal Finance*, 32, 3, 1977, pp. 875–900.

36. *Bank of Texas*, Vols. 1–3, Sheshunoff Information Services Inc. 1987.

37. Federal Deposit Insurance Corporation, 1987 Annual Report.

38. Significance level of the test is 5 percent.

39. Coefficients of the logit model were estimated using SAS LOGIT procedure.

40. The 1NN and 3NN models were constructed using the SAS NEIGHBOR procedure.

41. Usually, values slightly different from zero are used as initial weights to break up the symmetry.

42. J. Denker, D. Schwartz, B. Wittner, S. Solla, R. Howard, L. Jackal and J. Hopfield, "Large Automatic Learning, Rule Extraction and Generalization," *Complex Systems*, 1, 1987, pp. 877–922.

43. G. Whitred and I. Zimmer, "The Implications of Distress Prediction Models for Corporate Lending," *Accounting and Finance*, 25, 1985, pp. 1–13.

44. A. Shepanski, "Tests of Theories of Information Processing Behavior in Credit Judgement," *Accounting Review*, 58, 1983, pp. 581–599.

45. G. Cybenko, "Approximation by Superpositions of a Sigmoidal Function," *Math, Control, Signals, and Systems,* 2, 1989, pp. 303–314.

46. K. Funahashi, "On the Approximate Realization of Continuous Mappings by Neural Networks," *Neural Networks,* 2, 1989, pp. 183–192.

47. K. Hornik, M. Stinchcombe, and H. White, "Multilayer Feedforward Networks are Universal Approximators," *Neural Networks,* 2, 1989, pp. 359–366.

48. E. B. Baum and D. Haussler, "What Size Net Gives Valid Generalization?," *Neural Comput.,* 1, 1989, pp. 151–160.

49. G. F. Miller, P. Todd, and S. Hedge, "Designing Neural Networks Using Genetic Algorithms," *Proceedings of the Third International Conference on Genetic Algorithms,* Morgan Kaufmann, Palo Alto, CA, 1989, pp. 379–384.

50. D. E. Goldberg, *Genetic Algorithms in Search, Optimization, and Machine Learning* (Reading, MA: Addison-Wesley, 1989).

51. C. A. Mead, *Analog VLSI and Neural Systems,* (Reading, MA: Addison-Wesley, 1988).

52. B. Kosko, *Neural Networks and Fuzzy Systems* (Englewood Cliffs, NJ: Prentice-Hall, 1990).

53. The authors are grateful for the comments and suggestions of the associate editor and the four anonymous reviewers. They would like to thank Willliam Cooper and Patrick Brockett for their valuable comments on an early draft of this chapter.

13

NEURAL NETWORKS: A NEW TOOL FOR PREDICTING THRIFT FAILURES

Linda M. Salchenberger, E. Mine Cinar, and Nicholas A. Lash

INTRODUCTION

Recently, there has been considerable interest in the development of artificial neural networks (ANNs) for solving a variety of problems. Neural networks, which are capable of learning relationships from data, represent a class of robust, nonlinear models inspired by the neural architecture of the brain. Theoretical advances, as well as hardware and software innovations, have overcome past deficiencies in implementing machine learning and made neural network methods available to a

This article originally appeared in *Decision Sciences*, Vol. 23, No. 4, July/August, 1992, pp. 899–916. Reprinted with permission.

wide variety of disciplines. Financial applications that require pattern matching, classification, and prediction such as corporate bond rating,[1] credit evaluation, and underwriting[2] have proven to be excellent candidates for this new technology.

In this chapter, we present a neural network developed to predict the probability of failure for savings and loan associations (S&Ls), using the financial variables that signal an institution's deteriorating financial condition. We compare its performance with a logit model, since logit has frequently been used to discriminate between failed and surviving institutions. For all cases examined, the neural network performs as well or better than logit in classifying institutions as failed or nonfailed.

Even a moderate improvement in the ability to correctly classify insolvent institutions represents a significant contribution, given the magnitude of the current crisis in the thrift industry and the enormous costs of resolution.[3] Early identification of financial decline provides the opportunity for close monitoring of the problem institution and the ability to take immediate corrective actions.

The chapter is organized into four major sections. First, a selected group of past studies of thrift failures is presented. This is followed by a discussion of back-propagation neural networks and the relationship of the back-propagation learning to statistics. Next, we present a back-propagation neural network that uses financial data to predict thrift institution failures. Finally, we evaluate the ability of the neural network to predict thrift failures using a logit model as a performance benchmark.

PAST STUDIES OF THRIFT FAILURES

Past studies of thrift institution failures were typically devoted to either building early warning systems or explaining failures. The discriminatory variables included a set of financial ratios, determined from internal call report data and organized into a CAMEL framework. CAMEL is an acronym for the five major classes of financial data: capital adequacy (C), asset quality (A), management efficiency (M), earnings quality (E), and liquidity (L). Capital adequacy, determined largely by the extent of compliance with regulatory capital requirements, is important not only to absorb losses, but also to deter management from taking inordinate risks. Asset quality, measured by the volume and severity of problem loans, is often considered the most critical determinant of an institution's soundness and receives much of the examiners' attention. Other critical factors are the technical competence, leadership ability, and integrity of management. However, assessing management is highly subjective, and difficult to capture directly with specific financial ratios. In empirical studies, management efficiency is often evaluated in terms of the ability to control costs and expenditures.[4] Earnings are judged on the basis of level, trend, stability, and source. The final component refers to liquidity, and is gauged by the institution's liquid assets and ability to tap funding sources.

A review of past studies of thrift institution failures reveals that multiple discriminant analysis, logit, and probit models are frequently developed to classify institutions as failed or surviving. Altman[5] used a quadratic discriminant model to categorize 212 S&Ls as "serious problem," "moderate problem," and "no problem" using data from 1966 through 1973 (Table 13.1). Barth, Brumbaugh, Sauerhaft, and Wang[6] developed a logit model using semiannual data for 318 closed and 588 solvent institutions for the period 1981 through 1985. Logit was also used by Benston[7] in a study of 178 closed and 712 solvent S&Ls for the years 1981 through 1985. An early warning system based on multiple discriminant analysis was developed by Pantalone and Platt[8] for the S&Ls in the Boston district of the Federal Home Loan Bank System. Recently, a robust multivariate procedure, based on the evaluation of statistical outliers, was developed by Booth, Alam, Ahkam, and Osyk[9] to predict savings and loans failures.

Expert systems have also been used to predict bankruptcy in the thrift and other industries, as well. Elmer and Borowski[10] developed a rule-based expert system to compute an index that was a weighted average of measures of capital, asset quality, earnings, and liquidity. A system that incorporates this index performs as well as statistical models in identifying problem institutions 6 months before failure and achieves greater prediction accuracy in identifying problem institutions 12 and 18 months before failure.

A direct comparison of the performance of the statistical predictor models is difficult for a number of reasons. Each study differs with respect to modelling technique, a priori categories, and classification criteria. However, some common results do emerge from an examination of these past studies. First, predicting thrift institution failure is often formulated as a classification problem in which a group of independent variables are used to predict failure. Second, the relationship between failure or nonfailure and the financial variables is frequently

Table 13.1

Financial Variables Found to Be Significant in Selected Studies

Author	Statistical Technique	Significant Financial Ratios
Altman[5]	MDA	Net worth/Total assets (C) Net operating income/Gross operating income (E) Real estate owned/Total assets (A)
Barth et al.[6]	logit	Net worth/Total assets (C) Interest sensitive funds/Total funds (E) Net income/Total assets (E) Loans/Total assets (L) Liquid assets/Total assets (L)
Benston[7]	logit	Net worth/Total assets (C) Net income/Total assets (E) Change in interest and fee income/earning assets (E) Change in interest and depositor's dividends/Earning assets (E)
Pantalone and Pratt[8]	MDA	Net Worth/Total assets (C) Cash and securities/Total savings and short-term borrowing (L) Operating expense/Gross operating income (M)

Note: MDA = multiple discriminant analysis,
   A   = measure of asset quality,
   C   = measure of capital adequacy,
   E   = measure of earnings quality,
   M   = measure of management efficiency,
   L   = measure of liquidity.

assumed to be nonlinear. Finally, the financial predictor variables may be highly correlated. For classification problems in which the dependent variable is a nonlinear function of correlated independent variables, neural networks provide a promising tool. These observations motivated our decision to develop a neural network to discriminate between surviving and failed institutions.

NEURAL NETWORKS

Inspired by studies of the brain and nervous system, neural networks are composed of neurons, or processing elements and connections, organized in layers. These layers can be structured hierarchically, and the first layer is called the input layer, the last layer is the output layer, and the interior layers are called the middle or hidden layers. Feed-forward networks map inputs into outputs with signals flowing in one direction only, from the input layer to the output layer. A two-layer neural network consisting of an input layer and an output layer is shown in Figure 13.1. Each connection between neurons has a numerical weight associated with it, which models the influence of an input cell on an output cell. Positive weights indicate reinforcement; negative weights are associated with inhibition. Connection weights are learned by the network through a training process, as examples from a training set are presented repeatedly to the network.

Figure 13.1

A Two-Layer Neural Network

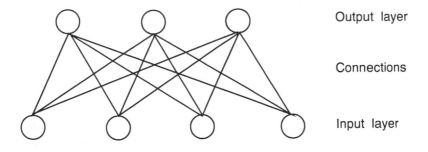

Output layer

Connections

Input layer

Each processing element has an activation level, specified by continuous or discrete values. If the neuron is in the input layer, its activation level is determined in response to input signals received from the
environment. For cells in the middle or output layers, the activation
level is computed as a function of the activation levels on the cells
connected to it and the associated connection weights. This function is
called the transfer function or activation function and may be a linear
discriminant function (i.e., a positive signal is output if the value of this
function exceeds a threshold level, and 0 otherwise). It may also be a
continuous, nondecreasing function. For example, the sigmoidal (logistic) function

$$f(\theta) = (1 + \exp(-\theta))^{-1} \tag{1}$$

(Figure 13.2) which assigns values between 0 and 1 (or –1 and 1) to
inputs is often used in back-propagation networks.

Figure 13.2

Graph of Sigmoidal Function

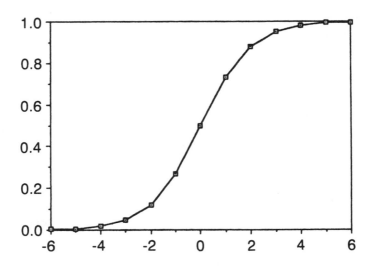

While basically an information processing technology, neural networks differ from traditional modeling techniques in a fundamental way. Parametric statistical models require the developer to specify the nature of the functional relationship between the dependent variable and the independent variables (e.g., linear, logistic). Once an assumption is made about the functional form, optimization techniques are used to determine a set of parameters that minimizes a measure of error. Neural networks with at least one middle layer use the data to develop an internal representation of the relationship between the variables so that a priori assumptions about underlying parameter distributions are not required. As a consequence, better results might be expected with neural networks when the relationship between the variables does not fit the assumed model. Nevertheless, many decisions regarding model parameters and network topology can affect the performance of the network.

Two-layer neural networks do not have the ability to develop internal representations. They map input patterns into similar output patterns. While these networks have proved useful in a variety of applications, they cannot generalize or perform well on patterns that have never been presented.

Neural networks with hidden layers have the ability to develop internal representations. The middle layer nodes are often characterized as feature detectors, which combine raw observations into higher order features thus permitting the network to make reasonable generalizations.

A two-layer neural network has an input layer that can be represented by a vector $\mathbf{x} = (x_1, x_2,...,x_n)$ of features and an output layer which can be represented by an output vector $\mathbf{y} = g(\mathbf{x})$. We assume, for the remainder of this discussion, that there is a single output node $y = g(\mathbf{x})$, the connection weights are represented by β_i, $i = 0,...,n$, and we have a linear transfer function. It follows that

$$y = g(\mathbf{x}) = \Sigma \beta_i x_i. \tag{2}$$

Thus, the familiar linear regression model is similar in form to a two-layer neural network that has a linear transfer function.

In the two-layer perceptron model with a linear discriminant transfer function, neurons are not activated until some threshold level θ_0 is reached, that is

$$y = F(\Sigma\beta_i x_i) \tag{3}$$

where $F = 1$ when $\Sigma\beta_i x_i > \theta_0$ and 0 otherwise. Since the transfer function F can be any continuous, nondecreasing function, F can represent a cumulative distribution frequency (cdf). When F is the normal cumulative distribution function, $F(\Sigma\beta_i x_i)$ is the conditional expectation of a Bernoulli random variable generated by a probit model. When F is the logistic cdf, $F(\Sigma\beta_i x_i)$ is the conditional expectation generated by the logistic model.[11] Therefore, in a two-layer neural network, the network output function can be compared to the familiar logit and probit regression models.

We now focus attention on multilayered neural networks. Consider a single middle layer, feed-forward network with a single output cell, k middle layer nodes, and n input nodes. Any middle layer cell receives the weighted sum of all inputs and a bias term and produces an output signal

$$m_j = f(\Sigma\omega_{ij}x_i), \quad j = 1,...,k, \, i = 0,...,n, \tag{4}$$

where f is the transfer function, x_i is the ith signal, w_{ij} is the strength of the connection from the ith input neuron to the jth middle layer cell. The activation levels from the middle-layer cells are transferred to the output layer cells in the same way so that the output cell sees the weighted sum of the outputs of the middle layer cells and produces a signal

$$y = F\left(\sum v_j f\left(\sum w_{ij} x_i\right)\right) = g(x,\theta) \tag{5}$$

where x is the vector of inputs, and θ is the vector of network weights. We can interpret (5) as a nonlinear regression function that represents a single middle-layer, feed-forward neural network.

The ability of multilayer networks to represent nonlinear models has been established through an application of an existence theorem proved by Kolmogorov.[12,13] This theorem has been used to show that, for any feed-forward network with a single middle layer, there exists a network output function

$$g(x,\theta) = \Sigma v_j f(\Sigma w_{ij}x_i) \tag{6}$$

that can provide an accurate approximation to any function of $(x_1, x_2,...,x_n)$, if the inputs are scaled to be within [0.1]. The number of middle units required by the theorem is $2n + 1$ where n is the number of input nodes, although representations with fewer middle nodes may also exist.[14] The implication of the Kolmogorov theorem is that classification problems which are not linearly separable can be solved with multi-layered neural networks.

It is interesting to note that research in neural networks was abandoned for almost 20 years when it was discovered that only linearly separable problems could be solved with two-layer networks. The linear perceptron network, a two-layer network using a linear threshold response function, was proposed by Rosenblatt[15] in the 1950s. While some theoretical limitations of the linear perceptron, including the requirement that data points be linearly separable for perfect classification, were recognized by Rosenblatt, a more complete analysis of its computational limitations was developed by Minsky and Papert.[16] They made extensive use of geometrical arguments to prove that properties like connectedness and parity could not be computed with perceptrons.[17]

Back-Propagation Networks and Learning Rules

Back-propagation is an approach to supervised network learning that permits weights to be learned from experience, based on empirical observations on the object of interest. Training consists of repeatedly presenting the network with examples that can be viewed as input/output vectors. Supervised learning methods require that for each input pattern, an appropriate response or classification of the output be presented to the network during training. These networks cannot learn from an input pattern for which no correct response has been provided.

In an approach to learning that does not require a teacher, no correct response is provided. These unsupervised learning methods take advantage of natural groupings that appear within the data by using a variety of approaches to learning. In the simplest form of competitive learning, an output node with the greatest net input is denoted winner and its weights are updated, using a learning rule.[18] Adaptive resonance theory (ART) overcomes some of the limitations and instability associated with competitive learning.[19] In self-organizing feature maps, the concept of neighbor is added to competitive learning and a group of associated nodes responds to an input pattern.[20]

Although the term *back-propagation* can be used to refer to the dynamic feedback of errors propagated backward through a network to adjust the weights, it is also commonly used to describe learning by the generalized delta rule. Rumelhart, Hinton, and Williams[21] described the generalized delta rule with the following three steps. First, the derivative of the square error with respect to the outputs and the target values of the network is computed. The chain rule is applied in the second step to calculate the derivatives of error with respect to outputs and weights within the network. Finally, the weights are updated using

$$\theta_t = \theta_{t-1} + \alpha \nabla f(X_t, \theta_{t-1})(Y_t - f(X_t, \theta_{t-1})) \tag{7}$$

$$t = 1, 2, ...,$$

where α is the learning rate, Y_t is the target, θ_0 is a random set of small initial weights, and ∇f is the gradient (vector of partial derivatives with respect to the weights θ). Thus, the learning process updates the current set of weights with a function of the difference between the system's response to an input vector and the associated correct category. The steepest descent algorithm is used in which changes are made in the direction of the gradient (i.e., direction of the largest change in the error).

Better results may be achieved by replacing the steepest descent algorithms with response surface methods. Response surface optimization does not require any functional form assumption, in contrast to the specification function required in current methods and thus represents a future research area that may improve neural network performance.

Under appropriate conditions, the learning rule given in (7) yields weights converging to a vector θ^* that solves

$$E[\nabla f(X_t, \theta)(Y_t - f(X_t, \theta)] = 0 \tag{8}$$

where the mathematical expectation is taken with respect to the joint distribution of the random variables X_t, Y_t. A solution θ^* to this equation satisfies the necessary conditions for a local solution to the least squares problem

$$\min_\theta E\left[(Y_t - f(X_t, \theta))^2\right] \tag{9}$$

A set of weights that solves (7) yields a network output that is mean square optimal for Y_t; it minimizes expected squared error as a prediction for Y_t. Also, the weights θ^* guarantee a network that is a mean square optimal approximation to the conditional expectation $E(Y_t \mid X_t)$. Thus, back-propagation learning is an approach for which convergence to a local optimal set of weights is guaranteed.[14]

The application of the generalized delta rule involves a forward pass through the network during which errors are accumulated by comparing actual outputs with the targets. This is followed by a backward pass during which adjustments in connections weights are made based on the errors, using a recursive rule such as (7).

Back-propagation is a gradient descent method that minimizes the mean squared error of the system by moving down the gradient of the error curve. The error surface is multidimensional and may contain many local minima. As a result, training the network often requires experimentation with starting position, adjusting the weights during training, and modifying various learning parameters. In particular, the learning rate α is usually adjusted downward during training and a momentum term may be increased to avoid getting stuck in local optima.

A NEURAL NETWORK TO PREDICT THRIFT INSTITUTION FAILURES

A back-propagation neural network that forecasts the probability of failure of thrift institutions has been developed using five financial variables as inputs. Back-propagation learning was selected because it has been successfully used to solve many pattern recognition and classification problems.

Selection of Variables

In past studies, the usual procedure was to select a rather large group of independent variables and reduce that to a smaller group of statistically significant variables. We wished to see how well the neural network would perform, when measured against the best logit model we could formulate. To reduce the dimensionality of the model, we experimented with 29 variables (Table 13.2), and performed stepwise regression that resulted in the identification of five variables. Each vari-

Table 13.2

Financial Ratios Tested

Capital	GNWTA*	GAAP net worth/Total assets
	ESTA	Earned surplus/Total assets
	RAPTA	RAP net worth/Total assets
Assets	RETA*	Repossessed assets/Total assets
	RLTA	High risk loans/Total assets
	REOTA	Real estate owned/Total assets
	ORATA	Other risky assets/Total assets
	TLS	Total loans/Savings
	ITA	Direct investments/Total assets
Management	NIGI*	Net income/Gross income
	TEOI	Total operating income/Other income
	OETA	Other expenses/Total assets
	OHAOI	Overhead/Adjusted operating income
Earnings	NITA*	Net income/Total assets
	NIM	Net interest margin
	ROA	Return on assets
Liquidity	CSTA*	Cash+securities/Total assets
	VLTA	Volatile liabilities/Total assets
	LATA	Liquid assets/Total assets
	ADRAP	FHLBB advances/RAP net worth
	ADGAP	FHLBB advances/GAAP net worth
	OBMTF	Other borrowed money/Total funds
	CSSB	Cash+securities/Savings + borrowed money
	BDS	Brokered deposits/Savings
	ADTA	FHLBB advances/Total assets
	ISFTF	Interest-sensitive funds/Total funds
	BFTA	Borrowed funds/Total assets
	IBLEA	Interest-bearing liabilities/Earning assets
Size	LOGTA	Log total assets

Note: GAAP = generally accepted accounting principles,
       Rap = regulatory approved principles.
*Used in results reported in Tables 13.3 through 13.5.

able selected represents one of the CAMEL categories. Although this is a rather small set of variables, we obtained the best results using logit with this group and consequently developed our models with these variables.

The predictor variables representing the categories of capital adequacy, asset quality, management efficiency, earnings, and liquidity were: GNWTA (GAAP net worth/Total assets), RATA (Repossessed assets/Total assets), NIGI (Net income/Gross income), NITA (Net income/Total assets), and CSTA (Cash securities/Total assets), respectively.

Since regulators use RAP (Regulatory Accounting Principles) net worth to close institutions, we experimented with models utilizing both GNWTA (GAAP net worth/Total assets) and RAPTA (RAP net worth/Total assets) as measures of capital adequacy. These variables were highly correlated for all our data sets and the best prediction rates on the training set were obtained with GNWTA.

The Data Set and Sampling Techniques

The data set consists of financial data on 3,479 S&Ls for the period January 1986 to December 1987. The data are taken from Federal Home Loan Bank Board quarterly tapes. The training sets, which were used to generate the logit model and to provide examples to the neural network during its training process, were developed from call report data for June 1986. For the first neural network and logit models, the 100 failures from January 1986 to December 1987 were matched with 100 nonfailed S&Ls, based on geographic location and value of total assets. For each failure, all the surviving institutions located in the same state were identified. Next, the absolute percentage differences in asset size between each failed institution and the survivors in the state were computed. These were ranked, and those that most closely matched the asset size of the failure were included in the appropriate sample.

For testing the predictive capabilities of logit and the neural network, a second sample consisting of call report data for each failed institution 6, 12, and 18 months prior to failure was used. Data were available for 58 failed and 58 surviving institutions 6 months prior to failure, 47 failed and 47 surviving institutions 12 months prior to failure, and 24 failed and 24 surviving institutions 18 months prior to failure.

A third sample was also tested, in which 75 failures were matched with 329 nonfailed institutions. Due to mergers and regulatory actions, data were available for the two-year period for only 75 of the 100 failures. The reasons for diluting this sample with surviving institutions were to develop a larger sample that more closely resembles the true population, and to test the robustness of our models with respect to sampling rates.

The Development of the Neural Network

The first step in the development of a neural network model is to select an appropriate neural network paradigm by matching the application requirements with the paradigm capabilities. The application is heteroassociative (i.e., it requires mapping one set of patterns onto a different set). Supervised learning was used since the network would be trained using examples that included the result. For this application, a single middle-layer, feed-forward, back-propagation neural network consisting of five input nodes, three middle-layer nodes, and one output node was developed (Figure 13.3). The input nodes represent the financial ratios selected, which measure capital adequacy (C), asset quality (A), management efficiency (M), earnings (E), and liability (L), and the output node is interpreted as the probability that an institution was classified as failed or surviving.

After experimentation with two middle layers did not result in better prediction rates, a single middle layer was adopted. This was consistent with other results with classification problems that demonstrated no improvement with more than one middle layer.[1,2]

Determining the proper number of nodes for the middle layer is more art than science, and experimentation and heuristics assisted in making this choice. Our initial network was constructed with three nodes in the middle layer, based on a rule of thumb which suggests that the number of nodes in the middle layer should be 75 percent of the number of nodes in the input layer. Other models using four and five nodes in the middle layer were also tested. Generally speaking, too many nodes in the middle layer, and hence, too many connections, produce a neural network that memorizes the input data and lacks the ability to generalize. Therefore, increasing the number of nodes in the middle layer will improve the network's ability to classify institutions

Figure 13.3

Neural Network for Predicting Thrift Failures

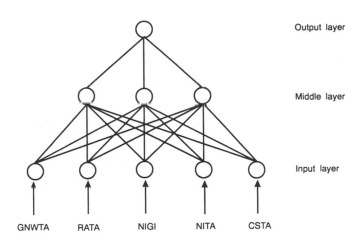

in the training set, but degrade its ability to classify institutions outside the training set. This proved to be true for our application.

The required output layer in this model consists of a single node, which would be interpreted as a classification node, indicating insolvency or solvency of the institution. Initially, we set a threshold of .5 (i.e., if the output value is greater than .5, failure is predicted, otherwise the institution is classified as surviving). We also used a threshold of .2 to test the sensitivity of the network to changes in this value.

The generalized delta rule was used with the back-propagation of error to transfer values from internal nodes. (For a more detailed explanation of back-propagation learning and the generalized delta rule, see Rumelhart and McClelland.)[22] The sigmoidal function is the activation function specified in this neural network and is used to adjust weights associated with each input node. This is the same transformation employed in logit analysis in which the dependent variable is assumed to be a logistic function of the independent variables and a constant. This function was the best choice for our application since its steepest slope occurs at .5. Therefore, the result of applying the sigmoidal function to a weighted sum of the independent variables will be greatest at the midpoint, and the transfer function will have less effect when an output transferred from the input layer is close to the extreme values (Figure 13.2).

The network was implemented using the software package Neural-Works Explorer running on a 386-based microcomputer with a math coprocessor. NeuralWorks Explorer, developed by NeuralWare, Inc. was selected because it can be used to implement over a dozen network paradigms.[23] It allows the user to easily alter learning parameters during training and to view the weights and output values associated with trained networks. Automatic scaling of input parameters and randomization of the training set reduce the development effort. The major limitation encountered when using NeuralWorks Explorer for this application was its inability to support the numerous experiments required to find a satisfactory combination of network architecture and set of learning parameters.

Training the Neural Network

Supervised learning was conducted with training sets consisting of five CAMEL ratios and the corresponding result (failure/surviving) for each S&L. For the input nodes in which the data were not in ratio form, the values were scaled to be within a range of 0 to 1. Automatic scaling was performed by the network software that computes the range of a set of values, and the difference between the input value and the minimum, and then divides the latter by the former. This minimizes the effect of magnitude among the inputs and increases the effectiveness of the learning algorithm. The selection of the examples for the training set focused on quality and the degree to which the data set represented the population. The size of the training set is important since a larger training set may take longer to process computationally, but it may accelerate the rate of learning and reduce the number of iterations required for convergence.

All the weights in the fully connected network were randomized before training. The learning rate and momentum were set initially at .9 and .6, respectively, and the learning rate was adjusted downward and the momentum was adjusted upward during training to improve performance. The learning rate is a constant of proportionality (see (7)) which determines the effect of past weight changes on the current direction of movement in the weight space. In back-propagation, it is usually set close to 1.0 for early iterations when larger changes take place as the optimum is approached. The learning rate should be set as high as possible, while avoiding oscillation. A momentum term can be added to the back-propagation learning rule (7), and this value is increased as an optimum is approached. This effectively provides the impetus to help the algorithm avoid becoming lodged in local minima. The NeuralWorks software allows the user to adjust these parameters dynamically, to maximize learning.

The training examples were presented to the network in random order to maximize performance and to minimize the introduction of bias. During each iteration, a training vector is presented to the network, the network error is computed, the error is propagated back through the network, and the weights are updated using this new information. In practice, the number of presentations made before the weights are updated is called the epoch size and is under the control of the user. Convergence was achieved after 40,000 iterations when the network errors remained relatively unchanged for subsequent iterations. In NeuralWorks, the user specifies the number of iterations to be performed, and the training process is stopped when an appropriate measure of network error is achieved. The training process can be interrupted at any point in time, and measures of network error can be displayed to assist the user in determining whether to stop or continue.

RESULTS

The performance of the neural network that was trained using 100 failures and 100 surviving institutions from January 1986 to December 1987 is compared to the logit model. The regression coefficients, significant variables, and the log likelihood function for the logit model are given in Table 13.3. Four of the five variables, representing capital adequacy, asset quality, management efficiency, and earnings quality, are significant at the 1 percent error level, as is the log likelihood ratio. The explanatory variables were checked for linear dependence by examining the correlation matrices. None were found to be linear combinations of any others, and this was confirmed by a principal components anal-

Table 13.3

Logit Results for Matched Sample

Intercept	–.0103
GNWTA	–55.7485*
RETA	28.7573*
NIGI	–1.2828*
NITA	–79.3499*
CSTA	6.4446
Log Likelihood Ratio	–51.000*

*Significant at the 1 percent error level.

ysis. Therefore, multicolinearity does not pose a serious problem for this model with these data.[24,25]

For both the logit and the neural network models, we classify the institutions as failed if the output values exceed a cutoff point. While some previous studies set a cutoff point of .5, this overlooks the fact that the costs associated with a Type I error (misclassifying a failed institution) are usually greater than those with a Type II error.[6] Thus, we present the results for cutoff points of .5 and .2, since lowering the cutoff point reduces the probability of committing a Type I error.

Results with the Matched Sample

In Table 13.4, we report the number of institutions correctly classified by each model and the p-values from the nonparametric test of equality of proportions.[26] The null hypothesis that the proportion of institutions correctly classified by each method is the same is tested using a non-parametric test since the data is categorical. The chi-square test statistic for equality of k proportions is

$$Q = \sum_{j=1}^{k} \frac{(f_j - n_j p)^2}{n_j p(1 - p)}$$

(10)

where p is the proportion of successes, f_j is the observed frequency of success, and n_j is the number of observations.

Table 13.4

Comparison of Logit and the Neural Network January 1986 to December 1987 (Matched Sample)

	All		Failed		Non-failed	
Cutoff=.5	Logit	Neural Network	Logit	Neural Network	Logit	Neural Network
Training Set	187/200 (93.5%)	194/200 (97.0%)	90/100 (90.0%)	96/100 (96.0%)	97/100 (97.0%)	98/100 (98.0%)
		$p=.10*$		$p=.10*$		$p=.60$
Six Months Before Failure	102/116 (87.8%)	107/116 (92.2%)	56/58 (96.6%)	56/58 (96.6%)	46/58 (79.3%)	51/58 (87.9%)
		$p=.25$		$p=1.0$		$p=.20$
Twelve Months Before Failure	79/92 (85.9%)	85/92 (92.4%)	43/46 (93.5%)	44/46 (95.6%)	36/46 (78.3%)	41/46 (89.1%)
		$p=.15$		$p=.99$		$p=.15$
Eighteen Months Before Failure	40/48 (83.3%)	44/48 (91.7%)	18/24 (75.0%)	22/24 (91.7%)	22/24 (91.7%)	22/24 (91.7%)
		$p=.25$		$p=.10*$		$p=1.0$
Cutoff=.2						
Training Set	166/200 (83.0%)	186/200 (92.5%)	95/100 (95.0%)	96/100 (96.0%)	71/100 (71.0%)	90/100 (90.0%)
		$p=.01**$		$p=1.0$		$p=.001**$
Six Months Before Failure	101/116 (87.1%)	104/116 (89.7%)	56/58 (96.6%)	56/58 (96.6%)	45/58 (77.6%)	48/58 (82.8%)
		$p=.60$		$p=1.0$		$p=.5$
Twelve Months Before Failure	79/92 (85.9%)	85/92 (92.4%)	44/46 (95.7%)	45/46 (97.8%)	35/46 (76.1%)	40/46 (87.0%)
		$p=.15$		$p=.60$		$p=.05*$
Eighteen Months Before Failure	41/48 (85.4%)	44/48 (91.7%)	19/24 (79.2%)	22/24 (91.7%)	22/24 (91.7%)	22/24 (91.7%)
		$p=.40$		$p=.25$		$p=1.0$

*Significant difference at the 10 percent level.
**Significant difference at the 5 percent level or less.

For the training set data and cutoff points of .5 and .2, each failed and nonfailed institution correctly classified using logit is also correctly classified by the neural network. In addition, the network commits fewer total classification errors for each cutoff point and the difference is significant at the 10 percent level for a cutoff point of .5. For the 6-, 12-, and 18-month predictions, the number of correct classifications made by the neural network is greater than or equal to those made by logit regardless of the cutoff point. For a cutoff point of .5, significant differences at the 10 percent level were indicated for the predictions made 18 months before failure. There was one institution, a failed S&L, which was correctly classified by logit and incorrectly classified by the neural network.

Differences between the misclassifications for the training set and 18-month forecasts made by the models were observed. Tables were developed to further analyze these misclassifications, with the rows as the misclassified failures and nonfailures made by the logit model and the columns as the misclassifications made by the neural network. We used Cohen's measure of agreement[27] to determine whether the categorizations developed by the models were in agreement. The maximum likelihood estimate of Cohen's K is computed as

$$K = \frac{N \sum x_{ii} - \sum x_{i+} x_{+i}}{N^2 - \sum x_{i+} x_{+i}}$$

where N = total number of observations, x_{ij} is the observed value in the $(i,j)^{\text{th}}$ cell, x_{i+} is the sum of the observed values in row i, and x_{+i} is the sum of the observed values in column i.

Since we observed a large number of cases in which the methods agreed, we computed K for the cases in which the models disagreed and using the asymptotic variance,[27] confidence intervals for K were developed. The 95 percent confidence interval for the true value of K was $(-.7, .25)$ for the training set and $(-.9, .58)$ for the 18-month forecasts. Since a value of 1 would indicate perfect agreement, these results lead to the conclusion that there is significant disagreement between the misclassifications made by the models at the 5 percent error level. When combined with the results of the test of equality of proportions, this shows that, for these two samples, the neural network did provide a better forecast of failures.

For the training set, changing the cutoff point had a greater effect on the number of correct classifications made by logit, because the neural network assigned fewer output values between .2 and .5. For example, when the cutoff point is changed from .5 to .2, logit correctly classifies 5 more failures, but the total number of nonfailures misclassified increases from 3 to 29. In contrast, the number of nonfailures misclassified by the neural network increases from 2 to 10. Changing the cutoff point had less effect on the prediction set for both models; this may be a consequence of the smaller sample sizes.

Results with Diluted Sample

The results of the logit and neural network models which included 75 failed and 329 nonfailed institutions are given in Table 13.5. The coefficients for the logit model, the number of S&Ls correctly classified, and the p-values for the nonparametric test for differences[26] are reported. The variables representing capital adequacy, management efficiency, and earnings quality are statistically significant at the 1 percent level. Logit correctly classifies 54 of 75 failures and the neural network correctly classifies 64 of 75 with this difference significant at the 5 percent level. The 95 percent confidence interval for the value of K are (.23, .55), indicating mild disagreement on misclassification errors. A significant difference is also observed for the classification of the nonfailed institutions when the cutoff is .2. Also, when the cutoff point changes from .5 to .2, the number of failures misclassified by logit is reduced from 21 to 10, and the number of misclassified nonfailures increases from 2 to 21. The number of failures misclassified by neural network is reduced from 11 to 7, and the number of misclassified nonfailures increases from 2 to 10. As with the matched sample, the neural network is less sensitive to reducing the cutoff point. Finally, each S&L correctly classified by logit was also correctly classified by the neural network.

CONCLUSIONS AND SUGGESTIONS FOR FURTHER RESEARCH

In our study, we evaluated the ability of a neural network to predict thrift institution failures by comparing it with the best logit model we could develop with our data. Since, for each data set we examined in

Table 13.5

Comparison of Logit and the Neural Network January 1986 to December 1987 (Diluted Sample)

Correctly Classified S&Ls

Cutoff=.5	All		Failed		Non-failed	
	Logit	Neural Network	Logit	Neural Network	Logit	Neural Network
	381/404	391/404	54/75	64/75	327/329	327/329
	(94.3%)	(96.8%)	(72.0%)	(85.3%)	(99.4%)	(99.4%)
	$p=.10*$		$p=.05**$		$p=1.0$	

Cutoff=.2						
	373/404	387/404	65/75	68/75	308/329	319/329
	(92.3%)	(95.8%)	(86.7%)	(90.7%)	(93.6%)	(96.9%)
	$p=.05**$		$p=.50$		$p=.05**$	

Logit Results	
Intercept	-1.0501**
GNWTA	-49.1956**
RETA	11.5391
NIGI	-1.3257**
NITA	-105.8590**
CSTA	-.1824
Log Likelihood Ratio	-80.6950**

*Significant difference at the 10 percent level.
**Significant difference at the 5 percent level or less.

our study, the neural network has performed as well or better than logit, neural networks may offer a competitive modeling approach for failure prediction. We also observe that, in some cases, when the cutoff point was lowered, the reduction in Type I errors committed was accompanied by greater increases in Type II errors for the logit model than for the neural network. This may be an important result when examiners factor in the cost of committing Type I and Type II errors. An examination of Table 13.5 shows a significant difference between the total number of correct classifications made by the two models when the sample is diluted with healthy institutions, for both cutoff points.

Since the diluted sample more closely resembles the total population of thrift institutions, the neural network may yield more consistent results when used with the data sets available to regulators. Finally, our results are consistent with those obtained in other studies[1,2] in which neural network technology is determined to be a promising tool for classification problems. For this application, the three-layer neural network gains some predictive power over logit, which can be viewed as a two-layer model. While model specifications such as the choice of activation function and learning parameters are required in neural network models, benefits may be derived when there is insufficient information available to make assumptions about population distributions.

Several limitations may restrict the use of neural network models for prediction. There is no formal theory for determining optimal network topology; therefore, decisions such as the appropriate number of layers and middle layer nodes must be determined using experimentation. The development and interpretation of neural network models requires more expertise from the user than traditional statistical models. Training a neural network can be computationally intensive and the results are sensitive to the selection of learning parameters. Poor results can also occur if the wrong activation function is selected. Finally, backpropagation neural network models seem to be most successful when solving pattern recognition and classification problems; more research is required to determine if there are other types of problems that may be good candidates.

The inability of neural networks to provide explanations of how and why conclusions may restrict the use of this modeling technique. This is in contrast to expert systems, which can provide explanations to the user about how inferences are made. One approach used to determine the relative importance of individual input variables is to design a special data set that exaggerates the values of the input variables to be tested. The activation levels of hidden nodes and the output nodes are examined as each observation is processed by the network.[28] Another approach which applies nonlinear statistical methods for misspecified models is under investigation.[14] Finally, some hybrid systems have been developed that include an expert system to provide explanations for the behavior of the neural network.[28]

There are many opportunities for conducting research in this area. Neural networks may be extended to other financial applications, particularly those requiring classification such as credit approval and bond rating. Further investigation into the relationship between the back-propagation network and traditional nonlinear statistical models may yield benefits to both areas of study.

ENDNOTES

1. S. Dutta and S. Shekhar, "Bond-rating: A Non-Conservative Application of Neural Networks," in *Proceedings of the IEEE International Conference on Neural Networks*, 2, 1988, pp. 443–450.

2. E. Collins, S. Ghosh, and C. Scofield, "An Application of a Multiple Neural-Network Learning System to Emulation of Mortgage Underwriting Judgments," *Proceedings of the IEEE International Conference on Neural Networks*, 2, 1988, pp. 459–466.

3. E. J. Kane, *The S&L Insurance Mess: How Did It Happen?* (Washington, D.C.: The Urban Institute, 1989).

4. In some studies of S&Ls, the management component is ignored, resulting in a CAEL framework. See references 5–7, 10.

5. E. L. Altman, "Predicting Performance in the Savings and Loan Industry," *Journal of Monetary Economics*, 1977, pp. 443–466.

6. J. R. Barth, R. D. Brumbaugh, D. Sauerhaft, and G. H. K. Wang, "Thrift Institution Failures: Estimating the Regulator's Closure Rule," in *Research in Financial Services*, ed. G. G. Kaufman (vol. 1), (Greenwich, CT: JAI Press, 1989).

7. G. J. Benston, "An Analysis of the Causes of Savings and Loans Failures," *Monograph Series in Finance and Economics*, 1986, Series 1985 (4).

8. C. Pantalone and M. Platt, "Predicting Failure of Savings and Loan Associations," *AREUEA Journal*, 15(2), 1987, pp. 46–64.

9. D. E. Booth, P. Alam, S. N. Ahkam, and B. Osyk, "A Robust Multivariate Procedure for the Identification of Problem Savings and Loan Institutions," *Decision Sciences*, 20, 1989, pp. 320–333.

10. P. Elmer and D. Borowski, "An Expert System Approach to Financial Analysis: The Case of S&L Bankruptcy," *Financial Management*, 1988, pp. 66–76.

11. G. S. Maddala, *Limited Dependent and Qualitative Variables in Econometrics*, (Cambridge: Cambridge University Press, 1983), pp. 12–41.

12. A. N. Kolmogorov, "On the Representation of Continuous Function of Many Variables by Superposition of Continuous Functions of One Variable and Addition," *Doklady akademii nauk SSSR*, 144, 1957, pp. 679–681.

13. A. N. Kolmogorov, "On the Representation of Continuous Function of Many Variables by Superposition of Continuous Functions of One Variable and Addition," *American Mathematical Society Translation*, 28, 1963, pp. 55–59.

14. H. White, "Some Asymptotic Results for Learning in Single Hidden Layer Feedforward Network Models," *Journal of the American Statistical Association*, 84, 1989, pp. 1003–1013.

15. F. Rosenblatt, "The Perceptron: A Probabilistic Model for Information Storage and Organization in the Brain," *Psychological Review*, 65, 1958, pp. 386–408.

16. M. Minsky and S. Papert, *Perceptrons*, (Cambridge, MA: MIT Press, 1969).

17. For a more complete discussion of the development of the perceptron by Rosenblatt, and the contributions of Minsky and Papert, see Anderson and Rosenfeld.[29]

18. D. E. Rumelhart and D. Zipser, "Feature Discovery by Competitive Learning," *Cognitive Science*, 9, 1985, pp. 75–112.

19. G. Carpenter and S. Grossberg, "ART2: Self-Organization of Stable Category Recognition Codes for Analog Input Patterns," *Applied Optics*, 26, 1987, pp. 4919–4946.

20. T. Kohonen, *Self-Organization and Associate Memory*, (New York: Springer-Verlag, 1988.)

21. D. E. Rumelhart, G. Hinton, and R. Williams, "Learning Internal Representation by Error Propagation," in *Parallel Distributed Processing*, ed. D. E. Rumelhart and J. L. McClelland, (Cambridge, MA: MIT Press, 1986), pp. 318–362.

22. D. E. Rumelhart and J. L. McClelland, *Parallel Distributed Processing*, (Cambridge, MA: MIT Press, 1986).

23. C. C. Klimasauskas, *NeuralWorks*: An Introduction to Neural Computing, (Sewickley, PA: NeuralWare, Inc., 1988).

24. M. D. Intrilligator, *Econometric Models, Techniques, and Applications*, (Englewood Cliffs, NJ: Prentice-Hall, 1978), pp. 151–156.

25. J. Kmenta, *Elements of Econometrics*, (New York: Macmillan, 1971), pp. 389–391.

26. J. Gibbons, *Nonparametric Methods for Quantitative Analysis*, (New York: Holt, Rinehart, & Winston, 1976), pp. 259–262.

27. Y. Bishop, S. Fienberg, and P. Holland, *Discrete Multivariate Analysis*. (Cambridge, MA: MIT Press, 1975.)

28. M. Caudill and C. Butler, *Naturally Intelligent Systems*, (Cambridge, MA: MIT Press, 1990).

29. J. A. Anderson and E. Rosenfeld, *Neurocomputing: Foundations of Research*. (Cambridge, MA: MIT Press, 1989.)

PART 4

DEBT RISK ASSESSMENT

14

BOND RATING: A NON-CONSERVATIVE APPLICATION OF NEURAL NETWORKS

Soumitra Dutta and Shashi Shekhar

INTRODUCTION

Domains of neural network applications can be classified into two broad categories—recognition and generalization.[1] For both classes, we first train the neural network on a set of input/output pairs (I_1, O_1), (I_2, O_2),...,(I_n, O_n). In recognition problems, the trained network is tested with the input I_j ($1 \le j \le n$) corrupted by noise as shown in Figure 14.1. The trained network is expected to reproduce the output O_j corresponding to I_j, in spite of the presence of noise. Shape recognition[2] and speech generation[3] are examples of recognition problems. On the other

Figure 14.1

Classes of Problems

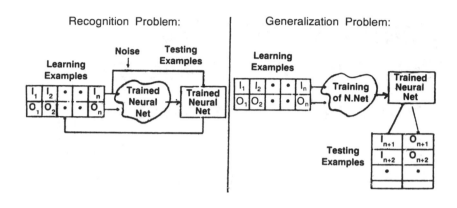

hand, in *generalization problems*, the trained neural network is tested with input I_{n+1}, which is distinct from the inputs $I_1, I_2,...,I_n$ used for training the network, as shown in Figure 14.1. The network is expected to correctly predict the output O_{n+1} for the input I_{n+1} from the model of the domain it has learned from the training input/output pairs. Typical examples of generalization problems are *classification* (e.g., diagnosis of diseases from symptoms) and *prediction* (e.g., of the future trends in the economy). It should be noted that for classification problems, the various O_is, $1 \le i \le n + 1$ may not necessarily be distinct and belong to a finite set of classes, $\{C_1, C_2,...,C_m\}$.

Generalization problems can be further subclassified on the basis of the underlying domain of application as shown in Figure 14.2. Some domains have well-defined domain models (e.g., electrical circuit analysis) while other domains have partially defined domain models (e.g., the diagnosis of diseases from symptoms and laboratory tests). Conventional techniques (e.g., statistical or systems analysis) can be applied to the former domain and many successful AI applications have been devised for the latter domain (e.g., expert systems such as MYCIN.[4] Yet another important class of problem domains are those that lack a do-

Figure 14.2

Recognition and Generalization Problems

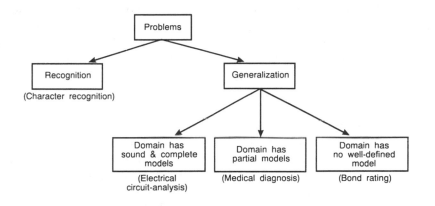

main model (alternatively termed as nonconservative domains), e.g., the problem of assigning ratings to corporate bonds.

Most of the earlier applications of neural networks,[2,3] has been to recognition problems. Lately, there have been some applications of neural networks to generalization problems in partially defined problem domains.[5,6] In this chapter, we explore the application of neural networks in domains lacking a well-defined model or theory. For such nonconservative domains, it is difficult to successfully apply either conventional mathematical techniques or standard AI approaches (e.g., rule-based systems). A neural network may be useful for such domains because it does not require the a priori specification of a functional domain model; rather, it attempts to learn the underlying domain model from the training input/output examples. We choose the ratings of corporate bonds as the practical domain for this study because it is a non-conservative domain of enormous importance in the real world of finance.

THE DOMAIN OF BOND RATING

The *default risk* of a bond is the possibility that the promised coupon and par values of a bond will not be paid. The default risks of the most actively traded bonds are rated by various independent organizations like Standard and Poor's (S&P) and Moody's. Table 14.1 gives some examples of the ratings given by S&P and Moody's. These ratings are used as a metric to reflect the risk of investment in bonds and are also used to define allowable bond purchases by certain investors. For example, the Comptroller of Currency has stated that bank investments must be of *investment grade*. (Investment grade includes bonds rated in the top four rankings.) These ratings also have a significant effect on the offering yield of a bond issue.

To evaluate a bond's potential for default, rating agencies rely on a committee analysis of various aspects of the issuing company such as the issuer's *ability* to repay, *willingness* to repay, and *protective* provisions for an issue. It is not known what model, if any, these rating agencies use for rating the various bond issues. The situation is complicated by the fact that all the various aspects analyzed by the ratings committee are not known completely, and some features such as *willingness* to repay are affected by a number of variables that are difficult to characterize precisely. Thus, it is not possible to accurately define a mathematical model that performs the required ratings of bonds. This is the main reason for the poor results yielded by conventional statistical analysis techniques. It is also difficult to develop a rule-based expert

Table 14.1

Definitions of Some Ratings Given by S&P and Moody's

Moody's	S&P	Definition
Aaa	AAA	The highest rating assigned. Capacity to pay interest and principal very strong.
Aa	AA	Very strong capacity to pay interest and principal. Differ from highest rated issues only in small degree.
A	A	Strong capacity to repay interest and principal but may be susceptible to adverse changes in economic conditions.
Baa	BBB	Adequate protection to repay interest and principal but more likely to have weakened capacity in periods of adverse economic conditions.

system for rating bonds as very few experts are available and most knowledge about the process of ratings is confidential. Developing a model for rating bonds is important as it enables a financial institution to independently evaluate the default risk of its bond investments.

RATING THE BONDS

The Problem Statement

The task of assigning ratings to the different industrial bond issues can be posed as a *classification* problem: given a set of classes and a set of input data instances, each described by a suitable set of features, assign each input data instance to one of the classes. For our study, the different bond issues form the set of input data instances and the various bond ratings (AA, B, etc.) form the set of possible classes to which the input bonds can belong. Each bond instance can be described by a set of features which represent important financial information about the company issuing the bond. Formally, we state the problem now:

Let B represent the space of n bonds, B_1, B_2,...,B_n, and R be the set of possible (mutually exclusive) m bond ratings, R_1, R_2,...,R_m. Let F represent the k dimensional feature space, F_1,...,F_k, describing each of the bonds. Each bond B_i can be considered as a k-tuple $(F1_{Bi}, F2_{Bi},...,Fk_{Bi})$ in the Cartesian space $F_1 \times F_2 \times ... \times F_k$. And rating the bonds involves finding the one to one mapping function f

$$f : F_1 \times F_2 \times ... \times F_k \to R$$

The mapping produced by this function f, i.e., the ratings assigned to the various bonds, is determined by the rating agencies, but a precise functional form or a mathematical model of this function f is not known. The exact feature space used by the rating agencies is not known, but there is some consensus among researchers in corporate finance on the feature space. Thus an *approximation* to this feature space can be defined. Past researchers have tried to approximate the function f by using various multivariate regression models, with limited success. In this chapter, we attempt to use a neural network for modeling the function f, with the input vector space being given by $F_1 \times F_2 \times ... \times F_k$ and the output vector space being given by R. We choose an input feature space similar to that chosen by past researchers (see below) for their statistical analyses.

Review of Past Research

For determining the ratings of bonds, rating agencies probably use both the financial data of the company and other qualitative factors, such as their subjective judgment concerning the future prospects of the firm. However, researchers in finance have mostly concentrated upon quantifiable historical data for the firm and provisions of the bond issue. The typical financial variables used include proxies for liquidity, debt capacity, debt coverage, size of issue, etc. They usually take coded bond ratings as an independent variable and use statistical techniques like regression to get a model of bond ratings.

Horrigan[7] regressed coded ratings with 15 financial ratios. Subject to the magnitudes of cross-correlations, he chose six ratios out of the 15 that had highest correlation with ratings. These were total assets, working capital over sales, net work over total debt, sales over net worth, profit over sales, and subordination. Another regression between the ratings and the new set of variables gave a model. This model was correct for 58 percent of Moody's ratings during the period 1961 through 1964. West[8] has a similar approach, using logarithmic forms of nine variables including earning variability, solvency period, debt equity ratio and outstanding bonds. His model correctly predicted 62 percent of Moody's rating during 1953. Pogue and Soklofsky[9] used a regression model with dichotomous (0 – 1) dependent variables, which represents the probability of group membership in one group of pair. They ran separate regressions for each pair of successive ratings (e.g., Aaa and aA, Aa and A, A and Baa) with the following independent variables: debt over total capital, income over assets, and income over interest charge. Dummy variables were used for broad industry effects. This approach involved at least $(n - 1)$ regressions for n-rating groups. A bond is assigned to the group in which its probability of occurrence is the highest. This method predicted eight bonds out of ten in holdout sample from the period 1961 through 1966. Pinches and Mingo[10] screened the initial 35 variables via factor analysis, and used multiple discriminant analysis to develop the final model. They used the following variables: subordination (0 – 1), years of consecutive dividend, issue size, income over assets, income over interest charge, and debt over assets. Bonds were classified on the probability of group membership. This model predicted roughly 65 percent and 56 percent of the Moody's ratings for holdout samples in the periods 1967 through 1968 and 1969.

Limitations of Regression Models

These approaches (based on multiple regression) have had limited success (approximately 60 percent correctness) in predicting bond ratings, even after considering as many as 35 financial variables and performing a large number of iterative regressions ($n - 1$ iterations for n ratings). This supports our premise that in the absence of well-defined domain models (such as in bond rating) the success of standard mathematical AND/OR statistical techniques is limited. Statistical techniques always require the assumption of a certain functional form for relating dependent variables to independent variables. When the assumed functional form is not correct, the statistical techniques merely confirm that, but do not predict the right functional form. Neural networks do provide a more general framework for determining relationships in the data and do not require the specification of any functional form. As shown later, neural networks do perform consistently better than regression.

NEURAL NET MODEL

We use a multilayer network consisting of simple processing elements called "units" that interact with each other using weighted connections. Each unit has a "state" or "activity level" determined by the input received from units in the layer below. The total input, x_j, received by unit j is given by equation $E1$ below where y_j is the state of the ith unit (which is in a lower layer), w_{ij} is the weight on the connection from the ith to the jth unit, and θ_j is the threshold of the jth unit. The lowest layer contains the input nodes and an external input vector is supplied to the network by clamping the states of these units. The state of any other unit in the network is a monotonic nonlinear function of its total input as given by equation $E2$.

$$E1: \quad x_j = \sum_i y_i u'_{ji} - \theta_j \qquad\qquad E2: \quad y_j = \frac{1}{1 + e^{-z_j}}$$

All the network's long-term knowledge about the function it has learned to compute is encoded by the magnitudes of the weights on the connections.

We experimented with two-layered and three-layered networks. In a two-layer network, the input units are directly connected to output units by a set of connections with modifiable weights. Given a set of input vectors and the desired output for each input vector, the back-propagation[11] learning algorithm can iteratively find a set of weights that will perform the mapping, if such a set exists. The two-layered neural network is more powerful than regression due to the non-linear summation at each unit. This is validated by our results (see below). We also experimented with three-layered networks with hidden nodes that combine the raw observations into higher order features. The number of input units connected to each hidden unit in a three (or more) layered network, determines the statistical order of high-order features extracted by the hidden unit.

The choice of the structure of the neural network is very dependent on the application domain of the neural network. If the input vector space consists of extremely low-level features, then we need a larger number of hidden layers to successively extract the higher-order features from the input data. A smaller number of hidden layers suffices if the input data is itself representative of some higher-order features. In our particular study, for reasons of efficiency, many higher order features were chosen in the input vector space, and thus, it was seen that the performance of the neural network did not improve significantly with an increase in the number of hidden layers.

Learning in Neural Nets

We used back-propagation[11] with simultaneous weight adjustments to learn the weights. The learning procedure is briefly described here. The error with a given set of weights is defined by equation E3 where y_{jc} is the actual state (weight) of unit j in input/output training example c (in the forward direction), and d_{jc} is its desired state (weight). This allows the network to compute, for each weight, the gradient of output error with respect to that weight. For a hidden unit, j, in layer J the only way it can affect the error is via its effects on the units, k, in the next layer K. So the derivative of the error $\partial E/\partial y_j$ is given by equation E4 where the index c has been suppressed for clarity. The weight is then changed in the direction to reduce the output error. Our neural network simulator uses global optimization for changing the weights

$$E3: \quad E = \frac{1}{2} \sum_{j,c} (y_{j,c} - d_{j,c})^2 \qquad\qquad E4: \quad \frac{\partial E}{\partial y_j} = \sum_k \frac{\partial E}{\partial y_k} \frac{dy_k}{dz_k} \frac{\partial I_k}{\partial y_k}$$

simultaneously and avoids the problems of conflicting local weight adjustments.

To verify how well the neural network has learned the underlying domain model, we use the same set of weights (on the connections) learned during the *learning phase* and check the accuracy of the predicted output for a new set of input vectors. We refer to the input vectors used for learning the weights as the *learning sample* and the input vectors used for testing as the *testing sample*. The success of the predictions of the neural network depends upon the range of the domain covered by the learning input/output vectors. Thus, for the case of bond ratings, it is desired that the neural network be shown examples of bonds belonging to all the different rating categories during the learning phase.

Regression Analysis versus Neural Net Models

Regression gives us the parameters of a given functional form but not the correct functional form. The neural network model helps us for determining the functional form as well as the parameters. It does not require us to guess any functional form, but determines the functional form by itself. It tunes the functional form and parameters to fit the learning examples, as closely as desired. We can specify both the desired size (number of parameters) of the model (neural network) and the error tolerance for the model. This gives us a more general framework for discovering relationships existing in data. As expected we found that it consistently outperformed regression methods for predicting bond ratings.

However, we note that the regression models are useful in determining the right set of independent variables, which determine the dependent variable to the largest extent. This is difficult to do with neural networks as the hidden layers (intermediate layers) of a neural network extract the higher-order features from the input variables to decide the output, so the output is not influenced directly by the inputs.

The weights on the connections for a two-layered network can give the relative importance of the input variables, but for any three- or higher layered network, such a discrimination from the weights on the connections becomes very difficult.

DESIGN OF THE EXPERIMENT

Selection of Variables

Based on the results of Horrigan[7] and Pinches and Mingo,[10] we selected ten financial variables for predicting bond ratings. The influence of a variable on the bond rating and ease of availability of data were the primary factors in the selection of the variables. These are listed in Table 14.2 and explained elsewhere. (The Valueline Index and the S&P Bond Guide).

Our first experiment uses all the ten variables in predicting the bond rating. Then, we used only the first six variables to predict the bond ratings. The correlations of the chosen variables were all small, and hence the chosen variables are independent (as desired).

Table 14.2

Financial Variables Used to Predict Bond Ratings

Variable	Definition
1	Liability/(Cash + Assets)
2	Debt proportion
3	Sales/Net worth
4	Profit/Sales
5	Financial strength
6	Earning/Fixed costs
7	Past five-year revenue growth rate
8	Projected next five-year revenue growth rate
9	Working capital/Sales
10	Subjective prospect of company

Data Collection

Bond ratings and values of the financial variables for a set of industrial bonds are taken from the April 1986 issue of the Valueline Index and the S&P Bond Guide. Bond issues of 47 companies were selected at random, and we used 30 of them to perform the *learning*, i.e., to train the neural network (obtain the weights on the different connections) and obtain the regression coefficients. The rest (17) of the bonds were used to test the neural network and regression performance. All the selected bonds had approximately the same maturity date (1998–2003).

A linear scale was used to convert the ratings of the bonds. We could have used a binary scale to convert the bonds (e.g., bonds rated A = 1; all other bonds = 0), but such a model would not be too accurate as there is a sort of linear relation in the rating of the bonds vs. the quality of the bonds (i.e., AAA is the best and the quality decreases progressively with lower rated bonds), and this is not captured by the binary model.

Linear Regression Model

We used the Berkeley ISP (The Interactive Statistical Package developed at the University of California, Berkeley) for multiple regression analysis to get a set of regression coefficients and their respective *t*-statistics. The *t*-statistics were significant for every regression coefficient. The regression coefficients obtained were then used to predict the ratings of both the learning sample (to see how well the regression model fitted the learning sample) and the testing sample of new bond issues (to see how well the regression coefficients predicted the ratings of the test bonds). The results are summarized in the next section.

Neural Net Model

We experimented with different neural network configurations (two-layered, three-layered, different number of hidden nodes in three-layered neural nets, etc.). The total permissible tolerance was kept constant for different neural network configurations. We compare the performance of the various neural networks against regression analysis and the performances of the various neural network configurations against themselves in the next section. Finally, we repeated all the above experiments with a smaller number of variables (variables one through six of the ten variables initially chosen).

RESULTS

Tables 14.3 through 14.6 summarize the results of our experiments. The models were expected to recognize if a given bond belongs to class of all bonds with AA rating. This problem naturally classifies the responses of prediction models into four different categories, described by the pairs of (actual, predicted) columns in Table 14.3.

The column *actual* is *Accept* if and only if the *given* bond is actually rated AA by S&P. For an ideal model, our test results should only belong to the first and fourth rows of Table 14.3 where the ratings given by S&P and the model coincide. Rows 2 and 3 of Table 14.3 are the undesirable cases and represent false-negatives and false-positives respectively. We report the statistics for the learning case and testing cases, separately to bring out the important features of our study. In Table 14.4 we list in detail the results of our study of the regression and neural network models for the four possible response classifications described in Table 14.3. High values in the columns under *Percent Correct Prediction* for the response pairs (Accept, Accept) and (Reject, Reject) point to a good model while high values for the response pairs (Accept, Reject) and (Reject, Accept) point to an inferior model. The values are listed separately for the learning and testing phases for both neural networks and the regression analysis. This helps us to better compare neural networks and regression analysis. For example (from Table 14.4 for ten

Table 14.3

Possible Classifications of Responses

Actual	Prediction	Description
Accept	Accept	S&P rating is AA and rating of model is also AA
Accept	Reject	S&P rating is AA and rating of model is not AA
Reject	Accept	S&P rating is not AA but rating of model is AA
Reject	Reject	S&P rating is not AA and rating of model is also not AA

Table 14.4

Performance of Regression and Neural Network Using Ten and Six Variables

Phase	Classification		Percent Correct Prediction Using Ten Variables			Percent Correct Prediction Using Six Variables		
	Actual	Predicted	Regression	Two Layer N-net	Three Layer N-net	Regression	Two Layer N-net	Three Layer N-net
Learning	Accept	Accept	61.5	76.9	92.3	61.5	76.9	76.9
	Accept	Reject	38.5	23.1	7.7	38.5	23.1	23.1
	Reject	Accept	29.4	17.6	0.0	35.2	17.6	17.6
	Reject	Reject	64.8	82.3	100.0	64.8	82.3	82.3
Testing	Accept	Accept	50	83.3	83.3	50	83.3	83.3
	Accept	Reject	50.0	16.7	16.7	50.0	16.7	16.7
	Reject	Accept	27.2	18.1	18.1	27.2	18.1	18.1
	Reject	Reject	72.8	81.9	81.9	72.8	81.9	81.9

Table 14.5

Results (Learning)

Number of Variables	Neural Net		Regression
	Two Layers	Three Layers	
6	80% tot_sq_err = 0.2365	80% tot_sq_err = 0.1753	63.33% tot_sq_err = 1.107
10	80% tot_sq_err = 0.2241	92.4% tot_sq_err = 0.0538	66.7% tot_sq_err = 0.924

Table 14.6

Results (Testing)

Number of Variables	Neural Net		Regression
	Two Layers	Three Layers	
6	82.4% tot_sq_err = 0.198	76.5% tot_sq_err = 0.1939	64.7% tot_sq_err = 1.528
10	88.3% tot_sq_err = 0.1638	82.4% tot_sq_err = 0.2278	64.7% tot_sq_err = 1.643

variables) during the learning phase, the regression model correctly classified 61.5 percent of AA bonds as AA bonds, and 64.8 percent of non-AA bonds as non-AA, using ten variables. Similarly (also from Table 14.4 for ten variables), during the testing phase the neural network model (both the two-layered neural network and the three-layered neural network) correctly classified 83 percent of the AA bonds as AA and 81.9 percent of the non-AA bonds as non-AA, using ten variables.

INTERPRETATION OF RESULTS

The data of Table 14.4 is condensed into Tables 14.5 and 14.6 for comparison. Table 14.4 condenses the results of the learning phase and Table 14.6 condenses the results of the testing phase. The percent of entries in Tables 14.5 and 14.6 essentially represent the percent of correctness of prediction of the two models (regression and neural network) and are obtained by computing a weighted average of the corresponding entries in Tables 14.4 for the response pairs (Accept, Accept) and (Reject, Reject). (The weights being given by the actual number of bonds in the respective categories.) We also list the absolute error as *tot_sq_err* for each model to give an idea of goodness of fit by various models. The *tot_sq_err* gives the sum of the squares of the errors in prediction in all the cases. Note that we converted bond ratings to a number in the range [0,1]. Thus, the total squared error is given by the sum of the squares of the differences between the numerical values of the actual and predicted bond ratings.

From Tables 14.4 through 14.6 we can draw the following conclusions:

1. Neural networks consistently outperform regression model in predicting bond ratings from the given set of financial ratios. Both in the training and learning samples the total squared error for regression analysis is about an order of magnitude higher than that for neural networks (see Tables 14.5 and 14.6). Also, the success rate of prediction for neural networks is considerably higher than that for regression analysis, e.g., the success rate during the testing phase for the two-layered neural network (ten variables) is 88.3 percent as compared to 64.7 percent for the regression model.

2. For the different configurations of neural networks, we observe that during the learning phase the total squared error decreases for a

neural network with a larger number of layers, but there are no significant differences in results during the testing phase. Given the training sample, we can obtain a better fit (with respect to the training sample) using a larger number of layers in the neural network but the additional layers do not seem to add to its predictive power as evidenced during the testing phase. This result can be understood in light of our earlier comments (see Neural Net Model, above) regarding the required number of hidden layers in a neural network. Our input financial features of a bond are relatively high level abstractions, and thus there is no significant improvement in prediction with an increase in the number of hidden layers.

3. The results obtained during the testing phase by our regression analysis are comparable to those obtained by previous researchers (see Neural Net Model, above). The poor performance of the regression models indicates that the linear multivariate model is inadequate for explaining the rating of bonds. There are substantial gains by applying neural networks to nonconservative domains such as bond rating.

4. It was observed that whenever the neural network model is in error, it is off by at most one rating. In contrast, regression analysis was often off by several ratings. We have not presented details here due to space limitations.

CONCLUSIONS

Domains of application of neural networks are not limited to recognition problems. They can be applied successfully to generalization problems, where the underlying application domain does not have any models. For nonconservative problem domains, neural networks perform much better than classical mathematical modeling techniques such as regression.[12]

ENDNOTES

1. P. D. Wasserman, et al., "Neural Networks, Part 2," *IEEE Expert Magazine*, vol. 3, no. 1, Spring 1988.

2. G. E. Hinton, "Learning to recognize shapes in parallel networks," in *Proceedings of the Fyssen Conference*, ed. M. Imbert, (Oxford: Oxford Univ. Press).

3. T. J. Senjowski, et al., "NETtalk: A Parallel Network That Learns to Read Aloud," (Baltimore, Md: Johns Hopkins University, EECS Department), Tech. Rep. 86-01.

4. E. H. Shortliffe, *Computer Based Medical Consulations: MYCIN*, (New York: Elsevier, 1976).

5. S. I. Gallant, "Connectionist Expert Systems," *Comm. of the ACM*, vol. 31, no. 2, February 1988.

6. H. V. Parunak, et al., "Material Handling: A Conservative Domain for Neural Connectivity and Propagation," *Proceedings AAAI Conference*, 1987, pp. 307–311.

7. J. O. Horrigan, "The Determination of Long Term Credit Standing with Financial Ratios," Empirical Research in Accounting: Selected Studies, *Journal of Accounting Research*, 1966.

8. R. R. West, "An Alternative Approach Predicting Corporate Bond Ratings," *Journal of Accounting Research*, Spring 1970.

9. T. E. Pogue, and R. M. Soklofsky, "What is in a Bond Rating?" *Journal of Financial and Quantitative Analysis*, June 1969.

10. G. E. Pinches, and K. A. Mingo, "A Multivariate Analysis of Industrial Bond Ratings," *Journal of Finance*, March 1977.

11. D. E. Rumelhart, et al., "Learning Internal Representations by Backpropagating Errors," *Nature*, vol. 323, pp. 533–536.

12. We would like to thank Professor Andrew Rudd, Business School, University of California at Berkeley for introducing us to the problem of bond rating and providing valuable insights from time to time. We also thank Rajesh Mehra of the quantitative finance research group, BARRA, for providing data related to several bond issues. We had fruitful discussions, about applicability of neural models in nonconservative domain, with Professor L. A. Zadeh, Computer Science, University of California at Berkeley. We are grateful to Dr. Shabbir Rangwala, Mechanical Engineering, University of California at Berkely, for his help with the neural network simulator.

NEURAL NETWORKS FOR BOND RATING IMPROVED BY MULTIPLE HIDDEN LAYERS

Alvin J. Surkan and J. Clay Singleton

INTRODUCTION

Choosing values for neural network architectural parameters that specify both the number of hidden layers and the number of active elements within those layers is still more an art than a science. Mathematical analysis that might answer such questions is made intractable by the complexity of the interactions among the many dimensions represented in simulated neural networks. Also, each trained network, in an incomprehensibly complex way, is dependent on the initial connection weight values and subsequent chance sequencing of their updating in training with backward error propagation,[1] which performs optimization through a non-deterministic, hill-climbing procedure. Until there is a better understanding of both the performance of backward-error propagation and the internal representation of problem knowledge over the connection weights, it is vital that alternative internal neural network architectures be explored by experimentation with data which is either real or truly representative of the problems for which neural networks have promise. In practice, this means frequently starting with very small training data sets, which themselves may have errors in patterns or have incorrect labels. For these one must establish the extent to which the resulting trained networks will generalize so as to classify the test patterns initially set aside from those used in training.

While it is assumed that infrequent labeling errors or even frequent small errors characteristic of patterns occurring in large training sets will have negligible permanent effect on training, it is clear that even one error in labeling a training pattern appearing in a small training set can drastically reduce the trained network's generalization performance. For this reason, when networks are trained to generalize from small training sets, it is necessary to study and filter incorrectly labeled patterns. Censoring may be required, independent of the reason the label is incorrect, i.e., erroneous label assignment or the presence of noise contaminating the pattern to such a degree that it, in fact, becomes effectively more representative of a class with a different label.

BOND RATINGS

Many researchers in economics and finance have studied the determinants of bond ratings. The essence of these investigations is to discover a model that mimics the ratings awarded by either of the major rating companies—Moody's or Standard & Poor's. These agencies claim their quality ratings combine analysis of financial variables with expert judgment to produce an estimate of the probability the company will default. Bond ratings also have economic significance as higher quality ratings command lower interest rates. Models of bond ratings, therefore, are of great interest to investors, who want to anticipate the rating given a change in company circumstances, and to financial managers, who seek to predict the rating (and accompanying interest rate) of a potential issue. Moody's ranks bonds from Aaa (highest quality), to Aa1, Aa2, Aa3 (medium quality) to A1, A2, A3 (investment grade, but lower quality).

DESCRIPTION OF THE FINANCIAL DATA USED

Bond raters publicly announce they consider leverage, coverage and profitability as prime determinants of bond issue quality. Peavy and Scott[2] modeled the bonds of 18 Bell Telephone operating companies divested by American Telephone and Telegraph Company (AT&T) in 1982. To construct a model, they surveyed bond rating research and found seven variables related to these three financial characteristics and often highly correlated with bond ratings in previous classification studies (mostly discriminant analysis). They used linear discriminant analysis to estimate their model and correctly classified 10 of the 18 bonds (56.6 percent) into four rating classes (Aa2, Aa3, A1, A2). For this study similar data (bond ratings and financial variables) were obtained for the same 18 telephone operating companies for the years 1982 through 1988. Specifically, the financial variables were:

1. Debt divided by total capital (LEVERAGE) — a measure of the bondholders' security.

2. Pre-tax interest expense divided by income (COVERAGE) — a measure of the company's ability to pay bondholders from current income.

3. Return on equity (ROE) or income — a profitability measure.

4. Coefficient of variation of ROE calculated over the past five years (CV of ROE) — an indication of the stability of profitability.

5. Logarithm of the total assets (TA) — a measure of size.

6. Construction costs divided by total cash inflow (FLOW) — a measure of the capacity to fund construction without increased borrowing.

7. Toll revenue ratio calculated as intradivided by inter-LATA (TOLL) — an indication of the effect of divestiture on profitability.

These financial variables should measure quality and, therefore, should be distinguishable by bond rating. A summary comparison of financial data is displayed in Table 15.1. This table gives the means of each of the seven financial variables and shows the distribution of the bonds by rating. The relationship between the rating classes among these variables is not obvious but suggestive of a complex interaction that is consistent with the rating agencies' claim of the need for expert judgment. These relationships may also be more amenable to a neural network than the traditional linear model. One advantage of the current research is that neural networks are trained with economic (not simulated) data and tested against a classification technique accepted by financial researchers.

CREATION OF NEURAL NETWORK MODELS

Each alternate configuration of an initially untrained PDP-type of layered connection network was emitted by a dynamic network generation program function called GENNET. Its operation requires only a few seconds and is initiated by evoking GENNET with a single vector argument, LL, on its right. The argument LL supplies the layer lengths first for the output, then the sequence of hidden layers, and finally the input. During each such synthesis of an experimental network, all the needed connection arrays and vectors are created. These are all correctly dimensioned to represent the connections and thresholding values for each simulated neuron. Also produced, simultaneously, are the input and activation vectors that supply the input to each successive processing layer and finally to the output. In all experiments, the number of elements in the input and output vectors were fixed at seven and two, respectively. The minimum and maximum number of elements provided in hidden layers ranged from 5 to 15. These would be introduced either all in a single hidden layer or divided between two layers. In experiments using two hidden layers, unequal numbers of elements were tested with trial combinations with the numbers of elements either increasing or decreasing, in the direction input to output.

Table 15.1

Means of Financial Variables by Bond Ratings for 18 Telephone Operating Companies (1982–1988)

BOND RATING SYMBOL

Variable	Aaa	Aa1	Aa2	Aa3	A1	A2	A3
Leverage	.39	.41	.39	.36	.36	.39	.39
Coverage	4.5	4.48	4.99	5.69	5.02	4.30	4.46
ROE	.25	.14	.14	.15	.12	.14	.15
CV of ROE	.1	.10	.08	.10	.14	.09	.07
TA	14.7	15.75	13.00	14.25	15.15	16.36	16.43
Flow	1.05	.92	1.05	1.05	.85	.74	.83
Toll	1.34	1.08	.82	1.24	1.04	1.01	.90
Frequency	30	23	20	27	10	11	5

TRAINING PROCEDURES AND DATA SELECTION AND SEQUENCING

Operation of the back-propagation updating during the training phase is managed in a specialized way tailored for training with small data sets. Besides having a schedule for diminishing the learning rate parameter as training proceeds, it is necessary to decide what useful role, if any, the momentum term should play in the weight update process. Besides this parametric control, the progress of training may be significantly influenced by the selection of the training patterns. Also, training is affected by any errors in the assigned pattern labels and how they are sampled and sequenced.

Unless training data sets are very large, experience suggests that using fewer prototypical training patterns with correct labels as training exemplars is preferable to using slightly larger training sets contaminated by even a very few labeling errors. In the absence of any knowledge of distribution of noise or errors in the pattern, it seems appropriate to provide an equal number of exemplars for representing each distinct output class. When this is made impossible by one or more too-poorly populated classes, the classes with smaller numbers of sample patterns are randomly sampled repeatedly with an increased frequency.

It was found experimentally that intentionally mislabeled real patterns inserted among the correct observed patterns could be identified early during the process of training a neural network. It follows that unless the patterns themselves are contaminated with too much noise, this same process for identifying mislabeled training patterns, soon after beginning training, provides a means of data censoring, which proved beneficial for producing trained networks with improved generalization capabilities. This is especially true when the training set size is rather small.

This staged training improves the data quality by identifying better training data, which is retained for producing the final model. Also, with small training sets the weight update process is implicitly rather than explicitly batched. This is done by performing a new weight update immediately after every training pattern makes its forward pass through the network. However, complete generations of such training passes are implicitly imposed by random sampling of each class without replacement. This is continued until all training patterns in a class are exhausted. As before, if one class becomes exhausted before others, it may be repeatedly sampled with replacement. Besides imposing this control on the random sampling within classes, an additional data sequencing constraint guarantees that samples representing differing output classes are chosen systematically. This ensures that classes will be randomly sampled repeatedly and without replacement among classes during each indirect training cycle or generation.

EXPERIMENTS ON EFFECTS OF NUMBER AND SIZE OF HIDDEN LAYERS

An APL^3 function GENNET was written and repeatedly used to generate various configurations of layered networks. All had a seven-element input layer which received the financial pattern values and a two-element output layer indicating into which bond class the data were finally mapped from the output of any intervening hidden layers. For these particular experiments, either a single or a pair of hidden layers were present. Usually, the number of intermediate elements was varied from 5 to about 15. When the number of elements was fixed, they were either all in one layer or redistributed among multiple layers.

Single Hidden Layer Experiments

When there is only a single hidden layer of neurons, its elements are activated by the signals arriving from the input. The activations on that hidden layer are processed by a second layer of processing neurons that finally activate the output. Each additional hidden layer introduced one set of processing neurons, which imposes an additional intermediate representation of the pattern as it is mapped from its input codes to the desired output codes. Experiments with single and multiple layers were performed by a fixed training set and by testing the performance of trained networks with a different number of elements placed either in a single hidden layer or divided between two hidden layers. With a pair of hidden layer lengths, it is also important to find out how pairs of unequal layer lengths should be sequenced in a mapping network that is optimal with respect to its ability to generalize. Here the word *generalize* is used to mean that the network constructed from the training patterns of presumably correct known class labels are able to predict the correct labels for those patterns that were set aside for testing and not permitted to be used during the training process.

RESULTS OF THE TRAINING AND TESTING EXPERIMENTS

It was found that the length of a single hidden layer could be varied over a relatively wide range (5 to 15) without significantly degrading the classification performance. This performance was measured simply by the number of patterns correctly labeled in the two classes. The results in the first row of Table 15.2 are for the typical sequence of layer lengths 7, 14, 2 proceeding from the input to the output. They are the same or representative of those obtained from the range of single hidden layers trained with the same 20 patterns of bond rating data. From the columns on the right half of Table 15.2, it is seen that the classification accuracy for the set-aside test patterns was 85 percent and 45 percent for classes 1 and 2, respectively. For 40 test samples of classes 1 and 2 combined, an overall performance of 65 percent was obtained. Because in practice all small sets of training samples can be preselected to include only that subset of data patterns that were correctly classified, the meaningful performance measure is the percent correct among only the test patterns. Also, it is of interest to examine the clarity of the network output code signals for those classifications for which the classes appeared incorrect. This is so because the discrepancy could arise from either a misclassification by the network or by humans who originally assigned the bond ratings. Frequently, inconsistency was accompanied by similar or almost equivocal pairs of activations of the two elements of the output layer.

Two Hidden-Layer Model Results

When a variety of networks with two hidden layers were trained on the same 20 dot patterns, they would consistently provide greater ac-

Table 15.2

Classification Accuracy Results

Samples	Both Training and Test Patterns				Only the Test Patterns		
Bond Class	1(Aaa)	2(A1, A2, A3)	1 and 2		1(Aaa)	2(A1, A2, A3)	1 and 2
Count	30	26	56		20	20	40
7, 14, 2	(27) [90%]	(15) [58%]	(38) [68%]		(17) [85%]	(9) [45%]	(26) [65%]
7, 5, 10, 2	(28) [93%]	(20) [77%]	(48) [86%]		(18) [90%]	(14) [70%]	(32) [80%]
7, 10, 5, 2	(30) [100%]	(21) [81%]	(51) [91%]		(20) [100%]	(15) [75%]	(35) [88%]

Entries give (number) and [percent] correctly classified by trained neural networks with a single pair of transposed hidden layer lengths as given in the leftmost column.

curacy in classifying the test data than did the single hidden layer network. This was true even when the hidden layer elements were distributed so that the shortest hidden layer preceded the longer one during the mapping process. In this case an immediate dimension reduction from 7 to 17 in the first layer suggests that the intrinsic dimension of the data is close to 5 or lower. As expected, when the longer hidden layer of neurons precedes the shorter and the training and test data are fixed for evaluating the action of permuting the hidden-layer length sequences with a constant number of elements, improved performance was obtained when the sequence decreased monotonically in the direction of the output.

The two lower rows of Table 15.2 — which contain the layer length sequences {7, 5, 10, 2} and {7, 10, 5, 2} — show marked improvement over the single hidden layer network in the top row. The {7, 10, 5, 2} architecture correctly classified 100 percent of the class 1, 75 percent of class 2, and 88 percent of the test patterns of classes 1 and 2 combined. It is important to explain that only six of the class 2 exemplars were explicitly assigned an A rating. The remaining four were, in fact, patterns chosen from higher-rated bonds assigned to rating category Aa3 adjacent to class 2 and distant from the class 1 exemplars, which were all assigned an Aaa rating.

COMPARISON WITH DISCRIMINANT CLASSIFICATION TECHNIQUES

These experiments show that both single and multiple hidden-layer networks for classifying patterns of a few variables (seven financial features) perform well. The results, however, do not necessarily establish neural networks as superior to simpler techniques, such as discriminant analysis. Discriminant analysis was selected as a benchmark because it has often been applied to bond classification problems. A valid comparison between various alternative hidden-layer configurations of simulated networks and discriminant analysis requires that both methods be applied fairly and to their best advantage. The neural networks classified the test patterns unavailable to it during training. Linear discriminant functions were estimated using the two groups as dependent and the seven financial features as explanatory variables. All 56 observations were used in a hold-one-out approach by iteratively calculating the model over 55 observations and classifying the 56th. Every observation was held out in turn, avoiding the bias of classifying the same observations used to estimate the model. The discriminant analysis may have been given a slight advantage in this comparison, as it was exposed to all the observations during training. Nevertheless, the superior ability of neural networks to classify bonds can be confirmed by comparing the results in Table 15.2 with the discriminant success rates of 40 percent (12 of 30) for group 1, 38 percent (ten of 26) for group 2 and 39 percent (22 of 56) overall. Even the earlier study by Peavy and Scott[2] (over a smaller, more homogeneous sample) only classified 56.6 percent (10 of 18) of the bonds correctly. Although neural networks are more complex than discriminant analysis, these results suggest the neural network may be the more powerful classification technique.

SUMMARY OF EXPERIMENTS WITH SINGLE AND MULTIPLE HIDDEN LAYER NETWORKS

The results shown in Table 15.2 and mentioned earlier demonstrate that neural networks with either single or pairs of hidden layers can provide 65 percent, 80 percent and 88 percent correct classification among the collections of 26, 32, and 35 test patterns not used in training each final network. This progression of improvements in classification accuracy corresponded with the reconfiguring from a single hidden layer (with network layer lengths of 7, 14 and 2) to double hidden layer configurations with layer lengths sandwiched in the sequences {7,5,10,2} or {7,10,5,2}. As expected, a classifier network trained one way and then retrained after swapping its two hidden layers so they were sequenced to decrease, rather than increase the number of processing elements, increased accuracy from 80 percent to 88 percent. At the same time, it is both surprising and not yet understood how the significantly improved classification accuracy was produced even when the pair of hidden layers was reversed so the layer length sequence was {7,5,10,2}. Similar improvement is realized even when the double hidden layer network has many different redistributions of the two layers, provided the number of simulated neurons is fixed at approximately the number used in a single hidden layer. This leads to the conjecture that redistributing an adequate number of single hidden layer elements to many optional pairings of hidden layers can produce a significant performance improvement without an unacceptable increase in training time.

GENERAL CONCLUSIONS

Bond rating by trained, layered, neural networks is an increasingly attractive area for the application of learning from limited numbers of examples when there are only a few variables known to be useful as class determinants. Also, this research provides real problems for neural networks to solve and a standard of comparison familiar in the field. The experimental evidence suggests the advantages of multiple hidden layers over a single one. The improvement in classification accuracy from redistributing the neurons from one to a pair of layers can be marked. Significant advantages arise even when the layers are ordered so that a smaller number of neurons receive their inputs directly from the inputs. This suggests that for this bond rating data, the problem of mapping from 7-features to 2-classes may have an inherent dimensionality of 5 or lower. The mapping of the five elements' (or neurons') output of the first layer down to two layers can be performed first. Then, there is still an advantage from the use of a subsequent hidden layer to provide another representation of useful classification information. There is a hope that some of the intermediate representations may be identified with concepts used by humans to analyze this bond classification problem. Finding such representations with correspondences to familiar higher level concepts remains a challenge for understanding the internal operation of neural networks.

ENDNOTES

1. D. E. Rumelhart, et al., "Learning Internal Representations by Back-Propagating Errors," *Nature*, vol. 323, 1986. pp. 533–536.

2. J. W. Peavy, III, and J. A. Scott, "The AT&T Divestiture: Effects of Rating Changes on Bond Returns," *Journal of Economics and Business*, vol. 38, 1986., pp. 255–270.

3. K. E. Iverson, "A Dictionary of APL," I. P. Sharp Associates Limited, 1987. (Also printed in *SIGATL Quote-Quad*, vol. 18, September 1987).

16

AN APPLICATION OF A MULTIPLE NEURAL NETWORK LEARNING SYSTEM TO EMULATION OF MORTGAGE UNDERWRITING JUDGMENTS

Edward Collins, Sushmito Ghosh, and Christopher Scofield

INTRODUCTION

Mortgage risk assessment begins with mortgage origination. A mortgage originator filters the general population of potential property owners according to a set of guidelines such as the proposed loan-to-value

© July 1988, IEEE. Reprinted with permission from *Proceedings of the IEEE International Conference on Neural Networks*, pp. II459–II466.

ratio, the ratio of proposed obligations to income, and other relevant measures of risk. In doing this simple analysis, the mortgage originator will decide that some of these applicants represent a greater than average risk. For these applicants, private mortgage insurance is required. The private mortgage insurance company then performs a second underwriting. If the applicant exhibits a low risk, he or she will be sold insurance. Mortgage insurance applicants are by nature a higher risk group than the general population of mortgage applicants. These applicants have already been underwritten by the mortgage originator and assessed as less secure cases. Thus, this second order underwriting performed by the mortgage insurer is bound to be more difficult and prone to greater ambiguity.

It is important to note that the mortgage insurance industry is undergoing a serious upheaval today with many of the weaker players suffering serious financial losses as well as bankruptcies. This upheaval, to a large part, can be attributed to the poor judgments made by an agency's underwriters. Poor judgments are especially prevalent on the more difficult applications that appear with a higher frequency in mortgage insurance.

Mortgage underwriting, at first glance, would seem to be an unlikely candidate for the application of neural networks. This is a problem in risk assessment that might seem to be best solved with a rule-based system, as the methodology applied by underwriters is thought to be well defined. Further, underwriters must be able to justify the decisions they make, and it is sometimes said that neural networks are not suitable for applications where this is a requirement. In addition, problems in this domain often involve the use of large numbers of features from diverse sources. A very large volume of data is required to develop a model that would be broad enough to handle the variability of such problems, and it is known that the training time of many of the popular algorithms grows rapidly with increases in the scale of problems, making them unsuitable for applications of this type.

However, the difficulty of getting underwriting "experts" to specify or agree on the rules they use in making their more subtle decisions, and the high economic value of reducing the number of bad risks presently accepted by underwriters, make the application of neural network decision systems potentially very valuable.

We have trained a multiple neural network learning system (MNNLS) on human underwriter judgments. This system is able to capture the complex data relationships necessary to mimic underwriting. The MNNLS is a specific architecture designed for rapid training on large amounts of data. We begin with a description of the properties of the multiple neural network learning system. Next, the application of this system to the problem of mortgage insurance underwriting is outlined and the results are presented. An analysis of the sources of disagreement between the system and the agency's underwriters is conducted in three ways. The first method explores case studies of loans on which the system disagreed with the human underwriter's judgment. The second method employs a single feature analysis of the population of files identified by the MNNLS. Finally, a rating of the quality of decisions was applied to the judgments made by the system and by human underwriters.

NEURAL NETWORK MODEL

Recent work on distributed memory systems has focused on single-layer, recurrent networks. Hopfield[1,2] introduced a method for the analysis of settling of activity in recurrent networks. This method defined the network as a dynamic system for which a global function called the "energy" (actually a Liapunov function for the autonomous system describing the state of the network) could be defined. Like its forerunners, the Hopfield network is limited in storage capacity. Degradation of memory recall with increased storage density is directly related to the proliferation in the state space of unwanted local minima, which serve as basins of flow.

Bachmann et al.[3] have focused on defining a dynamic system in which the locations of the energy minima are explicitly known. They have chosen a system isomorphic to the classical electrostatic potential between a positive test charge (corresponding to the test pattern), and negative charges located at the memory sites. The N-dimensional Coulomb energy function then defines exactly m basins of attraction to the fixed points located at the m memory sites. It has been shown that convergence to the closest distinct memory is guaranteed, independent of the number of stored memories m, for proper choice of system parameters.

An equilibrium feed-forward network with similar properties has been under investigation for some time.[4] This model employs the "square-well" limit of the N-dimensional Coulomb potential. The energy landscape consists of plateaus of zero potential outside of wells with flat, zero-slope basins. Since the landscape has only flat regions separated by discontinuous boundaries, the state of the network is always at equilibrium, and relaxation does not occur. This equilibrium model, referred to as the Restricted Coulomb Energy (RCE) model, shares the property of unrestricted storage density.

Reilly et al. have employed a three-layer feed-forward network that allows the generalization of a content addressable memory to a pattern classification memory. Because the locations of the minima are explicitly known in the equilibrium model, it is possible to dynamically program the energy function for an arbitrary energy landscape. This allows the construction of geographies of basins associated with the classes constituting the pattern environment. Rapid learning of complex, nonlinear, disjoint, class regions is possible by this method.[5,6]

The RCE network is an element in a novel architecture of multiple neural networks. This system has been described in detail elsewhere[5]; here we briefly review the system properties. The MNNLS employs an array of coupled subnetworks and a controller. For this application, we have chosen an architecture of nine coupled networks in a three-by-three arrangement. Each of the three networks at each of the three levels is focused on a nonexclusive subset of the full feature space. This partitioning of the full space has at least two advantages: each network space is smaller than the full space, making for a more efficient, easier-to-train system. In addition, the cooperative effect of three individual "experts" in a level of the system is used to determine the level of confidence for a system decision. Each of the expert networks renders a decision by itself. This group cooperates by searching for an agreement (or consensus) between networks of a level before the system yields a classification. The degree of agreement required can be varied during testing. When a high degree of consensus is required (maximum agreement is termed conservative mode), a smaller percentage of testing files will be unambiguously identified but with a higher accuracy.

If the networks at a particular level agree, the system gives an unambiguous response. However, if there is no consensus, the pattern is processed by the next level of networks. In this way, the three levels of the architecture serve as a hierarchical filter. Networks near the top of the structure handle obvious discriminations, while the networks near the bottom, unburdened with the majority of the decisions, focus on fine discriminations.

APPLICATION

This system was trained on the judgments of human mortgage insurance underwriters and learns to mimic their underwriting skill. The data used by the MNNLS consisted of examples of applications submitted to the insurance company and the subsequent classifications by the underwriters. The mortgage database on which this study was based consisted of 5,048 applications from all parts of the United States, collected in the period September 1987 to December 1987. The database consisted of 2,597 Certification files (which were accepted for mortgage insurance) and 2,451 Declinations (which were declined for insurance). This data was made up of one-, two-, and three-borrower cases. Results are reported for the one- and two-borrower cases. The three-borrower files appeared with low frequency and for this reason were not included in the system.

The feature set of the MNNLS consisted of approximately 25 fields selected from the full database. These fields included information related to the borrower's "cultural" status, such as the borrower's credit rating, the number of dependents, the number of years employed, as well as whether the borrower was self employed and whether he intended to occupy the property. Fields related to the borrower financial status included current income, portion of income due to sources other than salary, and amount of obligations other than the principal property. In addition, features were included that related to the mortgage instrument, such as the loan-to-value ratio, the type of mortgage, the ratio of income to mortgage payments, and the loan amount. Finally, there was a class of fields related directly to the property: these included the property age, the number of units, the appraised value, and the location of the property.

As mentioned previously, the MNNLS architecture employed here uses three experts per level with each focused on a nonexclusive subset of the available features. These experts were arranged such that one made greater use of the borrower financial information, the second looked in depth at the borrower's cultural and the mortgage instrument features, and the third focused equally on all four feature categories.

Figure 16.1 depicts the "accuracy" of the system (meaning agreement with human underwriters) on the patterns identified as a function of the fraction of files identified unambiguously (the system will not

Figure 16.1

MNNLS Performance When Applied to Mortgage Insurance Underwriting

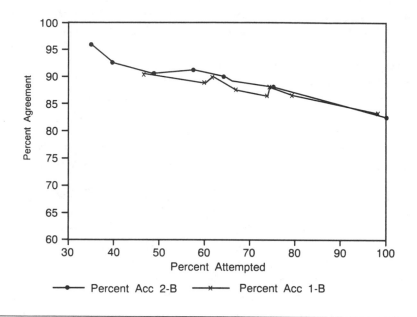

attempt a file lacking sufficient internal agreement). This particular kind of plot is possible with the MNNLS because the system can vary the degree of internal agreement among its constituent networks. The MNNLS is able to process over 30 percent of two-borrower applications for mortgage insurance with an accuracy of nearly 96 percent. The system, configured to process all applications, will perform with an accuracy of over 82 percent. One- and two-borrower performance is quite similar from a system agreement level of about 91 percent at 47 percent attempted to a system agreement level of 83 percent at 100 percent attempted.

This plot shows a clear trend of increasing confusion in the identifications as the attempt rate increases. This is due to inconsistencies in underwriting judgments in the training database. Analysis has shown that those files identified with high accuracy in the conservative (i.e., lowest attempted) mode are those on which underwriters agree. As the system is asked to attempt the more difficult cases, differences in underwriting practices lead to an ambiguity in the classification of files. Those files identified in the liberal (i.e., highest attempted) mode are in the difficult, "grey" area of underwriter judgment.

The goal of this study was to automate the mortgage insurance underwriting process and thus reduce processing costs. Much of the risk in mortgage insurance can be attributed to poor underwriter judgment, so an improvement in these judgments through more consistent use of underwriting guidelines would result in a significant reduction in risk. Here, consistency refers to the fact that when two similar loans are processed, they should be given the same judgment. If they are not, this demonstrates an inconsistent judgment. As was mentioned, human underwriters disagree with one another when making decisions. Therefore, the training examples, which the system used, contained ambiguities. One would expect that a system that mimicked these ambiguous judgments would exhibit similar behavior. However, we find that the MNNLS gives more consistent judgments than those of human underwriters. This improvement is a direct result of an informed consensus of network experts formed by the MNNLS architecture. The use of consensus allows the system to base its decisions on the combined expertise of past underwriting judgments.

In the following section we analyze the disagreements between the system and the human underwriter. This analysis will be performed using three methods: first, case studies of the disagreements; second, a distribution analysis of the files identified correctly and incorrectly; and finally, a quality analysis.

ANALYSIS

Case Studies

Case studies were performed on files in which the system's judgment disagreed with the actual underwriter. These studies were done when the system was run in the most conservative (i.e., lowest attempted) mode. Of the 12 errors that occurred, seven were underwriter declinations that were certified by the system. The remainder were underwriter-certifieds that the system declined. In nearly all the underwriting errors made by the MNNLS, very small differences in each of the several feature variables existed between the test application and the training example that the system used to make its judgments. The fact that applications existed in the training set that matched the test applications closely but were accompanied by opposite underwriter decisions indicates inconsistencies in underwriter practices. This shows that underwriters disagree with one another on different applications with similar characteristics.

On further observation, we note that in the case of the underwriter-declined applications, the reason given for the declination by the underwriting agency is generally not correlated with the features of the file. This is a second indicator of inconsistency as it suggests that the human underwriter was using the underwriting guidelines improperly. In particular, of the seven declinations, six were declined for reasons of credit. The credit rating field was a number between 1 and 8; a lower number generally indicated a more favorable credit rating than a large number. Of these six declined applications, half had credit ratings of 1 (generally considered a good credit rating), while only one had a credit rating worse than 2. An important point is that the system certified these files, which is apparently a reasonable judgment.

Single-Feature Analysis Using Histograms

The internal representation in the system memory formed through training on the database of underwriting decisions may be analyzed through the use of standard statistical tools. This form of analysis is not capable of fully describing the nonlinear, multidimensional decision surfaces that exist in the memory; however, it does provide a sense of the underwriting model which has been developed.

We have chosen to examine the model with a single-feature analysis. This procedure was carried out for many of the features used by the MNNLS; however, for brevity only three are presented here. For each feature, the distribution of correctly and incorrectly identified patterns has been plotted. The three features chosen are HSYS (the ratio of housing expenses to total income), OSYS (the ratio of total expenses to total income), and the Credit Rating. Each feature has been analyzed in the liberal (i.e., highest attempted) mode of operation. Figure 16.2 shows all three of these features. The left column of histograms depicts files identified correctly, while the right column illustrates the incorrectly identified files. Each graph depicts distributions for both certified (C) and declined (D) files. The white bars correspond to underwriter certified files and the black bars correspond to the underwriter declined files.

The graphs are normalized frequency histograms of the various groups of identified files. The horizontal axis of each graph illustrates the range of the feature in question. Values on this axis are center values of a bin. The bin range may be inferred from the graph. The vertical axis indicates the normalized frequency of occurrence of files at this particular feature value for this identification set. The certified and declined populations were normalized separately by their corresponding subpopulation totals.

Housing Obligations Ratio (HSYS).   HSYS is the ratio of housing costs to total income. It is generally felt that this ratio should not exceed the range of 25 percent to 28 percent.[7] The top row of histograms in Figure 16.2 depicts the frequency of files having HSYS values in the range from 0 to 45 percent. The leftmost graph plots all files identified correctly in the liberal (i.e., highest attempted) mode. The peak of the certification distribution occurs at a value of 21 percent with sharp fall-off occurring at 28 percent. This clearly demonstrates the fact that the system has learned the underwriting guidelines without prior knowledge. However, the fact that there are some applicants certified beyond this point shows that this is a loose or fuzzy boundary. As expected, a significant portion of the declination distribution occurs in the range of 35 percent and higher. A large number of files are declined in the acceptable range of 13 percent to 27 percent, presumably for reasons other than the value of HSYS: for example, an applicant with a good HSYS value may have a very bad credit rating.

The error distributions in liberal mode, illustrated in the top right-hand graph, are quite overlapping. Here again, we see a sharp falloff at 28 percent, which shows that this criterion was used properly even on files for which the system and the underwriter disagreed. Note that in the range of 30 percent to 35 percent, examples of both certifications and declinations occur. However, in the 34 percent to 36 percent bin, there is only a white bar, which represents underwriter-certified cases that were declined by the system. Thus, the system operates more conservatively: human underwriter-certified files with large HSYS values are declined by the system. This is advantageous since the system is adhering to its underwriting guidelines more strictly and will reduce risk in doing so.

Figure 16.2

Single-Feature Histograms of Correctly and Incorrectly Identified Files for HSYS, OSYS, and Credit Rating Features

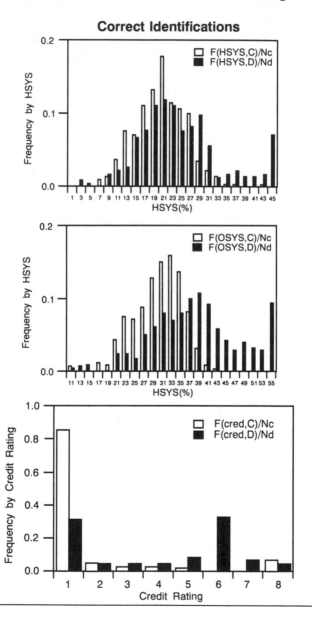

Figure 16.2 (continued)

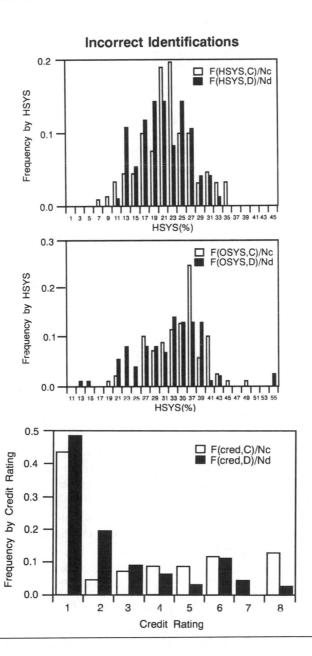

Total Obligations Ratio (OSYS). OSYS is the ratio of total expense to total income, and is indicative of the applicant's risk due to both the property in question and other borrower debt. This ratio is expected to be no greater than 33 percent to 36 percent.[7] The left graph of the middle row depicts the distribution of files correctly certified and declined in liberal mode, as a function of this feature. Note the drop-off in certified files after 36 percent. Again, the system has learned the guidelines inherent in the data, although it is not as pronounced as with the HSYS feature.

In the incorrectly identified distribution, all errors that occurred with OSYS greater than 44 percent were underwriter-certified files which were declined by the system. Again, it is seen that the system operates more conservatively than the human underwriters since it is declining files with high OSYS values that were certified by the agency's underwriters. This further reinforces the fact that the system is using its underwriting guidelines more consistently than the actual underwriters.

Credit Rating. The bottom left figure illustrates the credit ratings of the files identified in liberal mode. In general, a larger value in this field indicates a poorer credit rating than a small value. Nearly all certified files occur with a credit rating of 1, (a small number occur with ratings of 2, 3, 4 and 8). Declinations are spread across all credit ratings with a peak at the rating of 6. This behavior is expected as a credit rating of 1 indicates a nearly spotless record with at most only a small blemish. The rating of 6 is particularly poor as it indicates the occurrence of a bankruptcy or foreclosure at some point in the past. This again demonstrates the system's ability to learn this criterion without any prior knowledge.

In the error distributions, the general decreasing trend of the black bars as well as the general increasing trend (except for rating of 1) of the white bars are of particular interest. The decrease of the black bars corresponds to patterns that the system certified, while the white represent system declinations. Even in these cases, which disagreed with the actual underwriters, the system preserved its learning interpretation of this field. The fact that both classes have a peak in the error distribution at a value of 1 is likely due to the abundance of such ratings in the normal distribution of the data.

Quality Analysis

An analysis of the source of disagreement between the system and the human underwriters reveals that much of the disagreement occurs as a result of different human underwriter judgments based on the same file information. In difficult or marginal cases, different underwriters make different judgments based on the same information. It has been possible to assess the quality of the mortgages certified by a separate criterion.[8] We find that the quality of the neural network-certified files is consistently higher than those certified by human underwriters (Table 16.1). Here, quality is a function of the probability that loans will perform well (in terms of delinquencies) in the future. A lower quality means a greater frequency of predicted delinquency (negative quality means that more than 50 percent of the population had predicted delinquency in the future).

To further illustrate the benefit of a consensus judgment in the MNNLS, we have studied four basic subsets of files for quality. For each class, these subsets are: (1) files the system classified by itself, (2) files an underwriter classified independently, (3) files for which the underwriter's and system's judgments agreed and (4) files that they

Table 16.1

A Comparison of the Quality of Various Sets of Files Certified and/or Declined by the MNNLS (System) and the Human Underwriter (Underwriter)

Set	Quality
Certified by both system and underwriter	.87
Certified by system	.84
Certified by underwriter	.78
Certified by system, declined by underwriter	.50
Declined by underwriter	−.10
Declined by system, certified by underwriter	−.12
Declined by system	−.28
Declined by both system and underwriter	−.36

disagreed upon. Of particular interest is the fact that the certification files for which the system and underwriter agree have the highest quality. Correspondingly, the files in disagreement have the lowest quality. In this case, the underwriter can be thought of as another expert participating in the consensus. It is logical that these responses are of higher quality than the system's for the same reason that the system's decisions are better than the underwriter's. This highlights the finding that consensus judgment improves consistency and correspondingly the quality of judgments.

CONCLUSIONS

This application made use of a multiple neural network learning system. In essence, this system uses the consensus of a panel of expert networks to classify files according to risk. This system was used to replicate the decisions made by mortgage insurance underwriters. It should be noted that this is a real-world problem that possesses a significant economic benefit to the mortgage insurance industry. This problem is also difficult because it is a second-order problem. All applications to the mortgage insurance company have already been underwritten by a mortgage originator. Thus, all of these applications by nature have a higher risk.

The system was trained on several thousand previous underwriter judgments and learned to mimic their underwriting skills. When this system rendered decisions on a test set, the level of agreement with human underwriters (or accuracy) ranged from 96 percent to 82.5 percent depending on the degree of consensus desired between the system's expert networks. When a higher degree of consensus is required, a smaller percentage of the testing files will be unambiguously identified but with a higher accuracy. It is important to note that these results are for a system that performs underwriting on applications from all parts of the country. Thus, the system incorporates the geographic knowledge, and skills, among all of the underwriters in the company!

It was found that many of the disagreements between system and underwriter were caused by the inconsistent underwriting practices of human underwriters. Further, we found that the MNNLS is more consistent in its decisions than the human underwriters. This is a direct result of the consensus judgments of the MNNLS.

The system's improved use of underwriting guidelines was analyzed in three ways. The first method of analysis was the use of case studies of the applications in disagreement. It was found that in general, these applications were very similar to previous ones that were assigned the opposite classification. The second method was to perform a single-feature analysis of the certification and declination distributions for correctly and incorrectly identified patterns. This was reported for the HSYS, OSYS, and credit rating features. The HSYS and OSYS analysis showed that the system had learned the underwriting guidelines for these features and had represented it with a fuzzy boundary. In addition, errors that the system produced at high values of these features were applicants which the system declined yet the human underwriter had certified. This illustrates the system's attempt to use its learned guidelines more consistently. The system also learned the importance of a foreclosure in a borrower's credit rating. In this feature, as well, the errors demonstrate that the system is using its underwriting guidelines in a consistent manner.

Finally, a quality analysis of the files identified by the system and actual underwriters showed that the MNNLS-identified files were of higher quality. This is the case because the system makes an informed consensus judgment. It consistently outperforms a human underwriter because it looks for agreement among its cooperating networks. In contrast, an underwriter is one expert acting by himself. It would be quite labor intensive to have several agency underwriters process each application. However, the MNNLS does this automatically by design, and in this way can provide better judgments than a single underwriter. Thus, the system offers an economic benefit by reduced processing costs and further offers an economic gain by improved consistency in underwriting judgments.

ENDNOTES

1. J. J. Hopfield, "Neural Networks and Physical Systems with Emergent Collective Computational Abilities," *Proceedings of the National Academy of Science USA*, vol. 79, April 1982, pp. 2554–2558.

2. J. J. Hopfield, "Neurons with Graded Response Have Collective Computational Properties Like Those of Two-State Neurons," *Pro-*

ceedings of the National Academy of Science USA, vol. 81, May 1984, pp. 2088–3092.

3. C. M. Bachmann, L. N. Cooper, A. Dembo, and O. Zeitouni, "A Relaxation Model for Memory with High Density Storage," *Proceedings of the National Academy of Science USA,* vol. 21, November 1987, pp. 7529–7531.

4. D. L. Reilly, L. N. Cooper, and C. Elbaum, "A Neural Model for Category Learning," *Biological Cybernetics,* vol. 45, 1982, pp. 35–41.

5. D. L. Reilly, C. Scofield, C. Elbaum, and L. N. Cooper, "Learning System Architectures Composed of Multiple Learning Modules," *Proceedings of the First International Conference on Neural Networks,* 1987.

6. R. Rimey, P. Gouin, C. Scofield, and D. L. Reilly, "Real-Time 3-D Object Classification Using a Learning System," *Intelligent Robots and Computer Vision, Proceedings SPIE,* vol. 726, 1986.

7. *Underwriting Guidelines: Home Mortgages,* Freddie Mac, Publication no. 19, August 1984.

8. S. Ghosh, E. Collins, and C. Scofield, "Prediction of Mortgage Loan Performance with a Multiple Neural Network Learning System." *Proceedings of the First Annual Meeting of the International Neural Network Society,* September 1988.

17

RISK ASSESSMENT OF MORTGAGE APPLICATIONS WITH A NEURAL NETWORK SYSTEM: AN UPDATE AS THE TEST PORTFOLIO AGES

Douglas L. Reilly, Edward Collins,
Christopher Scofield, and Sushmito Ghosh

INTRODUCTION

Nestor's multiple neural network technology has been applied to many problems; among them, applications in signal processing for character recognition,[1] in medicine,[2] in vision,[3] industrial inspection,[4,5] diagnos-

© July 1991, IEEE. Reprinted with permission from *Proceedings of the IEEE International Conference on Neural Networks*, pp. II479–II482.

tics,[6] speech recognition.[7] Neural net applications have also been developed in the financial services arena. One particular problem domain that has been under investigation is that of automated decision-making and risk assessment for mortgage insurance underwriting. The application of Nestor's neural net technology to this problem has been previously reported.[8-10] This chapter presents an update to this work, returning to the risk assessment portion of the problem to analyze how well the risk prediction has fared for the mortgage portfolio under study, now that the portfolio has aged.

RISK ASSESSMENT

Mortgage risk assessment begins with mortgage origination. A mortgage originator filters the general population of potential property owners according to a set of simple guidelines on acceptable ranges for such risk measures as the proposed loan-to-value ratio, the ratio of proposed obligations to income, etc. Fannie Mae, and others in the secondary mortgage market, publish guidelines that serve to qualify and segregate the home loan applicant pool into risk categories. Some of the higher risk loans are referred for private mortgage insurance. The process of determining whether or not a loan applicant should be accepted for mortgage insurance involves in effect a second underwriting. If the applicant exhibits an acceptable level of risk, he or she will be sold insurance. Mortgage insurance applicants are by nature a higher risk group than the general originator and assessed as less secure cases. Thus, this second order underwriting performed by the mortgage insurer is bound to be more difficult, and prone to greater uncertainty.

The mortgage insurance problem can be divided into two parts. The first problem is that of automating the decision-making process of the underwriters. This can be served by constructing a system that can learn to emulate the decisions that underwriters make on mortgage applications. A system that correctly mimics the judgment of human underwriters on some subset of the loan applications presented to it can have economic benefit as a result of introducing consistency in underwriter judgments and in allowing an underwriting agency to better handle peak workloads. The strategy of applying a neural network approach to this phase of the problem is to capture data that represents loan application information together with the corresponding judgments that an underwriter has made on each application. The pool of data represents judgments from a number of underwriters. The neural net system trains to emulate the decision-making of this collection of experts on the problem.

A different aspect of the problem arises not from the use of the network in automating the human decision-making, but rather from the use of the network to improve on the quality of the decisions through its ability to learn to estimate some measure of the risk of a loan applicant's defaulting on his or her mortgage payments. Underwriters for loan originators and private mortgage insurance companies do not perform this task flawlessly. Although these insurance underwriters typically decline approximately 20 percent of the applications they review, of the remaining accepted group, some 20 percent will go delinquent during the course of the loan. Approximately 6 percent will eventually lead to losses as a result of claims. The peak in claims rates occurs some three to five years after the loan is granted. Because any feedback from an incorrect decision occurs some number of years after the decision is made, and because of the high turnover rate in underwriter staffing, there is little opportunity to improve on the underwriters' judgments from observations of historical outcomes.

Although the economic payoff of improving the quality of the underwriting decisions can be substantially greater than that of simply automating and replicating their current decision-making trends and practices, the acceptance of the former can require a higher level of commitment and reliance on the technology. It is relatively easy to immediately verify whether or not the system is deciding as the underwriter would decide. From the simple perspective of "trusting the machine," it requires more commitment to accept that the machine, when disagreeing with the underwriter, is actually making the *better* decision about something that might happen three to five years from now.

The neural network that was used for this application is a derivative of an RCE network that has been reported on elsewhere.[11] The RCE network is a three-layer network that has been described extensively.[12-15] Essentially, the network trains by committing cells on its single internal layer that represent prototypical "exemplars" of the pattern classes which it sees in the training set. It automatically selects from the training set the exemplars that are to be stored in memory, storing in its weights the values that define the prototype features. Associated with each prototype cell is a cell threshold, a number that captures the extent to which this prototype's exemplar will participate in the classification of incoming new patterns. This cell threshold represents a region of influence around the prototype in the pattern space.

Data used for the risk assessment study were taken from a collection of some 111,080 home mortgage loans from the period July 1984 to December 1986. The status of the loans was noted as of December 1987, and this served as the classification of "Good" and "Bad" loans. For the initial study, "Bad" was defined as any loan that had gone delinquent at least once in the period from origination through the end of 1987. A total of 758 good applications and 844 bad applications was used for the risk assessment study.

The results of the initial study are shown in Figure 17.1. For a certain percentage of the applications (10 percent), it is possible to predict with 95 percent accuracy the loans which, if granted, would go delinquent in payment. (Delinquency is not the same as default, but it is a necessary precursor.) If the system's decisions are accepted at this throughput (10 percent of applications), then some number of good applications will also be called "bad." Rejecting such loan applicants would amount to

Figure 17.1

Performance of Mortgage Risk Processor

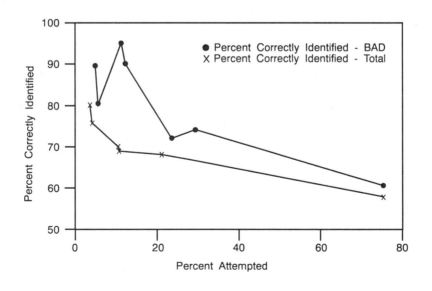

turning away good business. Since the cost of replacing this lost business is far less than the cost associated with underwriting loans that go to claim, this 10 percent throughput represents an operating point with a viable economic benefit.

As noted earlier, these results were reported on a portfolio of mortgages whose delinquency/default status was dated as of December 1987. Since the portfolio represented originations between July 1984 and December 1986, the age of the applications at the time of the study ranged from one to three and one-half years. Updates on the status of this portfolio were provided as of September 1988. Since claims begin to peak in the three- to five-year period after origination, we would expect to see significantly more claims in the updated portfolio. Special attention is paid to those loans that, at the time of the initial study had been labeled good, but have since gone bad.

Additionally, sensitivity of the model to the size of the training set is important. The collection of a portfolio for training purposes can often have some cost associated with it, if all the information that is typically available to underwriters is not available in electronic file format for the neural network to process. Consequently, it can be important to establish some measure of the additional marginal benefit in risk assessment as a function of additional loan examples made available for training. Figure 17.2 shows a learning curve for the neural net risk assessment system as a function of the percentage of the data set trained on.

ENDNOTES

1. D. Ward, C. L. Scofield, and D. L. Reilly, "An Application of a Multiple Neural Network with Modifiable Network Topology (GENSEP) to On-line Character Recognition," *Abstracts of INNS*, (Boston), 1988.

2. T. O. Carroll, H. Ved, and D. L. Reilly, "A Neural Network ECG Analysis," *Proceedings IJCNN*, June 1989, pp. II-575.

3. R. Rimey, P. Gouin, C. Scofield, and D. L. Reilly, "Real-time 3-D Object Classification Using a Learning System," *Proceedings SPIE Cambridge Symposium on Intelligent Robots and Computer Vision*, October 26–31, 1986.

Figure 17.2

Claims Prediction Learning Curve

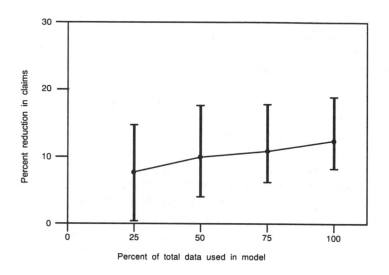

4. D. L. Reilly, C. Scofield, P. R. Gouin, R. Rimey, E. A. Collins, and S. Ghosh, "An Application of a Multiple Neural Network Learning System to Industrial Part Inspection," *Proceedings of ISA*, October 1988.

5. R. O. Fox, F. Czerniewjewski, F. Fluet, and E. Mitchell, "Neural Network Machine Vision," *Abstracts of INNS*, vol. I, 1988, p. 438.

6. K. Marko, J. James, J. Dosdall, and J. Murphy, "Automotive Control System Diagnostics Using Neural Nets for Rapid Pattern Classification of Large Data Sets," *Proceedings IJCNN*, vol. II, June 1989, pp. 13–16.

7. P. Zemany, W. Hogan, E. Real, D. P. Morgan, L. Riek, D. L. Reilly, C. L. Scofield, P. Gouin, and F. Hull, "Experiments in Discrete Utterance Recognition Using Neural Networks," *Proceedings of Second Biennial Acoustics Speech and Signal Processing Conference*, May 1989.

8. E. Collins, S. Ghosh, and C. L. Scofield, "An Application of a Multiple Neural Network Learning System to Emulation of Mortgage

Underwriting Judgments," *IEEE International Conference on Neural Networks II*, 1988, pp. 459–466.

9. C. Scofield, E. A. Collins, and S. Ghosh, "Prediction of Mortgage Loan Performance with a Multiple Neural Network Learning System," *Abstracts of INNS*, vol. 1, 1988, p. 439.

10. *DARPA Neural Network Survey Study*, AFCEA, November 1988, pp. 429–443.

11. C. L. Scofield, D. L. Reilly, C. Elbaum, and L. N. Cooper, "Pattern Class Degeneracy in an Unrestricted Storage Density Memory," *Neural Information Processing Systems*, ed. D. Z. Anderson, (New York), 1985, pp. 674–682.

12. D. L. Reilly, L. N. Cooper, and C. Elbaum, "A Neural Model for Category Learning," *Biological Cybernetics*, vol. 45, 1982, pp. 35–41.

13. L. N. Cooper, C. Elbaum, and D. L. Reilly, "Self Organizing General Pattern Class Separator and Identifier," U. S. Patent No. 4,326,259, awarded April 20, 1982.

14. L. N. Cooper, C. Elbaum, D. L. Reilly, and C. L. Scofield, "Parallel, Multi-Unit Adaptive Nonlinear Pattern Class Separator and Identifier," U. S. Patent No. 4,760,604, awarded July 26, 1988.

15. D. L. Reilly, C. Scofield, C. Elbaum, and L. N. Cooper, "Learning System Architectures Composed of Multiple Learning Modules," *IEEE First International Conference on Neural Networks II*, 1987, pp. 495–503.

PART 5

SECURITY MARKET APPLICATIONS

18

Economic Prediction Using Neural Networks: The Case of IBM Daily Stock Returns

Halbert White

INTRODUCTION

The value of neural network modeling techniques in performing complicated pattern recognition and nonlinear forecasting tasks has now been demonstrated across an impressive spectrum of applications. Two particularly interesting recent examples are those of Lapedes and Farber who apply neural networks to decoding genetic protein sequences,[1]

© July 1988, IEEE. Reprinted with permission from *Proceedings of the IEEE International Conference on Neural Networks*, pp. II451–II458.

and demonstrate that neural networks are capable of decoding deterministic chaos.[2] Given these successes, it is natural to ask whether such techniques can be of use in extracting nonlinear regularities from economic time series. Not surprisingly, especially strong interest attaches to the possibility of decoding previously undetected regularities in asset price movements, such as the minute-to-minute or day-to-day fluctuations of common stock prices. Such regularities, if found, could be the key to great wealth.

Against the optimistic hope that neural network methods can unlock the mysteries of the stock market is the pessimistic received wisdom (at least among academics) of the "efficient markets hypothesis." In its simplest form, this hypothesis asserts that asset prices follow a random walk.[3] That is, apart from a possible constant expected appreciation (a risk-free return plus a premium for holding a risky asset), the movement of an asset's price is completely unpredictable from publicly available information such as the price and volume history for the asset itself or that of any other asset. (Note that predictability from publicly unavailable (insider) information is not ruled out.) The justification for the absence of predictability is akin to the reason that there are so few $100 bills lying on the ground. Apart from the fact that they are not often dropped, they tend to be picked up very rapidly. The same is held to be true of predictable profit opportunities in asset markets: they are exploited as soon as they arise. In the case of a strongly expected price increase, market participants go long (buy), driving up the price to its expected level, thus quickly wiping out the profit opportunity that existed only moments ago. Given the human and financial resources devoted to the attempt to detect and exploit such opportunities, the efficient markets hypothesis is indeed an attractive one. It also appears to be one of the few well-documented empirical successes of modern economic theory. Numerous studies have found little evidence against the simple efficient markets hypothesis just described, although mixed results have been obtained using some of its more sophisticated variants.[3-6]

Despite the strength of the simple efficient markets hypothesis, it is still only a theory, and any theory can be refuted with appropriate evidence. It may be that techniques capable of finding such evidence have not yet been applied. Furthermore, the theory is realistically mitigated by bounded rationality arguments.[7,8] Such arguments hold that humans are inherently limited in their ability to process information, so that efficiency can hold only to the limits of human information processing. If a new technology (such as neural network methods) suddenly becomes available for processing available information, then profit opportunities may arise for the possessor of that technology. The technology effectively allows creation of a form of inside information. However, the efficient markets hypothesis implies that as the new technology becomes publicly available, these advantages will dwindle rapidly and ultimately disappear.

In view of the relative novelty of neural network methods and the implications of bounded rationality, it is at least conceivable that previously undetected regularities exist in historical asset price data, and that such regularities may yet persist. The purpose of this chapter is to illustrate how the search for such regularities using neural network methods might proceed, using the case of IBM daily common stock returns as an example. The necessity of dealing with the salient features of economic time series highlights the role to be played by methods of statistical inference and also requires modifications of neural network learning methods that may prove useful in general contexts.

DATA, MODELS, METHODS AND RESULTS

The target variable of interest in the present study is r_t, the one-day rate of return to holding IBM common stock on day t, as reported in the Center for Research in Security Price's security price data file ("the CRSP file"). The one-day return is defined as $r_t = (p_t - p_{t-1} + d_t)/p_{t-1}$, where p_t is the closing price on day t and d_t is the dividend paid on day t. The one-day return r_t is also adjusted for stock splits, if any. Of the available 5,000 days of return data, we select a sample of 1,000 days for training purposes, together with samples of 500 days before and after the training period, which we use for evaluating whatever knowledge our networks have acquired. The training sample covers trading days during the period 1974:II through 1978:I. The evaluation periods cover 1972:II through 1974:I and 1978:II through 1980:I. The training set is depicted in Figure 18.1.

Stated formally, the simple efficient markets hypothesis asserts that $E(r_t \mid I_{t-1}) = r^*$, where $E(r_t \mid I_{t-1})$ denotes the conditional expectation of r_t given publicly available information at time $t-1$, I_{t-1} (formally I_{t-1} is the σ-field generated by publicly available information), and r^* is a constant (which may be unknown) consisting of the risk-free return plus a risk premium. Because I_{t-1} includes the previous IBM price

Figure 18.1

Training Set

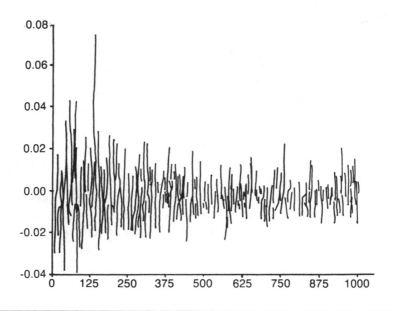

history, the force of the simple efficient markets hypothesis is that this history is of no use in forecasting r_t.

In the economics literature, a standard way of testing this form of the efficient markets hypothesis begins by embedding it as a special case in a linear autoregressive model for asset returns of the form

$$r_t = w_0 + w_1 r_{t-1} + \ldots + w_p r_{t-p} + \varepsilon_t, \, t = 1, 2, \ldots,$$

where $\underline{w} = (w_0, w_1, \ldots, w_p)'$ is an unknown column vector of weights, p is a positive integer determining the order of the autoregression, and ε_t is a stochastic error assumed to be such that $E(\varepsilon_t \mid I_{t-1}) = 0$.

The efficient markets hypothesis implies the restriction that $w_1 = \ldots = w_p = 0$. Thus, any empirical evidence that $w_1 \neq 0$ or $w_2 \neq 0 \ldots$ or $w_p \neq 0$ is evidence against the efficient markets hypothesis. On the other hand, empirical evidence that $w_1 = \ldots = w_p = 0$, while not refuting the efficient markets hypothesis, does not confirm it; numerous instances of deterministic nonlinear processes with no linear structure whatsoever are now well known.[9,10] The finding that $w_1 = \ldots = w_p = 0$ is consistent with either the efficient markets hypothesis or the presence of linearly undetectable nonlinear regularities.

An equivalent implication of the simple efficient markets hypothesis that will primarily concern us here is that $var\ r_t = var\ \varepsilon_t$, where var denotes the variance of the indicated random variable. Equivalently, $R^2 \equiv 1 - var\ \varepsilon_t / var\ r_t = 0$ under the simple efficient market hypothesis. Thus, empirical evidence that $R^2 \neq 0$ is evidence against the simple efficient markets hypothesis, while empirical evidence that $R^2 = 0$ is consistent with either the efficient markets hypothesis or the existence of non-linear structure.

Thus, as a first step, we examine the empirical evidence against the simple efficient markets hypothesis using the linear model posited above. The linear autoregressive model of order p $(AR(p)$ model) corresponds to a very simple two-layer linear feed-forward network. Given inputs $r_{t-1}, \ldots, r_{t-p}$, the network output is given as $\hat{r}_t = \hat{w}_0 + \hat{w}_1 r_{t-1} + \ldots + \hat{w}_p r_{t-p}$, where $\hat{w}_0, \hat{w}_1, \ldots, \hat{w}_p$ are the network weights arrived at by a suitable learning procedure. Our interest then attaches to an empirical estimate of R^2, computed in the standard way[11] as $R^2 \equiv 1 - \hat{var}\ \varepsilon_t / \hat{var}\ r_t$, where

$$\hat{var}\ \varepsilon_t \equiv n^{-1} \sum_{t=1}^{n} (r_t - \hat{r}_t)^2,$$

$$\hat{var}\ r_t \equiv n^{-1} \sum_{t=1}^{n} (r_t - \bar{r})^2,$$

$$\bar{r} \equiv n^{-1} \sum_{t=1}^{n} r_t,$$

and n is the number of training observations. Here $n = 1,000$.

These quantities are readily determined once we have arrived at suitable values for the network weights. A variety of learning procedures is available. A common learning method for linear networks is the delta method:

$$\underline{w}_{t+1} = \underline{w}_t - \eta\, \underline{x}'_t\, (r_t - \underline{x}_t\, \underline{w}_t) \quad t = 1, \ldots, 1{,}000$$

where $\underline{w}_t$ is the $(p+1) \times 1$ weight vector after presentation of $t-1$ target/input pairs, η is the learning rate, and $\underline{x}_t$ is the $1 \times (p+1)$ vector of inputs $\underline{x}_t = (1, r_{t-1}, \ldots, r_{t-p})$. A major defect of this method is that because of the constant learning rate and the presence of a random component ε_t in r_t, this method will never converge to a useful set of weight values, but is doomed to wander eternally in the netherworld of suboptimality.

A theoretical solution to this problem lies in allowing η to depend on t. As shown by White,[12,13] an optimal choice is $\eta \propto t^{-1}$. Nevertheless, this method yields very slow convergence. A very satisfactory computational solution is to dispense with recursive learning methods altogether, and simply apply the method of ordinary least squares (OLS). This gives weights by solving the problem:

$$\min_{\underline{w}} \sum_{t=1}^{n} (r_t - \underline{x}_t\, \underline{w})^2$$

The solution is given analytically as:

$$\underline{w} = (X'X)^{-1} X'r$$

where X is the $1{,}000 \times (p+1)$ matrix with rows $\underline{x}_t$, r is the $1{,}000 \times 1$ vector with elements r_t, and the -1 superscript denotes matrix inversion.

Network learning by OLS is unlikely as a biological mechanism; however, our interest is not on learning per se, but on the results of learning. We are interested in the performance of "mature" networks. Furthermore, White[12,13] proves that as $n \to \infty$ both OLS and the delta method with $\eta \propto t^{-1}$ converge stochastically to identical limits. Thus, nothing is lost and much computational effort is saved by using OLS.

When OLS is applied to the linear network with $p = 5$, we obtain $\hat{R}^2 = .0079$. By construction, $\hat{R}^2$ must lie between zero and one. The fact that $\hat{R}^2$ is so low suggests little evidence against the simple efficient markets hypothesis. In fact, under some statistical regularity conditions,

$n\hat{R}^2$ is distributed approximately as χ^2_p when $w_1 = \ldots = w_p = 0$. In our case, $n\hat{R}^2 = 7.9$, so we have evidence against $w_1 = \ldots = w_p = 0$ at less than the 10 percent level, which is below usual levels considered to be statistically significant. The plot of $\hat{r}_t$ also reveals the virtual absence of any relation between $\hat{r}_t$ and r_t (see Figure 18.2).

Thus, standard methods yield standard conclusions, although nonlinear regularities are not ruled out. To investigate the possibility that neural network methods can detect nonlinear regularities inconsistent with the simple efficient markets hypothesis, we trained a three-layer feed-forward network with the same five inputs and five hidden units over the same training period. The choice of five hidden units is not entirely ad hoc, as it represents a compromise between the necessity to include enough hidden units so that at least simple nonlinear regularities can be detected by the network (Lapedes and Farber[2] detected the deterministic chaos of the logistic map using five hidden units with the squashing functions; we use logistic squashes, but performance in that case at least is comparable, even with only three or even two hidden

Figure 18.2

Training Set

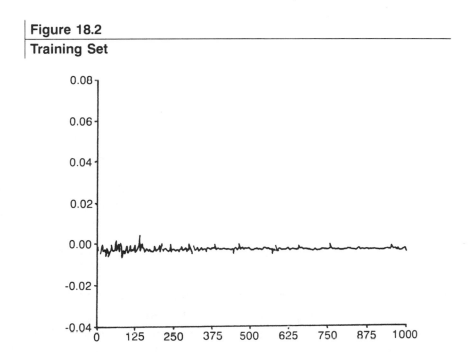

units) and the necessity to avoid including so many hidden units that the network is capable of "memorizing" the entire training sequence. It is our view that this latter requirement is extremely important if one wishes to obtain a network which has any hope at all of being able to generalize adequately in an environment in which the output is not some exact function of the input, but exhibits random variation around some average value determined by the inputs. Recent results in the statistics literature for the method of sieves[14,15] suggest that with a fixed number of inputs and outputs, the number of hidden units should grow only as some small power of the number of training observations. Overelaborate networks are capable of data-mining as enthusiastically as any young graduate student.

The network architecture used in the present exercise is the standard single hidden-layer architecture, with inputs x_t passed to a hidden layer (with full interconnections) and then with hidden layer activations passed to the output unit. Our analysis was conducted with and without a logistic squash at the output; results were comparable, so we discuss the results without an output squash.

The output of this network is given by:

$$\tilde{r}_t = \hat{\beta}_o + \sum_{j=1}^{5} \psi(\underline{x}_t \hat{\underline{y}}_j)\hat{\beta}_j = f(\underline{x}_t, \hat{\underline{\theta}})$$

where $(\hat{\beta}_o, \hat{\beta}_1, ..., \hat{\beta}_5)$ are a bias and weights from the hidden units to the output and $\hat{\underline{y}} = (\hat{\underline{y}}_1, ..., \hat{\underline{y}}_5)$ are weights from the input units, both after a suitable training procedure; and ψ is the logistic squashing function. The function f summarizes the dependence of the output on the input x_t and the vector of all connection strengths $\hat{\underline{\theta}}$.

As with the preceding linear network, the efficient markets hypothesis implies that $\tilde{R}^2 \equiv 1 - v\hat{a}r\, \tilde{\varepsilon}_t / v\hat{a}r\, r_t$ should be approximately zero,

where now $v\hat{a}r\, \tilde{\varepsilon}_t \equiv n^{-1} \sum_{t=1}^{n} (r_t - \tilde{r}_t)^2$ and $v\hat{a}r\, r_t = n^{-1} \sum_{t=1}^{n} (r_t - \bar{r})^2$ as before. This result will be associated with values for $\hat{\beta}_1, ..., \hat{\beta}_5$ close to zero, and random values for $\hat{y}_j$. A value for $\tilde{R}^2$ close to zero will reflect the inability of the network to extract nonlinear regularities from the training set.

As with the linear network, a variety of training procedures is available. One popular method is the method of back-propagation.[16,17] In our notation, it can be represented as:

$$\underline{\theta}_{t+1} = \underline{\theta}_t - \eta_t \nabla_\theta f(\underline{x}_t, \theta_t)' (r_t - f(\underline{x}_t, \underline{\theta}_t))$$

where $\underline{\theta}_t$ is the vector of all connection strengths after $t - 1$ training observations have been presented, η_t is the learning rate (now explicitly dependent on t) ∇_θ represents the gradient with respect to θ (a row vector) and the other notation is as before.

Back-propagation shares the drawbacks of the delta method previously discussed. With η_t a constant, it fails to converge, while with $\eta_t \propto t^{-1}$, it converges (in theory) to a local minimum. Unfortunately, the random components of r_t renders convergence extremely difficult to obtain in practice. In fact, running on an IBM RT at well over 4 MIPS, convergence was not achieved after 36 hours of computation.

Rather quick convergence was obtained using a variant of the method of nonlinear least squares described in White.[18] The method of nonlinear least squares (NLS) uses standard iterative numerical methods such as Newton-Raphson and Davidson-Fletcher-Powell[19] to solve the problem:

$$\min_{\underline{\theta}} \sum_{t=1}^{n} (r_t - f(\underline{x}_i, \underline{\theta}))^2$$

Under general conditions, both NLS and back-propagation with $\eta_t \propto t^{-1}$ converge stochastically to the same limit, as shown by White.[12,13]

Our nonlinear least-squares method yields connection strengths $\hat{\theta}$ which imply $\tilde{R}^2 = .175$. At least superficially, this is a surprisingly good fit, apparently inconsistent with the efficient markets hypothesis and consistent with the presence of nonlinear regularities. Furthermore, the plot of fitted $(\tilde{r}_t)$ values shows some very impressive hits (see Figure 18.3).

If for the moment we imagine that $\hat{\underline{y}}$ is given, and not the result of an optimization procedure, then $n\tilde{R}^2 = 175$ is χ^2_5 under the simple efficient markets hypothesis, a highly significant result by any standards.

Unfortunately, $\hat{\gamma}$ is the result of an optimization procedure, not given a priori. For this reason $n\tilde{R}^2$ is in fact not χ_5^2 ; indeed, its distribution is a complicated nonstandard distribution. The present situation is similar to that considered by Davies[20,21] in which certain parameters (γ here) are not identified under the null hypothesis. A theory applicable in the present context has not yet been developed and constitutes an important area for further research.

Given the unknown distribution for $n\tilde{R}^2$, we must be cautious in claiming that the simple efficient markets hypothesis has been statistically refuted. We need further evidence. One way to obtain this evidence is to conduct out-of-sample forecasting experiments. Under the efficient markets hypothesis, the out-of-sample correlation between r_t and $\tilde{r}_t$ (or $\hat{r}_t$) where $\tilde{r}_t$ ($\hat{r}_t$) is computed using weights determined during the training (sample) period and inputs from the evaluation (out-of-sample) period, should be close to zero. If, contrary to the simple efficient markets hypothesis, our three-layer network has detected nonlinear structure, we should observe significant positive correlation between r_t and $\tilde{r}_t$.

This exercise was carried out for a postsample period of 500 days, and a presample period of 500 days. For the postsample period we observe a correlation of –.0699; for the presample period, it is .0751 (for comparison, the linear model gives postsample correlation of –.207 and presample correlation of .0996). Such results do not constitute convincing statistical evidence against the efficient markets hypothesis. The in-sample (training period) results are now seen to be over-optimistic, being either the result of over-fitting (random fluctuations recognized incorrectly as nonlinearities) or of learning evanescent features (features that are indeed present during the training period, but which subsequently disappear). In either case the implication is the same: the present neural network is not a money machine.

CONCLUDING REMARKS

Although some might be disappointed by the failure of the simple network considered here to find evidence against the simple efficient markets hypothesis, the present exercise suggests some valuable insights: (1) finding evidence against efficient markets with such simple networks is not going to be easy; (2) even simple networks are capable of misleadingly overfitting an asset price series with as many as 1,000 observations; (3) on the positive side, such simple networks are capable of extremely rich dynamic behavior, as evidenced by time-series plots of $\tilde{r}_t$ (Figure 18.3).

The present exercise yields practical benefits by fostering the development of computationally efficient methods for obtaining mature networks.[18] It also highlights the role to be played by statistical inference in evaluating the performance of neural network models, and in fact suggests some interesting new statistical problems (finding the distribution of $n\tilde{R}^2$). Solution of the latter problem will yield statistical methods for deciding on the inclusion or exclusion of additional hidden units to a given network.

Of course, the scope of the present exercise is very limited; indeed, it is intended primarily as a vehicle for presenting the relevant issues in a relatively uncomplicated setting, and for illustrating relevant approaches. Expanding the scope of the search for evidence against the

Figure 18.3

Training Set

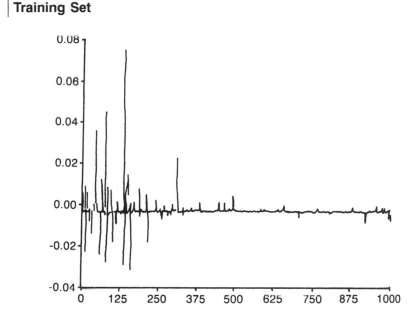

efficient markets hypothesis is a high priority. This can be done by elaborating the network to allow additional inputs (e.g., volume, other stock prices and volume, leading indicators, macroeconomic data, etc.) and by permitting recurrent connections of the sort discussed by Jordan.[22] Any of these elaborations must be supported with massive infusions of data for the training period: the more connections, the greater the danger of overfitting. There may also be useful insights gained by permitting additional network outputs, for example, returns over several different horizons (two-day, three-day, etc.) or prices of other assets over several different horizons, as well as by using within—rather than between — day data.

Another important limitation of the present exercise is that the optimization methods used here are essentially local. Although the final weight values were determined as giving the best performance over a range of different starting values for our iterations, there is no guarantee that a global maximum was found. A global optimization method such as simulated annealing or the genetic algorithm would be preferable.

Finally, it is extremely important to point out that while the method of least squares (equivalently, back-propagation) is adequate for testing the efficient markets hypothesis, it is not necessarily the method that one should use if interest attaches to building a network for market trading purposes. Such networks should be evaluated and trained using profit and loss in dollars from generated trades, not squared forecast error. Learning methods for this criterion are under development by the author.

ENDNOTES

1. A. Lapedes, and R. Farber, "Genetic Data Base Analysis with Neural Nets," paper presented to the IEEE Conference on Neural Information Processing System-Natural and Synthetic, 1987.

2. A. Lapedes and R. Farber, "Nonlinear Signal Processing Using Neural Networks," paper presented to the IEEE Conference on Neural Information Processing System-Natural and Synthetic, 1987,

3. B. G. Malkiel, *A Random Walk Down Wall Street* (New York: Norton, 1985).

4. R. T. Baillie, "Econometric Tests of Rationality and Market Efficiency," working paper, Michigan State University Department of Economics.

5. A. Lo, and A. C. MacKinley, "Stock Market Prices Do Not Follow Random Walks: Evidence From a Simple Specification Test," *Review of Financial Studies*, 1988.

6. R. J. Shiller, "The Use of Volatility Measures in Assessing Market Efficiency," *Journal of Finance*, vol. 36, 1981, pp. 291–304.

7. H. Simon, "A Behavioral Model of Rational Choice," *Quarterly Journal of Economics*, vol. 69, 1955, pp. 99–118.

8. H. Simon, *Models of Bounded Rationality* (Cambridge: MIT Press, 1982).

9. H. Sakai, and H. Tokumaru, "Autocorrelations of a Certain Chaos," *IEEE Transactions on Acoustics, Speech and Signal Processing* ASSP-28, 1980, pp. 588–590.

10. J. P. Eckmann, and D. Ruelle, "Ergodic Theory of Chaos and Strange Attractors," *Review of Modern Physics*, vol. 57, 1985, pp. 617–656.

11. H. Theil, *Principles of Econometrics*. (New York: Wiley, 1971.)

12. H. White, "Some Asymptotic Results for Learning in Single Hidden Layer Feedfoward Network Models," discussion paper 87–13, UCSD Department of Economics, 1987.

13. H. White, "Some Asymptotic Results for Back-Propagation," *Proceedings of the First Annual IEEE Conference on Neural Networks*, 1987.

14. U. Grenander, *Abstract Inference*. (New York: Wiley, 1981.)

15. S. Geman, and C. H. Hwang, "Nonparametric Maximum Likelihood Estimation by the Method of Sieves," *Annals of Statistics* vol. 70, 1982, pp. 401–414.

16. D. B. Parker, "Learning Logic," Office of Technology Licensing, Stanford University, 1982, Invention Report, S81-64, File 1.

17. D. E. Rumelhart, G. E. Hinton and R. J. Williams, "Learning Internal Representation by Error Propagation," in D. E. Rumelhart and J. L.

McClelland, eds., *Parallel Distributed Processing: Explorations in the Microstructures of Cognition*, vol. 1, (Cambridge: MIT Press, 1986), pp. 318–362.

18. H. White, "A Performance Comparison for Some On-Line and Off-Line Learning Methods for Single Hidden Layer Feedforward Nets," discussion paper, UCSD Department of Economics, 1988.

19. J. E. Dennis, *Numerical Methods for Unconstrained Optimization and Nonlinear Equations*, (Englewood Cliffs, N.J.: Prentice-Hall, 1983).

20. R. B. Davies, "Hypothesis Testing When a Nuisance Parameter Is Present Only Under the Alternative," *Biometrika*, vol. 64, 1977, pp. 247–54.

21. R. B. Davies, "Hypothesis Testing When a Nuisance Parameter Is Present Only Under the Alternative," *Biometrika*, vol. 74, 1987, pp. 33–43.

22. M. Jordan, "Serial Order: A Parallel Distributed Processing Approach," UCSD Institute of Cognitive Science Report 86-04, 1986.

19

PREDICTING STOCK PRICE PERFORMANCE: A NEURAL NETWORK APPROACH

Youngohc Yoon and George Swales

INTRODUCTION

The prediction of stock price performance involves the interaction of many variables, making prediction very difficult and complex. Many analysts and investors use financial statement data to assist in projecting future stock price trends. Qualitative information, while not as easily interpreted, may also have an effect on investment value. Both quantitative and qualitative variables help form the basis of investor stock price expectations and, hence, influence investment decision-making.

The multivariate analytical techniques using both quantitative and qualitative variables have been used repeatedly in finance and investments. However, the performance of multivariate analytical techniques is often less than conclusive and needs to be improved for more accurately forecasting stock price performance.

The neural network (NN) method has demonstrated its capability of addressing problems with a great deal of complexity. The neural network method may be able to enhance an investor's forecasting ability. However, comparatively few applications[1-3] using the neural network have been attempted in finance.

The purpose of this chapter is to apply the neural network approach to a dynamic and complex problem in a business environment and to investigate its ability to predict stock price performance. It also illustrates the methodology of applying this approach and compares its predictive power with that of multiple discriminant analysis (MDA) methods.

LITERATURE REVIEW

Discriminant analysis techniques are used to classify a set of independent variables into two or more mutually exclusive categories. It involves finding a linear combination of independent variables that reflect large differences in group means. The technique can be used for description as well as prediction.

Multivariate analytical techniques have repeatedly been used in finance. Applications are found in corporate finance, banking, and investments. Credit scoring of loan applications to estimate the probability of consumer or corporate default and bond rating analysis are examples of discriminant analysis applications in the finance discipline.

Perhaps the best known, seminal work in the field of multiple discriminant analysis methodology applied to finance was conducted by Edward I. Altman.[4] Altman's use of multiple discriminant analytical techniques focused on predicting corporate bankruptcy. After several early attempts, he settled on a discriminant model that contained five financial ratios used as independent variables. The model could reasonably predict corporate bankruptcy for up to two years in the future. Subsequent development and refinement of the model increased the two-year accuracy level and obtained a 70 percent accuracy rate for up to five years in the future.[5] A drawback of this linear approach is that it classifies some firms as likely to go bankrupt when in actuality they do not.

Since Altman's original work, there have been numerous attempts by researchers to modify and enhance his MDA model. Some of the results have been successful, while others have not. Gentry, Newbold, and Whitford[6] found that adding cash-based funds flow components to Altman's model provided superior results in predicting financial failure. They also concluded that cash outflow components were more closely related than cash inflow components to corporate failure.

Meyer and Pifer's method of predicting corporate bankruptcy utilized the same financial ratios as were found in Altman's model, but added financial data from more than one period prior to failure to determine a time trend. Collins[7] tested both models, using credit union financial data, and concluded that this approach adds little, if anything, to Altman's model.

Altman and Spivack[8] compared the Value Line relative financial strength system and the zeta bankruptcy classification methods of predicting corporate bankruptcy. Their findings reveal that although significant methodological differences do exist, a high correlation between the methods is evident, and that bond systems' scores correlate well with published bond ratings.

Pinches and Mingo[9] and others utilized the MDA concept to classify industrial bonds into multiple categories, using multiple independent variables. Most of these attempts have utilized quantitative financial variables to construct the model with reasonably good predictive results.

Direct applications of the use of the MDA technique to enhance corporate performance are found in the literature. An example is given by La Fleur Corporation, who, finding financial ruin at their doorstep, worked Altman's model backwards to turn the company around.[10]

While most of the development of MDA techniques involves the use of quantitative financial data, other approaches using qualitative assessments have been used in finance. Forecasting how a firm's stock will perform in equity markets, using qualitative variables found in the firm's annual report to the stockholders, has recently been attempted. McConnell, Haslem, and Gibson[11] and Swales[12] have found that qualitative data can provide additional information to forecast stock price performance.

As indicated above, using qualitative information to supplement an investor's forecasting ability in equity markets is beneficial. This type of information is often overlooked by investors, perhaps due to its subjective, not readily interpreted, form. While these techniques are valuable, other methods using nonlinear approaches may further enhance forecasting ability.

RESEARCH QUESTION

The studies mentioned above have generally indicated that multiple discriminant analysis, as used in the finance discipline, can be a valuable tool to the decision-maker. It has also been recognized that qualitative information can enhance an investor's stock price forecasting ability.

Given the above factors, can nonlinear methods significantly enhance an MDA model's stock price predictive power? Specifically, how does multiple discriminant analysis compare with the neural network approach in forecasting stock price performance? Additionally, can the use of neural network methods enhance the results of a recently published study, which used multiple discriminant analysis to assess the investor's ability to forecast stock price performance? These questions are addressed below.

DESCRIPTION OF THE DATA

As mentioned earlier, qualitative variables can provide an often neglected source of valuable information to the investor. Two independent research groups presented the results of the multiple discriminant analysis method, which used qualitative information found in the firm's annual report to the stockholder.[11,12] The study conducted by Swales serves as the basis for the application of the neural network approach, which this chapter addresses.

The data used in this study were gathered from two information sources frequently used by investors: the *Fortune 500* and *Business Week*'s "Top 1000."[13,14] These sources provide total return (dividends and stock price appreciation) and market valuation data, respectively, for widely followed companies. A stock's total return and market valuation are used by investors and financial analysts as performance measures.

For this experiment, two separate sets of data were gathered. From the Fortune 500 forms, five industries that offered investors the highest total returns in each year were selected; the sample consisted of 58 companies. The ten industries that were reported by *Business Week* to have the highest market valuations provided the data for the second set; 40 firms were included in this sample. It was felt that, if differences across the firms could be found among the top industries, then more pronounced differences were likely to exist in industries further down the line.

We classified the *Fortune* set of companies into two groups according to their total return. Group 1 provided investors with the highest total returns in their respective industries; Group 2 provided the lowest returns in their industries. We classified the *Business Week* set of 40 companies in each of 10 industries into 2 groups. Again, Group 1 consisted of those firms with the highest market valuations for their industries; Group 2 consisted of those firms with the lowest market valuations for their industries.

For each company in the study, the president's letter to stockholders from the annual report for the period immediately prior to the group selection year was studied. A qualitative content analysis technique was used to classify and tally recurring themes identified by similar words or phrases. An examination of president's letters to stockholders identified nine recurring themes commonly addressed in discussion of the future. These themes included reference to confidence, economic factors outside the firm's control, growth, strategic plans, new products, anticipated losses, anticipated gains, long-term optimism, and short-term optimism.

Each letter was read for content and references to the themes noted above. The frequency and percentage of each letter devoted to these themes was then recorded. When the letter did not contain a specific, direct reference to one of the themes, a subjective judgment was made by the researcher as to which, if any, theme should be credited with the phrase or statement. In those instances when reference was not made to a theme(s) in the letter, the data set reflected this finding. The frequency data set was then used for both MDA techniques and NN methods to predict stock price performance.

Content analysis techniques have been widely used in the social sciences.[15] Financial researchers have also applied these techniques to analyze narrative components of financial reports.[11,12,16,17] Refer to McConnell[11] and Swales[12] for further details of the content analysis technique used to analyze the president's letter to stockholders.

NEURAL NETWORK MODEL

Design of the Network

The neural network model is structured in a four-layered network, as shown in Figure 19.1: an input layer, two hidden layers, and an output layer. An input unit has excitatory (positive) or inhibitory (negative) connections to a hidden unit in the hidden layer, and a hidden unit has connections to an output unit in the output layer. Therefore, an input unit in this network structure has indirect connections to an output unit.

Input for the network was a list of nine variables: confidence, economic factors outside the firm's control, growth, strategic gains, new products, anticipated loss, anticipated gain, long-term optimism, and short-term optimism. Output was a classification of two patterns: a firm whose stock price performed well and a firm whose stock price performed poorly. In a network, each input parameter is represented in an input unit. Therefore, the network has the nine input units in the input layer and the two output units in the output layer. The number of

Figure 19.1

Four-Layered Network

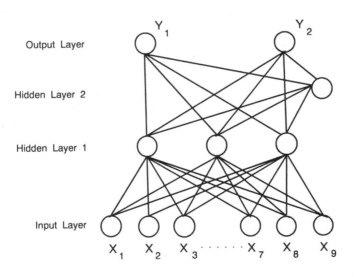

hidden units necessary to accurately predict the stock price performance was determined empirically.

The network for the prediction of stock price performance uses the following nine input ($X_1 - X_9$) and two output ($Y_1 - Y_2$) parameters.

Input Parameters

X_1: Confidence
X_2: Economic factors
X_3: Growth
X_4: Strategic plans
X_5: New products
X_6: Anticipated loss
X_7: Anticipated gains
X_8: Long-term optimism
X_9: Short-term optimism

Output Parameters

Y_1: Well-performing firms
Y_2: Poorly performing firms

Learning Process

Once a network structure was developed, a set of initial weights was assigned at random. Then, the back-propagation learning algorithm (BPLA)[18] was used with the *Fortune* set to estimate the weights of the feed-forward network. In this algorithm, the input vector with nine input values was assigned as the activation vector of an input layer propagates forward to the upper layer as the product of weights on the interconnections and the activation values. A sigmoid function in equation 1 was used to compute the activation value of a unit, A_j, on the upper layer.

$$A_j^{(L)} = \frac{1}{1 + Exp\left(\sum_{i=0}^{n} W_{ji} A_i^{(L-1)} - \theta_j^{(L)}\right)}$$

(1)

If the upper layer is not an output layer, its activation vector propagates forward to the higher layer in a network in the same manner. The superscript L and $L-1$ represents an upper and lower layer, respectively. If the upper layer is an output layer, an activation value of each output unit is compared to the desired one and the error is measured according to:

$$E = \frac{1}{2} \sum_{j=0}^{n} (D_j - A_j)^2$$

(2)

The learning algorithm iteratively modifies the set of weights in order to reduce this error. Thus, BPLA is a gradient descent algorithm in which weights in the network are iteratively modified to minimize the overall mean square error between desired and actual output values for all output units over all input patterns. The amount the weights are to be adjusted for each input pattern is determined by the derivative of the error function in equation 2 with respect to the weight as follows:

$$\Delta W_{ji} \propto -\frac{\partial E}{\partial W_{ji}}$$

(3)

This derivative yields the error signal,

$$\delta_j = (D_j - A_j)A_j(1 - A_j)$$

(4)

for an output unit, and

$$\delta_j = A_j(1 - A_j) \sum_{k=0}^{n} \delta_k W_{kj}$$

(5)

for hidden units.

Finally, the connection weight between the jth unit in the Lth layer and the ith unit in the $L - 1$st layer is modified according to:

$$\Delta W_{ji} = \alpha \delta_j^{(L)} A_i^{(L-1)}$$

(6)

where δ_j is defined above. A_i is the activation values of the ith unit, and α is the learning rate, which is used to control the speed of the training process. For further details and discussions of BPLA, see Rumelhart.[18] In this experiment, the initial training data consisted of 58 cases in the

Fortune set. A small learning rate of α = 0.1 was used. The experiment was conducted on a VAX 11/750 using the C programming language.

RESULTS

The performance of the trained network was tested with the *Business Week* set, which contains 40 cases. In the first experiment, the effect of varying the number of hidden units in a four-layered network was tested. The result of this experiment is represented in Figure 19.2. In a four-layered network, performance improved as the number of hidden units increased up to a certain point. This supports previous findings on the importance of the hidden layer for the different applications.[19,20] The best performance was achieved by a network with four hidden units on the first hidden layer and one hidden unit on the second hidden layer. Increasing the number of hidden units beyond this point produced no further improvement but impaired the network's performance.

Figure 19.2

Effect of Varying the Number of Hidden Units in a Four-Layered Network on Performance

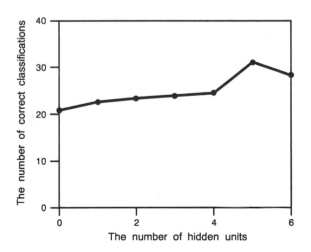

The performance of the NN model was also compared with that of MDA. Table 19.1 summarizes the result of this experiment. The report includes the performance of MDA and four-layered network on a training data set, as well as a testing data set, to demonstrate the important aspects of this study. The value indicates that MDA resulted in a 74 percent mean posterior membership probability for the training set: 21 of the 29 companies were correctly classified into Group 1, while 22 of the 29 companies were correctly classified into Group 2. However, during the testing phase, the model yielded only an overall 65 percent success rate for the testing data set: 14 and 12 of the 20 companies were correctly classified into Group 1 and 2, respectively.

The four-layered network correctly classified 91 percent of the mean training data and appropriately predicted 77.5 percent of the mean testing data: 18 of 20 companies were correctly classified into Group 1, whereas 13 of 20 companies were correctly classified into Group 2. During the training phase, the MDA model provided better predictive capability for firms in the lower performance category than for firms in the higher performance category. However, during the testing phase, all models demonstrated better predictive capability for firms in the higher performance category.

This study shows that the mean success rate during the testing phase for the four-layered network was 77.5 percent as compared with 65 percent for the MDA technique. This result shows that a NN method significantly enhanced the MDA model's stock price predictive power. Dutta and Shekhar[1] also reported the better performance in rating bonds by the NN approach than by the regression method. The higher performance of the four-layered NN model indicates that this nonlinear technique with hidden units in the network was a more appropriate

Table 19.1

Performance of the MDA and Four-Layered Network on the Training and Testing Data

Models	Training Data, Percent			Testing Data, Percent		
	Group 1	Group 2	Mean	Group 1	Group 2	Mean
MDA	72	76	74	70	60	65
Four-Layer	86	96	91	90	65	77.5

method to use to forecast stock price performance than the multiple discriminant analysis method.

However, the NN approach demonstrates a limitation. In general, MDA is useful for both descriptions, as well as predictions, since it can explain the characteristics of each group and the significance of each input parameter. In the NN model, it is a difficult task to analyze the characteristics of each group and the importance of input parameters in a NN model due to the hidden units employed in the network. The hidden unit is useful to extract the high-order mapping function between output and input; however, it makes separating the contribution of each input parameter to the output value very difficult.

CONCLUDING REMARKS

The study demonstrated that the neural network approach is capable of learning a function that maps input to output and encoding it in the magnitudes of the weights in the network's connection. The number of hidden units employed in the network contributed to its viability. The increase in the number of hidden units resulted in higher performance up to a certain point. However, additional hidden units beyond the point impaired the model's performance. Comparison of the NN technique with the MDA approach indicated that the NN approach can significantly improve the predictability of stock price performance.

While some limitations of this approach were noted, it is evident that its use can improve an investor's decision-making capability. Further research into the application of neural network techniques, using both quantitative and qualitative data, is suggested and encouraged.

ENDNOTES

1. S. Dutta and S. Shekhar, "Bond Rating: A Non-Conservative Application of Neural Networks," *Proceedings of the IEEE International Conference on Neural Networks*, vol. 2, 1988, pp. 443–450.

2. K. Kamijo and T. Tanigawa, "Stock Price Pattern Recognition: A Recurrent Network Approach," *Proceedings of the International Joint Conference on Neural Networks*, vol. 1, 1990, pp. 215–222.

3. T. Kimoto, K. Asakawa, M. Yoda, and M. Takeoka, "Stock Market Prediction System with Modular Neural Networks," *Proceedings of the International Joint Conference on Neural Networks*, vol. 1, 1990, pp. 1–6.

4. E. L. Altman, "Financial Ratios, Discriminant Analysis and the Prediction of Corporate Bankruptcy," *The Journal of Finance*, September 1968, pp. 589–609.

5. E. L. Altman, R. G. Haldeman and P. Narayanan, "Zeta Analysis: A New Model to Identify Bankruptcy Risk of Corporations," *Journal of Banking and Finance*, June 1977, pp. 29–54.

6. J. A. Gentry, P. Newbold and D. T. Whitford, "Predicting Bankruptcy: If Cash Flow's Not the Bottom Line, What Is?," *Financial Analysts Journal*, September–October 1985, pp. 47–56.

7. R. A. Collins, "An Empirical Comparison of Bankruptcy Prediction Models," *Financial Management*, Summer 1980, pp. 52–56.

8. E. L. Altman, and J. Spivack, "Predicting Bankruptcy: The Value Line Relative Financial Strength System vs. the Zeta Bankruptcy Classification Approach," *Financial Analysts Journal*, November-December 1983, pp. 60–67.

9. G. E. Pinches and K. A. Mingo, "A Multivariate Analysis of Industrial Bond Ratings," *Journal of Finance*, March 1977, pp. 1–8.

10. M. Ball, "Z Factor: Rescue by the Numbers," *Inc.*, December 1980, pp. 45–48.

11. D. McConnell, J. A. Haslem and V. R. Gibson, "The President's Letter to Stockholders: A New Look," *Financial Analysts Journal*, September-October 1986, pp. 66–70.

12. G. S. Swales, Jr., "Another Look at the President's Letter to Stockholders," *Financial Analysts Journal*, March–April 1988, pp. 71–73.

13. "The Fortune 500," *Fortune*, April 30, 1984; April 29, 1985; April 28, 1986.

14. "The Top 1000: America's Most Valuable Companies," *Business Week*, April 18, 1986.

15. B. Berlson, "Content Analysis in Communication Research," (New York: Hafner Publishing Company, 1971).

16. E. H. Bowman, "Content Analysis of Annual Reports for Corporation Strategy and Risk," *Interfaces*, January/February 1984, pp. 61–71.

17. K. B. Frazier, R. W. Ingram, and B. M. Tennyson, "A Methodology for the Analysis of Narrative Accounting Disclosures," *Journal of Accounting Research*, Spring 1984, pp. 318–331.

18. D. E. Rumelhart, G. E. Hinton, and R. J. Williams, "Learning Internal Representations by Error Propagation," in D. E. Rumelhart and J. L. McClelland [eds], *Parallel Distributed Processing: Exploration in the Microstructure of Cognition*, (Cambridge, Mass.: MIT Press), pp. 318–362.

19. R. P. Gorman and T. J. Sejnowski, "Analysis of Hidden Units in a Layered Network Trained to Classify Sonar Targets," *Neural Networks*, vol. 1, 1988, pp. 75–89.

20. Y. Yoon, R. W. Brobst, P. R. Bergstresser, and L. L. Peterson, "A Desktop Neural Network for Dermatology Diagnosis," *Journal of Neural Network Computing*, vol. 1, Summer 1989, pp. 43–52.

20

STOCK MARKET PREDICTION SYSTEM WITH MODULAR NEURAL NETWORKS

Takashi Kimoto, Kazuo Asakawa,
Morio Yoda, and Masakazu Takeoka

INTRODUCTION

Modeling functions of neural networks are being applied to a widely expanding range of applications in addition to the traditional areas such as pattern recognition and control. Its nonlinear learning and smooth interpolation capabilities give the neural network an edge over standard computers and expert systems for solving certain problems.

Accurate stock market prediction is one such problem. Several mathematical models have been developed, but the results have been disappointing. We chose this application as a means to check whether neural networks could produce a successful model in which their generalization capabilities could be used for stock market prediction.

Fujitsu and Nikko Securities are working together to develop a TOPIX buying and selling prediction system. The input consists of several technical and economic indexes. In our system, several modular neural networks learned the relationships between the past technical and economic indexes and the timing for when to buy and sell. A prediction system made up of modular neural networks was found to be accurate. Simulation of buying and selling stocks using the prediction system showed an excellent profit. Stock price fluctuation factors could be extracted by analyzing the networks.

ARCHITECTURE

System Overview

The prediction system is made up of several neural networks that learned the relationships between various technical and economical indexes and the timing for when to buy and sell stocks. The goal is to predict the best time to buy and sell for one month in the future.

TOPIX is a weighted average of market prices of all stocks listed on the First Section of the Tokyo Stock Exchange. It is weighted by the number of stocks issued for each company. It is used similar to the Dow-Jones average.

Figure 20.1 shows the basic architecture of the prediction system. It converts the technical indexes and economic indexes into a space pattern to input to the neural networks. The timing for when to buy and sell is a weighted sum of the weekly returns. The input indexes and teaching data are discussed in detail below.

Network Architecture

Network Model. Figure 20.2 shows the basic network architecture used for the prediction system. It consists of three layers: the input layer, the hidden layer, and the output layer. The three layers are completely connected to form a hierarchical network.

Figure 20.1

Basic Architecture of Prediction System

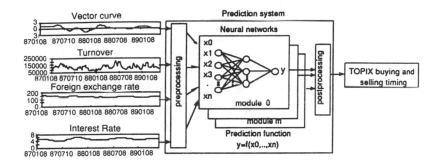

Figure 20.2

Neural Network Model

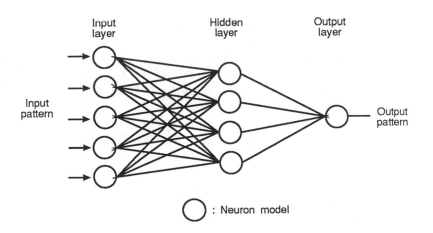

Each unit in the network receives input from low-level units and performs weighted addition to determine the output. A standard sigmoid function is used as the output function. The output is analog in the [0,1] section.

High-Speed Learning Algorithm. The error back-propagation method proposed by Rumelhart[1] is a representative learning rule for hierarchical networks. For high-speed learning with a large volume of data, we developed a new high-speed learning method called supplementary learning.[2]

Supplementary learning, based on error back-propagation, automatically schedules pattern presentation and changes learning constants.

In supplementary learning, the weights are updated according to the sum of the error signals after presentation of all learning data. Before learning, tolerances are defined for all output units. During learning, errors are back-propagated only for the learning data for which the errors of output units exceed the tolerance. Pattern presentation is automatically scheduled. This can reduce the amount calculation for error back-propagation.

As learning progresses, learning data for which tolerances are exceeded are reduced. This also reduces the calculation load because of the decreased amount of data that needs error back-propagation. High-speed learning is thus available even with a large amount of data.

Supplementary learning allows the automatic change of learning constants depending on the amount of learning data. As the amount of learning data changes and learning progresses, the learning constants are automatically updated. This eliminates the need for changing learning parameters depending on the amount of learning data.

With supplementary learning, the weight factor is updated as follows:

$$\Delta w(t) = (\varepsilon / \text{learning \_ patterns}) \, \partial E / \partial W + \alpha \Delta w(t - 1)$$

where

ε: learning rate
α: momentum
learning _ patterns: number of learning data items that require error back-propagation

The value of ε is divided by the number of learning data items that actually require error back-propagation. The required learning rate is automatically reduced when the amount of learning data increases. This allows use of the constants ε regardless of the amount of data.

As learning progresses, the amount of remaining learning data decreases. This automatically increases the learning rate. Using this automatic control function of the learning constants means there is no need to change the constants (ε = 4.0, α = 0.8) throughout simulation and that high-speed learning can be achieved by supplementary learning.

Learning Data

Data Selection. We believe stock prices are determined by time-space patterns of economic indexes such as foreign exchange rates and interest rates and of technical indexes such as vector curves and turnover. The prediction system uses a moving average of weekly average data of each index for minimizing influence due to random walk. Table 20.1 lists some of the technical and economic indexes used. The time-space patterns of the indexes were converted into space patterns. The converted indexes are analog values in the [0,1] section.

Teaching Data. The timing for when to buy and sell is indicated as an analog value in the [0,1] section in one output unit. The timing for when to buy and sell used as teaching data is weighted sum of weekly returns. When the TOPIX weekly return is r_i, teaching data $r_N(t)$ is defined as:

$$r_t = \ln (\text{TOPIX}(t)/\text{TOPIX} (t - 1))$$

TOPIX (t): TOPIX average at week t

$$r_N(t) = \sum_i \varphi^i r_{t+i}$$

φ : *Weight*

Preprocessing

Input indexes converted into space patterns and teaching data are often remarkably irregular. Such data is preprocessed by log or error func-

Table 20.1
Input Indexes

1. Vector curve
2. Turnover
3. Interest rate
4. Foreign exchange rate
5. New York Dow-Jones average
6. Others

tions to make them as regular as possible. It is then processed by a normalization function that normalizes the [0,1] section, correcting for the irregular data distribution.

Learning Control

In the TOPIX prediction system, we developed new learning control. The system automatically controls learning iterations by referring to test data errors, thereby preventing overlearning. The learning control allows two-thirds of data in the learning period to be learned and uses the rest as test data in the prediction system. The test data is evaluation data for which only forward processing is done during learning, to calculate an error but not to back-propagate it.

Our learning control is done in two steps. In the first step, learning is done for 5,000 iterations and errors against test data are recorded. In the second step, the number of learning iterations where learning in the first step suggests a minimum error against the test data is determined, and relearning is done that number of iterations. This prevents over-learning and acquires a prediction model involving learning a moderate number of times. In the second step, learning is done for at least 1,000 iterations.

Moving Simulation

For prediction of an economic system, such as stock prices, in which the prediction rules are changing continuously, learning and prediction must follow the changes.

We developed a prediction method called moving simulation. In this system, prediction is done by simulation while moving the objective learning and prediction periods. The moving simulation predicts as follows.

As shown in Figure 20.3, the system learns data for the past M months, then predicts for the next L months. The system advances while repeating this.

RESULT OF SIMULATIONS

Prediction Simulation

We verified the accuracy of the prediction system by simulating prediction of the timing for when to buy and sell. We used historical data of stock prices, technical indexes, and economical indexes.

The TOPIX prediction system improves its prediction accuracy by averaging prediction results of modular networks that learn for different learning data items. Four independent modular networks learn for four types of different learning data. Moving simulation is used with L as one month. The average of prediction outputs from these networks became the prediction output from the system. Prediction was thus repeated by moving simulation for each month to verify accuracy. Prediction was done for 33 months from January 1987 to September 1989.

Figure 20.3

Moving Simulation

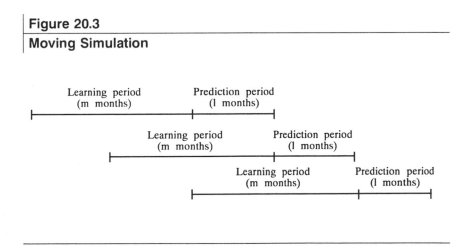

Table 20.2 shows the correlation coefficient between the predictions and teaching data and those of individual networks and prediction system. The prediction system uses the average of the predictions of each network. Thus, the prediction system could obtain a greater correlation coefficient for teaching data than could be obtained with neural network prediction.

Simulation for Buying and Selling Simulation

To verify the effectiveness of the prediction system, a simulation of buying and selling of stock was done. Buying and selling according to the prediction system made a greater profit than the buying and holding.

Buying and selling was simulated by the one-point buying and selling strategy, so performance could be clearly evaluated. One-point buying and selling means all available money is used to buy stocks and means all stocks held are sold at a time. In the prediction system, an output of 0.5 or more indicates buy, and an output less than an 0.5 indicates sell. Signals are intensified as they get close to 0 or 1.

The buying and selling simulation considered "buy" to be an output above some threshold and "sell" to be below some threshold. Figure 20.4 shows an example of the simulation results. In the upper diagram, the buy-and-hold performance (that is, the actual TOPIX) is shown as dotted lines, while the prediction system's performance is shown as solid lines. The TOPIX index of January 1987 was considered as 1.00; it was 1.67 by buy-and-hold at the end of September 1989. It was 1.98 by the buying and selling operation according to the prediction system. Use of the system showed an excellent profit.

Table 20.2
Correlation Coefficient

	Correlation Coefficient
Network 1	0.435
Network 2	0.458
Network 3	0.414
Network 4	0.457
System	0.527

Figure 20.4

Performance of the Prediction System

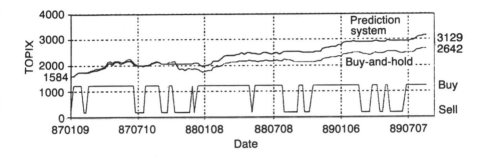

ANALYSIS

Comparison with Multiple Regression Analysis

The timing for when to buy and sell stocks is not linear, so statistical methods are not effective for creating a model. We compared modeling with the neural network and with multiple regression analysis. Weekly learning data from January 1985 to September 1989 was used for modeling. Since the objectives of this test were comparison of learning capabilities and internal analysis of the network after learning, the network learned 100,000 iterations.

The hierarchical network that had five units of hidden layers learned the relationships between various economic and technical indexes and the timing for when to buy and sell. The neural network learned the data well enough to show a very high correlation coefficient; the multiple regression analysis showed a lower correlation coefficient. This shows our method is more effective in this case. Table 20.3 shows the correlation coefficient produced by each method. The neural network produced a much higher correlation coefficient than multiple regression.

Table 20.3
Comparison of Multiple Regression Analysis and Neural Network

Correlation Coefficient with Teaching Data

Multiple regression analysis	0.543
Neural network	0.991

Extraction of Rule

The neural network that learned from January 1985 to September 1989 was analyzed to extract information on stock prices stored during that period.

Cluster analysis is often used to analyze internal representation of a hierarchical neural network.[3,4] In 1987 stock prices fluctuated greatly. The hidden layer outputs were analyzed to cluster learning data. The cluster analysis was applied to the output values in the [0,1] sections of the five units of hidden layers. Clustering was done with an inter-cluster distance determined as Euclidian, and the clusters were integrated hierarchically by the complete linkage method. Figure 20.5 shows the cluster analysis results of the hidden layers in 1987. It indicates that bull, bear, and stable markets each generate different clusters.

From cluster analysis, characteristics common to data that belong to individual clusters were extracted by analyzing the learning data. Figure 20.6 shows the relationships between TOPIX weekly data and six types of clusters in 1987.

This chapter analyzes the factors for the representative bull (clusters (2) and (3)) and bear (cluster (6)) markets in 1987 as follows.

Data (2) and (3) belong to different clusters but have similar characteristics. Figure 20.7 shows learning data corresponding to clusters (2) and (3). The horizontal axis shows some of the indexes of the neural network. The vertical axis show the value of each index. For example, New York Dow-Jones average is low when it is close to 0 and is high when close to 1.

This diagram suggests that the vector curve in the bull market during February to the beginning of April in 1987 were high enough to indicate a high-price zone. At the same time, however, the high

Figure 20.5

Cluster Analysis Results from 1987

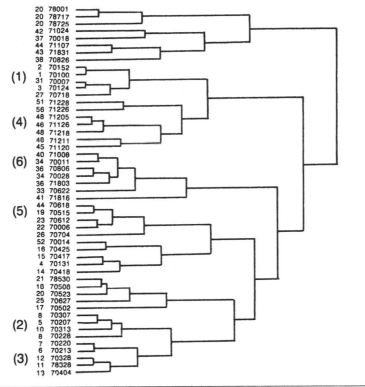

turnover kept the market going up. Also, the low interest rates and high New York Dow-Jones average helped push up stock prices.

Figure 20.8 shows the learning data corresponding to (6) in Figure 20.6. It is obvious that the high interest rate pulled prices down.

Part of the learning data in 1987 was analyzed. It was proved that the causes of stock price fluctuation could be analyzed by extracting the characteristics common to the learning data in the clusters obtained by cluster analysis of the neural network.

FURTHER RESEARCH

The following subjects will be studied.

❖ Using the system for actual stock trading

Figure 20.6

TOPIX in 1987

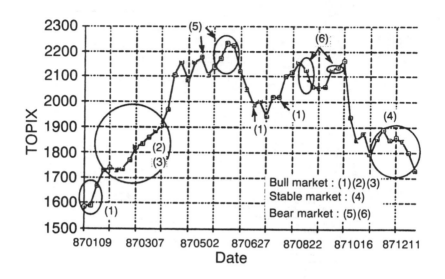

Figure 20.7

Input Indexes for Bull Market (2) (3)

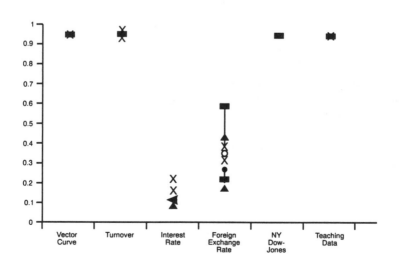

Figure 20.8

Learning Data in Bear Market (6)

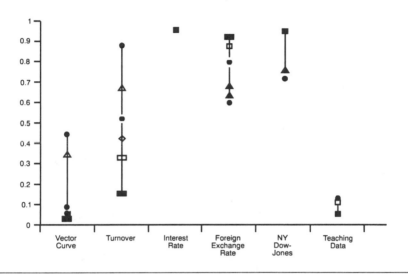

The current prediction system uses future returns to generate teaching data. A system in which teaching data is generated in combination with a statistical method must be developed.

❖ Adaptation of network model that has regressive connection and self-looping.

The current prediction system requires much simulation to determine moving average. Automatic learning of individual sections requires building up a prediction system consisting of network models to fit to time-space processing.

SUMMARY

This chapter has discussed a prediction system that advises the timing for when to buy and sell stocks. The prediction system made an excellent profit in a simulation exercise. The internal representation also was discussed and the rules of stock price fluctuation were extracted by cluster analysis.

For developing the prediction system, Nikko Securities offered investment technology and know-how of the stock market and Fujitsu offered its neural network technology. Fujitsu and Nikko Securities are proceeding further to build up more accurate economic prediction systems.

ENDNOTES

1. D. E. Rumelhart, et al., *Parallel Distributed Processing*, vol. 1 (Cambridge, Mass.: MIT Press, 1986).

2. R. Masuoka, et al., "A Study on Supplementary Learning Algorithm in Back Propagation," *JSAI*, 1989, pp. 213–217.

3. T. J. Sejnowski, C. R. Rosenberg, "Parallel Networks that Learn to Pronounce English Text," *Complex Systems*, vol. 1, 1987.

4. R. Paul Gorman, T. J. Sejnowski, "Analysis of Hidden Units in a Layered Network Trained to Classify Sonar Targets," *Neural Networks*, vol. 1, no. 1, 1988, pp. 75–90.

21

STOCK PRICE PATTERN RECOGNITION: A RECURRENT NEURAL NETWORK APPROACH

Ken-ichi Kamijo and Tetsuji Tanigawa

INTRODUCTION

This chapter proposes a recurrent neural network model for stock price pattern recognition and develops a new method for evaluating the network. In stock trading with technical analysis,[1] price patterns in Japanese-style stock charts,[2] such as *triangles*, indicate an important clue to the trend of future changes in stock price. An expert analyzes the charts to detect these patterns on the basis of his past experience. In practice, a few experts have continued to watch the charts, and they are engaged in stock trading for limited *names* of corporations. How-

© 1990, IEEE. Reprinted with permission from *Proceedings of the IEEE International Joint Conference on Neural Networks*, pp. I215–I221, San Diego, CA.

ever, it takes a long time to become a proficient expert, and the expert's capability life-span is short. Therefore, as the number of traded names increased, computer aid to the chart analysis has been strongly expected.

For recognizing specified patterns from a time sequence of stock prices, it is indispensable to develop a normalization method for eliminating the bias due to differences in time spans and names, and to investigate an algorithm for detecting the patterns. There is no successful rule-based approach to the stock price pattern recognition, because such recognition is based on the expert's subjectivities. For example, the *triangle* pattern has nonlinear time elasticity and definite oscillations. Therefore, it is difficult to recognize the patterns by means of existing statistical models and AI techniques.

In this work, a recurrent neural network model was applied to triangle recognition. Consequently, test triangles were appropriately recognized. Furthermore, a new method for examining recurrent networks was established by searching for temporal context transition in the model. It became clear that the model was effective in partial elimination of mismatching patterns.

STOCK DATA

Stock Price Patterns

An example of "candlestick" chart at every trading week commonly used in Japan is shown in Figure 21.1. A *triangle* pattern is enclosed by a large open circle in Figure 21.1. The candlestick is a symbol for describing opening, closing, high and low prices for a week at the same time. In case of a white (black) candlestick, the opening (closing) price is lower than the closing (opening), and the top and the bottom of the candlestick represent the closing (opening) and the opening (closing) prices, respectively. The top and the bottom of the line running through the candlestick depict high and low prices, respectively. Two oblique lines in the triangle pattern are called *resistance lines*. They are assistant lines that experts draw when judging whether a stock price pattern is a triangle.

The triangle refers to the beginning of a sudden stock price rise. Then, high and low prices appear mutually and the stock price oscil-

Figure 21.1

Candlestick Chart and Triangle Pattern Example

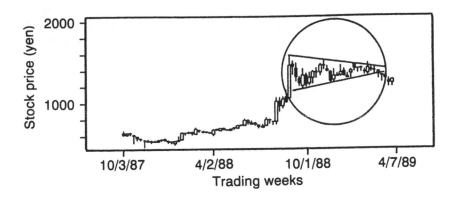

lates. The resistance lines joining peaks and troughs converge. Since the resistance line is hand drawn and the oscillation is vaguely defined, it is very difficult to formulate the triangle by means of a simple statistical model. Moreover, there is a difference in the degree of convergences among triangle patterns.

Data Collection

One expert extracted triangles by drawing resistance lines in candlestick charts during the past three years for 1,152 names of joint stock corporations listed in the First Section of Tokyo Stock Exchange. The 16 extracted patterns were clearly judged to be triangles by the expert. Also, beginning and ending weeks for these patterns were assigned by the expert. In the selected patterns, there is a difference in name and starting week. A triangle period varies from 13 to 35 weeks. Because the resistance line was marked on the basis of high and low prices for the candlesticks, these prices were used as the input data to the author's proposed neural network model.

Normalization

In general, the stock price data have bias due to differences in name and time spans. Eliminating this bias requires stock price data normalization. To accomplish this, the authors used the variation in stock price average rate every week as a normalized value. The stock price average, obtained by exponential smoothing, was adopted. Let C_t be a closing price at the tth week. Then, average A_t is given by:

$$A_t = s\, C_t + (1 - s)\, A_{t-1}$$

$$= s\, C_t + s(1 - s)\, C_{t-1} + s(1 - s)^2\, C_{t-2} + ..., \qquad (1)$$

$$s = \frac{2}{13} \qquad (2)$$

where s is a constant well known in the securies market, and the denominator is the number of recursive calculations. Therefore, normalized value $\tilde{V}_t$ is given by:

$$\tilde{V}_t = \frac{A_t - A_{t-1}}{A_{t-1}} \qquad (3)$$

Since both high and low prices are important for deciding whether there is a triangle pattern or not, it is necessary to utilize the prices as input data. The authors used a dissociation from stock price average as a normalized value. Let H_t and L_t be a high price and a low price at time t, respectively. Then, dissociation from a stock price average for the high price, $\tilde{U}_t$ and that from a stock price average for the low price, $\tilde{D}_t$, are given by:

$$\tilde{U}_t = \frac{A_t - H_t}{A_t} \qquad (4)$$

$$\tilde{D}_t = \frac{A_t - L_t}{A_t} \qquad (5)$$

respectively. Thus, a variation rate $\tilde{V}_t$ for stock price average, a dissociation $\tilde{U}_t$ for high price, and a dissociation $\tilde{D}_t$ for low price were
collected as normalized stock price data.

Although the frequency distribution of stock price data is roughly
approximated by the normal distribution, there are different averages
and variances for each of the normalized stock price data.

Since the sigmoid function is used as the output function for the
input layer, all the input data is linearly transformed, so that the data
are involved within the domain ranging from 0 to 1. For this purpose,
the average μ and the variance σ^2 were calculated for each normalized
value, from the data for 16 names during the past three years, and all
the data were transformed by means of the linear function, so that the
interval $[\mu - \sigma, \mu + \sigma]$ corresponds to the interval $[0,1]$. Moreover, V_t, U_t,
and D_t are obtained by linear transformations of $\tilde{V}_t$, $\tilde{U}_t$, and $\tilde{D}_t$, respectively. Consequently, about 68 percent of all the data was involved
in the interval $[0,1]$.

NEURAL NETWORK MODEL

The present network model has a recurrent connection structure, similar
to that proposed by Elman.[3] The structure does not rigidly constrain
the length of input sequences and represents a finite state grammar
implicitly.[4] For triangle pattern recognition, it is probable that variable
oscillations were represented by the transition to a recursive state of
internal grammar, and that nonlinear expansion and contraction were
represented by both the transition to a substate and the jumping over
states.

The network has a four-layer architecture, consisting of one input
layer, two hidden layers, and one output layer, as illustrated in Figure
21.2, for discriminating nonlinear patterns. Because of possibility that
the teacher signal is beyond the interval $[0,1]$, the output value for each
unit in the output layer is given by the following linear function:

$$f_1(x) = 0.4x, \qquad \left(x \equiv \sum_{i=1}^{m} w_i y_i - \theta\right)$$

$$(6)$$

Figure 21.2

Network Architecture

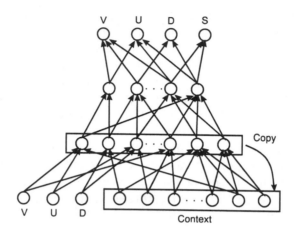

where y_i is the output value of the ith unit in a previous layer, w_i is the weight on the connection from the ith unit, θ is the threshold, and m is the number of unit in the previous layer. An output function for other layers is the sigmoid function:

$$f_2(x) = \frac{1}{1 + e^{-x}}$$

(7)

The input layer consists of two sets of units. The first set represents current stock data V, U, D. The second set of input units is called the *context* layer, and its units are used to represent the temporal context by holding a copy of the first hidden units' activity level at the previous time step. The output layer consists of prediction units for stock data and a triangle unit S, which represents the triangle pattern termination. In this chapter, the unit numbers for the first and the second hidden layers were set to 64 and 24, respectively.

TRAINING

The proposed network, with the back-propagation learning procedure,[5] was trained to acquire features of the triangles retroactively, by using V_t, U_t, D_t as input data and V_{t-1}, U_{t-1}, D_{t-1} and S_{t-1} as teacher signals at each point in time t. All the initial values for the context layer are zero. The training data for the triangle unit S_t, which extracts the triangle pattern termination, is set to be 0.5 during a period ranging from the beginning of the triangle pattern to the appearance of the earliest peak. Otherwise, it is to be zero. Periods differ for triangles ranging from 1 to 4.

Sixteen stock price patterns were divided into two groups, 15 training patterns and one test pattern. Sixteen experiments were carried out for the recognition, using these groups cyclically. In each experiment, the network was trained for 15 triangles in random sequence. This training was iterated 2,000 times. After the iterations were complete, the error of the trained network was very small and its variation rate hardly changed.

RESULTS

After training in each experiment, it was attempted to recognize the triangle for stock price data for 16 names during the past three years. The recognition started at the current week, then the network searched for triangles retroactively. When stock price data at any week is presented, the squared error was calculated between the prediction data and real data at a point in time one week past, transferring the values in the first hidden layer to the context layer. The error was retroactively accumulated. If the activation value of triangle unit S is beyond some threshold (0.3), the time period which exists until the activation is beyond some threshold is defined to be a triangle. When the network finished searching, during the past three years, the above procedure was accomplished after the current week was successively replaced with the previous week. If the difference in the triangle period between that for the present network and that indicated by an expert is within a few weeks, the period was assumed to be correctly recognized by the network.

Table 21.1 summarizes the experimental results. The given test triangle pattern was accurately recognized in 15 out of 16 experiments. The number of mismatching patterns, which an expert did not determine to be a triangle, but which the network did so indicate, was 1.06 per name on the average of 16 experiments. The expert, however, categorized these patterns into another kind of *unchanged* pattern. The difference between a true triangle and the patterns involves fluctuation. A similar feature is that they have definite oscillations.

Table 21.1
Recognition Results

	Triangles		Mismatch*
Experiment	Training (%)	Test	(total)
1	100	yes	1.06 (17)
2	100	yes	1.31 (21)
3	100	yes	0.69 (11)
4	100	yes	1.88 (30)
5	100	yes	0.75 (12)
6	100	yes	0.88 (14)
7	100	yes	1.44 (23)
8	100	yes	0.69 (11)
9	100	yes	0.88 (14)
10	100	yes	1.06 (17)
11	100	yes	1.00 (16)
12	100	yes	0.63 (10)
13	100	yes	1.88 (30)
14	100	yes	0.63 (10)
15	100	yes	0.63 (10)
16	100	no	1.56 (25)
Average	100%	93.8%	1.06 (16.9)

*Pattern(s) per name.

EVALUATION OF RECURRENT NETWORKS

In order to validate the recognition ability of the recurrent networks, the authors analyzed the performances for latent state transition, in particular, the temporal transition for the triangle sequences, using internal representations of the networks.[1] (Serven-Schreiber[4] analyzed *static* internal representations by a cluster analysis.)

The context vectors were successively generated in the first hidden layer at the recognition stage. The vectors must somehow encode features of stock price patterns at the time, according to rules on the basis of which the network was trained to recognize the triangle pattern. To clarify the features, a cluster analysis[6] was applied to the context vectors. Given stock data in the three pattern categories which are in training and test triangles and mismatched, a context vector in the first hidden layer is obtained in order. The dissimilarities between any two of the context vectors were given by standardized Euclidean distances. Then, Ward's clustering method was applied to the vectors.

For example, using the trained network for Experiment 4 in the Table 21.1, the analysis of the context vectors was carried out for three kinds of selected pattern sequences. The dendrogram is shown in Figure 21.3. Each leaf in the dendrogram denotes a context vector to any input just presented in stock pattern sequences. Twelve clusters were made by cutting the tree at distance dash-dotted line A in Figure 21.3. Then, they are alphabetically named, that is, categories a to l. By describing a transition chart of cluster classification with the context vectors for each stock price sequence, it is possible to verify performance for recurrent networks, that is, the ability to recognize a triangle. Then, the temporal transition charts were made by using the network for Experiment 4.

Figure 21.4(a) illustrates a training triangle chart and its context transition chart for the triangle. The transition chart indicates that the context category is retroactively transited. The same charts as in Figure 21.4(a) for a test triangle and a mismatching pattern are shown in Figures 21.4(b) and 21.4(c), respectively. It became clear that the context category transited recursively, according to triangle's oscillation, and that there are local category jumps at nonlinear time-elasticity points. Moreover, in this case, the mismatching pattern recognition finished according to a different category from others.

To verify the ability of classification, the finishing categories were checked for all triangles and all mismatching patterns in each experiment. Using these pattern's context vectors, a cluster analysis was car-

Figure 21.3

Cluster Analysis Result

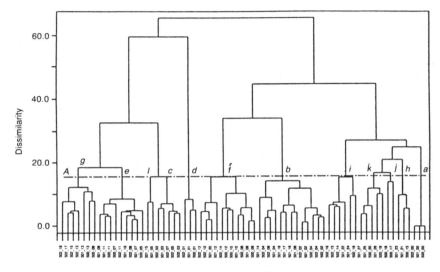

Leaves of Context Vector

ried out with 20 categories. The results concerning Experiments 1, 3, 4, 13, and 15 are shown in Table 21.2, and are similar to the results concerning the rest of the experiments. It is demonstrated that triangles are divided into a few major categories and some minor categories, and that the mismatching patterns are partially eliminated by checking the finishing categories. For example, in case of Experiment 13, training patterns were divided into two major categories and two minor ones. The mismatching patterns were divided into four categories identical to the training pattern categories (1st, 2nd, 3rd, and 4th categories), and remaining three categories (5th, 6th, and 7th categories). Therefore, the

Figure 21.4

Candlestick Charts and Context Transition Charts

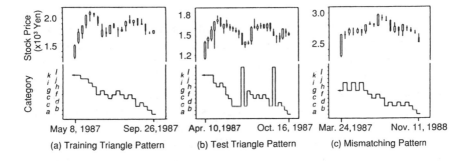

May 8, 1987   Sep. 26,1987   Apr. 10,1987   Oct. 16, 1987   Mar. 24,1987   Nov. 11, 1988

(a) Training Triangle Pattern   (b) Test Triangle Pattern   (c) Mismatching Pattern

Table 21.2

Number of Patterns in Finishing Categories

Experiment	Pattern Category	Finishing Category						
		1st	2nd	3rd	4th	5th	6th	7th
1	Training	5	4	2	2	1	1	-
	Test	1	-	-	-	-	-	-
	Mismatch	3	5	-	1	-	8	-
3	Training	11	2	1	1	-	-	-
	Test	-	-	-	-	1	-	-
	Mismatch	3	-	1	3	-	4	-
4	Training	10	2	1	1	1	-	-
	Test	1	-	-	-	-	-	-
	Mismatch	3	5	6	12	-	1	3
13	Training	5	5	3	2	-	-	-
	Test	1	-	-	-	-	-	-
	Mismatch	2	1	4	3	5	6	7
15	Training	9	3	1	1	1	-	-
	Test	1	-	-	-	-	-	-
	Mismatch	4	3	-	1	1	1	-

mismatching patterns in the remaining categories become candidates for rejection.

CONCLUSIONS

Recurrent neural networks were applied to recognition of stock price patterns. Among the patterns, triangle patterns indicate an important clue to trends in the stock market. From Japanese-style "candlestick" charts for names of corporations listed in the First Section of Tokyo Stock Exchange, 16 triangles were extracted by an expert. The patterns were divided into two groups, 15 training patterns and one test pattern. Sixteen experiments were accomplished using the groups cyclically. In order to eliminate the bias due to differences in name and time span, the variation rate for the stock price average obtained by exponential smoothing, and the dissociations from the average of high and low prices were utilized as normalized stock data. From these experiments, it was confirmed that the given test pattern was accurately recognized in 15 out of 16 experiments, and that the number of the mismatching patterns was 1.06 per name on the average in 16 experiments.

A new method for examining recurrent networks was established by searching for the temporal latent state transition. By applying a cluster analysis to context vectors generated in the networks at recognition stage, a transition chart for context categorization was obtained for each pattern sequence. It was found that the oscillations and the nonlinear time elasticity were represented by the recursive transition of context category and by the local jumps to other categories. Moreover, the finishing categories for context vectors in the charts are effective in triangle classification and partial elimination of mismatching patterns. The next step is to develop a method for determining the triangle period and to refine the method for eliminating mismatching patterns.[7]

ENDNOTES

1. M. J. Pring, "Technical Analysis Explained," (New York: McGraw-Hill, 1985).

2. S. Nison, "Learning Japanese-style 'Candlesticks' Charting," *Futures*, vol. 47, no. 13, 1989, pp. 46–47.

3. J. L. Elman, "Finding Structure in Time," Technical Report 8801, University of California, San Diego, Center for Research in Language, 1988.

4. D. Servan-Schreiber, A. Cleeremans, and J. L. McClelland, "Encoding Sequential Structure in Simple Recurrent Networks," Carnegie Mellon University, CMU-CS-88-183, 1988.

5. D. E. Rumelhart, H. E. Hinton, and R. J. Williams, "Learning Internal Representations by Error Propagation," in D. E. Rumelhart, J. L. McClelland, eds., *Parallel Distributed Processing: Explorations in the Microstructure of Cognition*, vol. 1, (Cambridge, Mass.: MIT Press, 1986).

6. H. C. Romesburg, "Cluster Analysis for Researchers," (Belmont, Calif: Lifetime Learning Publications, 1984).

7. The authors would like to thank Daiwa Securities Co. Ltd. for providing data related to stock and chart analysis. Meaningful discussions were held about applicability of neural networks to the securities domain, with M. Kinouchi, Y. Chiba, Daiwa Institute of Research Ltd., N. Kajihara and M. Asogawa, C&C System Research Laboratories, NEC Corporation.

22

ADAPTIVE PROCESSES TO EXPLOIT THE NONLINEAR STRUCTURE OF FINANCIAL MARKETS

W. E. Bosarge, Jr.

THE PROBLEM OF FORECASTING GLOBAL FINANCIAL MARKETS

The problem of forecasting directional movement within the highly complex financial markets during the 1990s will be difficult. We believe a new breed of financial technology is the answer. In fact, we believe

This paper was presented at the Santa Fe Institute of Complexity Conference: *Neural Networks and Pattern Recognition in Forecasting Financial Markets,* "Adaptive Processes to Exploit the Non-Linear Structure of Financial Markets," by W. E. Bosarge, Jr., February 15, 1991. Reprinted with permission.

that this technology will create major shifts in the global fund management industry during the 1990s.

A fundamental question in the evolution of money and risk management technology becomes, "How can I beat the index with some type of yield enhancement technology?" Yield enhancement technology is probably the highest and best use of the new adaptive investment technologies to be developed in the 1990s. There is a vast pool of international capital committed to index funds. Another use of the new technology is tactical asset allocation. Should a manager's capital be indexed to the Japanese market or should it be indexed to the U. S. market, or even in the West German DAX index? Where should I be invested daily? And how do I make that decision? Most of the major investment banking firms are attempting to answer these quantitative questions to provide new investment products for this decade. Salomon Brothers is offering a sophisticated product in this arena, although I am led to believe the underlying technology is linear.

The 1990s will be known as the decade of quantitative computer-driven strategies and nonlinear dynamical models. The major product trend for money management in the 1990s will center on passive/quantitative and international tactical asset allocation. Forecasting systematic risk for all instruments will become crucial for worldwide money management as well as risk control. This will be the decade that new software is designed for engineering workstations to automate the decision processes of the industry. The process of automation will take place quickly. Most firms that do not have an ongoing research effort in nonlinear dynamics, and those that do not have appropriately trained people, will be left behind.

The research team at Frontier has been working on the solution to the financial market forecasting problem for eight years. Our firm has spent about $8 million through December 31, 1990, on this R&D effort. We have designed and tested a new process technology for automated investment decision-making. So the process technology is an empirically discovered and validated technology that can backtest, simulate, or emulate, in real time, the solution to the financial forecasting problem.

MODELS FOR SYSTEMATIC RISK

In order to describe observed phenomena in the other branches of the physical world, researchers have devised models. Researchers also create models to describe economic phenomena. In this spirit we in the investment management industry have the efficient market theory of prices, which implies that past price time series behavior can provide no information about future prices. An efficient market is one in which prices should behave in accordance with this model.

An anomaly is defined to be a departure from a model. The history of all models is such that, initially, a wide body of research produces evidence that tends to support, and indeed leads to the formulation of, the model. It provides an orderly focus for thought, for discussion, and for further research. What is most interesting to the researcher is that a model is a context for the discovery of counterexamples, meaning exceptions to the models. As the state of knowledge matures, these exceptions, or anomalies, are discovered. Eventually, continued maturation, which produces more and more in the way of counterexamples, leads to the articulation of new modified structures that incorporate or subsume the previous models and theories.

Anomalies of such character may be found that cause the efficient market model to be totally rejected. In the context of the efficient market model, the anomalies have been called inefficiencies. Inefficiencies must always exist. Traders seek to exploit inefficiencies systematically. Most earlier inefficiencies have been typed as "pricing" differences between two instruments that should theoretically have the same value (based on an accepted theoretical framework). In so doing, it is one of the properties of financial markets that they make certain inefficiencies disappear (for high cost players). Thus, inefficiencies may be temporary, and it is the trader who may drive them away and make the markets more efficient. In fact, the brashest example of an inefficiency of some magnitude has been the recent use of stock-index arbitrage by Salomon, Morgan Stanley, and Goldman Sachs in Japan. The Americans developed their skills on Wall Street during the 1980s, learning to spot temporary valuation anomalies between the stock market and the futures market, and then using computers to execute baskets of trades (or program trades) at minimal cost that arbitrage the anomalies away. Just as program trading became a politicized issue after the October 1987 Wall Street crash, so American houses were widely reviled as the engine of the Tokyo stock market's precipitous decline in subsequent years.

Traders worldwide seek to profitably exploit inefficiencies because it is a way to obtain systematic (risk adjusted) excess returns. Any trading system which claims to produce systematic excess returns must at least implicitly be claiming to be exploiting an inefficiency. We quote Dr. H. Williams from a recent article[1]:

> I have just said that traders who are on to something have, in fact, discovered an inefficiency. What I have also said is that by the time an inefficiency can be clearly proven to exist, it is too late, for by then, it is almost certain that clever traders will have exploited these inefficiencies to the point of their disappearance. A typical scenario is this. An inefficiency is discovered. Capital is raised and a new investment firm is established to exploit this discovery and early results are extraordinary. The small amount of money under management, initially, becomes a bundle as accounts grow and new clients come to the window. By the time the track record is three to five years, everyone is signing on and the success of the strategy is essentially history. From here on it is doomed to languish and the best intentions are the source of built-in failure.

THE NON-LINEAR STRUCTURE OF FINANCIAL MARKETS

Seasoned traders and certain academics have observed that the movements of market prices are, in fact, not random. Rather, they behave in peculiar, nonlinear ways. Certain market observers possessing skills in mathematical physics observe that price time series must, in fact, be the output of a highly nonlinear (input/output), dynamic process. But the equations for that process are currently unknown to us. Although we do not know what they look like, we are gaining insight into the form these equations may take. We can establish certain properties of these equations. For example, the equations are most likely nonlinear, stochastic, delay-differential equations, because of a conclusion arrived at market response to certain real-world inputs.[2]

We have also observed that the market contains significant encoded inside information that can be extracted for profits and risk control. This inside information is contained in the data surrounding price (e.g., volume, open interest, call volume, call open interest, put volume, put open interest). In 1987, we found particular nonlinear transformations of price that were highly predictive of future price movements and remain useful today in the construction of our most predictive indicators for each market. We use this information to develop indicators in a methodical way, which we shall explain in a later section.

We have not discovered the equation that models the way the nonlinear financial market behaves (the systematic risk equation). We certainly know that we could use this information directly to forecast into the future if we knew the equation. We also know experientially that the forecasting horizon must remain very short because the casual forces driving the market change from day to day. Now, this does not surprise anyone. The last four weeks of August 1990, should deliver to each of us ample evidence that the safe forecasting horizon for financial markets is, in fact, very short (one to three days out). Within any nonlinear model (within the soft or hard physical sciences) where there are accepted fundamental equations, we have found only short-range forecasting to be feasible. We also have concluded that the predictive signals for the financial markets must be updated daily, or more often than daily. This is, we must track the swing cycle (three- to five-day cycle) to achieve a high degree of predictive accuracy. Finally, forecasting the direction of the financial market beyond five days increases the risk exponentially.

Similarity to Weather Forecasting

Now, let us view our last statement in the context of a highly important and timely nonlinear problem in science (a problem that was well researched in the mid-1940s at MIT). One of the earlier weather researchers asked, "Wouldn't it be wonderful to have a computer fast enough to forecast weather faster than the weather system moved, so we could forecast weather in real time and then perhaps even forecast forward in time." The problem was simply to forecast a weather system faster than a weather system moved. As computer performance increased, the required speed came.

That weather forecaster's dream was realized, and we have now installed the fastest weather forecasting computer in the world (a Cray YMK placed in Redding, England, rated at 800 megaflops). This system can forecast the weather for the entire northern hemisphere forward one week, requiring only one hour of CPU time. Thus, we can forecast the weather today far faster than real time. However, three or four days into our forecast, the forecast accuracy becomes unacceptable. Thus, we find that CPU cycles were, in fact, not the limit that researchers believed they would be in 1945. Therefore, it becomes no longer a CPU-bound problem. Something else is going on within the (nonlinear) structure of the problem.

The equations that govern all interesting real-world phenomena like the weather, the movement of the S&P, and like many economic, biological, and physiological systems (e.g., cancer cell growth) are, in fact, nonlinear. The future "activity" must be forecast over very short time frames and continually updated because the dynamic systems that must, in fact, describe these particular phenomena are:

❖ Nonlinear and nonstationary

❖ Sensitive to initial conditions (subject to chaotic behavior)

Is it sensitivity to initial conditions or is it the structure of the equations themselves causing poor forecast accuracy way out? Both![3] As for the weather equations, there are numerous problems: the data measurements are noisy and the required barometric pressure and air temperature grid does not, in fact, exist to the fineness required.

Chaos and the Challenge of the Efficient Market Model

Many financial market theorists believe that the death-knell for the random walk model (for financial markets) occurred in 1987. On October 19, the collapse (in tandem) of the world equity markets occurred. Now all the academicians who were grounded in an efficient market model said, "Wait a minute! There must be something drastically wrong with the theory if we can have a 500-point move in the Dow in one day." These markets cannot be efficient if they reflected all available information on Friday, October 16. They realized that there was more going on which must be far more profound. It was at this time when academics really began to take a serious look at the problem, especially with interest in nonlinear dynamics again on the rise.[3]

This event in the financial market typifies the behavior of complex, nonlinear, dynamic systems. Chaotic behavior can and will occur. We now have at least the correct view of the problem as it really exists! Therefore, we conclude that the best we can do is to predict the swing cycle or alpha cycle of the market. We can make statements today about the financial market of the following type: "The market is going to go down tomorrow, further down the next day, and then it is likely that the market will stabilize." That is the kind of "forecast" we can make about the financial markets today. So we are in the same position as the weather forecasters.

The Financial Modeling Problem

All of us who are interested in the market forecasting problem must begin to search for a new perspective. The financial data we have studied in the past may have been daily, weekly, or even monthly numbers; somehow, we had tried to build a model that would forecast future price movements from these numbers. We found first that econometrics did not work. The Wharton School of Finance models were inadequate. In fact, if we had studied each of the models that were used and marketed by the big econometric forecasting forms, we would have found that they had and still have almost no value in financial market forecasting. However, we do not dispute the validity of macroeconomic cause and effect. The system dynamics are such that going from macro (or micro) econometric data to forecasting daily price movements is simply unachievable (see Figure 22.1).

So, what must we try to do to build a framework for construction of a model? For example, suppose we are interested in modeling U. S. Treasury bonds. We ask, "What are traders doing in crude oil?" We have also discovered that there is "aggregation of intent" contained in six pieces of data (volume, open interest, call volume, put volume, call open interest, put open interest). Thus, if we are modeling bonds, we must study various time series data within the intermarket relationships, but primarily we research these six pieces of frontier data. Within these six pieces of data (which exist courtesy of the derivative instrument revolution) are encoded "directional footprints" of all classes of market players (hedgers, commercial speculators, and locals) and, within those footprints are, in fact, "patterns," which are predictive of short-term price movements. We call these data frontier data. The data are right on the "frontier" of price. We are simply as close as we can get to price. So price becomes, in the final analysis, an effect in our casuality spectrum.

In 1987, we entertained certain views from quantum mechanics which are, in fact, as predictive as the frontier data. We arrived at new classes of nonlinear transformations of intermarket price relationships, which we validated in real time in 1988, definitely refuting the strong form of the random walk hypothesis (i.e., "one cannot predict future

Figure 22.1

A Holistic Approach Design Assumptions Cause > Effect

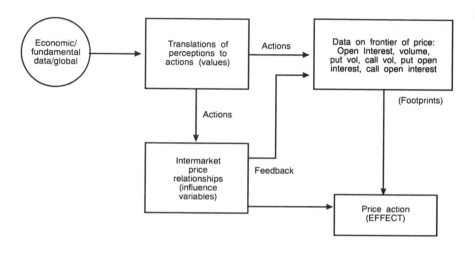

movement of prices from the study of past behavior of prices"). In fact, we have used daily transformations of the Swiss franc, S&P 500, and U. S. Bond prices that predict where the respective market will move over the next one to three days, with a predictive accuracy of over 65 percent for over three years. These represent fundamental discoveries that we wish to explain on a more theoretical basis in our research today.

The financial markets today are interlocked (coupled), and we, therefore, have new problems resulting from the globalization phenomenon. For example, the Japanese may raise a key interest rate, the Germans may raise another one, and the Swiss follow suit. Thus, our financial markets have become dynamically coupled, and thus have become part of a total worldwide dynamic system. In foreign exchange where a Central Bank (G-7) buffers either end of a trading range and places ceilings and floors that traders can play against, the trading profits come easier. However, in the laboratory we now seek to discover, synthetically, the fundamental equations describing the market system movements through "synthesis" using the new technologies that have recently been introduced and will be discussed at this conference.

We believe we have a substantial practical lead over our nearest competitors. This lead has tremendous value just like the early lead developed by earlier players in index arbitrage (a riskless price arbitrage strategy discovered in the U. S. financial markets in 1982). There were billions of dollars of profits made and the riskless arbitrage opportunity is still there. It will never go away because it represents a built-in inefficiency in the system. Remember, no matter how much energy we force into this arbitrage phenomenon, we cannot make the inefficiency go to zero. That would require infinite energy.

The total classes of inefficiencies in the Japanese financial market are enormous. So there is ample room to play the index arbitrage game, as well as model systematic risk. We are attempting to replicate the movements of the postulated, systematic risk equation, which describes the future movement of the actual price index itself.[4] And really, all we are interested in is the solution of that system of equations or an approximation to the solution that suits our purposes.

The thrust of our research has really been to detect a new class of inefficiencies in the liquid financial markets by using advanced forms of artificial intelligence. In particular, by using pattern recognition technology, fundamental principles of nonlinear dynamics, and some of the latest advances in adaptive neural networks, we are able to predict price movements associated with those inefficiencies, exploit these within the market, and generate trading profits and technology royalty fees. We have used our new vision to detect and harness these inefficiencies in numerous markets of interest. We have developed trading processes that we have tested in the market with live trading for a number of years. We now plan to use them for proprietary trading of firm capital. We have developed major world banks as partners to fund the extension of these generic discoveries to numerous other liquid world financial markets.[5]

SYNTHESIZING THE STRUCTURE

Pattern recognition was a budding technology in 1983 and was used often in the solution of defense problems and submarine warfare. As a matter of fact, its primary application in early years was for submarine detection through sonar imaging. Pattern recognition technology has been around now for about 25 years and has become very sophisticated. Although it is now being supplanted by newer technologies within artificial intelligence, it is still a useful technology, but will probably be relegated primarily to stationary nonlinear problems.

Another event that made the solution to the market forecasting problem possible was dramatic expansion in the use of derivative instruments. We may ask, in fact, "What are the characteristics of a market that Frontier's technology can predict well?"

❖ A primary liquid cash market must be present

❖ A liquid futures market on the primary cash instrument must be in place

❖ A liquid options market on the futures contract should be in place

The discrepancies in valuation mechanisms that exist on a daily basis are frequently related to the movements of the market over the swing cycle. We are interested in synthesizing a structure to predict these short-term movements. Computer CPU cycles are no longer an issue in the solution of the market forecasting problem. Furthermore, self-learning AI systems have taken a big leap in the last few years. Our R&D team has had great success in adaptive pattern recognition solutions to the market forecasting problem from 1987 through 1989. We discovered the generic, although highly nonstationary, driving forces of each for the financial markets studied. In fact, we found that they may be predictive for six months and then they may disappear for six months. We were looking for predictive pattern correlations, and we were trying to determine whether these correlations were sufficiently stable (robust) over a multitude of decision points. Pattern recognition achieved some interesting insights for us. It separated data streams that were spuriously correlated from those which were predictive.

We have recently built some simple pattern recognition models using our indicators, which use very simple patterns to determine whether the market is likely to go up and hit an objective or down and hit a stop. They have held their predictive capacity over live data tests during the past year.

ADAPTIVE TECHNOLOGY FOR EXTRACTION OF THE INEFFICIENCIES

We have now developed an automated decision technology for quantitative investment management that is adaptive and self-learning. The first requirement is that the technology process be adaptive and able to track the changing whims in the financial marketplace. The waxing and waning of totally quantitative influences (predictive indicators) must be handled by the modeling process. The core approach, as we have discussed, is essentially the determination of the current "causality spectrum" for the market in question. Once we have isolated and established a predictive influence, we fine tune the indicators into those segments that drove the market last year, last month, or last quarter. The approach and the selection process must be dynamic and deliver a catalog of predictive periods associated with various market conditions for each instrument (Figures 22.2–22.6).

The Clairvoyant Model

Often in presenting our approach to designing the dynamic model, we found that researchers could not frame the question. If the researcher does not ask the right trading or risk management question, then the research team is not going to get an answer that is useful to the trader. We create an objective function or clairvoyant trader. How might one create a perfect oscillator? We simply allow the computer to look ahead into the future. Thus, the computer becomes clairvoyant for training purposes. We say, "We know something about nonlinear dynamic systems. We know that we can only predict two or three days ahead, so we allow the computer to look two or three days ahead to see how it should trade today." Now if we do that, we should be able to trade pretty well. As a matter of fact, we trade with 100 percent accuracy. However, we are "cheating" over the past data. We created this perfect oscillator (or "artifice") which we call the "objective function" or the "clairvoyant trader." The result is simply an oscillator or a set of patterns of ones and minus ones. The oscillator is user defined in accordance with the exact way the user wants to trade. However, the user must define "perfection" incorporating the characteristics of the alpha cycle (Figures 22.7 and 22.8).

Figure 22.2

Eurodollar Call Open Interest

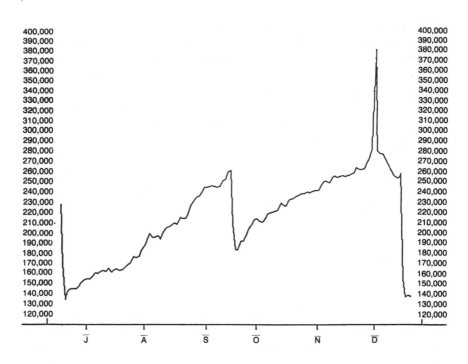

A trader may say, "I want to trade bond. Give me a perfect oscillator for bonds." And the question becomes, "What is your risk tolerance?" He responds, "Well, I can stand only a one point drawdown, after which I am stopped out." Once the trader defines his risk tolerance, the trader has implicitly defined his trading frequency.[6] That trading frequency invariably turns out to be a cycle frequency centered about the alpha cycle frequency (for most screen watching, discretionary traders). Five trades a month or six trades a month is the usual result. The alpha cycle for financial markets almost invariably turns out to be the same cycle over which we can predict any nonlinear dynamic system that models real-world processes. Thus, we develop, daily, this artifice in the computer, a so-called perfect model by continually allowing the computer to look three days ahead. If we could only hire this perfect trader! Why? Because this perfect trader is, in fact, programmed to be clairvoyant

Figure 22.3

Transformation of Eurodollar Call Open Interest

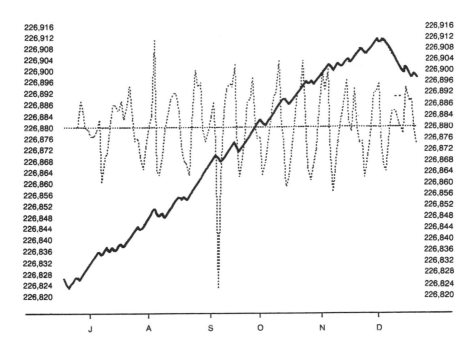

over past data. He would have done better than any other trader in the trading room. So that clairvoyant trader is used by the computer to train all indicators on a daily basis to deliver self-learning indicators.

We begin with any number of candidate indicators in the pattern selector (Figure 22.9). In general, most time series we believed were predictive delivered no predictive information. In 1989, numerous variables passed the predictivity test. Why? The derivative instrument revolution was in full swing on a global context. Now, several of these patterns which fall out of the pattern selector result from new transformations of price.[7] Put and call information, implied volatilities delivered into the pattern optimizer do deliver usable, predictive indicators. We optimize their predictive utility against this perfect oscillator. We ask, "How well did they do against this perfect model?" They are then ranked daily. We rank them univariately, then bivariately, then

Figure 22.4

A Direct Approach—Rocket Scientist/Rocket Equation

$$F = ma = \frac{d}{dt}(mv)$$

Futures market analog

$F \equiv$ Force $\equiv$ Effective volume $(NV = V_E)$

$M \equiv$ Mass $\equiv$ Open interest (effective) $(NOI = O_E)$

$V \equiv$ Velocity $\equiv$ Rate of change of price $(\frac{d}{dt}P\,)$

$$V_E = \frac{d}{dt}\left(O_E \times \frac{d}{dt}P\right)$$

$$V_E = VOL_{FUT} - \left(C_{VOL} - P_{VOL}\right) ; \qquad O_E = OI_{FUT} - \left(C_{OI} - P_{OI}\right)$$

$$V_E = \dot{O_E}\,\dot{P} + O_E\,\ddot{P}$$

---

trivariately, etc. We then test those combinations over randomly selected x-ante data sets. We have developed at this point an ability to rank predictive information in the context of what we require as a trader. These predictors, which do fall out as useful predictors, tend to always trade at the alpha cycle frequency.

In earlier years, we spent almost $1,000,000 on the Rice University main frame computer, building the original S&P and the bond models. Our research team was the second largest user of that computer while building these models. We were making eight- and ten-hour runs each night to solve this indicator selection problem. Today, at Frontier, we have 200 or 300 MIPS on UNIX-based IBM RIOS 320s and 540s to deal with this problem. A quantitative revolution is coming in the 1990s that will absorb huge market research teams. The problem is fiendishly complex. New software for indicator selection, validation, and testing must be created, developed, and placed in service. Our pattern selection technology and optimizer contains over 200,000 lines of C code and

Figure 22.5

BDHSVOLSP Equity Curve

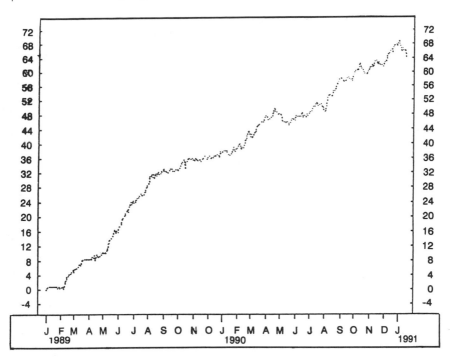

*1990 and 1991 real time — no slippage.

delivers daily self-learning indicators that can track this clairvoyant oscillator. The indicators trade five to six times a month. This software and hardware platform delivers us a dramatic edge over our competition (Figure 22.10).

Functional Synthesis with Neural Nets: An Introduction

The lure of intelligent decision machines goes back to the beginning of this century. Even before the advent of the first digital computer, science fiction writers dreamt of the day that machines could emulate complex human decision processes. Early research into intelligent machines took two paths. The first path modeled the devices and interactions that are

Figure 22.6

DMHSVOLQ Equity Curve

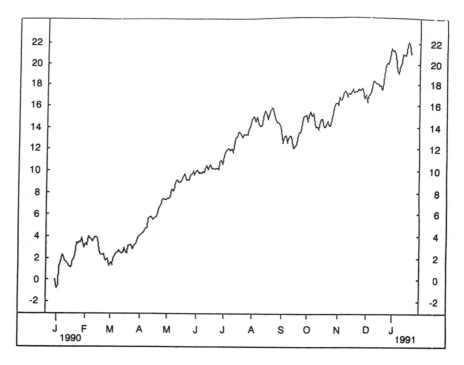

*1990 real time — no slippage.

found in the brain and nervous system. The second path also modeled the functions of the brain, but approached intelligence from a macroscopic or black-box perspective.

One of the earliest attempts at "black-box" machine intelligence was a program written by Minsky to do geometric proofs. Out of this research grew several basic information-processing and storage concepts: rules, implications, frames, etc. This and other early successes became the basis of what has become known as artificial intelligence. Expert systems is one of the children of this research, although a poor stepchild within the market forecasting arena.

Neural networks represent a new information-processing technology. From one perspective, the major information-processing technologies—procedural languages (BASIC, FORTRAN, COBOL, C), expert

Figure 22.7

U.S. Treasury Bond Futures

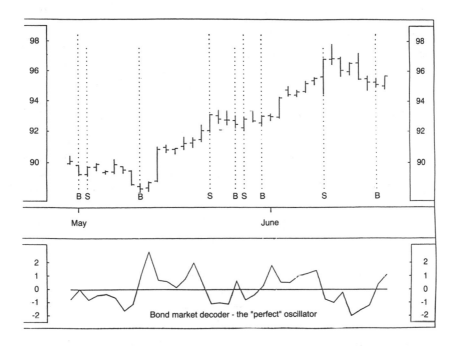

systems, and neural networks — run on the same hardware. At the hardware level, each accepts inputs, processes them, and produces outputs. Each is an information-processing technology. However, each of the three technologies brings unique insights into information processing, which make each good at solving specific types of problems.

Neural networks represent a parallel processing technology inspired by studies of the brain and nervous system. They are best at doing some of the things that biological systems are good at; in particular, pattern recognition and classification and complex functional synthesis such as that required to combine our predictive indicators to produce a model that emulates the perfect oscillator.

Pattern classification occurs at several levels. At a very low level, it is the ability to detect edges and connected areas in a picture, or to

Figure 22.8

Pattern Optimizer

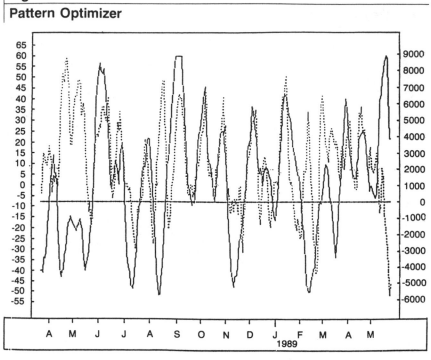

differentiate the sound of a bell and a whistle. At a higher level, pattern classification enables individuals to make "gut-level" judgments about the quality of a long or a short signal, or the risks involved in pursuing a particular strategy. Most of these decisions are based on previous experience weighted by the brain. Neural networks have now been applied to several similar problems. These include credit application evaluation and, most recently by our research team, the problem of forecasting daily, as well as intraday, price movements in over ten financial markets.

Functional synthesis consists of establishing relationships between our continuous-valued (or discrete) predictive indicators, our continuous-valued (or discretely valued) objective functions. For example, a trader decides to go long the Japanese yen against the deutsche mark. We must first teach our neural network how to evaluate and learn several complex nonlinear continuous-valued relationships that are predictive of this spread. At Frontier, neural network applications of func-

Figure 22.9

Frontier Process Design with Neural Networks

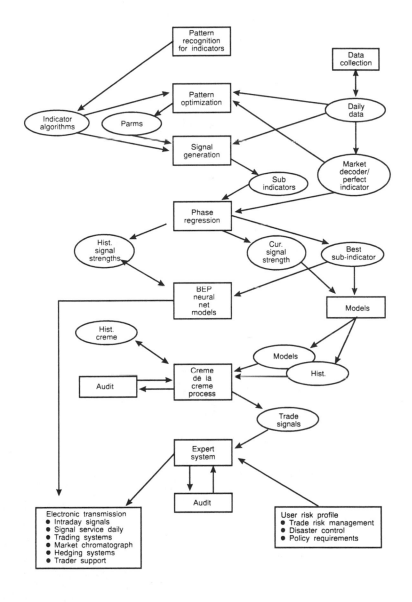

Figure 22.10

Frontier Real-Time Computing Facility

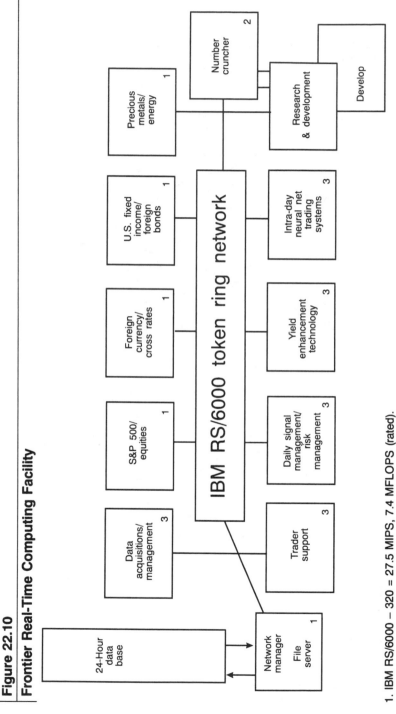

1. IBM RS/6000 – 320 = 27.5 MIPS, 7.4 MFLOPS (rated).
2. IBM RS/6000 – 540 = 41.1 MIPS, 13.0 MFLOPS (rated); 50.0 MFLOPS (Frontier Application mix, est.).
3. 486 Workstations = 11 MIPS, 1.0 MFLOPS (rated).

Figure 22.11

S&P 500: A Case Study Schematic Flow of an Adaptive Pattern Recognition Approach

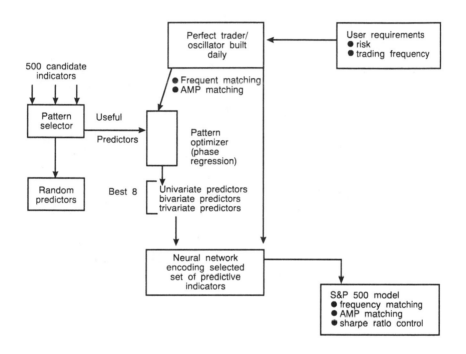

tional synthesis include filtering noise out of open interest data, primary forecasting, and estimating error in theoretically established reward/risk parameters.

Figure 22.12

Signal Generation — Darwinian Selector (A Creme de la Creme Expert System)

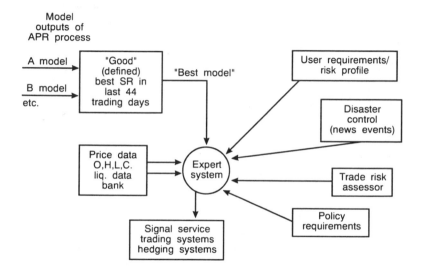

Putting It All Together

Although pattern recognition has been used to combine indicators as we earlier discussed, we have now proceeded with the function synthesis through adaptive neural networks. Suppose we possess a group of predictive indicators; we take the group (15 to 20 candidates). We now know that the perfect oscillator decodes the market in exactly the way the trader intends to trade. We build a function that combines these

Figure 22.13

S&P BISUM Equity Curve —Trading with Wide Stops and No Objectives

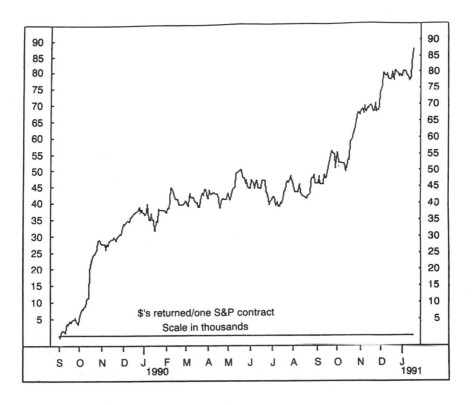

From: 09/01/89	Last	Last	Wins/	Pct	Net	Points/	Sharpe
To: 01/17/91	Stop	Obj	Trades	Wins	Points	Trade	Ratios
Long	7.50	0.00	41/72	57%	124.45	1.73	3.94
Short	3.50	0.00	31/65	48%	49.90	.77	2.18
Total			72/137	53%	174.35	1.27	3.17

Figure 22.14

Crude Light Trader Equity Curve —Trading with Wide Stops

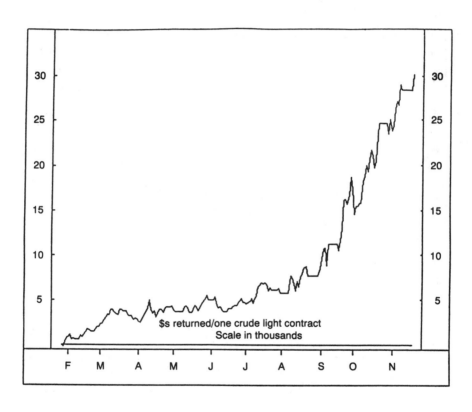

$s returned/one crude light contract
Scale in thousands

From: 01/26/90	Last	Last	Wins/	Pct	Net	Points/	Sharpe
To: 11/19/90	Stop	Obj	Trades	Wins	Points	Trade	Ratios
Long	999.00	0.00	16/27	59%	17.30	.64	3.89
Short	999.00	0.00	18/29	62%	12.91	.45	3.29
Total			34/56	61%	30.21	.54	3.61

Figure 22.15

Objective Function Optimization
S&P 500 – Best = 5 days, 75% of range

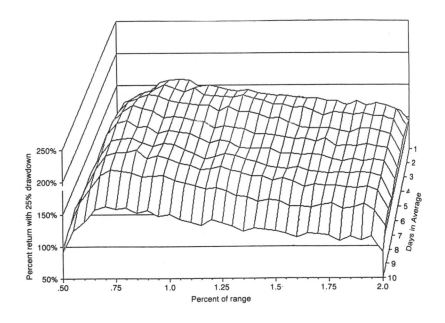

indicators into a neural network. For example, we place these indicators together and encode the perfect oscillator using only those indicators that are currently predictive. A neural network does the preselection. We train the final network to emulate the perfect oscillator for a period of time (training set). We then run the neural networks in real time. The neural network models appear to have a longer half-life than any of the adaptive pattern recognition models. In fact, the neural network models may last months in live trading before they deteriorate significantly. The neural network model that is produced maintains a high Sharpe ratio, and almost invariably the neural network models trade at the frequency of the perfect oscillator. As a bonus, the forecast of the amplitude match the amplitude of the perfect oscillator. In fact, we have emulated the perfect oscillator over the training set, but we can create an approximation to it in real time from data that is delivered daily.

Figure 22.16

Objective Function Optimization
Crude Oil – Best = 6 days, 95% of range

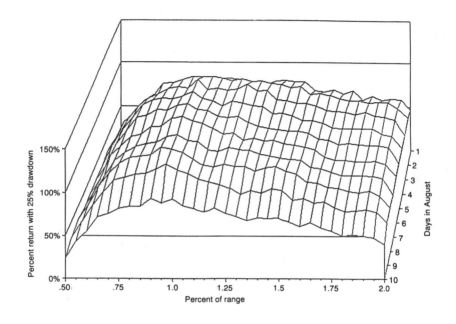

Thus, we have synthesized the solution to the fiendishly complex market forecasting problem (Figure 22.11).

We diversify by building a number of models which we allow to compete. We have built a Darwinian selector (an elementary genetic selector) that selects the winning individual models from over a dozen neural network models. For example, we build one model from our historical indicators, and others from different classes of various real-time indicators. All of these models can be used to develop a customized output and a technology signal service for our worldwide client base of banks and international oil companies. Applications of this technology are position taking; trading, market timing, portfolio hedging, hedging index funds, yield enhancement for equity funds, as well as fixed income portfolios, cross-hedging, and filtering of client-generated market timing signals (Figure 22.12).

Figure 22.17

Results from Combining Technologies: Frontier's Adaptive Indicators Combined with Neural Network Technology. S&P 500 Futures

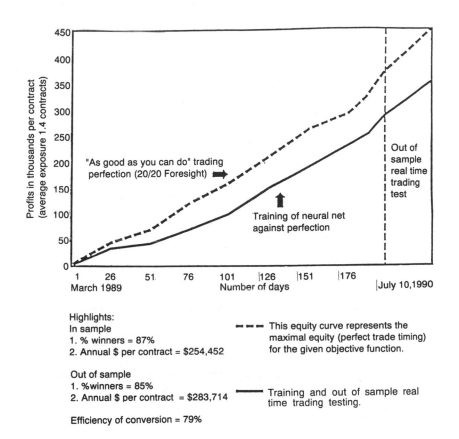

Highlights:
In sample
1. % winners = 87%
2. Annual $ per contract = $254,452

― ― ― This equity curve represents the maximal equity (perfect trade timing) for the given objective function.

Out of sample
1. %winners = 85%
2. Annual $ per contract = $283,714

━━━ Training and out of sample real time trading testing.

Efficiency of conversion = 79%

Figure 22.18

Results from Combining Technologies: Frontier's Adaptive Indicators Combined with Neural Network Technology. Crude Oil Futures (NYMEX)

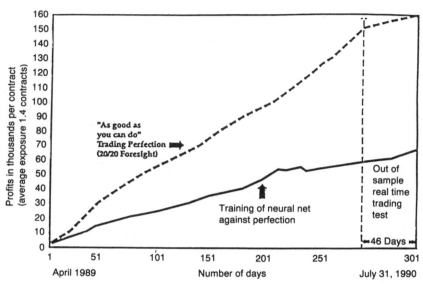

Highlights:

In sample
1. % winners = 71%
2. Annual $ per contract = $29,772

Out of sample
1. %winners = 68%
2. Annual $ per contract = $29,759

Efficiency of conversion =60%

▬ ▬ ▬ This equity curve represents the
maximal equity (perfect trade timing)
for the given objective function.

▬▬▬ Training and out of sample real
trading testing.

Figure 22.19

Trading Perfection and Frontier J-Yen Model

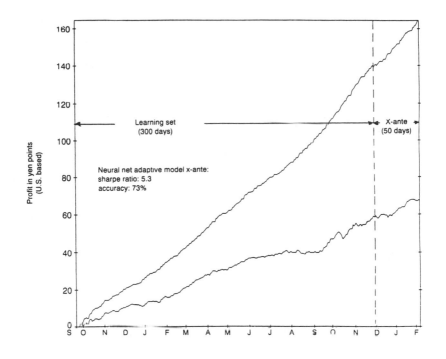

Results

Results of applying these new (nonlinear) technologies to making real-time predictions to the S&P 500 are shown in Figure 22.13. For real time signals in crude oil, we present the results in Figure 22.14. Figures 22.15 and 22.16 portray the optimization required to generate real time dynamical stops and objectives using Monte Carlo methods.

In Figures 22.17 through 22.21 we present the results of training and x-ante data set testing of a proprietary neural network paradigm on building automated decision trading models for the S&P 500, crude oil, Japanese yen, Eurodollar, and the NIKKEI respectively.

Figure 22.20

Trading Perfection and Frontier Eurodollar Model

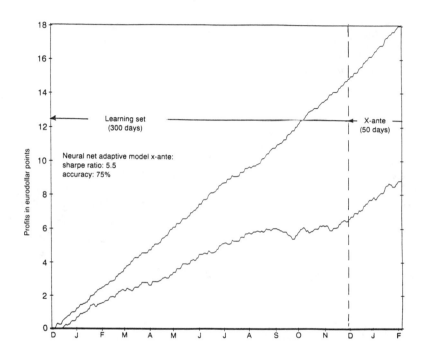

Figure 22.21

Trading Perfection and Frontier NIKKEI Model

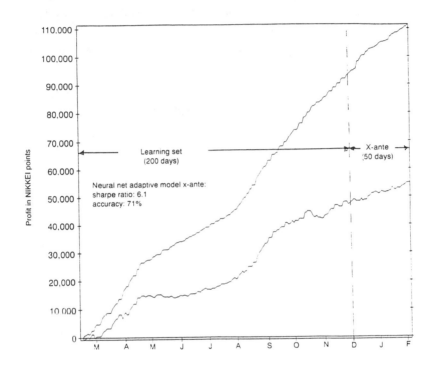

ENDNOTES

1. H. W. Williams, "Efficient Markets, Investment Management Selection, and the Loser's Game," research paper, University of Chicago, 1989.

2. N. Idelson, "Developing Real Time Technical Indicators and Trading Systems." *Innovations in Technical Analysis,* Conference, London, 1989.

3. J. Stewart, *Does God Play Dice?* (Ingram Books, 1989).

4. R. J. Shiller, "Market Volatility and Investor Behavior," *AEA Papers and Proceedings*, May 1990, pp. 58–62.

5. D. M. Cutler, J. M. Poterba, and L. H. Summers, "Speculative Dynamics and the Role of Feedback Traders," *AEA Papers and Proceedings*, May 1990, pp. 63–67.

6. R. Grinold, "The Fundamental Principle of Active Asset Management," research paper, BARRA, 1989.

7. W. E. Bosarge, Jr., "A Non-Random Walk Down Wall Street," (England: *Market Technician — The Journal of the STA*, 1989).

23

A Commodity Trading Model Based on a Neural Network-Expert System Hybrid

Karl Bergerson and Donald C. Wunsch II

Neural networks apply to problems that have proven difficult if not impossible to solve by programming a computer with algorithms. Problems such as predicting the market fall into this category because solving them involves the recognition of patterns—even patterns that are vaguely defined, buried in noise, or are otherwise difficult to decompose into the neat steps of an algorithm.

It is not necessary to solve the mysteries of human intelligence to make a useful system. Even the smallest insects have pattern processing, learning, and other capabilities that elude even the most powerful supercomputers. It is not surprising, then, that some insights in the field of neural networks have led to impressive gains in the capabilities of software-based trading.

Like several others who have tried market prediction with neural networks, we have used the back-propagation network,[1] with some parameters selected experimentally, as discussed below. However, we expended the majority of our efforts in providing good training data, which we believe sets our work apart. We wanted to control precisely what the network learned about market prediction, preferring that it only attempt to make a trade when the chances for profit were high. Therefore, it was not desirable to train the network purely on historical data, expecting it to predict gains and losses under all possible conditions. Instead, we used a human expert to implicitly define patterns, using hindsight, that an intelligent system might have been able to use for an accurate prediction. Desired outputs were found by a combination of observing the behavior of technical indices that normally precede a certain kind of market behavior, and by observing the actual market behavior in retrospect. Thus, the network learned to give signals based on data that looked favorable to a human expert, but tempered by the requirement that anything considered to be a "good example" must also be accompanied by a profitable history. The network also received a number of "bad examples," that is, examples where the indices looked good or borderline good, but were not borne out by historical data and therefore deserved an output indicating an unfavorable condition.

In contrast to merely pumping a neural network with massive amounts of historical data, our method was extremely labor intensive. Figures 23.1(a), 23.1(b), 23.1(c) and 23.1(d) show four technical indicators plotted against the daily Standard & Poor's 500 Index (S&P 500). The boxes show that the human expert felt that the patterns were clear enough to indicate that a "sell" decision could be made, and the triangles are where the human expert chose a "buy" decision. These points, chosen manually, were given as training examples to the network, together with technical data from the recently preceding days. The process demanded many hours of expert time, and careful consideration of each potential pattern in the data. These figures cover the period of September 19, 1980, to January 2, 1981. The triangles and boxes were chosen manually by the expert, and it took him about three hours to do this

Figure 23.1a – 23.1d

Buying ▲ and Selling ■ Decisions

Figure 23.1a Moving Average of Price — Normal

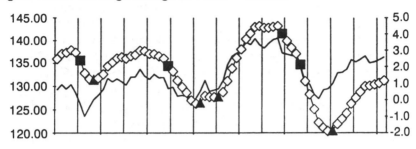

Figure 23.1b Moving Average of Price — Fast

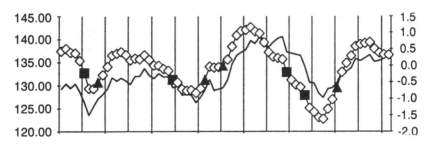

Figure 23.1c Moving Average of Advance Decline Line — Normal

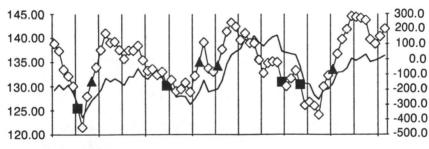

Figure 23.1d Moving Average of Advance Decline Line — Fast

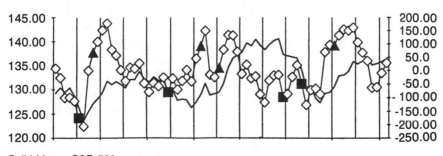

Solid Line = S&P 500

example. The total amount of data used for training covered approximately nine years.

The selection of parameters for the neural architecture also involved some extra effort. Two issues that were addressed experimentally were the number of hidden units to use, and the amount of training to provide. The number of hidden units was determined by pruning. We began with a full layer of 54 hidden units, the same as the number of input units. After training had stabilized, we removed those units whose weights were smallest, and retrained. In this way we corrected for any possibility of overfitting the training data. The amount of training to provide was also monitored. We did this by comparing the error on the test data to the error on the training data. When these were the same, we did no further training. Note, however, that the test data we used for the performance figures that we show includes data that were never seen by the network, even in this implicit manner.

It is very important to note that this hybrid approach offers strong advantages over either rule-based or unaided neural network approaches. Rule-based approaches are lacking in the flexibility to easily deal with the recognition of poorly defined patterns. Unaided neural networks are better at pattern recognition (in a theoretical sense) than they are at doing things that are naturally well-handled by rules, such as risk management. It is possible to make a theoretically excellent market prediction system using neural networks alone, but it is the combination of this capability with a rule-based system that makes a useful real-world investment system. Our system uses a risk-management rule that governs where stop-loss points are put to control losses when an incorrect prediction is made. Furthermore, these stops need to be increased when a trade goes well, so that one knows when to take profits. Also, certain extreme values of indicators are known to be a sign of extreme volatility in the market, making predictions more uncertain. These are best tracked by rules. The rule-based system thus has veto power over the neural networks' signals, but does not generate signals on its own. It is the synergy of the rule-based and neural system that permits the design of such an attractive reward-to-risk-ratio trading model. The reward-to-risk ratio for our system's performance to date is shown in Table 23.1.

Figure 23.2 shows the results of a rule-based daily trading system that has been augmented by a neural network market predictor.[2] The

Table 23.1

Hybrid System Performance

	Long	Short	All
Win Ratio %	58.33	91.67	75.00
Reward/Risk	5.82	3.81	4.81
Number of Trades	12.00	12.00	24.00
Average Gain Points	6.10	4.06	5.08
Maximum Loss Points	1.54	1.39	1.54
Average Loss Points	0.45	0.12	0.28
Average Duration	9.42	2.17	5.79
Maximum Drawdown	1.04	0.90	1.04
Average Drawdown	0.32	0.16	0.24

Report Dates: 89/01/04 through 91/01/29. Slippage: 0.50 [$250]

neural network was trained on data from 1980 to 1988, and then ran with an initial investment of $10,000 on January 4, 1989, to January 25, 1991. The final account value was $76,034, which represents a growth of 660 percent over 25 months. The maximum drawdown was for the period from September 15, 1989, to September 25, 1989. During this period, the account went from a value of $32,954 to $32,187, a 2.3 percent loss. The program easily recovered from this in a single successful trade. The reason for this resilient property is a conservative risk-management rule that limits the amount of losses that will be tolerated but allows maximal advantage of profit-making opportunities. It should be noted that these are theoretical gains, although we have been trading the system successfully with real dollars since August 1990.

Our point that learning can enhance the performance of trading systems is now clear. This enhancement is beyond that attainable with rule-based or neural network systems alone. The key issue is to move beyond mere theoretical prediction to profitability. As Figure 23.2 makes clear, that move has been made. The key technical insight that led to this achievement is that the neural network can be used as a knowledge acquisition tool, and when that tool is used with some real-world risk management expertise, the result is impressive. It is not a magic solution; in fact, it involved more hard work and more demands on the expert's time than traditional knowledge engineering approaches. The results, though, seem to justify the difficulty of the approach.

Figure 23.2

Plot of Neural$ System Performance versus the S&P 500

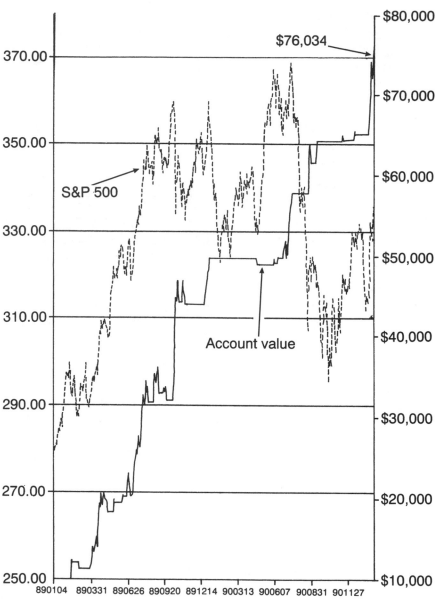

ENDNOTES

1. D. E. Rumelhart, G. E. Hinton, and J. R. Williams, "Learning Internal Representations by Error Propagation," in *Parallel Distributed Processing*, vol. 1 (Cambridge, Mass.: MIT Press, 1986).

2. Neural$ from Neural Trading Company.

24

COMMODITY TRADING WITH A THREE YEAR OLD

J. E. Collard

INTRODUCTION

This chapter reports on continuing work to train the ANN to recognize a long/short (buy/sell) pattern for the live cattle commodity futures market. The back-propagation of errors algorithm was used to encode the relationship between a LONG or SHORT position in the live cattle commodity futures market (the desired output) and fundamental variables plus technical variables into an artificial neural network (ANN). Trained on three years of past data, the ANN is able to correctly predict LONG or SHORT market positions for 178 trading days in 1991 yielding a profit of $1,547.50. If the account started with $3,000 this would represent a return of 52 percent for the 178 trading days or an annualized return of 81 percent.

Printed with permission of the author acknowledging support from Gerber Inc., Schwieterman Inc., and Martingale Research Corp.

NETWORK ARCHITECTURE

The ANN 044 was a simple feed-forward, single hidden layer network with no input units (inputs were prescaled), 30 hidden units, and one output unit.

TRAINING PROCEDURE

Back-Propagation of Errors Algorithm

The ANN was trained using the well-known ANN training algorithm called back-propagation of errors with the following optional features:

1. Use of a minimum slope term in the derivative of the activation function.

2. Momentum of .9.[1]

3. Weights changed once each epoch (data pass).[2]

DATA

The training data set for 044 consisted of 789 trading days in 1988, 1989, 1990, and 1991. Each trading day had associated with it a 37-component pattern vector consisting of 18 fundamental indicators, plus six market technical variables (Open, High, Low, Close, Open Interest, and Volume) for that trading day, six market technical variables for the previous trading day, six market technical variables for the two-days-previous trading day, and finally, the Target or TEACHER's long/short decision. The trained model was then traded in 1991 from April 11th through December 19th or 178 trading days.

TRAINING RESULTS

Figure 24.1 shows the extent to which network 044 was trained on the 789 trading days in the training data set. The network has not been able to correctly encode the LONG/SHORT position for 11 trading days in

Figure 24.1

Trained Network 044

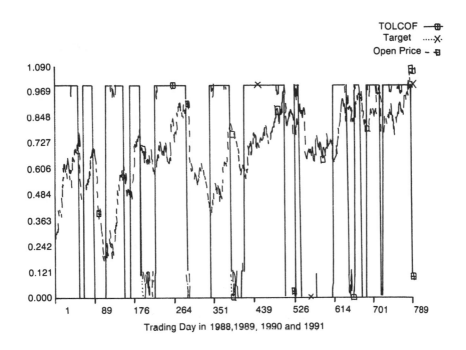

TOLCOF —⊞-
Target ....✕·
Open Price - ⊟

Trading Day in 1988,1989, 1990 and 1991

the training data set. Figure 24.2 shows that the resulting profit steps are relatively unchanged despite these 11 days of disagreement.

Figure 24.3 plots the profit and loss for the model during the training period as it exists on paper only. Each time a round turn (RT) is completed, the current paper profit or loss is recognized as real profit or loss and the curve goes to zero. As can be seen from the plot, the largest paper profit during the training period is $4,976 and the largest paper loss for the period is $120.

TRADING RESULTS

Table 24.1 shows the actual trading performance of network 044 for 178 trading days in 1991.

Figure 24.2

Profit Step Function for Trained Network 044

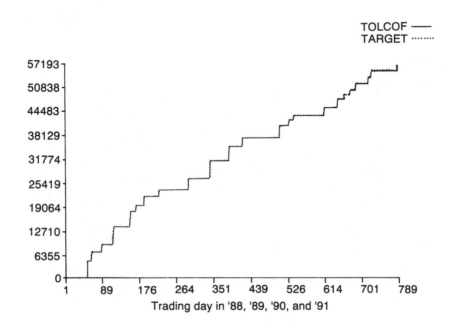

TOLCOF ——
TARGET ·······

Trading day in '88, '89, '90, and '91

Figures 24.4 and 24.5 show the actual long/short positions for network 044 for 178 trading days in 1991 and the profit step function for network 044 resulting from these positions.

OTHER RESULTS

Results for 16 trained networks are summarized in Tables 24.1 and 24.2.

Figure 24.3

Paper Profit for Trained Network

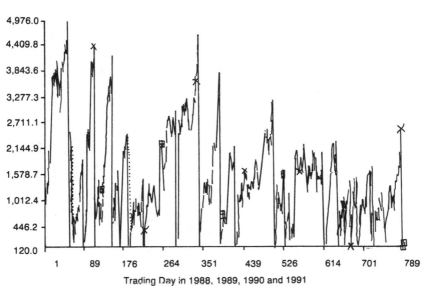

Trading Day in 1988, 1989, 1990 and 1991

Table 24.1

Actual Trading Results

DATE	PRICE	POSITION	PROFIT	CUMULATIVE PROFIT	BALANCE
4-11-91	77.18	SELL,1 - SHORT	$0.00	$0.00	$3,000.00
5-20-91	75.38	BUY,2 - LONG	$648.30	$648.30	$3,648.30
6-03-91	75.60	SELL,1 - OUT	$18.30	$666.60	$3,666.60
6-03-91	73.65	BUY,1 - LONG	$0.00	$666.60	$3,666.60
7-23-91	73.10	SELL,2 - SHORT	($291.74)	$374.86	$3,374.86
7-29-91	71.98	BUY,2 - LONG	$378.26	$753.12	$3,753.12
*8-01-91	*70.65	*SELL,1 - LONG	**($601.74)	$151.38	**$3,151.38*
8-01-91	73.40	BUY,1 - LONG	$0.00	$151.38	$3,151.38
9-27-91	74.88	SELL,1 - OUT	$488.26	$639.64	$3,639.64
10-01-91	76.85	SELL,1 - SHORT	$0.00	$639.64	$3,639.64
10-03-91	76.00	BUY,2 - LONG	$268.26	$907.90	$3,907.90
10-08-91	76.40	SELL,1 - OUT	$88.26	$996.16	$3,996.16
10-10-91	76.78	BUY,1 - LONG	$0.00	$996.16	$3,996.16
11-13-91	75.50	SELL,2 - SHORT	($581.74)	$414.42	$3,414.42
12-02-91	73.40	BUY,1 - OUT	$768.26	$1,182.68	$4,182.68
12-02-91	74.43	SELL,1 - SHORT	$0.00	$1,182.68	$4,182.68
12-12-91	72.83	BUY,2 - LONG	$568.30	$1,750.98	$4,750.98
12-17-91	71.70	SELL,2 - SHORT	($431.74)	$1,319.24	$4,319.24
12-19-91	70.95	BUY,1 - OUT	$228.26	$1,547.50	$4,547.50

*The trade on this date was necessitated by human error in not buying the second contract on the 29th of July (the previous trade) in October live cattle instead of August live cattle. This is contrary to the agreed-upon procedure and required a rollover trade two days later which cost the account $601.74. The model did not recommend a change in position on August 1, 1991.

**Without this error the profit would have been $2148.24 on 12 Round Turns (RTs). The profit step function in Figure 23.5 does not include this error.

Figure 24.4

044's Long/Short Positions in 1991

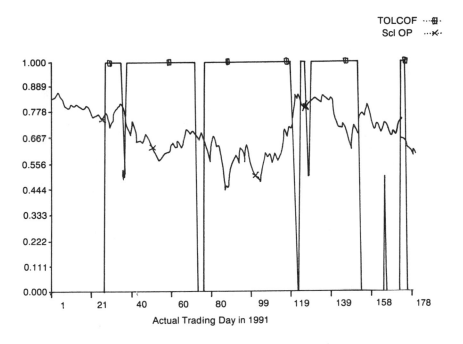

Figure 24.5

Profit Step Function for 1991

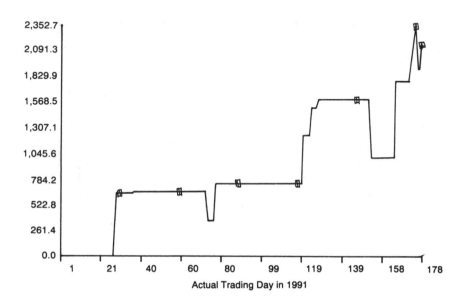

Table 24.2

Study Results

#	Size/In	Training Data	Training Profit/RTs	Test Data	Test Profit/RTs
Target >>		253-'88	$25,296/10	205-'89	$14,596/ 6
009	10-1 /24	253-'88	$24,173/14	205-'89	$ 7,272/ 6
010	6-1 /24	105-'88	$17,534/13	253-'88	80 percent
Target >>		251-'88	$24,819/10	205-'89	$14,596/ 6
011	10-1 /36	251-'88	$23,370/14	205-'89	$ 7,272/ 6
012	13-1 /36	251-'88	$22,965/12	205-'89	$ 6,554/14
013	16-1 /36	251-'88	$22,495/12	205-'89	$10,301/19
Target >>		253-'88	$25,232/ 9	252-'89	$16,576/ 7
Target >>				252-'89	$25,184/19
022	11-1/18*	251-'88	$23,360/19	252-'89	$ 5,936/ 4
023	16-1/24*	235-'88	$24,368/15	252-'89	$ 8,688/ 9
024	16-1 /24	235-'88	$25,008/11	252-'89	$ 6,848/11
Target >>		485-'8889	$49,936/27	85-'90	$ 7,840/ 7
025	23-1 /36	485-'8889	$49,712/29	85-'90	$ 2,752/ 6
Target >>		252-'89	$25,184/19	235-'88	$25,232/ 9
026	16-1 /24	252-'89	$ 5,472/23	235-'88	$ 4,368/ 3
027	16-1 /24	252-'89	$ 7,520/19		
Target >>		250-'89	$16,944/ 7	57-'90	$ 5,248/ 6
028	16-1 /36	250-'89	$16,944/ 7	57-'90	$(1,376)/6
029	10-1 /36	250-'89	$ 7,824/29	57-'90	$(480)/9
032	11-1 /36	6 mo-'8889		Next mo.	5 made, 2 lost
Target >>		737-88-90	$41,449/22	52-'91	$ 1,446/ 1
043	31-1 /36	737-88-90	$38,823/32	52-'91	$ 536 /8
Target >>		789-88-91	$57,471/22	178-'91	$13,498/6
044	31-1 /36	789-88-91	$57,257/29	178-'91 *S	$(1,169)/23
				178-'91 *A	$2,148/12

* = Pass-through connections, *S = Simulated Trades, *A = Actual Trades

= The numerical designation of the network

Size/In = The hidden-output layer dimensions/the number of inputs to the network

Data = The number of days and year of the data set

Profit RTs = The profit computed for the data and how many round turns (RTs) to generate that profit

ENDNOTES

1. D. E. Rumelhart and J. McClelland, *Parallel Distributed Processing*, (Cambridge, Mass.: MIT Press, 1986).

2. Y. H. Pao, *Adaptive Pattern Recognition and Neural Networks*, (Addison-Wesley, 1989).

25

Testability of the Arbitrage Pricing Theory by Neural Networks

Hamid Ahmadi

INTRODUCTION

The arbitrage pricing theory (APT) offers an alternative to the traditional asset pricing model in finance. It is an important study in evaluating and understanding the nature of asset pricing. This theory has given researchers great insight into asset prices, and it has provided the organized framework for much current research in finance. While the promise is great, this promise has not yet been achieved. In almost all of the published papers a statistical methodology called "factor analysis" is used to test or estimate the APT model. And the major shortcoming of this procedure is that it identifies neither the number nor the definition of the factors that influence the assets. This study offers a unique solution to this problem. It uses a simple back-propagation neural network with the generalized delta-rule to learn the interaction of the market factors and securities return. This technique helps us to investigate the effect of several variables on one another simultaneously without being plagued with uncertainty of probability distributions of each variable.

ARBITRAGE PRICING THEORY

Arbitrage pricing theory is based on the law of one price. The law of one price says that the same good cannot sell at different prices. If the same good sells at different prices, arbitrageurs will buy the good where it is cheap and simultaneously sell the good wherever its price is higher. Arbitrageurs will continue this activity until the different prices for the good are all equal. Equivalently, the law of one price says that securities with identical risks must have the same expected rate of return. More specifically, one of the fundamental theorems of APT says that assets with the same stochastic behavior must have the same expected returns.

THE MODEL

APT assumes that the rate of return on any security is a linear function of k factors.

$$R_i = E_i + b_{i1}F_1 + b_{i2}F_2 + \dots + b_{ik}F_k + e_i \qquad (1)$$

where

R_i = Rate of return on the ith asset
E_i = Expected return on the ith asset
F_j = jth factor (or communality) common to the returns of all assets under consideration.
$j = 1 \dots k$. This factor has a mathematical expectation of zero ($E[F_j] = 0$).
b_{ij} = Sensitivity of the ith asset's return to the jth factor
e_i = Random zero mean error term for the ith asset

To make Equation (1) more concrete, it is easy to think of several factors that might affect stock returns. Consider, for example, that the first factor in this equation be the rate of change in stock market (change in Standard & Poor's stock market index), the second factor as the change in GNP, and the third as change in inflation rates, and so on.

The b_{ij} coefficient in Equation (1) is a measure of *risk*—it indicates how sensitive the ith asset is to the jth factor. For instance, in above example b_{i1} indicates how sensitive the ith asset is to the stock market; incidentally the sensitivity of a security with respect to the stock market is called "beta" or "beta risk."

An arbitrage opportunity exists if one can form a portfolio with no risk and at no cost with a positive return. An arbitrage opportunity is expressed more formally in Equations (2) through (4) below.

$$\sum x_i = 0 \tag{2}$$

The x_i is the weight (or the dollar amount) invested in ith asset. In order to form an arbitrage portfolio with no change in wealth, the usual course of action would be to sell some assets and use the proceeds to buy others.

Secondly, if there are n assets in the arbitrage portfolio, we will choose x_i's in such a way that portfolio has no risk. The following condition eliminates all risk.

$$\sum x_i b_{ij} = 0 \quad \text{for each factor } j \ (j = 1 \dots k) \tag{3}$$

The rate of return of this n asset portfolio is:

$$R_p = \sum x_i R_i \tag{4}$$

The arbitrage opportunity exists if (R_p), the return of the above portfolio, is positive. At equilibrium all portfolios that satisfy the condition of no wealth and having no risk, must have no return on average.

To see how the equilibrium condition is constructed, let us write Equation (4) and substitute for R_i from Equation (1).

$$R_p = \sum x_i E_i + \sum x_i b_{i1} F_1 + \sum x_i b_{i2} F_2 + .. + \sum x_i b_{ik} F_k + \sum x_i e_i \tag{5}$$

Because the error terms, e_i, are independent, the law of large numbers guarantees that a weighted average of many of them will approach zero in the limit as n becomes large. Since the arbitrage portfolio has no risk or according to Equation (3), $\sum x_i b_{ij} = 0$, therefore Equation (5) becomes:

$$R_p = \sum x_i E_i \qquad (6)$$

If the return on the arbitrage portfolio were positive, then arbitrage opportunity exists. Such an opportunity is impossible if the market is to be in equilibrium and the return on arbitrage portfolios must be zero. In other words:

$$R_p = \sum x_i E_i = 0 \qquad (7)$$

Suppose we rewrite equations (2), (3), and (7).

$$\left(\sum x_i \right) \times 1 = 0 \qquad (2)$$

$$\sum x_i b_{ij} = 0 \qquad \text{for each factor } j \ (j = 1 \ldots k) \qquad (3)$$

$$\sum x_i E_i = 0 \qquad (7)$$

The above three equations are really statements in linear algebra. Any vector that is orthogonal to the constant vector (Equation 2), and to each of the coefficient vectors (Equation 3), has to be orthogonal to the 'E_i' vector. The vectors E_i, 1, and b_{ij} are in the same vector space and E_i is spanned by 1 and b_{ij}. In other words, there must exist a set of $k + 1$ coefficients, $\lambda_0, \lambda_1, \lambda_2, \ldots, \lambda_k$ such that:

$$E_i = \lambda_0 + \lambda_1 b_{i1} + \lambda_2 b_{i2} + \ldots + \lambda_k b_{ik} \qquad (8)$$

Recall that the b_{ij} represent the sensitivity of the return on the ith asset to the jth factor.

In the context of the APT it is impossible to construct two different portfolios, both having the same risk with two different expected returns. Equation (8) shows the general APT model, and the following equation shows the specific APT model that can be derived from the numerical values in Table 25.1.

$$E_i = 5 + 14b_{i1} + 2b_{i2} \tag{9}$$

Any three points, like E_i, b_{i1}, b_{i2}, for example, define a plane in geometry. Equation (9) is a formula for a specific three-dimensional plane that is an asset pricing model for three assets in Table 25.1. Figure 25.1 illustrates the APT plane of Equation (9). In equilibrium, the risks and return of every asset should conform to the APT model of Equation (8).

Table 25.1

APT Example

Asset (i)	Expected return (%)	b_{i1}	b_{i2}
A	16	.5	2.0
B	15	.5	1.5
C	28	1.5	1.0

Figure 25.1

Arbitrage Pricing Plane for Two Factors

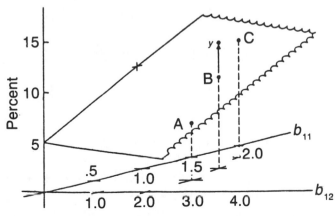

TECHNIQUES OF ESTIMATING LAMBDAS

To test or estimate the APT model, a statistical methodology called factor analysis is used. Factor analysis is a technique of statistical analysis with which most financial analysts were unfamiliar in 1976, when Stephen A. Ross's seminal article[1] introducing APT was published. Today, many empirical tests of the APT have been published. The dominant approach in testing APT still follows the initial empirical work published by Stephen Ross and Richard Roll.[2]

In their work, the factor analysis algorithm analyzes time-series data of 'T' periods rate of return over a cross-section of 'N' different assets and statistically extracts those factors that affect the returns. Factor analysis produces or extracts its own explanatory variables, called *factors* from the matrix of return below:

$$
\begin{array}{c}
r_{1,1} \ \ r_{1,2} \ \ r_{1,3} \cdot \cdot \cdot \cdot \cdot \cdot \cdot \cdot r_{1,T} \\
r_{2,1} \ \ r_{2,2} \ \ r_{2,3} \cdot \cdot \cdot \cdot \cdot \cdot \cdot \cdot r_{2,T} \\
\cdot \\
\cdot \\
\cdot \\
r_{N,1} \ \ r_{N,2} \ \ r_{N,3} \cdot \cdot \cdot \cdot \cdot \cdot r_{N,T}
\end{array}
$$

where $r_{N,T}$ is the return of the Nth asset at time period T. The purpose of factor analysis is to reduce the 'N by T' matrix of returns to a smaller 'K by T' matrix that explains all or most of the variation in the matrix of returns. The K factors ($K < N$) extracted by factor analysis have factor scores for each factor at each time period. For instance, $F_{K,T}$ represents the factor score for the Kth factor in time period T in the matrix below.

$$
\begin{array}{c}
F_{1,1} \ \ F_{1,2} \ \ F_{1,3} \cdot \cdot \cdot \cdot \cdot \cdot \cdot \cdot F_{1,T} \\
F_{2,1} \ \ F_{2,2} \ \ F_{2,3} \cdot \cdot \cdot \cdot \cdot \cdot \cdot \cdot F_{2,T} \\
\cdot \\
\cdot \\
F_{K,1} \ \ F_{K,2} \ \ F_{K,3} \cdot \cdot \cdot \cdot \cdot \cdot F_{K,T}
\end{array}
$$

The factor scores in the matrix above are used as the independent variables in Equation (1) to estimate the b_{ij} coefficients for every asset. For instance, the estimated coefficients for the first asset are derived from the following T equations; ($t = 1,...T$).

$$R_{1,t} = E_1 + b_{1,1} F_{1,t} + b_{1,2} F_{2,t} + \ldots + b_{1,K} F_{K,t} + e_{1,t} \qquad (10)$$

This process is repeated for all N assets. Therefore, we have N estimates for every coefficient, as shown in the matrix below.

$$
\begin{vmatrix}
b_{1,1} & b_{1,2} & b_{1,3} \cdots\cdots\cdots b_{1,K} \\
b_{2,1} & b_{2,2} & b_{2,3} \cdots\cdots\cdots b_{2,K} \\
& \cdot & \\
& \cdot & \\
& \cdot & \\
b_{N,1} & b_{N,2} & b_{N,3} \cdots\cdots b_{N,K}
\end{vmatrix}
$$

Using the above estimates, the following APT equation is employed to estimate the APT "factor risk premiums," denoted λ_j, $(j = 1, \ldots k)$.

$$E_i = \lambda_0 + \lambda_1 b_{i1} + \lambda_2 b_{i2} + \ldots + \lambda_k b_{ik} \qquad (8)$$

This regression was actually run by Ross and Roll in order to see whether or not the estimated λs are statistically significant. Ross and Roll employed factor analytic techniques to analyze 1,260 NYSE stocks randomly divided into 42 groups containing 30 stocks each, for 2,619 time periods. They repeated the above estimation 42 times to find the number of significant factors in each group. Their results show that 37 of the 42 groups had at least one statistically significant factor (at the 95 percent level of confidence). For 24 of the 42 groups, at least two factors were significant. In general, the results suggest that two or possibly even three risk factors exist that systematically influence common stock returns.

PROBLEMS WITH APT EMPIRICAL TESTS

The major problems with APT are essentially problems with factor analysis, not problems with the APT model. The usefulness of an APT model cannot be differentiated from the methodology used to estimate it. The theory may well be correct, but if it cannot be implemented or estimated in a meaningful sense, then, while it remains useful as a way of thinking, it cannot be used as part of the investment process. Apart from its economic and financial problems (many signs on the factor loadings have no logical meaning), we here just concentrate on the statistical problems in testing the APT model.

First, one problem inherent in any empirical application of factor analysis is that the statistical procedure is not capable of testing rigorously specified hypotheses. Factor analysis is a "flexible procedure"; it is capable of accidentally furnishing support for models that are illogical and/or erroneous, because sampling errors may influence the results.

A second problem, and a detrimental one, is that the ability of the factor analysis to specify factors to explain the securities' returns is highly dependent on the sample. Thus, for example, each of the 42 groups of 30 stocks used by Ross and Roll could conceivably contain *different* factors. In order words, if two significant factors were found in each of the 42 groups, for instance, this finding might actually represent as many as 84; $(2 \times 42 = 84)$ *different* factors, or as few as two factors or any number between 2 and 84. Thus, the principal disadvantage of this procedure is that it identifies neither the number nor the definition of the factors that influence the security returns.

SOLVING THE APT PROBLEM WITH NEURAL NETWORKS

In statistics, methods to estimate trends or recognize patterns are actually optimization methods. They all seek to minimize error. In addition to employing optimization techniques, in neural networks we also look at the whole pattern rather than sequentially looking at one feature at a time. However, the operation is generally presented as a mapping from one set of vectors to another set of vectors.

$$\{\text{vector space } v\} \rightarrow [\ W\ ] \rightarrow \{\text{vector space } u\}, \text{ or } u = Wv$$

This says that for each input vector v, the network searches for a weight-matrix W such that it produces vector u, whose components are very close to the output units. The process can be viewed as a search for a matrix W that when applied to a pattern v, yields an output u.

A typical neural network can be presented schematically in the form of an array of multiples and summing junctions. In a network with no hidden layer, inputs are connected to the output by a link such that the input to the output node is the sum of all the appropriately weighted inputs. In this work, a feed-forward net similar to Rumelhart, Hinton, and Williams,[3] illustrated in Figure 25.2, has been found to be an effec-

Figure 25.2

Feed-Forward Net

Output pattern

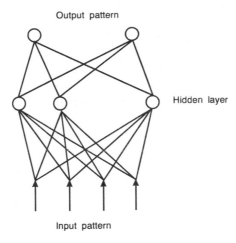

Hidden layer

Input pattern

tive system for learning risk factors of APT from a body of time-series examples.

Again, the network used in this study is, like Rumelhart, Hinton, and Williams, made up of sets of nodes arranged in layers. The outputs of nodes in one layer are transmitted to nodes in another layer through links that amplify, attenuate, or inhibit such outputs through weighting factors. Each node is activated in accordance with the input, the activation function, and the bias of the node.

The net input to a node in layer j is:

$$net_j = \sum w_{ji} x_i$$

Where x_i is the ith input, and the output of node j is:

$$y = f\,(net_j)$$

Where f is the activation function, and (Φ) is the bias.

$$y = f(net_j) = \frac{1}{1 + e^{-(net + \Phi)}}$$

In this study the NeuralWare Professional II software has been used. The learning rules employed here are the generalized delta-rule in a back-propagation schedule. The net is presented schematically in Figure 25.3. The inputs are the rate of returns of assets and also several factors that generally are believed to have an effect on stock returns have been added to the inputs. These are the rate of change in stock market, the change in GNP, the unemployment rate, and the inflation rate. The inputs are normalized such that they are scaled to fall between the values 0 and 1. In the learning process there were 3,000, 5,000, 8,000, and 10,000 presentations of data to the network. After testing the network there was not a significant improvement after 5,000 times. The success of the system did depend on the number of hidden layers. At this time it is not known why two hidden layers were the best choice. One hidden layer did not produce a better system but more than two hidden layers definitely reduces the effectiveness of the network. Consequently, there are two hidden layers; one is capturing the effect of other stocks on a particular asset. The other hidden layer is designed to capture macroeconomic factors. Therefore, every asset at the output layer is influenced by other assets, market factors, and macroeconomic factors.

Applying neural nets with hidden processing elements to the APT problem eliminates all the shortcomings of the factor analysis mentioned above. This system is distribution free, that is, we do not need to know the probability distribution of the rate of returns. Additionally,

Figure 25.3

Back-Propagation Network

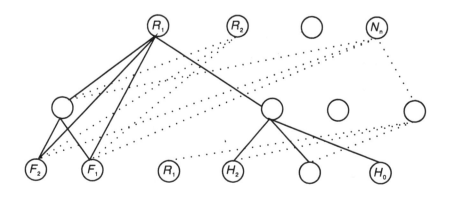

this system is not concerned with the number of factors. The researcher can add as many factors as desired, and the network learns that some factors are not relevant to this problem.

OTHER NEURAL NET POSSIBILITIES

Economists and financial analysts, at this point, are very much concerned about the meaning of the "weights" in a trained network. They would like to relate them to slope, sensitivity, and rate of change or marginal effects. Interpreting these weights in finance is not an easy task, especially when the network has several hidden layers. The only solution to this problem is to create a Functional-Link Network. This system is suggested by Klassen and Pao,[4] and has been tested by Pao.[5] This network actually eliminates the effect of hidden layers and makes the interpretation easier, and according to Pao, "improves the rate of learning" too. In this model, each input vector is acted on by the functional link to yield input-related values.

Pao suggests, "the net effect is to map the input pattern into a larger pattern space. We associate and represent each component x with the quantities x, x^2, x^3,..... or with x, sin πx, cos πx, sin2 πx, cos2 πx, and so on depending on the set of functions that we deem to be appropriate. No intrinsically new ad hoc information is introduced, but the representation is enhanced." This concept is shown schematically in Figure 25.4.

ENDNOTES

1. S. Ross, "The Arbitrage Pricing Theory of Capital Asset Pricing," *Journal of Economic Theory*, December 1976, pp. 344–360.

2. R. Roll, and S. Ross, "An Empirical Investigation of the Arbitrage Pricing Theory," *Journal of Finance*, vol. 35, December 1980, pp. 1073–1103.

3. D. E. Rumelhart, G. E. Hinton, and R. J. Williams, "Learning Internal Representations by Error Propagation," in *Parallel Distributed Processing*, (Cambridge, Mass.: MIT Press), pp. 318–362.

Figure 25.4

Alternative Representation

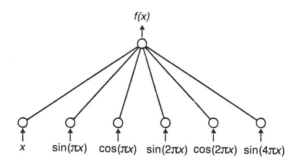

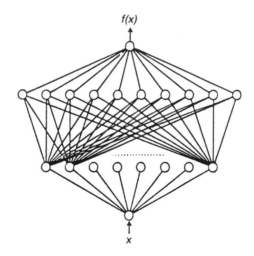

4. M. S. Klassen, and Y. H. Pao, "Characteristics of the Functional Link Net: A Higher Order Delta Rule Net," *IEEE Proceedings of Second Annual International Conference on Neural Networks*, 1988.

5. Y. H. Pao, *Adaptive Pattern Recognition and Neural Networks* (Addison-Wesley, 1989).

PART 6

NEURAL NETWORK APPROACHES TO FINANCIAL FORECASTING

26

NEURAL NETWORK MODELS AS AN ALTERNATIVE TO REGRESSION

Leorey Marquez, Tim Hill, Reginald Worthley, and William Remus

INTRODUCTION

Linear statistical models are well established and useful tools in the quantitative analysis. A survey by Ledbetter and Cox[1] ranks regression analysis as the most popular of all quantitative methods used in business and finance.

Artificial neural network (ANN) models provide a viable alternative to classical regression models. According to Wasserman, these models can learn from experience, can generalize and "see through" noise and distortion, and can abstract essential characteristics in the presence of

© 1991, IEEE. A modified version of a paper is reprinted with permission from *Proceedings of the IEEE 24th Annual Hawaii International Conference on Systems Sciences*, pp. 129–135, Vol. VI.

irrelevant data. According to Lippman,[2] these models provide a high degree of robustness and fault tolerance. In addition, artificial neural network models can find the right transformations for variables,[3] detect weak linear relationships, and deal with outliers.

In spite of the popularity of neural networks, these assertions have not been tested. In this chapter we report a study that filled this void. Our general approach was to generate data representing common functional forms encountered in regression modeling and then to compare neural networks to regression models using that data.

EXPERIMENTAL DESIGN

The purpose of the experiment described below is to evaluate the performance neural networks in estimating simple functional forms. To perform this kind of research, social scientists advocate testing alternative models side-by-side in critical experiments.[4] There is precedent for this kind of study using neural networks[5,6] and in statistics.[7-9] Thus, our experiment is a side-by-side comparison of two competing methods, neural networks and regression.

To be able to generalize to many settings, the estimates were compared in 27 different conditions. The study examines three functional forms, three noise levels, and three common sample sizes for the data set as described below. Since the true underlying functional form is often unknown, we also examined the performance of mis-specified regression models with the true model and neural networks. We chose the most logical mis-specifications as would be predicted by the ladder of re-expression; this technique is described in more detail in Exhibit 26.1. The details of this simulation study will be described below.

The performance of the regression models and neural network models were evaluated across the three functional forms commonly encountered in regression analysis. These are the linear model ($Y = B_0 + B_1 \times X + e$), the logarithmic model ($Y = B_0 + B_1 \times \log(X) + e$), and the reciprocal model ($Y = B_0 + B_1/X + e$). These will be termed the true functional form or true model.

For each true model, 100 samples of n (x,y) pairs each (to be used for model estimation) were generated. Each sample of n (x,y) pairs was used to compute the parameters for the three regression estimates, one based on the true model and the others based on the nearest models on the ladder of re-expression. The last two models represent "close,"

Exhibit 26.1

The Ladder of Re-Expression

Mosteller and Tukey[10] introduced the concept of a ladder of re-expressions as a tool to straighten out simple curves. The basic notion starts with the observation that most simple curves can be represented by a relation of the form $Y = X^p$. When p takes on the values such as 3, 2, 1, -1, -2, and -3, a series of curves appears as a ladderlike formation.

Given a set of points from an unknown curve, the idea is to move up and down the ladder searching for the expression that will transform the points into a straight line. For example, given a set of data points based on the relation $Y = X^2$ ($p = 2$), the correct model to use would be $Y = B_0 + B_1 \times X^2 + e$. However, since this correct model is not usually known, estimates based on other models might be used. It would be expected that the model $Y = B_0 + B_1 \times X + e$ ($p = 1$) would provide better estimates than $Y = B_0 + B_1/X + e$ ($p = -1$) since the first lies closer to the true relation in the ladder than the second model.

Since the value $p = 0$ leads to a constant, Mosteller and Tukey use the symbol # instead of 0; it represents $Y = \log(X)$. This was important addition since the logarithm transformation is widely used. In this scheme, the series can be thought of as coming from the $\int X^{(p-1)} dX$. For positive values of X, the curves are monotonically increasing and concave upward for $p > 1$, straight for $p = 1$, and monotonically decreasing and concave downward for $p < 1$.

In this simulation study we generated data based on the linear ($p = 1$), log ($p = $#), and reciprocal ($p = -1$) functional forms. When displayed using the ladder of re-expressions, there would be three curves in the middle. If we also added the two curves adjacent to each functional form, we would also have two "close" mis-specifications of a true functional form. Since the p values of the true functional forms are 1, #, and -1, the additional adjacent curves needed are 2 and -2. The five models and their corresponding values of p in the ladder of re-expression are summarized as follows:

P	Model		Description
2	$Y = B_0 + B_1 \times X^2$	$+ e$	Squared Model
1	$Y = B_0 + B_1 \times X$	$+ e$	Linear Model
#	$Y = B_0 + B_1 \times \log(X)$	$+ e$	Log Model
-1	$Y = B_0 + B_1/X$	$+ e$	Reciprocal Model
-2	$Y = B_0 + B_1/X^2$	$+ e$	Squared-Reciprocal Model

but mis-specified, regression estimates of the true model. The same data were also used to generate the neural network estimates. The true, mis-specified, and neural network models were then evaluated using an additional 100 data pairs set generated for testing the model.

In this study, we varied the size of the error. Three different R^2 values were used; these were 0.30, 0.60, and 0.90. These three values represent weak, medium, and strong relationships. We also varied the sample size (n) used to derive the regression models and train the neural network; we used samples of size 15, 30, or 60. These sample sizes were chosen to represent the small, medium, and large samples that characterize most regression studies. The number of replications and the sample sizes are consistent with the numbers used in the prior simulation studies.[7-9]

As noted earlier, the models were evaluated in terms of their forecasting accuracy using a test sample of 100. Our measure of performance was that most commonly used by forecasters: the mean absolute percentage error (MAPE). To compare across the conditions, the paired t-test was used. Given Wasserman's assertion that neural networks were able to see through noise and distortion and to perform data transformations automatically, we would expect the neural networks to perform as well as the true regression model in each condition.

ESTIMATING THE NEURAL NETWORKS

An important part of the above experiment was the proper estimation of the regression and neural networks. The regression analysis was straightforward, but the neural network estimation was more complex. In this section we will detail the latter process.

The neural networks are based on the back-propagation learning algorithm.[11,12] These models were obtained using the Rumelhart and McClelland[11] software written in C.

We experimented with many parameter values but ultimately settled on the Rumelhart and McClelland defaults since other parameter combinations gave little or no improvement. The only parameter that was modified was momentum. We used a momentum value of 0.8 instead of the default of 0.9 since preliminary tests showed that this value resulted in a slightly improved overall performance.

Back-propagation will minimize the least squared error if (1) the model does not get trapped in a local optimal and (2) there are an adequate number of nodes in the hidden layer. To assure that the error is minimized, it is customary to build neural networks with one hidden layer and keep doubling the number of nodes until the error is no longer reduced.[13] In the preliminary tests, we experimented with networks containing 3, 6, 12, and 24 nodes in the single hidden layer. We found the improvement in error after six nodes insignificant, while the processing speed and convergence rate were significantly worse.

The neural network weights were adjusted following the presentation of each (x,y) pattern. Convergence was within 800 training periods or epochs. The neural network estimates used the structure 1-6-1; that is, one input node, six nodes in the hidden layer, and one output node. It is worth noting that the CPU time required by the regression models was in seconds whereas the neural network models required tens of minutes.

THE RESULTS OF THE SIMULATION

Tables 26.1 to 26.3 present the performance of the estimates of each of the three true models; the measure of performance is mean absolute percentage errors (MAPE). Each table gives the results for the nine possible combinations of sample sizes and R^2 values for one of the true models.

Table 26.1 shows the results of the simulation study when the true model was linear. The results include the performance of the linear model, the performance of the two nearest mis-specified models on the ladder of re-expression (the log and squared models), and the neural networks. In general, the neural networks fit this true model well; the maximum difference in MAPE was 2 percent and the median difference in MAPE .62 percent. However, the difference in MAPE was lowest for small sample sizes and low noise where there were no significant differences. Overall, the mis-specified models also fit the data well. At their worst, the neural networks seemed to perform as well as the mis-specified models.

Table 26.2 shows the results of the simulation study when the true model was logarithmic. The results include the performance of the true logarithmic model, the performance of the two nearest mis-specified models on the ladder of re-expression (the reciprocal and linear models), and the neural networks. In general, the neural networks fit this true model well; the maximum difference in MAPE was 4 percent and the

Table 26.1

MAPE Paired Difference T-test for Model 1 (LINEAR)

H0: delta MAPE ≤ 0   vs.   H1: delta MAPE > 0

* z(.05) = 1.645   ** z(.01) = 2.33   Test sample = 100

Training Sample	True Model: Alternate Model:	Linear Quadratic	Linear Log	Linear ANN
n = 15	R-square = .30			
	MAPE (true model)	15.68	15.68	15.68
	MAPE (alt. model)	15.74	15.82	15.38
	Mean diff.	0.06	0.14	− 0.30
	Std. Dev. of diff.	0.26	0.26	1.55
	Paired t-value	2.44 **	5.34 **	−1.93
	R-square = .60			
	MAPE (true model)	11.66	11.66	11.66
	MAPE (alt. model)	11.80	11.95	11.70
	Mean diff.	0.14	0.29	0.04
	Std. Dev. of diff.	0.29	0.30	1.33
	Paired t-value	4.84 **	9.75 **	0.32
	R-square = .90			
	MAPE (true model)	5.59	5.59	5.59
	MAPE (alt. model)	6.12	6.16	7.98
	Mean diff.	0.52	0.57	2.39
	Std. Dev. of diff.	0.40	0.52	2.13
	Paired t-value	13.21 **	10.89 **	11.24 **
n = 30	R-square = .30			
	MAPE (true model)	14.44	14.44	14.44
	·MAPE (alt. model)	14.29	14.70	14.83
	Mean diff.	− 0.15	0.26	0.39
	Std. Dev. of diff.	0.14	0.16	0.70
	Paired t-value	−10.55	15.87 **	5.50 **
	R-square = .60			
	MAPE (true model)	11.59	11.59	11.59
	MAPE (alt. model)	11.73	11.63	12.49
	Mean diff.	0.14	0.04	0.89
	Std. Dev. of diff.	0.12	0.18	0.59
	Paired t-value	11.54 **	2.29 *	15.26 **

Table 26.1 (continued)

MAPE Paired Difference T-test for Model 1 (LINEAR)

Training Sample	True Model: Alternate Model:	Linear Quadratic	Linear Log	Linear ANN
	R-square = .90			
	MAPE (true model)	5.70	5.70	5.70
	MAPE (alt. model)	6.44	6.31	6.90
	Mean diff.	0.74	0.61	1.20
	Std. Dev. of diff.	0.18	0.32	0.41
	Paired t-value	40.89 **	19.31 **	29.29 **
n = 60	R-square = .30			
	MAPE (true model)	13.87	13.87	13.87
	MAPE (alt. model)	14.19	13.69	14.34
	Mean diff.	0.32	− 0.18	0.46
	Std. Dev. of diff.	0.09	0.14	0.34
	Paired t-value	36.84 **	−12.78	13.60 **
	R-square = .60			
	MAPE (true model)	10.25	10.25	10.25
	MAPE (alt. model)	10.71	10.50	10.87
	Mean diff.	0.46	0.25	0.62
	Std. Dev. of diff.	0.16	0.22	0.29
	Paired t-value	29.03 **	11.10 **	21.67 **
	R-square = .90			
	MAPE (true model)	5.20	5.20	5.20
	MAPE (alt. model)	5.68	5.67	5.97
	Mean diff.	0.48	0.47	0.76
	Std. Dev. of diff.	0.11	0.27	0.37
	Paired t-value	41.77 **	17.36 **	20.55 **

Table 26.2

MAPE Paired Difference T-test for Model 2 (LOG)

H0: delta MAPE ≤ 0   vs.   H1: delta MAPE > 0

* z(.05) = 1.645   ** z(.01) = 2.33   Test sample = 100

Training Sample	True Model: Alternate Model:	Log Linear	Log Reciprocal	Log ANN
n = 15	R-squared = .30			
	MAPE (true model)	15.68	15.68	15.68
	MAPE (alt. model)	17.49	17.38	15.60
	Mean diff.	1.82	1.70	−0.08
	Std. Dev. of diff.	2.24	1.20	1.73
	Paired t-value	8.11 **	14.13 **	−0.45
	R-squared = .60			
	MAPE (true model)	11.66	11.66	11.66
	MAPE (alt. model)	14.89	14.96	12.24
	Mean diff.	3.23	3.31	0.58
	Std. dev. of diff.	1.96	1.56	1.38
	Paired t-value	16.44 **	21.24 **	4.22 **
	R-squared = .90			
	MAPE (true model)	5.59	5.59	5.59
	MAPE (alt. model)	11.72	11.61	9.72
	Mean diff.	6.13	6.02	4.13
	Std. Dev. of diff.	1.59	2.65	2.21
	Paired t-value	38.60 **	22.74 **	18.67 **
n = 30	R-squared = .30			
	MAPE (true model)	14.44	14.44	14.44
	MAPE (alt. model)	14.70	15.94	14.12
	Mean diff.	0.26	1.50	−0.32
	Std. Dev. of diff.	0.68	0.65	0.46
	Paired t-value	3.85 **	23.15 **	−6.90
	R-squared = .60			
	MAPE (true model)	11.59	11.59	11.59
	MAPE (alt. model)	14.08	13.78	12.11
	Mean diff.	2.48	2.19	0.52
	Std. Dev. of diff.	0.81	1.44	0.39
	Paired t-value	30.64 **	15.24 **	13.24 **

Table 26.2 (continued)

MAPE Paired Difference T-test for Model 2 (LOG)

Training Sample	True Model: Alternate Model:	Log Linear	Log Reciprocal	Log ANN
	R-squared = .90			
	MAPE (true model)	5.70	5.70	5.70
	MAPE (alt. model)	11.35	12.24	7.83
	Mean diff.	5.66	6.54	2.13
	Std. Dev. of diff.	0.79	2.07	0.62
	Paired t-value	71.24 **	31.63 **	34.16 **
$n = 60$	R-square = .30			
	MAPE (true model)	13.87	13.87	13.87
	MAPE (alt. model)	16.00	15.06	14.57
	Mean diff.	2.13	1.19	0.70
	Std. Dev. of diff.	0.46	0.64	0.40
	Paired t-value	45.95 **	18.49 **	17.39 **
	R-square = .60			
	MAPE (true model)	10.25	10.25	10.25
	MAPE (alt. model)	13.86	13.36	11.10
	Mean diff.	3.61	3.11	0.85
	Std. Dev. of diff.	0.70	0.74	0.38
	Paired t-value	51.79 **	42.29 **	22.19 **
	R-square = .90			
	MAPE (true model)	5.20	5.20	5.20
	MAPE (alt. model)	10.59	9.76	5.76
	Mean diff.	5.39	4.56	0.56
	Std. Dev. of diff.	0.70	1.18	0.29
	Paired t-value	77.13 **	38.46 **	19.17 **

Table 26.3

MAPE Paired Difference T-test for Model 3 (RECIPROCAL)

H0: delta MAPE ≤ 0   vs.   H1: delta MAPE > 0

* z(.05) = 1.645   ** z(.01) = 2.33   Test sample = 100

Training Sample	True Model: Alternate Model:	Reciprocal Log	Reciprocal Sq-Recip	Reciprocal ANN
n = 15	R-square = .30			
	MAPE (true model)	15.68	15.68	15.68
	MAPE (alt. model)	15.82	15.74	15.67
	Mean diff.	0.14	0.06	− 0.01
	Std. Dev. of diff.	0.26	0.26	1.67
	Paired t-value	5.34 **	2.44 **	− 0.04
	R-square = .60			
	MAPE (true model)	11.66	11.66	11.66
	MAPE (alt. model)	11.95	11.80	12.20
	Mean diff.	0.29	0.14	0.54
	Std. Dev. of diff.	0.30	0.29	1.71
	Paired t-value	9.75 **	4.84 **	3.15 **
	R-square = .90			
	MAPE (true model)	5.59	5.59	5.59
	MAPE (alt. model)	6.16	6.12	8.75
	Mean diff.	0.57	0.52	3.15
	Std. Dev. of diff.	0.52	0.40	2.53
	Paired t-value	10.89 **	13.21 **	12.45 **
n = 30	R-square = .30			
	MAPE (true model)	14.44	14.44	14.44
	MAPE (alt. model)	14.70	14.29	14.76
	Mean diff.	0.26	− 0.15	0.32
	Std. Dev. of diff.	0.16	0.14	0.71
	Paired t-value	15.87 **	−10.55	4.47 **
	R-square = .60			
	MAPE (true model)	11.59	11.59	11.59
	MAPE (alt. model)	11.63	11.73	12.43
	Mean diff.	0.04	0.14	0.84
	Std. Dev. of diff.	0.18	0.12	0.55
	Paired t-value	2.29 *	11.54 **	15.33 **

Table 26.3 (continued)

MAPE Paired Difference T-test for Model 3 (RECIPROCAL)

Training Sample	True Model: Alternate Model:	Reciprocal Log	Reciprocal Sq-Recip	Reciprocal ANN
	R-square = .90			
	MAPE (true model)	5.70	5.70	5.70
	MAPE (alt. model)	6.31	6.44	7.15
	Mean diff.	0.61	0.74	1.45
	Std. Dev. of diff.	0.32	0.18	0.45
	Paired t-value	19.31 **	40.89 **	32.26 **
$n = 60$	R-square = .30			
	MAPE (true model)	13.87	13.87	13.87
	MAPE (alt. model)	13.69	14.19	14.28
	Mean diff.	− 0.18	0.32	0.41
	Std. Dev. of diff.	0.14	0.09	0.36
	Paired t-value	−12.78	36.84 **	11.36 **
	R-square = .60			
	MAPE (true model)	10.25	10.25	10.25
	MAPE (alt. model)	10.50	10.71	10.74
	Mean diff.	0.25	0.46	0.49
	Std. Dev. of diff.	0.22	0.16	0.21
	Paired t-value	11.10 **	29.03 **	23.21 **
	R-square = .90			
	MAPE (true model)	5.20	5.20	5.20
	MAPE (alt. model)	5.67	5.68	6.00
	Mean diff.	0.47	0.48	0.80
	Std. Dev. of diff.	0.27	0.11	0.34
	Paired t-value	17.36 **	41.77 **	23.34 **

median difference in MAPE was .58 percent. However, the difference in MAPE was lowest for small sample sizes and low noise. In all cases, the mis-specified models did not fit the data as well as the neural networks.

Table 26.3 shows the results of the simulation study when the true model was reciprocal. The results include the performance of the true reciprocal model, the performance of the two nearest mis-specified models on the ladder of re-expression (the reciprocal of the square of X and log models), and the neural networks. In general, again the neural networks fit this true model well; the maximum difference in MAPE was 3 percent and the median difference in MAPE was .48 percent. The difference in MAPE was lowest for small sample size and low noise. In all cases, the mis-specified models fit the data better than the neural networks although all performed well.

DISCUSSION

The overall MAPEs for the neural network models were very good. Also, the median differences in MAPE between the neural networks and true models were generally around .6 percent. Even when there were statistically significant differences between the true and neural network model, these differences may not hold any practical significance. The level of MAPE encountered is considered excellent in most real-world situations. In some of the cases (usually low sample size and low noise), the t-test indicated that the neural network estimates did not differ significantly from the true model.

It is clear from this experiment that the nature of the true functional form is an important consideration in the use of neural network models. It was shown that the neural network model estimated the linear model best. However, neural networks were comparatively successful when compared with mis-specifications of the log model but not with the reciprocal model. This means that one cannot just build a neural network model and expect it always to perform best.

The size of the samples used specified the amount of data available in defining the underlying relationship, while the magnitude of the R^2

value described the amount of error or noise in the data. These two variables specified the level at which the underlying relationship is defined by the data. The results show that the neural network models perform reasonably close to the true model when the relationship is not sufficiently defined.

This study only considered linear models, log models, and reciprocal models in the role of the true model. Other important transformation relationships need to be tested. Also combinations of these transformations will have to be examined. The R^2 value used in this study is one way of introducing noise into the model. It would be interesting to examine the impact of outlying or highly influential data on these models. Other considerations worthy of examination include the effects of multicollinearity and heteroschedasticity on neural networks.

This study has shown that neural network models possess considerable potential as an alternative to regression models. Within the limitations of this study, neural network models have been shown to be especially useful in modeling data that do not strongly exhibit underlying relationships between the variables. The study also showed that a neural network's capacity to continuously learn and self-transform as the true relationship becomes more defined depends to some extent on the underlying relationship.

The potential offered by neural network models is tempered by several basic problems. Guidelines are needed to deal with the enormous number of choices and decisions the model builder has to make. Without these guidelines, the procedure for selecting the structure of a neural network will continue to be essentially a trial and error process. The selection of the training parameters also remains a trial and error process. Even the trial and error process itself can be done interactively or in batch mode. It is hoped that more systematic guidelines will be developed soon.

This situation can be viewed both as a blessing and a misfortune. On one hand, it gives the researcher such a wide array of model parameters and properties for fine-tuning of the model. On the other hand, there exists the danger that finding the "best" model may turn out to be a laborious undertaking.

ENDNOTES

1. W. Ledbetter and J. Cox, "Are OR Techniques Being Used?" *Industrial Engineering*, vol. 9, no. 2, 1977, pp. 19–21.

2. R. P. Lippman, "An Introduction to Computing with Neural Nets," *IEEE ASSP Magazine*, April 1987, pp. 4–22.

3. D. Connor, "Data Transformation Explains the Basics of Neural Networks," *EDN*, May 12, 1988, pp. 138–144.

4. R. M. Hogarth, "Generalizations in Decision Research: The Role of Formal Models," University of Chicago, Graduate School of Business, 1986.

5. D. H. Fisher, and K. B. McKusick, "An Empirical Comparison of ID3 and Back-Propagation," *Proceedings of International Joint Conference on Artificial Intelligence*, 1989, pp. 788–793.

6. S. M. Weiss, and I. Kapouleas, "An Empirical Comparison of Pattern Recognition, Neural Nets, and Machine Learning Classification Methods," *Proceedings of International Joint Conference on Artificial Intelligence*, 1989, pp. 781–787.

7. A. Mitra, and R. F. Ling, "A Monte Carlo Comparison of Some Ridge and Other Biased Estimators," *Journal of Statistics, Computation and Simulation*, vol. 9, 1979, pp. 195–215.

8. H. Paarsch, "A Monte Carlo Comparison of Estimators for Censored Regression Models," *Journal of Econometrics*, vol. 24, 1984, pp. 197–213.

9. B. Pendleton, I. Newman, and R. Marshall, "A Monte Carlo Approach to Correlational Spuriousness and Ratio Variables," *Journal of Statistics, Computation and Simulation*, vol. 18, 1983, pp. 93–124.

10. F. Mosteller, and J. Tukey, *Data Analysis and Regression: A Second Course in Statistics*, (Addison-Wesley, 1977), pp. 79–84.

11. D. E. Rumelhart, and J. McClelland, *Parallel Distributed Processing* (Cambridge, Mass.: MIT Press, 1986).

12. R. Hecht-Nielsen, "Theory of the Backpropagation Neural Network," *Proceedings of International Conference on Neural Networks*, vol. 1, 1989, pp. 593–605.

13. O. Ersoy, Tutorial at Hawaii International Conference on Systems Sciences, January 1990.

27

A CONNECTIONIST APPROACH TO TIME SERIES PREDICTION: AN EMPIRICAL TEST

Ramesh Sharda and Rajendra B. Patil

INTRODUCTION

Forecasting has been mentioned as one of the most promising applications of artificial neural networks. The autoassociative memory of certain neural network models can be tapped in prediction problems. Smolensky (1986) specifies a dynamic feed-forward network in the following way:

$$u_i\,(t+1) = F\left[\sum_k W_{ki}\,G(u_k(t))\right]$$

This article appeared in the *Journal of Intelligent Manufacturing,* published by Chapman and Hall, 1992. Reprinted with permission.

where $u_i(t)$ is the activation of unit i at time t, F is a nonlinear sigmoid transfer function, G is a nonlinear threshold function and W_{ki} is the connection strength or weight from unit k to unit i. This relationship can, in principle at least, be used for predicting future values of variables.

Several authors have attempted to apply this idea for forecasting a time series. Werbos[1] states that he laid the foundations for use of back-propagation in forecasting in his doctoral dissertation.[2] In his chapter,[1] he describes an application of back-propagation to locate sources of forecast uncertainty in a recurrent gas market model.

Lapedes and Farber[3] used a multilayered perceptron to predict the values of a nonlinear dynamic system with chaotic behavior. They illustrated the method by selecting two common topics in signal processing, prediction and system modeling, and showed that the nonlinear applications can be handled extremely well by using nonlinear neural networks. They reported that neural networks gave superior prediction for their dynamic system.

Sutton[4] introduces a class of incremental learning procedures specialized for prediction—that is, for using experience with an incompletely known system to predict its future behavior. Whereas conventional prediction-learning methods assign credit by the difference between predicted and actual results, the method used by the author assigns credit by the difference between temporally successive predictions. The author also proves the convergence and optimality for special cases, relates them to supervised-learning methods, and claims that the temporal-difference method requires less memory and less peak computation than conventional methods and produces more accurate predictions. He argues that most problems to which supervised learning is now applied are really prediction problems of some sort, to which temporal-difference methods can be applied to advantage.

Fozzard et al.[5] discuss a neural nets-based expert system for solar flare forecasting and claim that its performance is superior to human experts. Tang et al.[6] discuss the results of a test of the performance of neural networks and conventional methods in forecasting time series. The authors experimented with three time series of different complexity using different feed-forward, back-propagation models, and the Box-Jenkins model. Their experiments demonstrated that for time series with long memory, both methods produced comparable results. However, for series with short memory, neural networks outperform the Box-Jenkins model. The authors conclude that neural networks are robust, parsimonious in their data requirements, and provide good long-term forecasting. All of these results are based on comparison of the techniques using three time series.

However, the experiences with neural networks in forecasting are not all positive. Fishwick,[7] for example, reports that the forecasting ability of neural networks was inferior to simple linear regression and surface response methods. There are some trade magazine articles about use of neural networks in stock price forecasting, but no concrete descriptions can be found (perhaps for confidentiality reasons). Even when the use of neural networks in forecasting has been shown to be positive, it is usually based on test data sets from a particular problem domain.

Sharda and Patil[8] reported the results of an empirical test of neural networks which shows that neural networks may be used for time series forecasting, at least for a single period forecasting problem. The authors tested and compared a sample of 75 data series containing annual, quarterly, and monthly observations using neural network models and traditional Box-Jenkins forecasting models. The simple neural network models tested on 75 data series could forecast about as well as an automatic Box-Jenkins ARIMA modeling system. Each method outperformed the other in about half of the tests. These tests were based on one particular set of learning parameters and one architecture.

This chapter also reports results of a forecasting competition between a neural network model and a traditional forecasting technique, Box-Jenkins forecasting. Several data series from a comprehensive forecasting competition were analyzed using a neural network model and the Box-Jenkins time series forecasting techniques. The data series came from a variety of sources. This chapter reports the performance of a neural network model using several different learning parameters. Further, it compares the forecasting ability of a neural net model and the Box-Jenkins technique in forecasting multiple horizons ahead. Previous research has not studied the issue of single-step versus multiple step ahead forecasting with neural networks.

DATA, MODELS AND METHODS

Data

The time series were selected from the famous M-Competition to compare the performance of various forecasting techniques.[9] Out of 1,001
series collected, only 111 series were analyzed in the M-Competition
using Box-Jenkins methodology. This was done because the Box-Jenkins
approach requires an analyst's intervention and is thus quite time consuming. Pack and Downing[10] examined this 111 series subset and concluded that several series were not appropriate for forecasting using
the Box-Jenkins technique. Sharda and Patil[8] took a sample of 75 series
from this 111 series set after considering Pack and Downing's recommendations. The tests reported here are based on the full 111 series. Of
course, the comparisons between Box-Jenkins technique and the neural
network can only be made using the subset where both techniques were
able to build a model. Our test set contains 13 annual, 20 quarterly, and
68 monthly series. In Table 27.1, series numbers ≤ 112 are annual, series
numbers 382 and > 112 are quarterly, and the rest are monthly.

Method

One hundred and eleven data sets were analyzed using the following
approach. For each data set, $n - k$ observations were used to build the
forecast model (to train the network), and then the model (the trained
neural network) was used to forecast the future k values, where $k = 6$,
8, 18 for annual, quarterly, and monthly series respectively. These values
are well established for such comparisons in the forecasting literature.
The generated forecasts were compared with the actual values for the
k periods, and mean absolute percent error (MAPE) was computed for
each series. We also computed the absolute percent error by forecast
horizon for monthly series.

Models

Box-Jenkins Method. This approach to time series forecasting is well
known and has been applied in practice.[11] It is considered to be a
sophisticated approach to forecasting, but is quite complex to use. Es-

sentially, the analyst examines both the auto and partial autocorrelations and identifies models of the form:

$$\varphi(B)\Phi(B^s)\nabla^d\nabla_s^D(Z_t - c) = \theta(B)\Theta(B^s)a_t$$

where

B is the back-shift operator (i.e., $Bx_t = x_{t-1}$);

$\nabla = 1 - B$; s = seasonality, a_t = white noise;

$\varphi(B)$ and $\Phi(B^s)$ are nonseasonal and seasonal autoregressive polynomials respectively;

$\theta(B)$ and $\Theta(B^s)$ are nonseasonal and seasonal moving average polynomials respectively;

Z_t = series (transformed if necessary) to be modeled.

After identification of several candidate models, the analyst can iterate through the process of estimation and diagnostic checking. Once the final model has been selected, the forecasting process can begin.

The process of model identification, estimation, and diagnostics-checking has been automated and is available in the form of a forecasting expert system. The performance of such an automatic "expert" system has been reported to be comparable to real experts.[12] For our tests, we used such an automatic Box-Jenkins modeling expert system, AUTOBOX.[13] This program can take a data set and iterate through the model identification, estimation, and diagnostics process to develop the best model. The series were run in AUTOBOX using its default setting with no intervention detection.

Neural Network Model. A back-propagation rule was used to train a multilayered perceptron network. We used one hidden layer. The number of neurons in the input, hidden layers, and output was based on an input test to be described shortly.

Different architectures, with increasing numbers of hidden-layer neurons, were trained over different values of learning parameters to find the optimal learning parameters first and then find the optimal architecture for a given class of data series. MAPE and Me-APE (median absolute percent error) were used as the measure of performance. Nine combinations of three learning rates (0.1, 0.5, 0.9) and three momentum values (0.1, 0.5, 0.9) were tried.

Ten data series were trained over different architectures and learning parameter sets, and the optimal learning parameters and architecture were found. These parameters were then taken to model remaining data series. All the models discussed above were nonlinear neural network models. Each hidden neuron and output neuron had a nonlinear sigmoidal transfer function.

The neural network software used for this test was the popular PDP software.[14] This program requires that the data be normalized. The data series were normalized by row. While normalizing the file two different data files were created: training file and testing file. The format of these two files was the same as the unnormalized data file, except each number was now normalized using the minimum and maximum value over the corresponding complete pattern. Each pattern had different minimum and maximum values. While normalizing, the output was written to two different files. The number of patterns written to training file and testing file were:

# of test patterns = 18, 8, 6 for monthly, quarterly, and yearly data series respectively

# of training patterns = total patterns – # of test patterns

The normalizing technique over the testing file was slightly different than for the training file. In the training file the minimum and maximum was found over each complete pattern (input and output part) and each number in the pattern (input and output) was normalized using:

normalized number = (number – min) / (max – min)

Note that maximum and minimum values are over all numbers of the input and output part of each training pattern, and each pattern was normalized by its own minimum and maximum values. In the case of the test file the maximum and minimum values were only over the input part of the testing patterns because the output part of the pattern is not supposed to be known but is needed in the pattern for calculating the pattern error and total sum of squares error (tss) while testing. The same formula was used for the normalization of the test file. The maximum and minimum values were saved only over the test file for denormalization purpose.

Once the above described preprocessing was done, the neural network model was trained with learning rate = 0.1 and momentum = 0.1. These values were found to be optimal from the tests. Maximum cycles trained were 1,000. Training was stopped if total sum of squares error reached 0.04 before training reached 1,000 cycles. If a series converged in less than 1,000 cycles, the total sum of squares error over all the training patterns was less than 0.04. The same seed was used in all our tests to initialize the network in order to facilitate the best comparison of their performances.

Once a network was trained, the test file was tested over the network, and the activation values of output neurons were logged into a file and denormalized using the normalization parameters saved during normalization of test file. The log file was the forecast generated by the trained network using the test file.

RESULTS AND DISCUSSION

Table 27.1 exhibits the MAPEs of AUTOBOX and the neural network approach. These are the averages of absolute percent errors overall forecasting horizons for each series. It shows that the simple (training algorithm) neural network approach performed as well as a forecast expert system. The mean of the MAPE's for neural nets model is slightly less than that for the Box-Jenkins modeling system. However, due to a large standard deviation, the difference is insignificant. A pairwise means test also indicates the same result. Forecasts using AUTOBOX resulted in lower MAPEs for 22 series, and thus the neural network model was able to do better in the other 50 series. However, the large standard deviations still make these differences insignificant.

When the series are grouped on the basis of periodicity, the MAPE's are still insignificantly different between the two approaches. This suggests that the periodicity of the series being modeled does not affect a technique's performance. It was quite interesting, at least for us, that the neural network model was able to incorporate seasonality automatically, just as AUTOBOX is able to do.

Figure 27.1 shows a graphic comparison of MAPEs of the 43 monthly series included in Table 27.1. This chart indicates that the pattern of MAPEs for both approaches is quite similar.

Table 27.1

MAPE Comparison of Box-Jenkins (AUTOBOX) and Neural Network Performance as Forecasting Experts

Series	AUTOBOX	NN-PDP	Series	AUTOBOX	NN-PDP
SER4	23.53	6.43	SER499	13.50	10.02
SER13	6.58	2.59	SER508	16.11	5.89
SER31	18.07	0.55	SER526	9.95	14.75
SER40	10.16	1.03	SER544	2.72	3.98
SER49	24.77	7.65	SER571	5.57	5.82
SER58	72.57	1.34	SER580	3.03	3.28
SER85	37.00	0.29	SER589	9.66	8.20
SER112	4.55	0.10	SER598	23.49	6.36
SER184	20.61	6.92	SER616	7.22	4.62
SER193	44.43	32.52	SER634	13.70	18.67
SER202	21.51	3.95	SER643	18.92	20.29
SER211	26.31	36.03	SER652	15.23	15.54
SER220	37.10	47.59	SER661	19.80	20.52
SER229	42.19	4.19	SER670	28.39	30.27
SER238	14.22	4.79	SER679	20.42	40.01
SER265	21.15	5.52	SER688	12.86	11.12
SER292	12.67	13.94	SER697	4.13	3.63
SER301	2.91	2.25	SER706	20.11	9.66
SER310	4.46	2.90	SER715	61.31	83.83
SER319	14.30	4.39	SER724	17.43	22.44
SER328	8.02	3.14	SER733	14.21	21.52
SER337	8.52	3.86	SER742	5.00	2.05
SER346	20.23	11.15	SER751	5.19	8.17
SER355	4.75	3.92	SER760	7.75	8.05
SER364	3.73	1.25	SER787	3.17	1.87
SER382	32.78	18.25	SER796	17.68	15.96
SER400	14.14	11.42	SER805	7.93	1.18
SER409	42.80	32.09	SER823	1.29	0.65
SER418	19.23	27.37	SER832	7.96	1.29
SER427	9.89	8.53	SER877	3.73	3.38
SER436	7.09	1.85	SER904	3.88	3.22
SER445	25.71	12.87	SER913	58.53	48.90
SER454	8.48	6.85	SER922	26.35	5.22
SER463	6.19	19.95	SER958	13.67	11.36
SER472	19.21	20.76	SER967	38.74	20.68
SER481	32.36	31.00	mean	15.94	14.67
SER490	7.90	8.71	stdev	15.18	15.39

Figure 27.1

MAPEs for Monthly Series

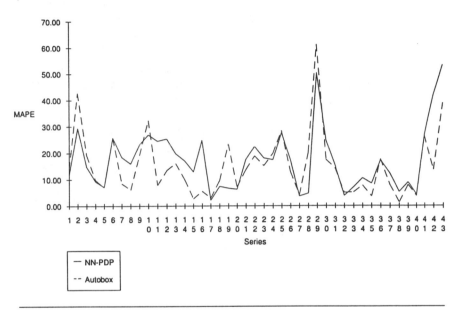

These results are quite encouraging for the proponents of neural networks as a forecasting tool. Obviously, this work needs to be replicated to assess the full potentiality of neural networks for forecasting. Possible use of other neural network architectures and more sophisticated training algorithms may improve the results.

Different Parameter Effects

One of the objectives here was to examine the effect of different architectural and learning parameters on the performance of neural networks over time series modeling. This test was carried out with monthly data. Different values of learning rate and momentum were used to train a 12-12-1, 12-12-2, 12-12-4, 12-12-6, 12-12-8, 12-12-12 architecture, generating forecasts over 1, 2, 4, 6, 8, and 12 periods ahead respectively. These architectures were trained over nine different combinations of learning rate (0.1, 0.5, 0.9) and momentum (0.1, 0.5, 0.9) values. Observations over this test gave the optimal learning parameters. These optimal learning parameters were then used to train remaining monthly data series over different architectures as: 12-6-1, 12-12-1, 12-18-1, 12-24-1, to observe the effect of different number of hidden neurons. The architecture that performed well in average analysis was then considered as the optimal architecture. The optimal architecture was carried out only over a 1-step forecast.

Figure 27.2 shows the average $n + 1$ forecast error with different network architectures. These results are over ser400 and ser409 data series. It is interesting to observe the effect of increasing the number of output neurons. It is observed that, as the number of output neurons was increased from 1 to 12 the $n + 1$ (single step) forecast improved. Figure 27.2 also shows the effect of different learning parameters on the network performance. It is seen that the learning parameters with learning rate = 0.1, and momentum = 0.1 gave the best results. The performance was poor whenever the momentum value was high. Again, the optimal parameters were, learning rate = 0.1 and momentum = 0.1.

Figure 27.2

Effect of Learning Parameters and Architecture

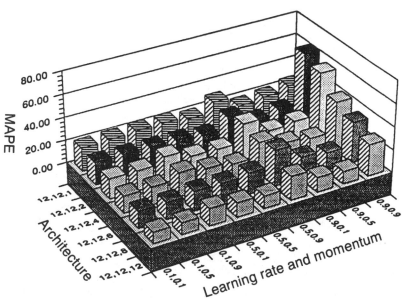

Optimal learning parameters found in the above test were then used to train the remaining set of data series to find the optimal architectures. This test was carried out only for the single step forecast. On average analysis, 12-12-1 appeared to be the best architecture. This architectural parameter (equal number of input and hidden neurons) was then used in further tests.

Multiple Horizon Forecasting

We analyzed 43 monthly series further using AUTOBOX and the neural approach. As before, 18 observations were held back. Remaining data were used to build a model, and forecasts were made at one origin so that the performance of a technique can be evaluated in terms of forecasting multiple horizons. AUTOBOX was used in its default mode. The neural network model was a simple 12-12-18 network. Table 27.2 gives the average absolute percent error for the 43 series at each forecasting horizon. Figure 27.3 depicts these same results graphically. It is apparent that AUTOBOX had a lower MAPE than the neural network models at most of the forecasting horizons. However, the MAPE for neural networks is more stable than for AUTOBOX. Again, the closeness of errors between these two approaches suggests that the neural network models should be investigated further.

CONCLUSIONS AND FUTURE RESEARCH DIRECTIONS

Neural networks provide a promising alternative approach to time series forecasting. The neural networks ability to forecast in a fuzzy sense is more appropriate than the other forecasting methods. Our present study was limited to univariate forecasting, but it is expected that neural networks may be used for multivariate forecasting also. For time series with long memory, both Box-Jenkins models and neural networks perform well, with Box-Jenkins models slightly better for short-term forecasting. With short memory, neural networks outperform Box-Jenkins.[6] By approximating the underlying mapping of the time series, a neural network provides robust forecasting in cases of irregular time series. Neural networks can be trained to approximate the underlying mapping of time series, albeit the accuracy of approximation depends on a number of factors such as the neural network

Table 27.2

MAPEs of AUTOBOX and NN Model at Various Horizons
(43 Series)

LAG	AUTOBOX	NN-PDP
1	10.75	15.35
2	18.19	14.97
3	10.31	15.17
4	14.00	15.49
5	13.32	16.30
6	16.79	17.16
7	15.17	17.30
8	11.53	17.21
9	16.53	17.22
10	12.57	17.75
11	12.72	17.36
12	13.41	17.10
13	16.48	18.57
14	28.45	19.60
15	14.84	19.12
16	14.61	19.08
17	14.34	19.46
18	17.78	19.36
Average	15.10	17.42

structure, learning method, and training procedure. Without a hidden layer, the linear neural network model is functionally similar to Box-Jenkins ARIMA model.

The neural network structure and training procedure have great impact on its forecasting performance. This fact is evident from the present work that we are doing. The learning algorithms used in our study are by no means the best. We believe that there is still much room for improvement in neural network forecasting.

Figure 27.3

Mean APE by Forecasting Horizon (43 Monthly Series)

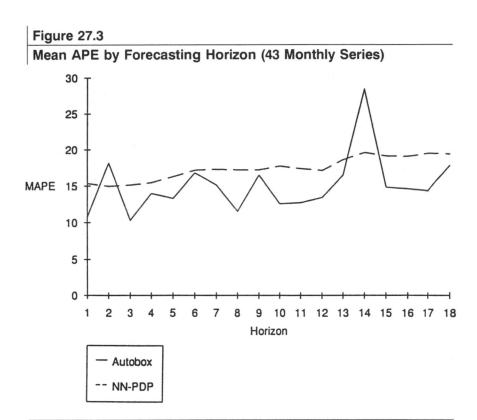

ENDNOTES

1. P. Werbos, "Generalization of Backpropagation with Application to Recurrent Gas Market Model," *Neural Networks*, vol. 1, 1988, pp. 339–356.

2. P. Werbos, "Beyond Regression: New Tools for Prediction and Analysis in the Behavioral Sciences," Harvard University, Ph.D. thesis, 1974.

3. A. Lapedes and R. Farber, "Nonlinear Signal Processing Using Neural Networks: Prediction and System Modeling," Los Alamos National Lab Technical Report LA-UR-87-2261, July 1987.

4. R. S. Sutton, "Learning to Predict by the Methods of Temporal Differences," *Machine Learning*, vol. 3, 1988, pp. 9–44.

5. R. Fozzard, G. Bradshaw, and L. Ceci, "A Connectionist Expert System for Solar Flare Forecasting," in *Advances in Neural Information Processing Systems I*, ed. by D. S. Touretzky (Morgan Kaufmann Publishers, Inc., 1989), pp. 264–271.

6. Z. Tang, C. de Almedia, and P. A. Fishwick, "Time Series Forecasting Using Neural Networks vs. Box-Jenkins Methodology," International Workshop on Neural Networks, Auburn, Ala., February 2–4, 1990.

7. P. Fishwick, "Neural Network Models in Simulation: A Comparison with Traditional Modeling Approaches," *Proceedings of Winter Simulation Conference* (Washington, D. C., 1989), pp. 702–710.

8. R. Sharda, and R. Patil, "Neural Networks as Forecasting Experts: An Empirical Test," International Joint Conference on Neural Networks, IJCNN-WASH-D.C., vol. II, January 15-19, 1990, pp. 491–494.

9. S. Makridakis, et al., "The Accuracy of Extrapolation (Time Series) Methods: Results of a Forecasting Competition," *Journal of Forecasting*, vol. 1, 1982, pp. 111–153.

10. D. J. Pack, and D. J. Downing, "Why Didn't Box-Jenkins Win (Again)?" *Proceedings, Third International Symposium on Forecasting* (Philadelphia), 1983.

11. G. E. P. Box, and G. M. Jenkins, "Time Series Analysis: Forecasting and Control," (San Francisco, Calif.: Holden-Day, 1976).

12. R. Sharda and T. Ireland, "An Empirical Test of Automatic Forecasting Systems," ORSA/TIMS Meeting, New Orleans, May 1987.

13. AUTOBOX, *Software User Manual*, (Hatboro, Pa.: Automatic Forecasting Systems), 1988.

14. J. McClelland and D. E. Rumelhart, *Exploration in Parallel Distributed Processing: A Handbook of Models, Programs and Exercises*, (Cambridge, Mass.: MIT Press, 1988).

28

CONSTRUCTIVE LEARNING AND ITS APPLICATION TO CURRENCY EXCHANGE RATE FORECASTING

A. N. Refenes

INTRODUCTION

Forecasting the behavior of a given system follows two distinct approaches. The first and most powerful approach depends on exact knowledge of the laws that underlie a given phenomenon. When this knowledge is expressed in terms of precise equations, which can in principle be solved, it is possible to predict the future behavior of system once the initial conditions are completely specified. The main problem

Printed with permission of the author.

with this approach is that the knowledge of the rules governing the behavior of the system are not readily available. This is particularly true for most macroeconomic problems. One possible source of this weakness is parameter instability, but it is more likely that the cause is lack of nonlinearities in the models.

A second, albeit less powerful method for prediction relies on the discovery of strong empirical regularities in observations of the system. There are problems, however, with the latter approach. Regularities are not always evident, and are often masked by noise. There are phenomena that seem random, without apparent periodicities, although recurrent in a generic sense.

Several researchers have attempted to use feed-forward neural networks[1,2] to predict future values of time series by extracting knowledge from the past. One common approach is to use time-space patterns of economic indexes, such as interest rates, to relate the changes in one time series to other phenomena in the economy. Others believe that currency exchange rates embody all the knowledge that is necessary to predict future behavior. The underlying assumption in this approach is that any changes in economic policy and/or other indexes are ultimately reflected in the currency exchange rate, e.g., through direct central bank interventions.

Neural network architectures have drawn considerable attention in recent years because of their interesting learning abilities. However, two main problems are associated with the use of fixed-geometry networks and back-propagation in nontrivial applications.

1. *Convergence*: Back-propagation performs learning by steepest descent in weight space, and may be trapped in local minima. The classification may not be learned, and the learning can be extremely slow.

2. *Network configuration:* A main problem is that a priori no realistic estimate can be made of the number of hidden units required to learn the classification. For good generalization, the network must be sufficiently large to learn the problem but also necessarily small to generalize well. Network design is currently something of a "black art" and depends heavily on manual experimentation and fine tuning of the learning parameters. The aim here is to develop learning procedures that will achieve optimum network configuration.

Recently, several methods have been proposed that attempt to get around the problems of slow convergence and dynamic network construction. They include Cascade Correlation,[3] the Tiling algorithm,[4] the Neural Decision tree,[5] the Upstart Algorithm,[6] and others. In some of these techniques the hidden units are constructed in layers one by one as they are needed. By showing that at least one unit in each layer makes fewer mistakes than a corresponding unit in the earlier layer eventual convergence to zero errors is guaranteed. Other techniques operate in the opposite direction by pruning the network and removing "redundant" connections.

The above techniques differ in complexity, convergence speed, and most importantly in their generalization performance. Although most, but not all, methods will guarantee to learn the classification, no realistic statement can be made about their generalization performance. For example, the upstart algorithm shows a rate of generalization between 50 percent and 70 percent,[6] which is unrealistic for most real-life applications.

This chapter describes and evaluates a procedure for constructing and training multilayered perceptrons by adding units to the network dynamically during training. Units are added as they are needed. By showing that the newly added unit makes fewer mistakes than before, and by training the unit not to disturb the earlier dynamics, eventual convergence to zero errors is guaranteed. By training each unit to solve a simpler problem than the entire network, faster convergence is achieved.

The CLS+ procedure is a development from earlier work[7] and is designed to perform well with continuous-valued networks.

BASIC NOTIONS

Constructive techniques are based on the principle that the hidden units of a network are constructed incrementally, one by one as they are needed. The basic building block for constructive techniques is a *linear classifier*. A linear classifier is defined as a simple node with a set of input weights w_i, a set of output weights w_o, and a simple learning rule (Figure 28.1a). The components, $< v_1,...,v_n >$, of an input vector V are

Figure 28.1a, b, c

Generic Algorithm for Constructive Learning

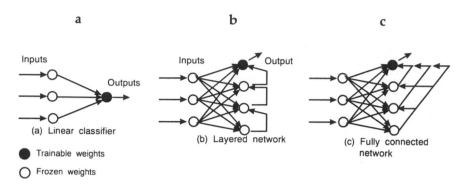

1. Construct a good (preferably optimal) set of weights for a linear classifier L_1. This is always possible and can be achieved using any of the gradient descent training algorithms (i.e., back-propagation, quickprop, etc.). If all (or the maximum number possible) of the training examples are correctly classified, exit. Otherwise, freeze the weights for L_1.

2. Construct a good (preferably optimal) set of weights for linear classifier L_{i+1} having inputs from the training examples and from linear classifier L_i. Depending on the training technique, it can be shown that D_{i+1} can correctly classify a greater number of training examples than D_i. Freeze the coefficients for D_{i+1}.

3. Repeat from Step 2, a finite number of times until all, or the maximum number possible of training examples are correctly classified.

mapped into a new vector, V^*, whose components, V_j^*, are computed according to the following rule:

$$V_j^* = w_{oj} f\left(\sum_{i=0}^{n} w_i v_i\right)$$

(1)

A linear classifier can be trained to maximize (or minimize) the correlation (or error) between its outputs and some arbitrary quantity. Constructive learning starts with a fixed architecture. By showing that the addition of a new *linear classifier* produces fewer errors than the earlier architecture, eventual convergence to zero errors is guaranteed. An obvious way to use linear classifiers of this type is as mechanisms for correcting errors that the earlier network is making. This can be done by training the linear classifier to further minimize the error or to maximize the correlation between its output and the error that a specific node in the network is making. In this way, the classifier will develop corrective weights in its output connections. Once added into the network the weights of the linear classifier are frozen and the procedure is repeated. Linear classifiers can be connected to the network in at least two ways.

Firstly, they can be inserted between the last hidden node and the output units (Figure 28.1b). Secondly, they can be inserted in the same way but connected to all the hidden units (Figure 28.1c). In the simple case where the linear classifier produces binary values, it is called a linear discriminant.

Figure 28.1 shows a linear classifier and two ways of constructing networks with one output unit, by repeatedly extending the output until convergence is achieved. In this case, the construction of L_i is achieved by training to minimize the error between the desired output and the classifier's actual output.

The convergence, generalization, and scalability properties of these techniques depend on the type of linear classifier used, the way in which its weights are calculated (i.e., learning rule), the type of subclassification it is asked to learn, and finally, the way in which it is inserted in the network.

Suppose we are given a training set to be learned. Each input vector $i^{(r)}$ of N continuous values has an associated target $t^{(d)}$. Each unit has a "state" or "activity level" that is determined by the input received from the other units in the network. Information is processed locally in each unit by computing a dot product between its input vector and its weight vector (x_i).

$$x_i = f\left(\sum_{j=0}^{n} y_j w_{ji}\right)$$

(2)

This weighted sum, x_i, which is called the "total input" of unit i, is then passed through a squashing function to produce the state of unit i denoted by f. We consider the family of squashing functions $F_n = \{f = f(x, k, T, c) \mid x, k \in R; T, c \in R - \{0\}\}$, which are defined by (3):

$$f(x) = k + \frac{c}{1 + e^{Tx}}$$

(3)

Note that for suitable values of k, c, T the typical sigmoid, hyperbolic tangent, and similar are obtained. In this chapter we shall use $k = A$, $C = -2A$, and $T = 2S$ to obtain the symmetric scaled hyperbolic tangent function:

$$f(x) = A \tanh S(x) = A \frac{e^{Sx} - e^{-Sx}}{e^{Sx} + e^{-Sx}}$$

$$= A \frac{e^{2Sx} - 1}{e^{2Sx} + 1} = A - \frac{2A}{1 + e^{2Sx}}$$

(4)

where A is the amplitude of the function and S determines its slope at the origin, and the entire squashing function is an odd function with horizontal asymptotes $+A$ and $-A$. Symmetric functions are believed to yield faster convergence, although the learning can become extremely slow if the weights are too small.[8] The cause of this problem is that the origin of the weight space is a stable point for the learning dynamics, and although it is a saddle point, it is attractive in almost all directions. For our simulations, we use parameter values similar to Le Cun's with $A = 1.7159$ and $S = \frac{2}{3}$. With this choice of parameters, the equalities $f(1) = 1$, and $(-1) = -1$ are satisfied. The rationale behind this is that the overall gain of the squashing transformation is around 1 in normal operating conditions, and the interpretation of the state of the network is simplified. Moreover, the absolute value of the second derivative of f is a maximum at $+1$ and -1, which improves the convergence at the end of the learning session.

Before training, the weights are initialized with random values. Training the network to produce a desired output vector $o^{(r)}$ when presented with an input pattern $i^{(r)}$ involves testing the network to see if the actual output vector $a^{(r)}$ is in agreement with the desired output, $d^{(r)}$, and then adding a new hidden unit to correct the residual error. The new unit, and only it, is then trained to recognize those patterns for which the network was in error. The basic idea is that a hidden unit is constructed with the purpose of correcting the mistakes at the output layer. If we are considering binary valued networks, an output unit O_i, can make two types of error[6,7]:

wrongly ON $\quad a^{(r)}i = 1 \quad$ but $d^{(r)}i = 0$

wrongly OFF $\quad a^{(r)}i = 0 \quad$ but $d^{(r)}i = 1$

Consider patterns for which O_i is wrongly ON: O_i could be corrected by a large negative weight from a new hidden unit in the hidden layer, say h_i. The new hidden unit h_i is active and has an inhibitory effect for those vectors for which O_i is wrongly ON. For the remaining patterns, h_i remains silent. Likewise when O_i is wrongly OFF it could be corrected by a sufficiently large positive weight. Again, h_i has an excitatory effect only for those vectors.

For networks with continuous output, the CLS+ procedure uses a generalization of the above described in the next section.

THE CLS+ PROCEDURE

Overview

The CLS+ procedure is illustrated in Figure 28.2. It begins with some N inputs and M outputs and at least one hidden unit. The number of inputs and outputs is dictated by the problem and by the I/O representation. Every input is connected to the unit in the hidden layer which is in turn connected to every unit in the output layer.

We add hidden units to the network one by one. Like cascade correlation,[3] each hidden unit receives a connection from each of the networks input and also from the last (but not all) hidden unit. The hidden unit's weights are frozen after the unit is added to the network.

The learning is on-line, and the algorithm begins with only a single, fully connected hidden unit with randomized connection strengths. The learning algorithm proceeds as follows:

Figure 28.2

The Constructive Learning Procedure

The network grows sideways; new units are added to correct the mistakes at the output and are then trained to remain silent for those patterns for which there are other feature detectors.

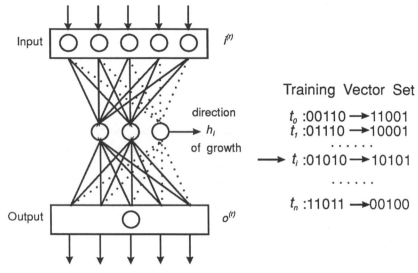

Training Vector Set

t_0 :00110 →11001
t_1 :01110 →10001
......
t_i :01010 →10101
......
t_n :11011 →00100

Step 1. Feed-forward test for training vector t_i. If the output o_r makes an error then add a new unit h_k. Connect h_k to the output unit o^r with a connection strength that corrects the error. The connection strength w_{hk} can be calculated analytically as follows. Prior to adding the new unit h_k, the output at o^r is given by:

$$o^r = f\left(\sum_{i=0}^{k-1} w_{h_{i,o}} v_{h_{i,o}}\right) = t^d{}_i \pm \varepsilon$$

(5)

where $\varepsilon = |o^r - t^r d|$. After adding $h_{k,0}$ the error at o^r will be eliminated. Thus:

$$o^r = f\left(\sum_{i=0}^{k-1} w_{h_{i,o}} v_{h_{i,o}} + w_{h_k} v_{h_k}\right) = t^d{}_i$$

(6)

Using (4) we expand (6), and solving for $w_{h_k} v_{h_k}$ we obtain:

$$w_{h_k} v_{h_k} = \frac{\log_e \left(\frac{2A}{A - t^{d_i}} - 1 \right) - 2S \sum\limits_{i=0}^{k-1} W_{h_{i,o}} V_{h_{i,o}}}{2S} \qquad (7)$$

There are two unknowns in (7); the weight for h_k and its value. If we fix the value that h_k has to produce for pattern t_i, we can compute the weight and vice versa.

Step 2. Connect the newly added unit h_k to all the input units and to h_{k-1}. The connection's strength must be such that the unit recognizes the current vector t_i and none of the previous vectors, $t_0, t_1, ... t_{i-1}$, so that the cognitive properties of the network are not disturbed. This is achieved by gradient descent learning.

The main point to note here is the method of training the new units. The current unit is trained using the current pattern and all the patterns that appear before the current pattern in the training set. The new unit is trained such that it will be active for the current pattern but be inactive for all the patterns that appear before the current pattern in the training set. The patterns that appear after the current pattern in the training set are not taken into consideration. It is possible that different patterns appearing after the current patterns in the training set may activate the current unit. This is done to increase the generalization capabilities of the network. The rules for training the newly added unit are summarized in Figure 28.3.

The procedure now moves to the next pattern in the training set. In practice, t_i is not selected sequentially, but on the basis of a largest error condition. Exactly the same procedure that is used for training pattern t_i is used to train pattern t_{i+1}. This carries on until the algorithm has been through all the training patterns in the training set.

Convergence of the CLS+ Procedure

The convergence result follows immediately from the training method because the error at the output units has been corrected, so the newly added hidden unit is given a easier problem to solve than the output unit. The proof consists of two parts.

Figure 28.3

Rules for Training a Hidden Unit to Correct the Mistakes Made for Pattern t_i

The unit is trained to produce $0 < |v_k| < A$ for the current pattern, and a zero on all the previous patterns. In practice, t_i is not selected sequentially but on the basis of a largest error condition.

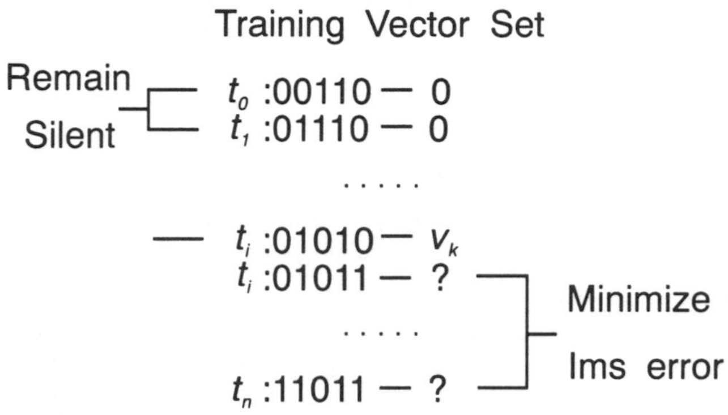

Training Vector Set

$$
\begin{array}{ll}
\text{Remain} & t_0 :00110 - 0 \\
\text{Silent} & t_1 :01110 - 0
\end{array}
$$

. . . . .

$$
\begin{array}{l}
t_i :01010 - v_k \\
t_i :01011 - ? \\
\end{array}
\quad \text{Minimize}
$$

. . . . .

$$
t_n :11011 - ? \quad \text{lms error}
$$

Part 1. In Part 1 we prove that after we have added a new unit h_i in the hidden layer, we will always have fewer errors than before.

Proof. Assume we have a training set with n patterns. The CLS+ algorithm goes through the training set a pattern at a time.

Before we add a new unit h_i to the hidden layer, we correctly recognize all the patterns that appear before the ith pattern in the training set. i.e., $t_0 \rightarrow t_{i-1}$ patterns recognized correctly.

At this point t_i and all the patterns that appear after t_i in the training set have not been learned by the network. So inputting any patterns from t_i to t_n will make an error.

At t_i the total error is:

$$
E = e_r(t_i) + \dots + e_r(t_n) = \sum_{j=i}^{n} e_r(t_j).
$$

(8)

by adding the new unit h_i the error term $e_r(t_i)$ has been eliminated. The total error is now given by:

$$E' = | \sum_{j=i+1}^{n} e_r(t_j) | \quad < \quad | \sum_{j=i}^{n} e_r(t_j) | . \tag{9}$$

By adding unit h_i we have reduced the total error. Therefore the algorithm converges.

Part 2. In Part 2 we need to show that the new unit h_i will always learn the following condition simultaneously.

1. *To be active at pattern t_i*: This condition is required so that the new unit h_i can become a feature detector. The output of the unit will then excite the corrective weights.

2. *To be inactive at patterns $t_0,...,t_{i-1}$*: This condition is necessary due to the fact that all the previous patterns are already recognized correctly and this should not be disturbed.

This is a linearly separable problem and can be learned by the delta rule[9] provided that the training data set does not contain a malicious (one-to-many) training vector.

Generalization of the CLS+ Procedure

Neural networks are interesting because of their learning properties: i.e., the ability to perform well on all patterns taken from a given distribution after having seen only a subset of them. The generalization properties of the CLS+ procedure depend solely on the way in which hidden units are trained. For the purposes of convergence, it is necessary to train a hidden unit at t_i to acquire the inhibitory and excitatory behavior described earlier. As long as conditions 1 and 2 above are obeyed, we could train the hidden unit in several ways.

If the hidden unit were trained to recognize only pattern t_i and no other patterns, convergence could still be possible (in fact it is much faster). However, because each unit could only recognize a specific vector, the overall network would not be able to recognize anything outside the training set. The minimal conditions for a lower bound on generalization are as shown:

1. Unit h_i must be trained to be active at pattern t_i.

2. Unit h_i must be trained to be inactive at patterns $t_0, ..., i-1$.

3. Unit h_i must be active for at least one other pattern in $t_{i+1}, ..., t_n$.

Any arbitrary pattern would suffice, but the higher the correlation of the unit's behavior to the regularities within the training set, the higher the probability of good generalization. Such behavior can be achieved by increasing the sophistication of h_i. There are several ways of doing so. Figure 28.4 shows a construction in which h_i is composed of three subsidiary units: A, B, C.

In this construction, the tasks of the subsidiary units are defined as follows:

A. Is a linear discriminant. It is connected to all input units and to the previous hidden unit h_{i-1}. A is trained to produce the desired output for pattern t_i and 0 for all other patterns.

B. Is a similarity approximator. It is connected in the same way as A but it is trained to minimize the least square error between its output and the desired output for pattern $t_{i+1}, ..., t_n$.

C. Is an arbitrator unit. It is connected to both A and B and sees the output of previous A_j, j ε $\{0, ..., i\}$. When A is active, C inhibits B and simply passes on the output of A. The connection strength

Figure 28.4
Hidden Unit Construction

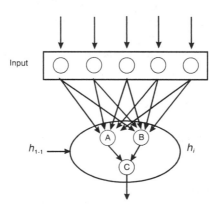

between C and the output is calculated as in (7). When A_j is inactive, C inhibits B and simply passes on the output of A (o^A) suitably adjusted to cancel the effect of W_h by a simple division, i.e.:

$$o^c = \frac{o^A}{w_{h_i}}$$

(10)

The rationale behind this method of construction has a simple geometric interpretation. Here, an analogy is made between learning and curve fitting. There are two problems in curve fitting: finding the *order* of the polynomial, and finding the *coefficients* of the polynomial once the order has been established. For example, given a certain data set, one first decides that the curve is second order, thus has the form $ax^2 + bx + c$, and then computes somehow, the values for a, b, c, e.g., to minimize the sum of squared differences between required and predicted $f(x_i)$ for x_i in the training set. Once the coefficients are computed, the value of $f(x_i)$ can be calculated for any x_i including those not present in the training data set. Orders smaller than the appropriate ones risk not to lead to good approximation even for the points in the data set.

On the other hand, choosing a larger order implies fitting a high-order polynomial to the low-order data. Although one hopes that the high order terms will have zero coefficients to cancel their effect, this is not the case in practice. Typically, it leads to perfect fit to points in the data set but very bad $f(x_i)$ values may be computed for the x_i not in the training data—the system will not generalize well. Similarly, a network having a structure simpler than necessary cannot give good approximations even to patterns in the training set. A structure more complicated than necessary "overfits" in that it leads to good fit for the training set but performing poorly on unseen patterns.

By adding units to correct the output for the patterns with the largest errors, the CLS+ procedure has the effect of increasing the order of the polynomial approximator, and by recomputing the connection strengths of the newly added hidden unit, the procedure makes a better approximation to the values of the coefficients. Because only part of the network is retrained, the degrees of freedom in exploring the search space are reduced dramatically.

In our work so far and in the simulation results reported here, hidden units were trained using the construction in Figure 28.4.

EXPERIMENTAL SET-UP AND SIMULATION RESULTS

Network Architecture

The network architecture at the input and output levels is largely determined by the application. A common method of identifying regularities within a data set contaminated by noise is *windowing* (Figure 28.5).

The basic idea is to use two windows W^i and W^0 of fixed sizes, n and m respectively, to look into the data set. For a given window size the assumption is that the sequence of values $W^i_0, ...W^i_n$ is somehow related to the following sequence $W^0_0, ...W^0_m$, and that this relationship, although unknown, is defined entirely within the data set. Various methods can then be used to correlate the two sets of values. In the case of neural networks, $W^i \rightarrow W^0$ can be used as a training vector. Both windows are shifted along the time series using a fixed step size s (Figure 28.5).

The choice of window and step sizes is critical to the ability of any prediction system to identify regularities and thus approximate the hidden relationship accurately. Quite often some preprocessing of the data set is required to obtain a sensible starting point for n, m, and s.

Figure 28.5

Windowing: Looking for Hidden Correlations and Regularities in Time Series

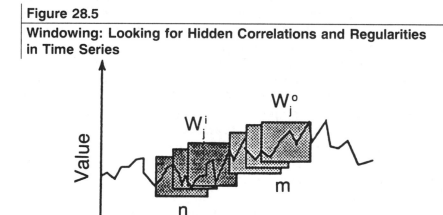

Two types of forecasting are valuable in normal operating conditions in currency trading:

1. *Multistep prediction:* First, there is the requirement for long-term forecasting that aims to identify *general* trends and *major* turning points in a currency exchange rate. In multistep prediction, the system uses a set of current values to predict the value of the exchange rate for a fixed period. The prediction is then fed back to the network to forecast the next period. We show that neural networks can use their smooth interpolation properties to produce extremely good multistep predictions, even with difficult training datasets.

2. *Single step prediction:* For the single-step prediction there is no feedback. The network predicts the exchange rate value one step ahead of time, but uses the actual rather than the predicted value for the next prediction. Single-step prediction serves two purposes. Firstly, it is a good mechanism for evaluating the adaptability and robustness of the prediction system by showing that even when its prediction is wrong, it is not dramatically wrong and that the system can use the actual value to correct itself. Second, it can act as an alarm generator and would allow traders to buy or sell in advance of a price increase or decrease respectively. We show that neural networks are very robust and adaptive prediction systems, but careful network design and training are required to achieve reasonable turning point prediction in noisy data.

In the following section, we describe the use of the CLS+ procedure for identifying underlying regularities in time-series. The system described here is designed and trained to predict the exchange rate between the U.S. dollar and the deutsche mark.

Training and Test Sets

The *training set* and *test set* consist of currency exchange data for the period 1988 through 1989, on hourly updates for the 260 trading days.

The first 200 items of the data set were used for training, while the second part was used for testing. The problem is particularly difficult to solve since the training set has a positive slope (i.e., general increase of the exchange rate), while the test set has a negative slope (i.e., a general decrease; see Figure 28.6).

Figure 28.6

Training and Test Set

The data set consists of currency exchange data for the period 1988–1989 on hourly updates, i.e., 260 trading days.

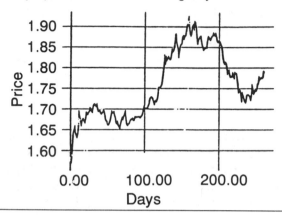

The choice of window and step sizes is critical to the ability of any prediction system to identify high-order regularities in time series and thus approximate the hidden correlations accurately. Quite often some preprocessing of the data set is required to obtain a sensible starting point for the sizes of W^i, W^0, and the step sizes. For our simulations we use the following parameter values:

$$n = \text{size of } (W^i) = 12$$

$$m = \text{size of } (W^0) = 1$$

$$s = \text{size of (step)} = 4$$

The rationale behind this is that a day's trading ($n = 12$) would capture the underlying regularities quite accurately and would eliminate much of the noise. The rationale behind the small size of $m = 1$ is to avoid overloading the smooth interpolation properties of the learning procedure. Moreover, the overall effect of $s = 4$ is to take the moving average over a four-day period. This would dampen the effect of trading near the beginning and end of the week where the processing of backlogs might affect the markets and introduce further noise.

The resulting training set consists of overlapping snapshots of the time series each of length 12 hours, moving along the curve at an interval of 4 hours. More formally:

$$
\begin{aligned}
t_0: \quad & W^i_0 = \{V_0, ..., V_{11}\} &&\rightarrow& W^o_0 = \{V_{12}\} \\
t_1: \quad & W^i_1 = \{V_4, ..., V_{15}\} &&\rightarrow& W^o_1 = \{V_{16}\}
\end{aligned}
$$

$$\cdots\cdots\cdots$$

$$
t_j: \quad W^i_j = \{V_{j+s}, ..., V_{j+n}\} \quad\rightarrow\quad W^o_j = \{V_{j+n+1}\}
$$

The overall size of the training set therefore, is given by:

$$
d \times y \times n \times s = \frac{2}{3} d \times n \times s = \frac{2}{3}\, 260 \times 12 \times 4 = 8{,}236
$$

The intermediate size of the *training set* and *test set* makes the problem nontrivial and also allows for extensive tests of learning speed and generalization performance.

In our simulation experiments, we investigate the influence of varying learning time, and varying the learning rate on the convergence and generalization performance. We start with the multistep prediction.

Multistep Prediction

For the multistep prediction, the network would use the inputs of the past 12 hours of trading to predict the value of the exchange rate for the $(12 + 1)^{th}$ hour. The prediction is then fed back to the network to forecast the next value. This process is repeated for all the values in the last 60 trading days of the year 1989.

The result of the multistep prediction is shown in Figure 28.7. The prediction for the general trend in the exchange rate is very accurate. The network predicted a sharp fall and then a rise in the exchange rate. For the first 30 days, the prediction is very accurate both in terms of trends, and also in terms of absolute values. The network predicted a turning point at approximately the time that it took place, and estimated correctly the pace of the recovery.

Figure 28.7

Multiple-Step Prediction

The solid line shows the whole time series, while the dotted line shows the exchange rate predicted by the neural network for the days 200 to 260.

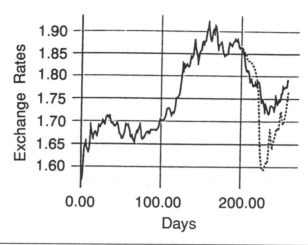

The problem as defined by the training data alone is particularly difficult to solve since the training set has a positive slope (i.e., general increase of the exchange rate), while the test set has a negative slope (i.e., a general decrease).

Evaluation

Although the prediction performance of the network is intuitively quite accurate, a more rigorous evaluation would be required. It is generally difficult to quantify the prediction performance of such systems, and evaluations are often applicant dependent. The evaluation we use here is based on a simple trading strategy:

> We buy or sell in advance according to the prediction. We buy or sell when the system predicts a turning point. The volume of the transaction can be fixed or variable, i.e., proportional to the predicted rate of change. Certain market imperfections such as transaction costs, and the cost of borrowing are assumed away.

We define the following:

P_{t_0}—Actual price at time t_0 the decision time.

P_{t_k}—Actual price at the time t_k, which according to the prediction is a turning point.

$P^*_{t_k}$—Predicted price at time t_k which according to the prediction is a turning point.

λk—Amount of units bought or sold. For transactions with fixed amounts of money we use $\lambda = 1$.

p_i—Profit that the system makes for transaction i. This can be negative as well as positive.

The profit is then related to the predictions as follows:

$$p_i = (P_{t_0} - P_{t_k})\lambda k \tag{11}$$

The network has predicted one major turning point and four minor ones (Figure 28.7). The first was to occur approximately 30 days ahead of prediction, while the second would occur approximately ten later and so on. According to the strategy outlined above, we would have made six transactions: at the 200th, the 230th, 240th, 245th, 255th, and 257th. The corresponding profits are given by direct substitution in (11).

$$p_1 = (P_{t_0} - P_{t_k})\,\lambda k = (1.87 - 1.72)\,\lambda k = 0.15\lambda k \tag{12}$$

$$p_2 = (P_{t_0} - P_{t_k})\,\lambda k = (1.72 - 1.72)\,\lambda k = 0\lambda k \tag{13}$$

$$p_3 = (P_{t_0} - P_{t_k})\,\lambda k = (1.72 - 1.72)\,\lambda k = 0\lambda k \tag{14}$$

$$p_4 = (P_{t_0} - P_{t_k})\,\lambda k = (1.78 - 1.72)\,\lambda k = 0.06\lambda k \tag{15}$$

$$p_5 = (P_{t_0} - P_{t_k})\,\lambda k = (1.78 - 1.78)\,\lambda k = 0\lambda k \tag{16}$$

$$p_6 = (P_{t_0} - P_{t_k})\,\lambda k = (1.79 - 1.78)\,\lambda k = 0.01\lambda k \tag{17}$$

Thus, for fixed $\lambda = 1$, there is an overall positive profit p of 22 percent on the amount of monies invested in the transactions, i.e.:

$$p = p_1 + p_2 + p_3 = (0.15 + 0.05 + 0.02)\, k = 0.22k$$

A more sensible strategy is to make the number of units bought or sold proportional to the predicted changes in prices. In this case, profits on correct predictions are increased but so are losses on incorrect predictions. The choice of this strategy is directly related to the confidence in the robustness of the system. As we shall see later, there are good reasons to have a high level of confidence in the prediction accuracy of the network.

A sensible measure for λ is the ratio between the current price and the predicted one. This ratio is often suitably scaled by a factor c, dependent on the degree of confidence in the prediction system:

$$\lambda = \frac{P_{t_0}}{P^*_{t_k}}\, c \tag{18}$$

Using (18) and (12, 15, 17) we obtain a more realistic estimate of the profit. For $c = 1$, we have:

$$p = p_1 + p_2 + p_3 = (0.175 + 0.064 + 0.01)\, k$$

$$= 0.25k$$

For this type of prediction system, it is often sensible to scale λ by values of $c > 1$ near the beginning of the prediction and to use values of $c < 1$ as the prediction gets further away. In our case, such scaling would have increased the profit c-fold.

Single-Step Prediction

For the single-step prediction there is no feedback. The network predicts the exchange rate value one hour ahead of time, but uses the actual rather than the predicted value for the current hour.

Figure 28.8 displays the results for the single-step prediction in which the input values are the values of the observed time series. The prediction is quite accurate in that it follows the actual prices closely. Even when it makes a mistake with respect to predicting a turning point, it is capable of adjusting itself as soon as the actual price is made available at the next cycle. This type of performance measure is often

Figure 28.8

Single-Step Prediction

The solid line shows the whole time series, while the dotted line shows the actual exchange rate produced by the neural network for the days 200 to 260.

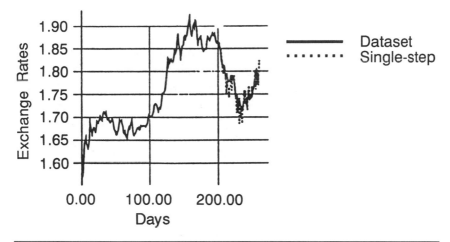

cited by researchers to indicate the robustness of the system. In practical terms, however, this is of little use, as the system has to predict ahead of time the exchange rate price.

To analyze the behavior of the system further we compare the "gradients" of the two curves to identify turning points (strictly speaking, these are first differences, not true gradients, because the time series are not continuous).

Define t as the number of turning points in the curve, p as the number of perfect matches on turning points, within two time steps, and s as the number of slope corrections within two time steps. The following measures are of interest:

$a = \frac{p}{t}$ is the prediction accuracy of the system at the turning points;

$r = \frac{s}{t}$ denotes the robustness of the system and shows how well the system adapts its prediction in response to real events.

For the simulations in our single-step prediction we obtain the following:

$$a = \frac{p}{t} = \frac{18}{26} = 0.69 \tag{19}$$

$$r = \frac{s}{t} = \frac{23}{26} = 0.88 \tag{20}$$

The measures in (11) and (12) show that the system predicted correctly 69 percent of the turning points, and when it was wrong it corrected its prediction within two time steps 88 percent of the time. A closer analysis of those results showed that 90 percent of the correctly predicted turning points are in the positive direction. The main reason for the poor performance of the system lies in the training data itself, which generally follow a positive trend, but the test data follow a general negative trend (Figure 28.6). In general, this problem need not arise. It is possible to select a more representative training set, one that contains both negative and positive trends, except for its availability.

The overall result is good. The network under evaluation here was designed to identify *major* rather than *minor* turning points and was carefully trained to avoid overfitting the noise. In practice short-term prediction networks would be trained to overfit.

COMPARISON TO OTHER TECHNIQUES

Since 1973, with the implementation of the floating exchange rate system by the industrialized countries, a large amount of research work has been carried out in an attempt to explain the movements of exchange rates. In this section we compare the performance of classical smoothing techniques and fixed geometry networks with that of the CLS+ procedure.

Statistical Forecasting

For the purposes we use three smoothing techniques typical of those employed in everyday use by financial institutions: simple autoregression, and exponential smoothing methods.[10] In order to make these methods work at all we found that this was necessary to reduce the noise in the data set and have compiled *daily* observations by taking the average of our *hourly* data set.

Exponential Smoothing. Exponential smoothing is a convenient way of expressing the forecast y_{t+T} in terms of exponentially smoothed statistics. If the time series is not flat but has linear trends, *second order* exponential smoothing is used. This can model the trend and hence exponentially smooth the de-trended data set. The *second order* exponential smoothing model is given by:

$$y_{t+T} = \left(2 + \frac{\alpha T}{1 - \alpha}\right) S_t - \left(1 + \frac{\alpha T}{1 - \alpha}\right) S_t(2) \tag{21}$$

where $S_t(2) = \alpha S_t + (1 - \alpha)S_{t-1}(2)$. T is the time trend and

$$S_t = \alpha y_t + (1 - \alpha)S_{t-1} \tag{22}$$

where $0 < \alpha < 1$ and y_{t+T} denotes the exchange rate. The statistic $S_t(2)$ is called the double smoothed statistic and is a smoothing of the smoothed values. $S_t(2)$ gives an indication of the trend of the averages S_t over time. Hence, its inclusion in the model accounts for a linear trend of y_t with time. The estimated values for the parameters are $\alpha = 0.62$ and $T = -0.0015$.

The predicted values for y_1 are depicted in Figure 28.9a. They form a straight line *sf*1 of positive slope and fail to pick up the change of pattern in the actual data.

If the time series is neither constant nor linear with time, it is best to use a triple exponential smoothing model. Higher-order exponential

Figure 28.9

Multiple-Step Prediction Using Statistical Methods

a. Second-order exponential smoothing
b. Third-order exponential smoothing
c. Autoregression

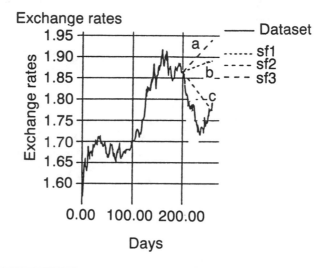

smoothing models exist but the difficulties in computing the forecasting equation for models of an order higher than the three are considerable. It is generally accepted that unless a time series is extremely volatile, third-order exponential smoothing would suffice. The *third-order* exponential smoothing model is given by:

$$y_{t+T} = \left[6(1-\alpha)^2 + (6-5\alpha)\alpha T + \alpha^2 T^2\right] \frac{S_t}{2(1-\alpha)^2}$$

$$- \left[6(1-\alpha)^2 + 2(5-4\alpha)\alpha T + 2\alpha^2 T^2\right] \frac{S_t(2)}{2(1-\alpha)^2}$$

$$+ \left[2(1-\alpha)^2 + (4-3\alpha)\alpha T + \alpha^2 T^2\right] \frac{S_t(3)}{2(1-\alpha)^2}$$

The *triple smooth statistic* $s_t(3)$ is, in a sense, describing the average rate of change *of the average rates of change*. It is computed as follows:

$$S_t(3) = \alpha S_t(2) + (1 - \alpha)S_{t-1}(3)$$

The predicted values for y_t using third order exponential smoothing are depicted in Figure 28.9b. Again, they form a straight line *sf2* of positive slope and fail to pick up the change of pattern in the actual data.

The main problem with exponential smoothing is that essentially they perform piecewise linear approximation and find it quite difficult to model "volatile" time series. An additional obstacle is that an a priori estimate of the degree of nonlinearity of time series is required in order to select the order of smoothing. In practice, this is not always readily available.

Autoregression.   The autoregression forecasting methodology consists of two main parts: a large class of time series models and a set of procedures for choosing one of these models to use for forecasting. The class of *autoregressive integrated moving average* models (ARIMA) contains all time series of the form:

$$y_t = \sum_{i=1}^{p} \varphi_i\, y_{t-i} + \varepsilon_t - \sum_{j=1}^{q} \theta_j\, \varepsilon_{t-j} \tag{23}$$

The first summation term in (23) is the autoregressive part of the model, with the second summation term being the moving average part of the model. The terms $\varepsilon_t, \varepsilon_{t-1}, \ldots, \varepsilon_{t-q}$ are the current and past q error terms of the series. The constants φ_i are called the autoregressive parameters of the model, and the terms in θ_i are the moving average parameters.

We have used several autoregressive models, with the best being a purely autoregressive model with four lags. The estimated equation from the 200 observations is listed below:

$$y_t = 0.00972y_{t-1} + 1.37448y_{t-2} - 0.54810y_{t-3} + 0.16870y_{t-4}$$

with regression parameters $R^2 = 0.99$, and D. W. = 2.03.

Using the above estimated coefficients, we predicted the exchange rate for the remaining observations. The predicted values form a straight line of negative slope as shown in Figure 28.9c. This model provides the most satisfactory forecasts amongst classical forecasting methods and using (11) would give profit of 9 percent.

Fixed Geometry Networks

Fixed geometry networks are sensitive to network size, to training times, and to the choice of control parameters for the gradient descent. We have experimented with several configurations of standard back-propagation networks. The best result was obtained with a network of a single layer of 32 nodes, trained for 4,500 iterations, and $\lambda = 0.4$. The predicted result is shown in Figure 28.10.

For the first 20 days, the prediction is very accurate both in terms of trends, and also in terms of absolute values. The network predicted a turning point slightly earlier than it actually took place, and overestimated the strength of the recovery. As expected the smooth interpolation properties of back-propagation eliminated the short-term noise in the prediction.

Using the evaluation procedure in the previous section (11) and (18), the corresponding profit levels are 18 percent for fixed k, and 20 percent for variable k and scaling factor $c = 1$. This is much better than the statistical techniques but not as accurate as with the CLS+ procedure.

Figure 28.10

Multiple-Step Prediction: By Error Back-Propagation

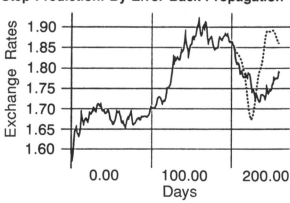

The same type of prediction was possible with several network configurations of fixed geometry networks. However, as one varies network size so one must vary training times appropriately; we were not able to establish a linear relationship between the two. In general it is not possible to have an a priori estimate of these two parameters. Another interesting discovery was that almost all fixed geometry networks developed two attractor dynamics: if the network was overfitting it would predict a curve with a shape similar to that in Figure 28.9, but with a smaller periodicity; if the network was underfitting it would predict a curve which was in effect averaging the time series (i.e., with a larger periodicity but much smaller amplitude and a mean around 1.82). Interestingly, there was no smooth transition from one attractor dynamics to another; the change from would happen within a single iteration (around the 4,000th pass through the data set).

CONCLUSIONS AND FURTHER WORK

One of the main problems with neural network design is that a priori no realistic estimate can be made of the number of hidden units that are required to solve a problem. We have presented a new strategy for dynamically configuring a feed-forward multilayered network for any function. The CLS+ algorithm is designed for general purpose supervised learning for neural networks. With respect to previous approaches to learning in layered system, such as back-propagation, our approach presents a completely new way of addressing the problem. The geometry, including the number of hidden units and the connections, is not fixed in advance but generated by the growth process.

The CLS+ algorithm offers the following advantages over network learning algorithms currently in use:

❖ There is no need to guess the size, and the connectivity pattern of the network in advance. A network (though not optimal) is built automatically.

❖ The CLS+ procedure convergence learns fast. In back-propagation the hidden units engage in complex calculation before they settle into distinct useful roles; in CLS+, each unit sees a fixed problem and can move decisively to solve that problem.

❖ At any given time we train just one unit in the network. The rest of the network is not changing, so the results can be cached.

The principal difference between the CLS+ algorithm and other learning architecture are the dynamic creation of hidden units, the way we add units to a single layer with a fixed input and output layer and the freezing of units as we add them to the network. An interesting discovery is that by training one unit at a time, instead of training the whole network at once, we can speed up the learning process considerably.

We have explained the different parts of the application and the relationship between them. The result is good. For multistep prediction, the network learns the problem well and makes at least 20 percent profit. This compares well with normal trading strategies which normally achieve levels of profit between 2 percent and 5 percent.

The system described here is designed and trained to predict the exchange rate between the U. S. dollar and the deutsche mark, but it is easy to see how to apply the methodology to other time series problems. The next step will be to train the network for a realistic trading environment. For example, the current model assumes that there is a risk-free rate of interest at which borrowing (and lending) takes place.[11] In addition, taxes, and other market imperfections (such as transaction costs) are assumed away.[12]

ENDNOTES

1. A. S. Weigend, B. A. Huberman, and D. E. Rumelhart, "Predicting the Future: A Connectionist Approach," Stanford University Technical Report, Stanford-PDP-90-01. Submitted to the *International Journal of Neural Systems*.

2. T. Komoto et al., "Stock Market Prediction with Modular Neural Networks," poc., IJCNN-90, San Diego, 1990.

3. S. E. Fahlman and C. Lebiere, The Cascade-Correlation Learning Architecture. Carnegie Mellon University. *Technical Report CMU-CS-90-100*, 1990.

4. M. Mezard, and J. Nadal, "Learning in Feedforward Layered Network: The Tiling Algorithm," *J. Physics A.*, vol. 22, 1989, pp. 2191–2203.

5. S. I. Gallant, "Three Consecutive Algorithms for Neural Learning," Proceedings of the 8th Annual Conference of Cognitive Science Society.

6. M. R. A. Frean, "The Upstart Algorithm: A Method for Constructing and Training Feed-Forward Neural Networks," Technical Report, Department of Computer Science, University of Edinburgh, 1989.

7. A. N. Refenes and S. Vithlani, "Constructive Learning by Specialization," *Proc. ICANN-91*, Helsinki, June 1991.

8. Y. Le Cun, *Generalization and Network Design Strategies*, (University of Toronto, 1985).

9. M. Minsky and S. Papert, Perceptrons: An Introduction to Computational Geometry. (Cambridge, Mass.: MIT Press, 1969).

10. W. Mendenhall, et al. "Statistics for Management and Economics," (Boston, Mass.: PWS-KENT Publishing Company, 1989).

11. One possible candidate for this rate are short-term treasury bills because they are fixed in nominal terms and the probability of default is practically zero. However, in an inflationary environment, there is always uncertainty about the real rate of return.

12. We would like to thank S. Vithlani for implementing a simulator for the CLS+ procedure, and Dr. G. Karoussos of Credit Swisse & First Boston for his advice on financial forecasting models.

Name Index

SUBJECT INDEX

About the Publisher

PROBUS PUBLISHING COMPANY

Probus Publishing Company fills the informational needs of today's business professional by publishing authoritative, quality books on timely and relevant topics, including:

- Investing
- Futures/Options Trading
- Banking
- Finance
- Marketing and Sales
- Manufacturing and Project Management
- Personal Finance, Real Estate, Insurance and Estate Planning
- Entrepreneurship
- Management

Probus books are available at quantity discounts when purchased for business, educational or sales promotional use. For more information, please call the Director, Corporate/Institutional Sales at 1-800-PROBUS-1, or write:

Director, Corporate/Institutional Sales
Probus Publishing Company
1925 N. Clybourn Avenue
Chicago, Illinois 60614
FAX (312) 868-6250